PSYCHOANALYTIC ENERGY
PSYCHOTHERAPY

PSYCHOANALYTIC ENERGY PSYCHOTHERAPY

INSPIRED BY THOUGHT FIELD THERAPY, EFT, TAT, AND SEEMORG MATRIX

Phil Mollon

KARNAC

First published in 2008 by
Karnac Books Ltd
118 Finchley Road
London NW3 5HT

British Library Cataloguing in Publication Data

A.C.I.P. for this book is available from the British Library

   ISBN-13: 978-1-85575-566-6

Edited, designed, and produced by Sheffield Typesetting
www.sheffieldtypesetting.com
e-mail: admin@ sheffieldtypesetting.com

Printed in Great Britain by the MPG books Group,
Bodmin and King's Lynn

www.karnacbooks.com

CONTENTS

CHAPTER 19

For Olivia

DISCLAIMER

- Although some of the ideas and principles described here are *related* to psychoanalysis, and the author is a psychoanalyst, the methods described here are not psychoanalysis. No implication is intended, or should be assumed, that any other psychoanalyst would agree with the contents of this book.

- Although inspired by Thought Field Therapy, the work described here is not intended to teach Callahan Techniques Thought Field Therapy. Every effort has been made to provide an accurate account of Thought Field Therapy and other approaches, but the material here is not endorsed by Dr Callahan or any other developer of methods described here. For training in Thought Field Therapy, the reader should seek an approved trainer: www.tftrx.com or www.thoughtfieldtherapy.co.uk.

- Practitioners wishing to use any of the methods or ideas presented here are responsible for ensuring they have appropriate training and experience—and that the work is within their legitimate scope of practice.

- None of the ideas or methods described here is intended as a substitute for, or alternative to, appropriate medical care.

- The contents of this book express the personal observations, impressions, and thoughts of the author. Some of these may differ from those embraced within the broad consensus and dominant paradigms of psychotherapists, psychoanalysts, or clinical psychologists.

ACKNOWLEDGEMENTS

I am particularly grateful to the following who have influenced and contributed to this work: Beatrice Salmon-Hawk and other members of the Special Interest Group in Energy Psychology who have worked at the applications of these methods within the NHS; Edina Dzeko, Dr Shoshana Garfield, and an anonymous client, who contributed valuable accounts of their work and experiences; the many clients and workshop participants who have explored and delighted in the energy realms; the wonderful Association for Comprehensive Energy Psychology [ACEP]; Dr Jill Padawer for her encouragement; my teachers in the informational-energy methods: Dr Roger Callahan; Robin Ellis; Charles Stone; Sandra Hillawi; Tapas Fleming; Dr Asha Clinton; Shu-Fang Wang; Dr Judith Swack; Dana How—and many others. In thanking these teachers and innovators, I intend no implication that they have endorsed or agree with the contents of this book.

ABOUT THE AUTHOR

Dr Phil Mollon PhD. trained first in clinical psychology before qualifying in psychotherapy at the Tavistock Clinic in London. Subsequently he trained in psychoanalysis at the London Institute of Psychoanalysis and became a member of the 'Independent Group' of analysts. More recently he has studied energy psychology extensively—including Thought Field Therapy, Emotional Freedom Techniques, Seemorg Matrix, Freeway-CER, Tapas Acupressure Technique, Theta Healing, Healing from the Body Level Up, Emotrance, and Quantum Techniques—and is a Diplomate in Comprehensive Energy Psychology and a Certification Consultant for The Association for Comprehensive Energy Psychology. He is also a certified trainer of Tapas Acupressure Technique. His previous books have included: The Fragile Self; Multiple Selves, Multiple Voices; Remembering Trauma; Releasing the Self, the Healing Legacy of Heinz Kohut; Shame and Jealousy; EMDR and the Energy Therapies. He can be contacted at phil_mollon@ yahoo.co.uk. Dr Mollon is a member of the British Complementary Medicine Association [BCMA].

CHAPTER ONE

Introductory remarks—and rationale for psychoanalytic energy psychotherapy

"… when I began using my new cure, I wasn't sure it would work. I certainly was not prepared for its spectacular effect. I was amazed. More amazed, possibly, than my patients."
[Callahan, 1985, p. 36]

Psychoanalytic Energy Psychotherapy is the outcome of one psychoanalyst's encounter with the field known generically as 'energy psychology', which reveals how the conflicts and traumas active within the psyche are encoded as information within the body's energy system. It is inspired primarily by the remarkable and far-reaching work of Dr Roger Callahan in his development of Thought Field Therapy. There were important figures before Dr Callahan in the lineage—notably George Goodheart, the founder of Applied Kinesiology, who first explored muscle testing as a source of information about the body's organs and functions, and psychiatrist Dr John Diamond, who extended this enquiry into the emotional and psychological domains—and many have built substantially on his work since. However, in my perception, he remains the principle figure to whom we owe gratitude for discovering how to identify and treat the perturbations in the energy field that cause psychological and other

1

forms of disturbance, and for distilling this into a highly effective and simple procedure that is easily taught. Like almost all who learn to use Thought Field Therapy and its derivatives, I am compelled to the conclusion that purely talk-based forms of psychotherapy, although not without value, are simply not able to engage effectively with the realm in which the patterns of emotional distress are encoded—the area at the interface of the psyche and the soma, the body's energy field. For this reason, I encourage psychotherapists to consider the implications of TFT and the wider domain of energy psychology.

In using Thought Field Therapy, typically what happens is as follows. The client is asked to think about a target trauma, anxiety, or other source of emotional distress, whilst the therapist guides him or her to tap on a sequence of energy-sensitive points on their own body. After a minute or two, or even a few seconds, of this procedure, the distress or anxiety has gone—and remains gone. Although there are many complexities and subtleties in the process, that, in essence, is it! Further aspects or 'thought fields' may then emerge, each with their own emotional charge; each of these can then be addressed in the same way through attention to the body at the same time as the mind. Insight and further understanding may (or may not) follow. The method is *not* based on suggestion, hypnosis, or charisma, although these are common hypotheses on first hearing of this approach. Callahan comments:

> "Another indication that this treatment is neither based on suggestion nor hypnosis is that I have successfully treated a number of people who not only did not have an open mind regarding what was taking place—they obviously were convinced I was some kind of madman." [Callahan, 1985, p. 34]

For me, this realm of the body and its energy is entirely congruent with—and indeed an extension of—the psychoanalysis originally developed by Freud (as distinct from most contemporary forms of psychoanalysis that have jettisoned the roots in the study of the libido and its flow through the zones of the body). As Kennedy (2001) comments:

> "... libido is a scientific concept on the 'frontier' between the mental and the somatic; it is a psychical entity, and yet it refers to bodily phenomena" [p. 7]

Freud's 'libido' is extremely close to the concepts of subtle energy that we work with in energy psychology (and similarly elusive). Just as Freud tracked the vicissitudes of the libido, its pathways, its flow and blockages in its flow, the ideas, images, and memories 'cathected' by the libido, the effects of trauma on the libido, developmental regression of the libido—and so forth—similarly, in energy psychology we track the vicissitudes of subtle energy, the information encoded within it, the disruptions in its flow, the reversals in its flow, and their consequences, and the regressive emergence of previously subsumed anxieties in response to toxic factors. Just as Freud observed the influence of libido on both mind and body, so the energy psychologist studies the interplay of psyche, soma, and energy. Moreover, just as Freud (1920g) discerned the malignant traces of the 'death instinct', in states of severe depression, trauma, perversion, and negative therapeutic reaction, so in the realm of energy psychology we detect psychological and energetic reversal, wherein the person's system becomes oriented towards illness, hopelessness, and self-sabotage. Dr Callahan regards 'psychological reversal' as one of his most important discoveries.

Thought Field Therapy reveals something else that is both crucially important and startling. Quite often, seemingly psychological states, of anxiety and depression, are caused or exacerbated directly by non-psychological factors of 'energy toxins' (Callahan & Callahan, 2003). These are foods or chemical substances which cause havoc in the individual's energy system. It was not until the development of such a rapidly effective and precise psychological therapy as TFT that the effects of energy toxins could be identified. If an energy toxin is acting on a person's system, TFT does not work; when the toxin is eliminated or neutralised by a simple procedure, the same TFT now works easily. This is not merely Dr Callahan's claim; it is readily confirmed in routine clinical observation by any TFT practitioner who has trained to the appropriate level. As well as being of immense interest and relevance within Thought Field Therapy itself, this finding of the role of energy toxins has considerable implications for psychological therapies in general since it seems likely that all therapies will be affected in this way. Not all that masquerades as psychological is actually psychological in essence.

Some within the psychoanalytic world are recognising and correcting the trend for psychoanalysis to have lost the roots in the body that were so crucial for Freud—returning to a concern with the embodied psyche (e.g. Bloom, 2006). Emotions are bodily events. In a state of anxiety, the body's physiology is highly aroused and organised. Similarly, when we access an emotionally charged memory, our body is in a correlated physiological state. And yet, in much psychotherapy, we work as if relating to an unembodied psyche, rarely addressing physiological experience. In Thought Field Therapy and its derivatives we work with psyche *and* soma, accessing the coding in the body to bring about rapid shifts in psychosomatic experience. Dr Callahan has further added to our understanding of mind-body interaction by identifying the significance of Heart Rate Variability as not only a crucial marker of both physical and psychological health and sickness, but also an indicator that is highly responsive to TFT (but not to other interventions that have been tested). This highly innovative development promises to be an important outcome measure for identifying effective psychotherapeutic interventions (Callahan, 2001e; 2001f; Callahan & Callahan, 2003; Pignotti & Steinberg, 2001).

How did a psychoanalyst become interested in Thought Field Therapy and energy psychology? Here is how it came about. In the late 1980's I began working in a general psychiatric setting, having trained first as a clinical psychologist and then as a psychoanalytic psychotherapist at the Tavistock Clinic. Although my training in psychotherapy was excellent and I had had a number of years experience, I found that, with many of the more disturbed patients I was asked to see, my skills and knowledge were of limited help. I became aware of how extensive the experience of trauma had been in the childhood and adult lives of many of these patients—and how unhelpful conventional talking therapy, of whatever kind, often was in relation to trauma. Although the troubled people I saw might begin to tell me about their experiences, and we might achieve some understanding of their development and of the dynamics of their mind, this did not seem to help. Sometimes it would make people worse; self-harm would be a common outcome. Talking of trauma, to an empathic and receptive psychotherapist, may leave a person *re-traumatised*. The trauma and its associated affect is activated but left unresolved—the affect simply cycling around the psychosomatic system. This presented an agonising clinical dilemma: many people who have suffered traumas need help in processing their traumatic memories, but accessing the memories leads to a worsening in their mental and behavioural state. As Figley (1999) and Seligman (1995) noted, effective treatments for trauma were simply not available. In the early 1990s Eye Movement Desensitisation and Reprocessing (EMDR) emerged and I began to hear from colleagues of excellent results using this method. After training in EMDR and using it extensively, I recognised that at last we had a truly effective therapy for trauma—one which, moreover, seemed to be able to engage with all the depths of psychoanalysis (Mollon, 2005). However, there was still one problem. Although EMDR is a very effective therapy, it can be distressing for clients, and for those who have been most severely and extensively traumatised it can be hazardous (although there are ways of addressing this). Towards the end of the 1990s, I started to hear of some EMDR practitioners incorporating strange tapping methods into their work and reporting even better results. EMDR itself contains a sensory tapping variant, but these new tapping procedures appeared different, involving tapping on particular parts of the body. I learned that this method was called Emotional Freedom Techniques (EFT), a derivative of TFT—and, after training in this I found that it did indeed map easily onto EMDR protocols. As I became more experienced in its use, EFT opened up extraordinary new realms of clinical work, enabling much more to be achieved and more rapidly with a wide range of patients. Deep psychodynamic material and trauma could often be addressed easily and gently. Gradually I became aware of the wider field of energy psychology and its many approaches, represented by the Association for Comprehensive Energy Psychology. Within this, I studied widely and deeply, taking workshops in Seemorg Matrix, Tapas Acupressure Technique, and many others. Relatively late in my learning, I realised that although EFT is a derivative of TFT, there was considerably more to grasp in TFT itself. Robin Ellis and Charles Stone taught me the basics of TFT, using the algorithms of tapping sequences that have been found applicable for a wide range of problems, as well as the role of individual energy toxins. Subsequently I took the TFT 'diagnostic' training with Dr Callahan, learning how to use muscle testing to diagnose meridian sequences, in which it is possible literally to see and feel the perturbations in the energy field. This was an astonishing revelation for me as I pondered its significance: that more or less any state of psychological or physical distress has an energetic coding that can be located through a simple, replicable, and teachable procedure.

Whilst there are many important and valuable energy psychology approaches and trainings available now, I would recommend the potential practitioner to take a training in TFT with Dr Callahan or an approved Callahan Techniques teacher,[1] in addition to any other method that may be of interest. This provides a firm grounding in observing and working with the body's energy system and its perturbations that are linked to the thoughts and emotions experienced in the mind. Dr Callahan feels, with good reason, that his Thought Field Therapy protocol is now so simple and efficient, pared down to its most essential elements, that it would be hard to improve on. This being so, why would I bother to write a substantial further book about energy psychology methods? It is because I feel it is possible to apply the principles of TFT, and other methods derived from it, to psychological problems that are deep and complex, pervading the personality, making use of all the knowledge and observations accumulated over the last century of psychoanalysis. This follows quite naturally, since we know from TFT that whatever is in the mind is also encoded in the body. Rather than purporting to improve on TFT itself, I am writing about its applications to different levels and domains of the psychosomatic system. In addition, I have attempted to draw upon the strengths and methodological nuances of a range of energy psychology approaches, most of which (but not all) are derived, in one way or another, from TFT.

There is another reason for this book. Those of us who have a background in clinical psychology, in addition to other trainings in psychotherapy, are obliged through the nature of this discipline to enquire and question and, where possible, engage in research. There is much to study and reflect upon here. One of the features of energy psychology approaches is that they are not fundamentally based on theory but on observation of reality. Thus the pioneers discovered aspects of how the psychosomatic system responds, and how to work with it to cure distress and disturbance, leaving a task then of how to explain and theorise about these processes. Different innovators have proposed subtly different theories, some more sophisticated than others. Whilst the concept of a subtle energy system, involving both flow and information, is shared by most within the field, not all practitioners embrace this concept. Some propose, for example, that the somatosensory stimulation of tapping creates a bodily and brain state that is conducive of plasticity in hitherto inflexible and entrenched cognitive-emotional patterns. Moreover, it seems possible that somewhat different mechanisms or processes may be involved in different procedures—for example, in TFT and EFT. I have attempted carefully to examine and unpack these issues and also to review relevant research. In so doing, this is a book *inspired* by TFT but is not itself a manual of TFT—and no implication is intended that it is a text approved by Dr Callahan.[2]

TFT and its immediate derivatives work with the energy meridian system, as used in acupuncture. There are other approaches, such as Tapas Acupressure Technique (TAT) and Seemorg Matrix, that work also with chakras. TAT uses one chakra and Seemorg uses several. Both of these have a quietly meditative quality, allowing deep insights to emerge alongside the gentle clearing of the energetic patterns of turmoil. They also both illustrate how the energy system responds to intention—as does EFT and the approach known as BeSetFreeFast (BSFF). TAT and Seemorg are able to address deep patterns and roots of distress and maladaptive beliefs, even ones that are not accessible to consciousness. Seemorg was conceived in a Jungian psychotherapist's exposure to energy-based therapy and explores all the ways in which we become internally divided and disconnected from Self and from the source of life. TAT seems to enable a dis-identification from trauma and pain, creating a mental space in which spontaneous healing can rapidly occur. This field of energy psychology is immensely rich, endlessly fascinating, and a source of continual teaching. Because the methods usually work rapidly, feedback is more or less immediate. Therefore we learn quickly. I think most practitioners find that our ways of working are continually evolving subtly on a daily basis as we attempt to engage with the more complex and difficult areas psycho-somatic disturbance. Even though energy methods usually work fast, there can still be much to do. Many clients have extensive, multifaceted and multilayered, networks of psychological and somatic disturbance. All the details of these may have to be addressed. Thus, although energy methods work efficiently, they do not bypass the details of what needs to be done—they are not 'magic' (although they can appear so!).

I have aimed to make this book of particular relevance to those with a background in psychotherapy. Therefore, I have included discussion of how to incorporate the energy perspective within psychotherapy and also consideration of the implications in relation to transference. A recurrent theme is my perception of a distorted view of transference that has become prevalent in some psychoanalytic cultures, such that interpretive comments relating to unconscious aspects of the 'here-and-now' relationship between patient and therapist are regarded as the exclusive legitimate activity of the therapist (Mollon, 2005). This was not Freud's approach and I believe it is basically unhelpful. It detracts from a proper focus on the internal processes of the client, by assuming that all must be resolved via an external dramatisation in the 'transference'. Amongst the many problems arising from this excessive preoccupation with the interaction and relationship is that the sexual and libidinal are less likely to emerge, for the simple and obvious reason that the relationship between therapist and client may not be one which facilitates or naturally encourages the sexual, as contrasted with aspects of relating to do with dependence and nurturance. Whilst Freud found sexual material to be ubiquitous, in much contemporary practice, as Kennedy (2001) comments: "sexuality as the central issue for psychoanalysis has been replaced by object relations theory, with its emphasis on early development before the child becomes recognisably sexual" [pp. 11–12]—perhaps to its detriment (Green, 1995; 2000; Mollon, 2005b). When working with energy methods, we can thankfully jettison this anti-libidinal 'transference' preoccupation, relegating true transference to its proper position as an occasional form of expression of the client's inner conflicts and traumas, and get on with the task of enabling the client to become free of the perturbations that disrupt his or her libidinal energy and optimum functioning in the here-and-now of life.

Psychoanalytic Energy Psychotherapy [PEP] provides, I hope, a window into the deep sources that give rise to the vicissitudes of emotional currents that flow through the mind. From this energetic vantage point we can survey the parts, the multiple levels, and the hidden programmes of the psychosomatic system. We have access to realms that are not available through the psyche alone. I have tried to provide sufficient information within each chapter such that any can be read in any order. One point of advice may be helpful. Some sections may, on first reading, seem a little dense, obscure, or confusing. There is a general tendency for the brain to react with a certain perplexity and confusion when first presented with entirely novel phenomena or information.[3] If you return to it later, it will make sense!

Notes

1. In the UK, consult www.thoughtfieldtherapy.co.uk. In the U.S.A., consult www.tftrx.com.
2. For example, the term 'energy psychology' is not one that is used by Dr Callahan to describe his work. He emphasizes that it is *information* and not merely energy that is addressed in TFT.
3. Some might feel that certain ideas in this book are rather fanciful—perhaps requiring credulity or belief for their acceptance. As I have got older, I find I am less inclined to believe anything. My assumptions and beliefs have often turned out to be incorrect in various ways. Indeed, beliefs seem merely limiting—an obstruction to open enquiry. Instead, I consider possibilities as working hypotheses—to be accepted, revised, or discarded in the light of accumulating evidence and information.

CHAPTER TWO

The essence of energy psychology

Whilst there are many variants and complexities of energy psychology, with its roots in applied kinesiology and the pioneering work of psychiatrist John Diamond and clinical psychologist Roger Callahan, it is possible to describe the essence of the approach rather simply and succinctly as follows. The psychodynamics and traumas of the *mind* are manifest also in the body's *energy system*, with its meridians, chakras and other traditionally recognised components. When a person thinks of a target anxiety or trauma, the subjective experience of this in the mind and body is accompanied by a patterning in the energy system that can be detected by muscle testing. If this pattern that is manifest in the energy system is eliminated, by tapping or holding a sequence of meridian or chakra points, the subjective disturbance in the mind and body (the experience of anxiety or distressing emotion) is also eliminated.

It is this phenomenon of the 'thought field' — the informational field of influence in the energy system — that is the key to the astonishing speed and effectiveness of energy psychology methods. Roger Callahan, building on the slightly earlier work of John Diamond, brought for the first time an awareness and understanding of the thought field, enabling rapid resolution of many emotional problems to an extent never previously imagined possible. Without this awareness and understanding, work purely at the mental level is relatively inefficient and ineffective. Conversely, work purely with the body's energy system, without linking this to the thought field, is also relatively ineffective in relieving emotional problems. It is the linking of thought and energy that provides the powerful synergistic combination.

The understanding of the thought field lies outside the dominant psychological and mental health paradigms. Therefore, most psychologists, psychotherapists, and psychiatrists are unaware of this area of knowledge. Since the phenomena described are impossible to understand within purely psychoanalytic or cognitive-behavioural paradigms, they fail to engage the majority of professional mental health practitioners' interest. Most people do not like to step outside their preferred or familiar framework, paradigm, or set of constructs for understanding the world, and thus the realm of energy psychology is largely ignored. Some who are heavily invested in a prevailing paradigm, financially and professionally as well as emotionally, may react with hostility on encountering reports of energy psychology methods. Little can be done in relation to this latter group, other than counter their misleading arguments and assertions wherever possible. However, there are many others in the professions of psychotherapy who are potentially deeply interested in energy methods once their nature and potential are explained. Such people are ready and willing to embrace new perspectives if an understanding and bridges to existing familiar frameworks are provided. It is for these open-minded people that this book is written.

A crucial observation made by Dr Callahan was that the *resistances* to therapeutic resolution in the mind-body-energy system are also manifest in the same informational field—again clearly detectable through muscle testing. Unless cleared, these resistances will completely block therapeutic progress. Fortunately they usually take only seconds to clear. Most such obstacles in the energy field seem to have a psychological basis, but some appear due to 'energy toxins'— substances or other forms of energetic interference that profoundly disrupt the individual's energy system (either throwing it into reverse, or causing disorganisation). This non-psychological component of what might appear to be purely psychological problems was not apparent before Dr Callahan's discoveries.

There are two further features of the informational energy field that are important in their therapeutic implications. First is the point that *physical* dysfunction and symptoms are also manifest in the energy field, again detectable through muscle testing. By focussing the mind on the physical issue, the informational energy field associated with it is activated and can be cleared, just as can be done in relation to emotional issues, with a resulting improvement in the physical condition or symptom. The second point is that if given a target problem, the mind will search for it and activate its correlates in the informational energy field, *even if the precise nature and content of this target in not in conscious awareness*. Thus the mind-body-energy system can be given the task of finding, for example, "the original trauma behind this symptom", which will then become activated in the energy system so that its accompanying perturbations can be eliminated. From a conventional perspective, such a phenomenon is extraordinary—but is commonplace in energy psychology work (although not a standard feature of Callahan Techniques Thought Field Therapy).

Dr Callahan's original Thought Field Therapy is grounded in observation through muscle testing. The procedures and observations of this method are precise and clear. However, many variants of this original approach have developed—and some that have become very popular and simple to learn, such as Emotional Freedom Techniques, no longer use muscle testing. The information obtained through muscle testing is retained, but the procedure itself is eliminated.

One point that is implicit in many of the energy psychology perspectives—and, indeed in the whole procedure of muscle testing, is that there is an inherent knowledge and intelligence in the energy system. If the right question is asked, phrased in a manner that permits a yes-no answer, the system will obligingly provide the information. This is not a magical or mystical process—nor a method of divination. The system appears computer-like—perhaps akin to what John Lilly (1974) called the 'human biocomputer'. Its answers are 'digital', in that there are only two responses, the muscle is either 'on' (strong) or 'off' (weak). Not only does the system provide the information necessary to guide the work, but also, if any internal objections are cleared, it will display enormous 'processing capacity' and speed in identifying and healing the target issues. Although the work of energy enquiry is sometimes termed 'diagnostic', it is not a matter just of the knowledge and expertise of the practitioner, but of the cooperation between the enquirer-therapist and the energy system. Crucially, the practitioner does not tell the client what is wrong with him or her, but rather is engaged in a process of translating for the client's conscious mind the muscle testing information that the client's energy system is providing. The language of the energy system, revealed through muscle testing is digital; once this is grasped, the possibilities of enquiry and communication are truly awesome.

A point of controversy within energy psychology is worth brief comment here. Thought Field Therapy, at the 'diagnostic level', makes use of a muscle testing procedure in order to determine the encoding of perturbations in the energy field. A precise sequence is usually found, although this is somewhat dynamic and fluctuating rather than fixed. When the client taps or otherwise stimulates the correct sequence, taking account of reversals, the effect is usually a marked drop in distress or anxiety—much more so than if another sequence is used. On the other hand, the founder of Emotional Freedom Techniques, Gary Craig, argues that precise sequence is unimportant (although he does teach an intuitive form of diagnosis—see pages 51–67 of the transcript of his DVD: Steps Towards Becoming the Ultimate Therapist)—and many practitioners of EFT around the world do indeed find that the method works very well despite its lack of concern for finding a coded sequence to represent the specific perturbation in the thought field. Some argue that EFT is merely an inefficient version of TFT, in that if the client keeps tapping around on all the points the embedded sequences will eventually be covered. There may be something in this argument, but there are other energy psychology methods that also do not involve specific sequences for particular thought fields and which nevertheless are found very beneficial—such as Tapas Acupressure Technique (TAT),[1] Seemorg Matix,[2] BeSetFreeFast (BSFF),[3] and Freeway-Cer[4]— even though they do not use the tapping points of TFT. All these seem to combine stimulation of the energy field with the use of intention, words and thoughts designed implicitly to 'request' the energy system to heal the problem. It is the greater use of words and phrases that distinguishes EFT from TFT, in addition to the omitting of sequence. In TFT the client is asked simply to think of what is troubling him or her—and a diagnosed sequence is found, or an 'off the shelf' algorithm sequence is used. By contrast, in EFT, there is much more elaborate verbalisation of the target problem during the initial tapping of the side of the hand, and then more emphasis on the repetition of words relating to the problem as the client taps each point. To use EFT effectively, the client often must articulate various sensory, cognitive, or emotional components of the target problem, tapping for each one—whereas in TFT, it seems to be more a matter of targeting the correct sequence that encodes that various aspects of the problem. Thus EFT and TFT seem to work in subtly different ways.

The success of EFT despite its lack of detailed attention to the meridian energy system, and to sequences of tapping, lends support to those, such as Ruden (2005) and Andrade (www.bmsa-int.com), who propose that it is the neurobiological effects of somato-sensory stimulation that create the observed therapeutic effect, rather than a process of clearing perturbations in the energy field. Not surprisingly, this is a view with which Dr Callahan strongly disagrees, arguing that the loosening of his precise and carefully developed protocol, of detailed attention to the energy system and the information encoded in the perturbations, leads to potential dilution of an originally powerful method. My own current working hypothesis is that both mechanisms apply—the neurobiological effect of somato-sensory stimulation, *and* the clearing of information encoded in the perturbations within the energy field.

A further aspect of the energy psychological approach involves the function of the therapist. An analogy with homeopathy may be relevant here. When a homeopath selects a remedy based on a substance that in its dense form would create symptoms similar to those currently suffered, what is being presented to the client's system is a frequency signal representing the nature of the problem that requires healing. This effect is clearly nothing to do with any direct biochemical effect of the substance since the dilutions are such that no molecule may be left in the dosage provided. Modern devices that provide homeopathic frequencies simply read the client's body frequency, or a sample of body fluid or product, and then potentise and imprint that frequency into a vial of water (www.eagleresearchllc.com), The process appears to be one in which the body-energy system is presented with feedback in the form of a frequency signal that announces what requires to be healed. In conventional psychotherapy and counselling, the empathic therapist may offer reflective feedback regarding the emotions and thoughts that have been conveyed. This feedback helps the client to process experiences, traumas, and conflicts. An analogous process may go on during energy psychology work, particularly when carried out be experienced and skilled practitioners who have proceeded beyond the mechanistic level of tapping procedures. The therapist's energy system 'reads' that of the client—either intuitively or with muscle testing—and, in effect, presents this energetic information back to the client's system. The feedback may consist of a mixture of words and guidance regarding where and how to tap on meridians, chakras, and so forth. It is common for practitioners to report enhanced capacities for relevant intuition when using these methods. Thus it appears that client and therapist form a combined energetic field which can then create a healing intention—and within this energetic context, all kinds of methods appear to work.

How I incorporate energy psychology into my psychotherapy

Although the work with each client is different, there is a simple pattern to how I use the phenomena, knowledge, and methods of energy psychology. First of all, I listen to the client in the way I always would have done as a psychoanalyst and psychotherapist—taking note of the emotional themes, conflicts and traumas inherent in the client's discourse. My aim is to identify, as rapidly as possible, the most important psychodynamic, cognitive, and trauma-derived psychological content that underpins the presenting problem. Having clarified this—which may take anything from five minutes to several sessions—I then aim to address the material also at the level of the energy system. As a preliminary to this work, there may need to be checks to ensure that the client's energy system is not in a state of disorganisation—and to correct this if it is. The next step in this process is to check for resistances ('reversals') against resolution of, or recovery from, these target problems—and to locate these both within the client's psyche and his or her energy system. This may, or may not, involve direct energy testing (muscle testing) of the client's own system. These resistances are then cleared from the energy system through a simple procedure involving tapping on particular meridian points.

By this point, the target psychodynamic, cognitive, and traumatic contents of the mind-body-energy system have been identified and the resistances and disorganisations in the system have been cleared. As a result, the client's system is therefore willing and able to resolve the target issues—and will use its innate intelligence to accomplish this when invited to do so. The next step is to have the client think of the target issue or problem whilst he or she taps or holds particular meridian or chakra points. The patterning in the informational energy field means that the tapping may need to be carried out in a particular sequence of meridian points for the best result. Usually, if the energy field has been adequately prepared (made free of resistances and disorganisation) the perturbations giving rise to the subjective disturbance rapidly clear. The client is then able to think about the target issues without experiencing distress. If this process does not occur rapidly, then it is likely that some factor (usually a hidden resistance or 'reversal') is interfering and must be identified and cleared before the therapeutic process can continue.

Presenting problems, particularly in people with complex and pervasive psychological disturbance, may be underpinned by many specific experiences, traumas, conflicts, and other aspects. Often it is necessary to target a representative range of these underlying aspects before the presenting problem gives way. On the other hand, when done with skill, it is sometimes possible to work quite globally, allowing the inherent healing intelligence of the mind-body-energy system to do its work.

If deep rooted patterns of belief, self-image, or self-sabotage are apparent, I may focus also on clearing these from the chakra system. Some in the energy psychology field have the impression that deeper patterns are encoded more in the chakra system than in the meridians.

As one psychological issue is cleared from the system, another is likely to present itself. The traumas and conflicts of the mind appear to be organised in networks and layers, and to form a kind of 'queue'—rather like the paper napkins in a spring-loaded dispenser, whereby as one is taken out the next one is immediately there at the front. This feature of the work can sometimes lead the client to feel that no progress is being made because he or she is still experiencing distress and difficulty—but, on reflection, the client is likely to acknowledge that the issues that have been targeted previously are no longer troubling. Such shifts of emotional distress may occur very rapidly. For example, in working through a traumatic experience, the client may report a continuing high level of distress following a meridian tapping sequence, but on enquiry it may emerge that it is now a different emotion that is in the foreground. In this way, the work with energy methods is no different from ordinary verbal psychodynamic (or cognitive) therapy, as the layers and networks of trauma, conflict, cognition and fantasy, are explored. The work can still be relatively long-term, especially with complex problems that pervade the personality, but the addition of the energy psychology dimension does powerfully and synergistically add to the effectiveness and efficiency of the process.

Advice to psychotherapists on incorporating the energy psychology dimension into the work

Many psychotherapists are very interested in the possibilities of energy psychology but feel bewildered as to how this dimension can be incorporated within psychotherapy without grossly violating existing frameworks of knowledge and skill, and, in effect, throwing out what has previously been learned over many years of hard training and practice. Some preliminary words of advice and reassurance can be offered.

First, it is important to continue to use your existing skills. These might include, for example: establishing rapport; taking a history; discerning patterns of emotional/psychodynamic conflict; inferring deep cognitive schemas (self-related core beliefs); understanding unconscious communications and making interpretations; observing transference; applying knowledge of human development, especially that of attachment; understanding neurobiological concomitants of trauma—and many other routine applications of the knowledge of the contemporary psychoanalytically and cognitively informed psychotherapist. All of these are still relevant.

The energy psychology dimension provides an additional perspective and method for rapidly clearing emotional distress and the deep patterning in the psycho-somatic-energy system. Much of a psychotherapy session may remain as before—the client speaking fairly free-associatively of his or her problems and current preoccupations, whilst the therapist listens and from time to time makes clarifying, enquiring, or interpretive remarks. The actual application of an energy method may take only a couple of minutes—or, in other cases, may take up the bulk of the session. Many practitioners find that longer sessions than the standard 50 minutes may be required—just as is the case when using EMDR.

In addition to the inclusion of the actual technique of working with the energy system, there are, however, some subtle shifts of emphasis that follow from the new perspective. Less emphasis on the interpretative activity of the therapist is appropriate—and also a greatly diminished privileging of the transference as the focus of the work. In previous writings (e.g. Mollon, 2005), I have emphasised the point that the current fashion for focusing exclusively on the so-called 'transference'—the patient's unconscious relationship with the therapist in the here-and-now of the consulting room—may be unhelpful and may even have adverse effects. A significant minority of analysts share my caution about the 'here-and-now'technique, which I believe is likely increasingly to fall out of favour as its negative consequences become more widely apparent (Bollas, 2007). My use of the phrase "so-called 'transference'" reflects the point that this approach is a far cry from what Freud had in mind when he gave us the concept of transference.

As late as 1920 [*Beyond the Pleasure Principle*], Freud indicates unequivocally that transference should not be encouraged, a position that appears radically at odds with much contemporary practice. Regarding the relationship between remembering and repeating in the patient's communications and actions, he wrote:

"He is obliged to *repeat* the repressed material as a contemporary experience instead of, as the physician would prefer to see, *remembering* it as something belonging to the past. These reproductions, which emerge with such unwished-for exactitude, always have as their subject some portion of infantile sexual life … and they are invariably acted out in the sphere of the transference, of the patient's relation to the physician. When things have reached this stage, it may be said that the earlier neurosis has now been replaced by a fresh, 'transference neurosis'. *It has been the physician's endeavour to keep this transference neurosis within the narrowest limits: to force as much as possible into the channel of memory and to allow as little as possible to emerge as repetition."* [1920g pp. 18–19 italics added]

Even when the analysis of transference is not viewed as the essential focus of the psychotherapy, there can still be a tendency to place too much emphasis upon the therapeutic relationship as the healing vehicle. The seductive implicit promise of a healing relationship can lead to malignant and addictive forms of regression and bestows a burden of reparative restoration that a professional dyad may be ill-equipped to carry. The best outcome of such aspirations may be a gradual disillusionment, such that the patient eventually gives up the search for gratifications of thwarted childhood needs and desires and more or less comes to terms with present reality—and less favourable outcomes are not uncommon. Instead of striving for healing through the *interpretation* of the relationship with the therapist, or through the *gratifications* in that relationship, it may be much more helpful to shift the focus back to the intrapsychic—i.e. back to the client's internal traumas, conflicts, core beliefs etc. that have brought him or her in search of help. When the client's internal problems, the dysfunctions in the software of his or her psycho-somatic-energy system, are in focus, then the relationship with the therapist fades into its appropriate place as a reliable and non-intrusive backdrop to the work. The succinct advice flowing from these considerations is as follows: do not focus on the relationship with the client any more than is necessary to ensure the flow of the work, the focus of which is normally on the problems within the client's system. However, if the client becomes preoccupied with the therapist in a way that is interfering with the work, then this issue must temporarily be addressed before it is possible to move on. This stance may be close to that originally outlined by Freud when he wrote about transference.

An energy psychology view of transference is expressed as follows by Dorothea Hover-Kramer (2006), in her aptly titled book *Creating Right Relationships: A Practical Guide to Ethics in Energy Therapies.*

"Transference occurs when a client personalises the professional relationship with the therapist, thereby diminishing its effectiveness. The more disorganised, disempowered, and lacking in internal resources clients are, the more susceptible they will be to transferences." [p. 43].

Such a view may seem astonishing to many who have been schooled in contemporary approaches to psychoanalytically oriented psychotherapy. Nevertheless, I believe this stance to be profoundly correct: that transference and other forms of excessive preoccupation with the relationship with the therapist are essentially interferences with the therapeutic work.

Sometimes during energy psychological work, a client's thoughts may become briefly focused on the therapist before shifting to a memory—thus the intrapsychic content is momentarily externalised as a transference preoccupation but then returns to the intrapsychic. For example, a man who presented with pronounced feelings of shame suddenly, during a tapping process, reported that he was experiencing intense impulses to shame me—but then, after a few seconds spoke of intense rage towards his father, whom he had experienced as bullying, and of wishes to shame his father. A few minutes later, still engaged in the tapping process, he reported a sudden shift to various related images and memories involving his father. The content of his thoughts required no comment from the therapist as this intrapsychic-energetic process was worked through, my words being restricted to advising him where to tap.

The energy psychology dimension can greatly facilitate the work of psychotherapy. By using conventional skills in exploring and clarifying the psychodynamic and cognitive issues underlying the client's presenting problems—and then, *in addition*, using an energy method to clear the distress and the dysfunctional emotional patterning encoded in the system, the client is enabled to move on. Without the attention to the energy system where the dysfunctional emotional information is encoded, the cognitive-emotional patterning remains and the affect has nowhere to go except to be recycled around the psycho-somatic system. The inclusion of an energy method at the end of the session may take only a few moments—but these can be crucial moments that make all the difference.

Because energy psychology methods are so effective, it becomes reasonable to expect definite therapeutic shifts in each session. No longer is it appropriate to maintain a vague hope that in time there will be some progress. When using an effective and efficient method we can know more or less immediately whether it has worked or not. If it has not, then we can try to figure out why. The rapid, and often clear, feedback—through the client's reports of his or her subjective experience, or through the data of muscle testing—mean that we can be continually guided towards resolution of the problem.

What is psychoanalytic about energy psychology?

Energy psychology methods are certainly not necessarily psychoanalytic. Some may seem closer to cognitive-behavioural approaches, with acupoint tapping simply taking the place of other methods of desensitisation. This similarity is most apparent in the case of simple forms of Emotional Freedom Technique (EFT), where the tapping on the body may be more or less substituted for the tapping used in the tactile variants of EMDR. Indeed, many EMDR practitioners do interweave their work with EFT—and this was in fact my own initial bridge to energy psychology methods. Energy psychology can certainly be used in a relatively technique-based way, easily dovetailing with techniques of cognitive-behavioural therapy. By contrast, psychoanalytic practitioners are less focused on particular techniques, apart from the general stance of endeavouring to respond thoughtfully to the unconscious communications of the patient that are embedded in the free-associative discourse.

The psychoanalytic stance tends to be characterised by a receptive and exploratory attitude, a tolerance of initially not knowing and understanding, and an assumption that underlying the surface conscious presentation there may be layers of psychodynamic material—the latter consisting of constellations of thought and emotion involving warded off (defended against) motives, perceptions, and traumatic experience. Is it possible to sustain this attitude whilst working within energy psychology? I believe it is. Since I am a psychoanalyst, my way of working energetically is inevitably psychoanalytic. I listen receptively, as in conventional verbally-based psychotherapy, but in addition I try to sense the patient energetically. Once one is attuned to the energy dimension this is not difficult. Just as the unconscious mind of one person can read that of another person [Freud, 1912c, p. 116], so the energy fields of people continually communicate—although mostly this communication is not processed into conscious awareness. And just as one might offer the client a psychoanalytic interpretation based on his or her verbal and non-verbal communications, in a similar way we may offer an energetic intervention which also reflects what has been communicated energetically. Energy information may be communicated broadly in two ways: through the therapist's capacity to sense the client's energetic state more or less directly (which comes more fluently with practice); and via muscle testing, which is a way in which we enable the body to provide a language that can engage with our conscious verbal enquiry.

Usually, in working with a client, I begin by listening as he or she speaks of what is troubling. Just as in my conventional psychoanalytic practice, I may say little, but simply allow the client's discourse to unfold. After some time, perhaps a few minutes, or maybe half an hour, some clear psychodynamic themes emerge, usually with indications of traumatic or other adverse experiences that may lie behind these. Often these are rather obvious, once the trauma paradigm is grasped. For example, today I listened to a new client telling me about her states of anxiety and feelings of helplessness when she is faced with aggressive male customers for her business. She went on to tell me of her childhood years of being subject to the intimidating rages of her stepfather. The link was conscious for her—but this awareness had made no difference to the affect. We proceeded then with energy work, guided by muscle testing. After clearing the perturbations associated with a representative series of the most distressing experiences with her stepfather, including also the thoughts linked to these, I asked what came to her mind next. She said she was thinking of how her mother had not protected her. We tapped through this perturbation. Following this she reported feeling 'neutral' about the events of her childhood. We then focussed on some typical recent experiences where she had felt intimidated by angry or aggressive men, clearing these perturbations too. In addition we cleared inherited traumas from her biological father's family line. However, a quick Diamond check of her energy system (Diamond, 1985) revealed a remaining problem in her gall bladder meridian, reflecting a continuing issue of lack of forgiveness of her mother. Moreover, she muscle tested strong to 'I hate my mother'. Thus it became apparent that her persisting hatred of her mother and lack of forgiveness was weakening her system. We used tapping and Diamond affirmations to clear this. A re-check of her energy system revealed that it was now balanced. She looked very happy and reported a sense of surprise at how good she was now feeling.

This work had taken about an hour and a half. As she stood up, she remarked "It feels like we have really covered a lot". I think it is quite likely that she will not require a further session.

So what was involved in this session? Insofar as it is possible to isolate the components, my own contributions included the following:[1] Listening, without interruption, to the client's free discourse—and, from this, discerning the potential targets for energy work; [2] sensing the client's energy field; [3] free-floating attention to all my impressions, feelings, thoughts, and fantasies about the client; [4] being guided by muscle testing; [5] being guided by intuition; [6] testing meridian 'alarm points'; [7] waiting to see what emerges (rather than following an agenda), thus following the inherent layering of emotional problems; [8] responding to emerging indications of energetic perturbations by guiding the client in clearing these by tapping on meridians and holding chakras; [9] following the content of the client's thoughts, memories, and emotions—and locating the energetic correlates of these; [10] checking the meridians to see whether the work was, at that point, complete. Transference, in terms of the relationship to the therapist, did not form a significant feature of this clinical encounter. The work was focused on the perturbations *within* the client's own mind-body-energy system. However, transference did feature in terms of the obvious way in which the client's reactions to aggressive men were influenced by her childhood experiences—a clear transference of images of her raging stepfather. For many analysts and psychotherapists, this case might appear puzzlingly simple. In long term work, we are used to complexities of psychodynamic material whose meaning is unravelled only through many hours of hard analytic work. My response to such concerns is that complexity may not lie in the essence of a client's difficulties, but only in the varied derivatives of the basic core traumas, conflicts, and dilemmas. In becoming immersed in the details of a conventional psychoanalytic session within a long on-going therapeutic process, it is easy to lose sight of the 'wood' by attending to the individual and varied 'trees'.

Here is another case I worked with today. A young woman asked for help with a lack of self-motivation for activities that consciously she wished to do, such as going to the gym or getting on with studying. On the basis of what she told me of her life and childhood experiences within an immigrant family, I muscle tested the statements "I am responsible for my own life" and "I make my own decisions". Both of these tested weak—as did the subsequent statement we tested "I am permitted to be responsible for my own life". Testing the meridians, in accord with the Diamond procedure, revealed persisting weakness in the large intestine and gall bladder meridians. In view of the large intestine problem (and its common relationship with guilt), I enquired whether she thought she might feel a continued deep guilt about going against her parents' wishes. She readily affirmed this and began to speak with some vehemence about the pressures she had experienced to conform to her parents' expectations of what a girl from their culture should be like—and acknowledged the depth of her rage about this, and her guilt about this rage. I guided her to tap on these meridians whilst speaking of these emotions. The gall bladder and large intestine meridians then tested strong. However, the next meridian to reveal a weakness was the governing vessel—indicating, not surprisingly, conflicts in relation to the *governance* of her body, mind, and life. She also muscle tested weak to the statement "I can make my own choices" and "I can tell myself what to do". We spoke briefly of her difficulty in accepting that she could make her own decisions and exert executive control of herself from within. Accordingly I then invited her to tap on the governing vessel point under the nose, whilst making statements affirming her capacity to make her own decisions and tell herself what to do. After a little further talking and tapping around these issues, she tested strong to assuming governance of her own life. I asked what else she would like to address. She spoke of difficulties in accepting the ending of a relationship with an ex-boyfriend. Again the large intestine meridian seemed particularly involved in this issue—leading me to wonder aloud whether she tended to blame herself for the ending and to think that if she were somehow better the relationship would have continued. She agreed that she had been blaming herself in this way. We continued tapping through the perturbations as they were encoded in the energy field, until a few minutes later she felt calm and free of distress on thinking of the ex-boyfriend. At this point, I felt that probably we had reached the end of what we needed to do in that session. However, she muscle tested strong to the statement "there is more we need to do today". I asked her what came to mind. She thought for a moment, and then, looking surprised, said that what she found herself thinking of was church. Elaborating, she explained that during her teenage years her family had been involved with an evangelical church that she had ultimately come to experience as rather controlling—like another version of her parents. She spoke angrily of what she perceived as contradictions in the characteristics and requirements of God, giving us free-will and then condemning us if we did not follow His will. Further tapping through the perturbations of rage at the arbitrary and contradictory demands of this 'God the Father and Mother' led her to feel calm. Now her meridian system tested as balanced—and she muscle tested strong to "We've done all we need to do".

With this young woman, the clear psychodynamics behind her presenting problem of lack of self-directed volition revolved around core conflicts relating to her autonomy and sense of identity. These conflicts had originated in the pressures she had experienced between the requirements of her parents and their cultural values, on the one hand, and the demands of the culture of her peer group. Rebellion and rage against her parents gave rise to guilt and feelings that she was not good enough. She felt she was not entitled to be responsible for her own life. These struggles over autonomy had later been transferred to her perception of a church that she had been involved with. Her feelings of being not good enough also manifested in relation to an ex-boyfriend. Thus a great deal of core psychodynamic material was revealed, and its energetic perturbation correlates unravelled, during this single session.

Psychological reversal—the expression of psycho-energetic conflict

A concept crucial to much energy psychological work derives from Dr Callahan's original observation that some clients who did not initially benefit from a TFT type of treatment showed a paradoxical muscle test result. The indicator muscle would test weak to a statement such as "I want to be over this problem" and strong to "I want to keep this problem". When this reversal was corrected, by having the client think of it and tap the side of the hand (or neurolymphatic 'sore spot'), the muscle test would show a normal result and the client would be able to benefit from the TFT. With further enquiry (and when the effect is not directly due to an individual energy toxin), it is often possible to identify more precise motivational conflicts underlying the reversal—such as a belief that it is not safe to be free of the problem, or that the person does not deserve to be free of it. Dr Callahan himself does not emphasise psychodynamic conflicts, probably seeing no need for this level of conceptualisation since his TFT protocol effectively clears the reversals. Nevertheless, the psychodynamics behind reversals are there to be observed, and Dr Callahan has given us the key to do so. I find that in working with people with complex personality problems, whose childhood backgrounds have involved much trauma and other adverse circumstances, it can be very helpful to be able to locate the precise psychodynamic conflict behind a reversal. In this way we can unravel what used to be thought of, in psychoanalytic terms, as the resistances and the negative therapeutic reactions. Since, in a state of general or massive psycho-energetic reversal, good will register as bad and bad will register as good, it is also possible to grasp the energetic underpinnings of what may otherwise be conceptualised as 'perversion' (Meltzer, 1973). Moreover, it becomes possible to observe how addictive substances, such as alcohol and other energy toxins, may bring about these pervasive states of reversal. By observing these reversal phenomena at the energetic level, and also appreciating how easy they can be to clear at this level, it becomes possible to view human motivations and behaviour more objectively and with less judgement.

Notes

1. www.tatlife.com
2. www.seemorgmatrix.org
3. www.besetfreefast.com
4. www.freeway-cer.com

CHAPTER THREE

History: how did we get to modern energy psychology?

> "Most of my psychiatric colleagues are still giving electro-shock, still poisoning their patients with drugs, and still devoting years to life-energy depleting psychotherapy. In their hearts they know it is not really working. But they are too frightened to change, too frightened to explore the wonderful new ways that are available." [John Diamond M.D., 1986, p. 70]

On first encounter, for those steeped in conventional verbal forms of psychotherapy, the procedures of energy psychology are likely to seem so utterly astonishing—even bizarre—that it may seem impossible to imagine how anyone could have dreamt up such a preposterous method. Did some unusually creative person wake up one day with the thought that perhaps asking people to tap on their body, whilst humming and counting, might cure them of anxiety and other distress? Was there a single eccentric genius to whom we owe eternal thanks for this gift to mankind of energy psychology? The reality is more mundane—and all falls into place when the history is appreciated. All of it was developed one step at a time, each person building on what had been done before. No single person grasped the whole picture in one fell swoop. A number of notable individuals did make substantial contributions, but many practitioners all around the world have played a part in developing the versions of energy psychology that we know today.

Understanding the history and evolution of energy psychology is important because through that understanding it is possible to grasp essential points about its nature that can otherwise be missed. We need to understand, for example, that the whole field is originally derived from muscle testing, each step having been tested in that way. This is easily overlooked when people are exposed predominantly to those energy psychology methods, such as Emotional Freedom Techniques, that have jettisoned muscle testing. Indeed muscle testing is not essential to the work, but it is essential to know about it in order to understand the field.

There are broadly two roots of modern energy psychology. Kinesiology is one—the study of muscle strength and weakness as a form of body language providing a guide to diagnosis and treatment. Muscle testing provided a window into the body—and then the mind. It tells us what is wrong, what to do, and provides immediate feedback on the results of our efforts. The other root is the ancient knowledge of the energy pathways in traditional Chinese medicine (subsequently broadened to include the chakra systems of Hindu and other eastern thought).

It is necessary first to explain a little about the origins of muscle testing and its initial use in essentially non-psychological applications.

Detroit Chiropractor, George Goodheart

It was 1964 when Chiropractor George Goodheart made an observation marking the beginnings of what he came to call Applied Kinesiology, which, in turn, led to energy psychology. As a chiropractor, Goodheart naturally focused upon structural imbalances in the body, to do with postural problems, false alignment of bones etc. He did not, up to this point, test muscles. However, he had a particular patient whose presenting problem was that one of her shoulder blades stuck out from the body. This appeared to reflect a muscle weakness on one side, although there was no indication that the muscle was less developed on that side. Goodheart was startled to discover that when he rubbed certain nodules where the tendons held the muscle to the ribs, the muscle immediately functioned with more strength and the shoulder blade moved into a normal position. Further details of this particular case need not concern us—but the important point is that a muscle was found to display a weakness that was immediately corrected when Goodheart carried out a simple massage. This led Goodheart to begin to study an existing, but, at the time, not widely known, tradition of muscle testing. From these rudimentary beginnings, the vast potential of muscle testing as a language of the body, and as a means of interrogating the body-mind system, eventually unfolded.

The beginnings of muscle testing

Goodheart—links disease, muscle response, and neurolymphatic reflex

Manual muscle testing was first developed by Boston orthopaedic surgeon, R. W. Lovett in the early 20th century. He used muscle testing to trace spinal nerve damage because muscles that tested weak often had a common spinal nerve. His work, describing five levels of muscle testing, was published in 1932. Henry and Florence Kendall modified and systematised Lovett's ideas and published a pioneering book: *Muscle testing and function.* [1949]

Kendall and Kendall's work inspired Goodheart, who went on to discover further ways in which certain muscles would test weak when associated with particular diseases. He then linked his work with the ideas of an early osteopath, Frank Chapman, who had observed that many symptoms seemed to have an origin in sluggish lymph flow, the fluid that carries nutrients to organs and carries toxins away. Chapman found that many points on the bodies of people showing symptoms of diseases would be tender when palpated or massaged—but regular massage of these places would result in improvement in the disease condition. He called these Chapman Reflex Points and published his findings in the 1930s. Goodheart made the link between the Chapman Reflex Points, muscle weaknesses, and particular disease conditions. He found that rubbing the Chapman Reflex Point would result in strengthening of a particular muscle associated with the disease.

Another chiropractor, Terence Bennett had developed his own model of restoring health based on proper blood flow. This was based on similar ideas to those of Chapman regarding the lymph flow. Bennett developed his own set of reflex points, most of which were on the head and upper body. He found that applying light pressure to these points would stimulate increased blood flow to the associated tissues and organs—with ensuing improvements in the disease condition. Goodheart also incorporated Bennett's work.

Goodheart–Applied Kinesiology incorporating Chinese Medicine

As Goodheart continued to explore the possibilities of muscle testing, he gathered a group of interested chiropractors (who came to be known as the Dirty Dozen) and developed the new field that he called Applied Kinesiology (Walther, 1988). However, it was Goodheart himself who, in the 1960s, took the major step of exploring and integrating ideas that were filtering into the West regarding traditional Chinese medicine. He found that when muscle strength was not restored by stimulating either the Chapman or Bennett reflex points, he could do this by running his hand along a particular energy meridian in the direction of flow. In 1966 he wrote a manual on strengthening muscles by holding acupuncture points called Tonification Points. Goodheart began to appreciate the complex relationship between muscle response and imbalances in the lymphatic system, the vascular system, the energy system, and particular organs (in Chinese medicine, particular meridians are associated with particular organs). Goodheart's achievement was to have found a way of accessing the subtle energy systems of Chinese medicine by using the immediate biofeedback of muscle testing.

Goodheart and his colleagues also recognised that muscle strength could also vary in response to different thought processes. Thus it was found that muscle testing could be used to give indications of areas of stress and emotional disturbance in a person's life, if the clinician monitored the muscle whilst enquiring about different subjects. It was this application to the study and treatment of emotional and psychological life that psychiatrist John Diamond pioneered, paving the way for the new wave of energy psychology methods. Diamond's work is discussed separately below.

The emergence of Touch for Health

Another member of Goodheart's 'Dirty Dozen', was chiropractor Dr John Thie. Like Goodheart, he became immersed in principles of Chinese medicine and developed a method for the general public to balance their energy on a regular basis as a means of maintaining health. This became known as 'Touch for Health'—a therapeutic movement that began in the 1970s and is popular in over 50 countries. One Touch for Health method is that of Emotional Stress Release. In this technique, the person thinks of a stressful event whilst applying gentle finger pressure to the frontal eminences, the broad bumps on the forehead above the eyes (which are also the Gall bladder 14 acupoints)—and this may be combined with holding the base of the back of the skull with the other hand. This seems to help restore blood flow to the frontal lobes, which are important in thinking and new learning. When a person is stressed, blood may be withdrawn from these areas and directed towards the lower survival centres of the brain (limbic system)—hence the impaired thinking shown by people under stress. Using Emotional Stress Release, the emotional charge associated with the stressful situation is reduced or eliminated.

John Barton, a health practitioner in California also saw the possibilities of kinesiology for a popular holistic approach, which he developed in the 1970s under the name Biokinesiology

Beardall discovers the thumb-finger energy loop

One of Goodheart's protégés, Dr Alan Beardall, made several additional important discoveries. One of these (in 1983) was that when a patient touched a painful area with an open hand, the muscle being monitored became weak, but when the same area was touched by the patient holding thumb and little finger together, the muscle strengthened. It thus appeared that the thumb and little finger had energy flows that somehow related to the energy flow of the meridian system, and that muscle monitoring provided a means of assessing these flows. Gradually, Beardall established the following: thumb to index finger responded to structural stresses in the body; thumb to middle finger responded to nutritional stress; thumb to ring finger responded to emotional stress; thumb to little finger responded to energetic stresses such as meridian imbalance.

The broadening scope of kinesiology

As kinesiology developed further from these beginnings, all manner of new insights and applications emerged. To summarise some of the overall conclusions, it was found that a muscle may test weak in response to: [1] a physical factor; [2] a disturbance in a related organ system (with restricted lymph or blood flow); [3] a disturbance in an associated meridian; [4] a disturbance of emotion or thought. It is the latter aspect that became the basis of the emerging field of energy psychology. Kinesiology, through muscle testing, was found to offer a means of 'eavesdropping' on the unconscious mind, and of accessing emotions that might be at odds with the person's conscious view.

Neurological disorganisation—applications to education

Dr Paul Dennison suffered from severe dyslexia, and after becoming aware of Touch for Health, began to see the value of 'cross crawl' or cross patterning, that had been developed by kinesiologists as a treatment for neurological disorganisation, as well as the Emotional Stress Release method. He saw the potential for understanding many kinds of learning difficulties and behavioural disorders in children as expressions of neurological disorganisation, a lack of coordination of brain activity. Out of this work, initially called Educational Kinesiology, came the approach called Brain Gym, now used in many educational contexts.

Another related educational application was that of Three-in-One or One Brain Kinesiology, developed by Gordon Stokes, Candice Callaway, and Daniel Whiteside. This approach gave greater emphasis to the role of unresolved emotional problems in learning difficulties—and gave rise to a deeper and more focused stress relief method called Emotional Stress Defusion.

The work of John Diamond M.D.

[Dr Diamond has told me that he no longer endorses all that he wrote in his earlier books. Nevertheless, they are relevant as an important part of the history and evolution of what has come to be called 'comprehensive energy psychology'. Aspects of Dr Diamond's current work can be found at his website http://www.drjohndiamond.com/. Dr Diamond cautions against the use of muscle testing by those with insufficient training]

John Diamond was the first to make the link from the largely physical health focus of Applied Kinesiology to its applications in relation to emotional, psychological and psychiatric problems—although he is truly holistic in his approach, attending to the multiple levels of a person's physical, emotional, mental, and spiritual health. Indeed, Diamond, who received the Distinguished Pioneer award at the 2006 ACEP conference, may justifiably be regarded as the father of all the many contemporary approaches based on using muscle testing to identify and subsequently treat the meridian basis of psychological distress or dysfunction.

Diamond found that it is possible to muscle test for a person's response to almost any kind of stimulus—whether this be a particular food, a facial expression, a visual symbol, a kind of music, and so forth. This work was outlined in his 1979 book *Your Body Doesn't Lie*. Exploring a person's 'life energy', he found that the thymus gland, in the centre of the upper part of the chest, is a key to the strength or weakness of this—and developed ways to enhance this, including the 'thymus thump'. He went on to discover links between the different meridians and particular emotions. Using muscle testing, he was able to identify which meridians were unbalanced and were thereby linked to a person's emotional state. He discovered also that certain affirmations would correct the weakness in particular meridians. By working through layers of weak testing meridians, he could clear the different levels of emotional disturbance that lay behind a presenting symptom or problematic state of mind. Diamond's work draws upon many different traditions of knowledge, but is particularly interwoven with allusions to psychoanalysis. If his insights are followed, the therapeutic work can indeed be, in certain ways, much deeper than that afforded by conventional psychoanalysis in many of its forms.

The thymus gland

In his 1985 book, *Life Energy*, Diamond emphasises the importance of the thymus gland:

"The thymus gland monitors and regulates energy flow throughout the body's energy system, initiating instantaneous corrections to overcome imbalances as they occur so as to achieve a rebalancing and harmony of life energy. Further, it is the link between mind and body, being the first organ to be affected by mental attitudes and stress. A healthy, active thymus gland makes for vibrant and positive health." [p. 15].

Diamond would muscle test whilst the person placed their fingers of one hand in the vicinity of the thymus gland. Frequently he would find that whilst the indicator muscle (e.g. the deltoid muscle tested with the subject's arm outstretched) would test strong 'in the clear', it would test weak when the person touched their thymus gland area. He found he could check that the procedure was testing the thymus gland by having the person chew a tablet of thymus extract, which would then result in a strong muscle test when the thymus area was again touched whereas previously it had tested weak. He came to view the thymus as the "master switch, the master controller, of the acupuncture energy system of the body" (1985, p. 20), since actions that enhance the functioning of the thymus will automatically correct imbalances or weaknesses in other parts of the energy system. Diamond found that feelings of fear, anger, hatred, and envy would undermine the strength of the thymus gland.

The cerebral hemispheres

Diamond (1985) writes of the differential functions of the two cerebral hemispheres and their interdependence for optimum creative activity. Thus, although this is an oversimplification, the right hemisphere is concerned with music, rhythm, imagination, intuition, humour, and dreams—and the sympathetic nervous system; the left hemisphere deals with logic, arithmetic, and ordered sequential relationships— and the parasympathetic nervous system. The two hemispheres relate to different acupuncture meridians. By performing a simple test of cerebral hemispheric dominance at any one time, Diamond found he could identify more quickly which of the meridians were out of balance. When in a state of stress, it is common for a person's cerebral hemispheres to become unbalanced.

Diamond's test for hemispheric dominance is as follows. The person is first muscle tested 'in the clear'; then he or she places the palm of the right hand two to four inches from the left side of the head, opposite the ear, and the muscle test is repeated. If the person tests weak with their hand in this position against the left side, this indicates left hemisphere dominance. If he or she tests weak with the right hand held against the right side, this indicates right hemisphere dominance.

- Right hand against left hemisphere—muscle test weak = left hemispheric dominance.
- Right hand against right hemisphere—muscle test weak = right hemispheric dominance.

Diamond found that most people test as left hemisphere dominant:

> "They are caught in a verbal and intellectual struggle with their environment and have sacrificed the aesthetic and intuitive aspects of the right hemisphere." [1985, p. 88]

Each hemispheric weakness/dominance is associated with a particular set of meridians. Six meridians run down the midline of the body and another six run bilaterally down either side—and each has a particular test (or 'alarm') point, these points having been previously established in Applied Kinesiology. If the person is left hemisphere dominant, the meridians with midline test points are tested to find which is out of balance. If he or she is right hemisphere dominant, the meridians with bilateral alarm points are tested.

- Right hemisphere dominant—test the bilateral alarm points.
- Left hemisphere dominant—test the midline alarm points.

The meridians, emotions, and affirmations

Diamond's testing and treatment procedure is described below, after an outline of the meridians, their associated emotions, test points, and affirmations.

Diamond writes extensively about the emotional qualities associated with each meridian. Brief summaries are provided below, along with indications of the test points and the affirmations that Diamond found would help to correct imbalances in each meridian. Diamond's

1985 book provides photographs illustrating the test points (which are also illustrated in other texts, such as Feinstein, 2004, p. 261).

The following meridians have test points bilaterally (either side) of the body:

- Lung,
- Liver,
- Gall bladder,
- Spleen,
- Kidney,
- Large intestine.

Lung Meridian

Test point: the hollow of the shoulder: "the first intercostal space on the anterior paraxillary". [Diamond, 1985, p. 102]
Diamond calls this the meridian of humility. Negative emotions linked to the lung meridian include: disdain; scorn; contempt; haughtiness; false pride; intolerance; and prejudice.
Affirmations: I am humble/tolerant/modest.

Liver Meridian

Test point: an inch or two below the nipple: "in line with the nipple at about the costal border, usually just above it." [Diamond, 1985, p. 112]
Diamond calls this the meridian of happiness. The negative emotion linked to the liver meridian is unhappiness.
Affirmations: I am happy/have good fortune/am cheerful.

Gall bladder meridian

Test point: an inch or so up from the base of the ribs at the front, under the nipple but an inch or so to the side: "at or just below the junction of the ninth rib and the costal border." [Diamond, 1985, p. 118]
Diamond calls this the meridian of adoration. Negative emotions include rage and fury.
Affirmations: I reach out with love/with forgiveness.

Spleen meridian

Test point: on the side, where the waist bends: "tip of the eleventh rib." [Diamond, 1985, p. 123]
Diamond calls this the meridian of confidence. Negative emotions are to do with realistic anxieties about the future.
Affirmations: I have faith and confidence in my future; My future is secure; I am secure.

Kidney meridian

Test point: in the vicinity of one of the kidneys: "tip of the twelfth rib." [Diamond, 1985, p. 129]
Diamond calls this the meridian of sexual assuredness. Negative emotions are to do with sexual indecision.
Affirmations: I am sexually secure; My sexual energies are balanced.

Large intestine meridian

Test point: an inch or so under the navel, and a couple of inches or so to one side: "approximately six centimetres lateral to the umbilicus and two centimetres below." [Diamond, 1985, p. 133]
Diamond calls this the meridian of self-worth. The negative emotion is guilt.
Affirmations: I am basically clean and good; I am worthy of being loved.

Midline meridians

The following meridians have test points down the centre of the body:

- Circulation-sex/heart protector
- Heart
- Stomach
- Thyroid/Triple heater
- Small intestine
- Bladder

Circulation-sex meridian

Test point: centre of the chest level with the nipples.
Diamond calls this the meridian of relaxation and generosity.
Negative emotions include: regret and remorse; sexual tension; jealousy; stubbornness.
Affirmations: I renounce the past; I am relaxed; My body is relaxed; I am generous.

Heart meridian

Test point: just under the ribs in the centre under the chest: "tip of xiphoid process below sternum." [Diamond, 1985, p. 149]
Diamond calls this the meridian of forgiveness.
Negative emotion is anger.
Affirmations: I love; I forgive; There is forgiveness in my heart.

Stomach meridian

Test point: in the centre, around the area of the stomach: "halfway between the xiphoid process and umbilicus." [Diamond, 1985, p. 154]
Diamond calls this the meridian of contentment and tranquillity.
Negative emotions include: disgust; disappointment; bitterness; greed; emptiness; deprivation; nausea; hunger.
Affirmations: I am content; I am tranquil.

Thyroid/triple heater meridian

Test point: an inch or two below the navel: "one third down an imaginary line between the umbilicus and symphysis pubis." [Diamond, 1985, p. 164]
Diamond calls this the meridian of hope.
Negative emotions include: depression; despair; grief; hopelessness; despondency; loneliness; solitude.
Affirmations: I am light and buoyant; I am buoyed up with hope.

Small intestine meridian

Test point: "two-thirds down an imaginary line between the umbilicus and symphysis pubis." [Diamond, 1985, p. 178]

Diamond calls this the meridian of joy.
Negative emotions: sadness and sorrow.
Affirmations: I am full of joy; I am jumping with joy.

Bladder meridian

Test point: just above the pubic bone: "just above the symphysis pubis." [Diamond, 1985, p. 182]
Diamond calls this the meridian of peace and harmony.
Negative emotions: restlessness; impatience; frustration.
Affirmations: I am at peace; I am in harmony; Conflicts within me have been resolved; I am balanced.

The Conception/Central and Governing Vessels

These are not organ-related meridians, but are regarded more as vessels collecting energy that has passed through the organ meridians. Diamond links the governing vessel to embarrassment and the central vessel with shame. However, he believes these are more like secondary emotions rather than the more fundamental ones based around love and hate, and he finds the governing and central meridians tend to correct themselves when the more fundamental underlying emotional state is resolved.

Test point for governing vessel: "slightly above the midpoint of the upper lip." [Diamond, 1985, p. 188]
Test point for conception/central vessel: "slightly below the midpoint of the lower lip." [Diamond, 1985, p. 190]

Diamond's testing and treatment process

The following is, schematically, the procedure Diamond [1985] describes for ascertaining and correcting the predominant emotional state of a person at the time of testing.

- The person is muscle tested whilst he or she touches the thymus.
- If the thymus tests weak, the hemisphere test is performed.
- If this test indicates left hemisphere dominance, the midline meridian points are tested; if right hemisphere dominance, the bilateral meridian points are tested.

- The meridian that tests weak is located.
- The person repeats several times, with feeling, the appropriate affirmation.
- On retesting, the previously weak-testing meridian may now be found to test strong; the cerebral hemispheres are balanced; and the thymus also tests strong. If not, then another meridian may now need balancing.
- The procedure is continued, treating each weak-testing meridian with an appropriate affirmation until the thymus tests strong.
- NB. Normally only one meridian will test weak at a time. Diamond found that occasionally more than one might test weak, but only one of these would be important—the other being more like static in the system, easily eliminated by taking a couple of relaxing breaths.

Diamond recommends a daily programme for life energy, whereby the affirmations for each meridian are repeated whilst the person touches each test point (although he finds that just saying the affirmations alone is also effective).

The significance of 'layering' of meridian imbalance

Diamond realised that the layering of meridian imbalance reflected an underlying layering of emotional disturbance. They are revealed one at a time, just as in traditional psychoanalytic therapy layers of emotion are gradually revealed as the more unconscious levels move to the surface. However, Diamond makes another interesting point, that the last or deepest meridian to be corrected before the thymus tests strong is the most important or most basic one. Often he finds that this is the lung or thyroid meridian—and, of these two, the lung meridian is traditionally seen as the fundamental route of Chi into the energy system through the breath, and thus is regarded as the primary meridian. Diamond relates the lung meridian to Melanie Klein's primary paranoid-schizoid position, driven by envy, and the thyroid to her depressive position.

Diamond's treatment of fears and phobias

Diamond's procedure for treating a specific fear or phobia is as follows.

- The person is asked to think about the feared situation as vividly as possible.
- He or she is then tested to find which meridian registers as weak.
- The appropriate affirmation for that meridian is used.
- The person repeats the affirmation prior to and during the feared situation.

Diamond finds that often the circulation-sex meridian is involved in phobias.

When the indicator muscle tests weak without touching the thymus

Diamond adds a crucial point that at times when a person thinks of a stressful situation, his or her indicator muscle will test weak without touching the thymus gland. Then, when the person touches the meridian test points, one will be found that registers strong. Note that this is different from the situation previously described where the search was for the meridian that registered weak (when the indicator muscle registered strong). If the indicator muscle is registering weak when the person thinks of the stressful situation, then what is sought is the meridian that makes the muscle register strong. Diamond explains this as being like a 'double negative'—hence the seemingly paradoxical result that the problematic meridian registers as strong.

The basic problem: hatred of the mother

In a number of Diamond's writings, he states that the fundamental emotional problem for human beings is often hatred of the mother, and, most basic of all, a doubt of the mother's love:

> "The single most important fact I have learned in my years in psychiatry and preventive medicine is that love is the great healer. And yet we all know that there is something inside ourselves that prevents us loving fully, completely opening our hearts and making a total commitment. The basic reason for this lies in our inability to totally love our mothers. This problem begins in the first minutes of life as a result of the unnatural manner of our births." [Diamond, 1986, p. 1.]

He finds that simple muscle tests demonstrate this. For example, if a woman thinks of comforting her upset child or husband, she will often muscle test weak. If a man thinks of putting his head in his wife's lap for comfort, he will often test weak. Looking at a woman's lower belly will often lead a person, of either sex, to test weak. Looking at a card with one's mother's name, plus the word 'mother', will usually cause a person to test weak, whilst the mother's name on its own does not. Moreover, Diamond finds that almost everyone will test strong to the statement "I want to kill my mother":

> "This desire to kill your mother is the most primitive destructive force in you. It is not just hate. It is the murderous impulse and it is the recognition of this that led Freud and Melanie Klein to postulate the death instinct." [Diamond, 1986, p. 19]

Diamond explains that when he tests people for this level of murderous hatred, he prefaces it by pointing out that there are parts of us that love our mother and parts that hate her and that the test is to determine which part is affecting the person at that point:

> "It is not to say that all of you hates her, or necessarily to imply that all of you loves her. But there is a part of you that hates her, and that part is ruling your life at the moment and is causing you to test strong when you say 'I want to kill my mother'. You may protest that this is an extreme statement. You may admit that you have some difficulties with her, and that, yes, you dislike her, but kill her, no. That is going too far. And I reply that the unconscious does not work that way. The unconscious does not have modifiers and qualifiers. It deals in black and white—you love or you hate … The unconscious is a binary system. And of course as it is the unconscious that rules us, it is the unconscious that is revealed by the testing." [Diamond, 1986, p. 19]

It is this attunement to the deeper layers of human destructiveness—and indeed the eternal tension between life and death instincts—that makes Diamond's work so congruent with psychoanalysis. Just as Freud (1900) revealed how dreams may function as a 'royal road' to the unconscious mind, Diamond has shown how muscle testing functions as another, and more direct, window to hidden motives and emotions.

Reversal of the body morality

Diamond noticed that sometimes a person will display a reversal of normal responses, such that good (or love) will test as bad, and bad (or hate) will test as good. The person may test strong to "I want to be ill/to die" and weak to "I want to be well/to live" [Diamond, 1988]. In such conditions healing cannot occur.

Diamond does not offer quick fixes for profound problems. He finds that many difficulties, including those found in fundamental reversals of the body's morality, are very deep rooted. Recovery from illness requires effort. Moreover, he recognises the element of choice in whether a person embraces a positive attitude and becomes well:

> "The start of all illness is the loss of the inherent will to be well. In fact, I believe that the illness itself is this loss of the will to be well, just differently manifested depending on various lesser etiological factors." [Diamond, 2002, p. 71]

For Diamond, illness and health are physical, emotional, and also spiritual matters, fundamentally to do with our relationship with love.

On holistic practice

Diamond is truly a holistic practitioner. In this respect he defies categorisation. Something of the quality of his stance is revealed in the following quote:

> "Forget the medical diagnosis. It is only a name. It is only an Orion's belt in the whole firmament of the universe of the sufferer. The therapist must breach the narrow confines that most institutions want him to work within. He must think of the totality of the sufferer. To see him as anything less, to reduce his existence to a diagnosis, is an insult. To see him in his totality is to worship him as a Being.
>
> Holistic therapy really implies the absence of using any diagnostic label. The best label is the name of the patient, because we each suffer from the disease which is ourselves. The diagnostic label for John Smith is "John Smith". [Diamond, 2002, p. 17]

Crucial components of John Diamond's contribution

Diamond's work has proceeded in many directions, resulting in a vast and complex network of observations, insights, and methods. Only a small area of this has been summarised here. However, it may be worth highlighting those components of his contribution that seem particularly important in the evolution of the field of 'energy psychology' (a term, it should be said, that Diamond neither likes nor uses). As I perceive it, the crucial steps that Diamond took are as follows:

- He extended the field of muscle testing, exploring emotional truth, as well as the impact of all manner of stimuli upon the human system.
- He identified the links between specific meridians and emotions.
- He discovered how muscle testing of meridian test/alarm points could be used to identify the meridian imbalance underlying an emotional state.
- He discovered how meridian imbalance may occur in layers, and how these may correspond to layers of emotions. Thus, he used muscle testing to identify the sequence of meridians that required treatment in relation to a particular emotional problem.
- He discovered how meridians that are out of balance can be corrected by specific affirmations.
- Thus he discovered an efficient way of identifying how the meridian system is out of balance in relation to an emotional problem, fear or phobia, and how to correct this.
- He also identified profound obstacles to healing, such as the reversal of the body's morality.

Roger Callahan and the emergence of Thought Field Therapy

Dr Roger Callahan is a clinical psychologist—originally a pioneer cognitive therapist, a colleague of Albert Ellis—who had been working with some of Goodheart's group, including John Diamond. His breakthrough that led to TFT came in 1979. By this point, many ingredients and possibilities were in place on the basis of the discoveries and methods developed by Goodheart and Diamond and others. These included: [1] links between meridians and emotions, including fear; [2] muscle testing for diagnosing meridian imbalance in relation to particular states of mind, using meridian test/ alarm points; [3] the knowledge of layers or sequences of meridian imbalance in relation to particular emotional states; [4] ways of treating meridians, by stimulation with needles or tapping or touch (Goodheart) or by the use of affirmations (Diamond). What Callahan learned to do was similar to all of these, but subtly different and startlingly effective.

Mary

Callahan had been working for about eighteen months with a woman called Mary Ford, who had a long-standing and severe phobia of water. She could not bear to be near water, bathed and drank as little as possible, avoided venturing out if it rained and did not like to see water on television or in views of the ocean or rivers. This had troubled her for as long as she could remember. It was a true phobia, in that there appeared to be no traumatic antecedents. Using conventional cognitive and behavioural and hypnotherapeutic methods of the time, Callahan had enabled Mary to make sufficient progress to tolerate sitting with her feet dangling in his swimming pool, but she would do this and feel intense distress—she had learned to tolerate her anxiety but the phobia was as strong as ever. On the basis of muscle testing, Callahan knew that there was a problem in Mary's stomach meridian—but he did not know quite what to do about this. One day, acting on a whim, he suggested to her that she tap on a point at the end of the stomach meridian. This procedure of tapping on the first (or last) point of a meridian was not in general use. To his amazement, Mary leapt up, declaring "it's gone!" and ran exuberantly to the swimming pool. Callahan describes how he thought she had gone mad and called after her not to jump in—but she called back to reassure him that she was fully aware she could not swim. She subsequently explained that what she meant by "its gone!" was that the anxiety she had always experienced in her stomach had suddenly been released and she no longer experienced any anxiety. Her phobia had disappeared in an instant—and never returned. Callahan was astonished, but, fortunately, rather than dismissing this event as just some strange fluke, he persisted in exploring what it meant and how he could use the same principles to help other patients.

Sequences of tapping

He found that many patients required more than one point to be tapped and that these needed to be done in a particular sequence— just as Diamond found that meridian imbalance emerges in layers. Callahan used a similar procedure to that described by Diamond, except that instead of having the patient make affirmations to correct each meridian (as Diamond had done) he had them tap the beginning or end of the meridian. An exception to the general principle of tapping a beginning of end of a meridian is the kidney meridian, which is tapped at the K27 points under the collar bones. In an early outline of his method for treating phobias (Callahan, 1985), he described having the patient tap on the big toe (for the spleen meridian) and the second toe (for the stomach meridian)—points which are no longer routinely used.

Callahan's muscle testing procedure for diagnosing sequences of tapping for the particular individual in relation to the particular target problem cannot properly be learned from a book. The interested reader is best advised to obtain the 'Step A' material from Dr Callahan [www.tftrx.com] and to take a 'Step B' diagnostic workshop with Dr Callahan or other authorised trainer. Once grasped, the TFT causal diagnostic method is enormously effective and simple—and can be applied to any state of psychological or physical distress. It reveals the meridian coding for any dysfunctional state.

Callahan's v Diamond's diagnostic procedure for meridian sequence

There was one difference between Callahan's diagnostic procedure for determining the meridians requiring treatment and that described by Diamond. Both of them used the same test/alarm points (described above in the account of Diamond's work), and both would usually press on the arm, thus using the deltoid muscle as an indicator. However, the impression from Diamond's writings (1985) is that, after the initial investigations using muscle testing with the patient touching the thymus, he would continue by muscle testing 'in the clear' with a strong muscle—and would then look for the meridian test point that made the muscle weak, which he would then correct with an affirmation. By contrast, Callahan would ask the patient to tune into the target problem, which would normally make the muscle test weak. He would then search for the meridian test point that made the muscle strong—and then treat this meridian by having the patient tap on the appropriate meridian point. Diamond did mention in passing that sometimes thinking of a stressful situation would make an indicator muscle test weak, and that then he would search for the meridian test point that made the muscle strong—a 'double negative', as he called it—but this did not, according to his published account, form the normal basis of his procedure as it did for Callahan. The basic principle here seems to be that if we start with a weak muscle we look for the meridian that makes it strong, and if start with a strong muscle (but know from other data, such as the thymus test that there is a meridian problem) then we look for the meridian test point that makes it weak.

Common sequences—algorithms

Callahan found that very often the same sequences would emerge when different people were muscle tested for similar mental states. Thus *anxiety* would usually involve the following meridian sequences: [stomach] under eye, [spleen] under arm, [kidney] collar bone; *claustrophobic anxiety and spider phobia* might involve: [spleen] under arm, [stomach] under eye, [kidney] collar bone; *trauma* might involve: [bladder] eye brow next to the nose; [kidney] collar bone; *anger* might involve [heart] little finger; *rage* might involve [gall bladder] side of the eye. Extensive lists of these common sequences, or 'algorithms', have been published in books such as Dr Callahan's *Tapping the Healer Within* (2001) and Suzanne Connolly's *Thought Field Therapy: Clinical Applications* (2004). The important point that Callahan found was that sequence is usually crucial. Incorrect sequences would not work.

Good and effective work can be done using TFT algorithms. These do not involve knowing how to muscle test. Thus, algorithms can readily be incorporated into other forms of psychotherapy without any need for physical contact with the client. On the other hand, the diagnostic muscle testing procedures allow the practitioner a much deeper and clearer knowledge of what is going on in the energy system on a moment-to-moment basis.

Quantum drops in the subjective units of distress

Using the Callahan methods, the practitioner works with the client until the 'subjective units of distress', a widely used Likert scale of 0-10, have collapsed to zero—the point when the client can no longer locate any distress at all when thinking of the target problem. Usually the distress drops in significant 'quantum' jumps—of at least two points, and sometimes more. The effect is normally quite startling, on first encounter.

Psychological reversal

Callahan discovered two complications in the work with some patients: psychological reversal, and neurological disorganisation. He noticed that some patients, the ones who did not initially respond to the tapping method, would display a paradoxical muscle test response when asked to make certain statements. Normally, a person will muscle test strong to the statement 'I want to be over this problem' and weak to 'I want to keep this problem'. Some patients showed a reverse reaction, testing strong to wanting to keep the problem and weak to wanting to be free of it. For a time, Callahan did not know what to do about psychological reversal; it completely blocked treatment, whether by tapping or conventional therapy. One solution he found worked was to have the patient ingest a small amount of Bach Flower Rescue Remedy. A problem with this was that some patients did not like to take a seemingly strange herbal concoction and were suspicious of it. Subsequently Callahan found that having the client tap on the side of the hand, on the small intestine meridian, whilst thinking of the problem, usually corrected the reversal. Initially he combined this with having the patient make a statement of self-acceptance—a strategy he developed from the work of Carl Rogers—but subsequently he found this to be unnecessary, although it is an effective correction for reversal in its own right (Callahan, 2001d). More recently, as Callahan and colleagues have explored the ways in which psychological reversal is actually manifest as electrical voltage changes on the surface of the body, measurable with a simple voltmeter (Callahan, 2006), he has a renewed enthusiasm for the remarkable effectiveness of Rescue Remedy in correcting reversals. Thus Dr Callahan discovered, through trial and error, three corrections for psychological reversal: [1] Bach Rescue Remedy; [2] a statement of self-acceptance; [3] tapping the side of the hand on the small intestine meridian.

Callahan also found that there could be different layers of psychological reversal. Commonly, after a person's subjective units of distress have dropped quite low (perhaps to 2 or 3), further dissipation of distress will appear to stall. When the person is muscle tested to the statement 'I want to be *completely* over this problem' he or she will test weak. Callahan called this a 'mini-reversal' and applied the same correction of having the patient tap the side of the hand, this time whilst thinking of being completely over the problem. He also identified reversals relating to the future, expressed in the testing statement 'I *will* be completely over this problem'. Sometimes reversals would occur recurrently, so that a few minutes, or even seconds, after a correction the reversal would reappear. Callahan eventually realised that these recurrent reversals were often an indication of the action of 'individual energy toxins', chemical substances (in food, the environment, or grooming products) that directly disrupted that person's energy system. The discovery of individual energy toxins was possible only as a result of the development of a highly potent and efficient therapeutic method such as TFT and the use of muscle testing which allows a direct observation of the effects of certain substances; when using less effective methods, the role of energy toxins would never become apparent. Fortunately, in the last few years Dr Callahan has developed a simple method of neutralising energy toxins, known as the '7 second toxin treatment' [training material known as the 'toxin pack' is available from www.tftrx.com or from a Callahan Techniques licensed trainer].

Neurological disorganisation and the collar bone breathing technique

The second complication that Callahan identified was that of 'neurological disorganisation', long-recognised within Applied Kinesiology as subtle forms of incoherence in the neurological and energy systems. This would make both diagnosis and treatment within TFT more difficult. Like psychological reversal, it may sometimes be a result of individual energy toxins. Callahan devised an effective and efficient treatment for this, known as the collar bone breathing technique—which appears to be derived partly from the 'respiratory challenge' combined with various components used in Applied Kinesiology to correct 'switching' (Frost, 2002, pp. 70, 86–89). This involves sequenced breathing of five steps ([1] breathing in fully, hold; [2] breathe out halfway, hold; [3] breath out all the way, hold; [4] breath in halfway, hold; [5] breathe normally), whilst the client holds finger tips to the K27 collar bone point and at the same time tapping on the 'gamut' thyroid meridian point between the knuckles of the little and ring finger of the back of the hand. The fingers are then moved to the other collar bone point, and then the knuckles (in effect, the back of the hand) are held to the collar bones. This is repeated with the other hand. Thus the 5-stage breathing and tapping procedure progresses through 8 different finger/knuckle positions—a total of 40 different steps. It is an essentially simple procedure that is best learned through direct tuition in a Callahan Techniques workshop.

The '9 gamut' procedure

When a person's distress has fallen to near zero, it sometimes needs a little more help to clear it fully. Callahan noticed that if a person is muscle tested at this point, he or she might register weak when performing any one of the following 9 actions: [1] closing the eyes; [2] opening the eyes; [3] moving the eyes down right; [4] moving the eyes down left; [5] moving the eyes in a circle one way; [6] moving the eyes in a circle the other way; [7] humming a few notes; [8] counting a few numbers; [9] humming again. This observation, linked partly to the Applied Kinesiology tests for 'ocular lock' (Frost, 2002, p. 85), would appear to indicate that certain brain activities, expressed in one or more of these movements, were still associated with a disruption in the energy system in a way that was linked with the target problem. It may also be regarded as a form of neurological disorganisation. This would be corrected by performing the action and tapping the thyroid meridian point on the back of the hand between the knuckles of the little finger and ring finger. One further odd observation was that step 7 could actually be *either* humming or counting, which would then be followed by counting or humming (whichever step 7 had not been)—but then step 7 might have to be repeated in step 9. It appeared that although step 7 might register strong initially, it might register weak after step 8. Like many other phenomena in this field, the precise reason for this is unclear, but the method is based on direct observation. Although it is simple enough to muscle test for each of these steps, it is actually quicker just to do the whole lot routinely if it appears needed (taking less than thirty seconds). Because a gamut of 9 different actions are conducted whilst tapping on the thyroid meridian on the back of the hand, Callahan called this the '9 gamut point'.

Why is it called Thought Field Therapy?

Callahan points out that the TFT procedure is crucially dependent on the client thinking of the problem whilst the muscle testing and meridian tapping takes place. Although it does not matter to an acupuncturist what the client thinks of during the treatment, in TFT this is all important. He reasoned therefore that the *thought* is expressed within the energy *field* of the body. The thought is encoded in the patterning of the energy field, which is expressed in the *sequence* of meridians that require to be treated. This sequence is analogous to a code for a combination lock. It is not just a matter of a 'blockage' or 'imbalance' in a meridian, but of the *information* encoded in the energy system. This information—which Callahan calls a *perturbation*—generates the disturbance in the body that is experienced as the troubling emotion. When the perturbation—the active information in the field—is cleared, then the disturbance in the body collapses. Perturbations can be cleared very quickly since they contain little mass or inertia; they are *signals*, which can shift in an instant.

Callahan links his observations and theory with the ideas of biologist Rupert Sheldrake and the concept of the morphogenic fields that contain information guiding the form and behaviour of living organisms. These insights are suggestive of ways in which perturbations, such as phobias, might be inherited through the generational energy fields or the 'collective unconscious'. True phobias, without traumatic antecedents in the person's life history, usually relate to situations that might, at some time in the history of the species, actually have been very dangerous, when the fear would have been potentially life-preserving—for example, of snakes and spiders in certain parts of the world. Callahan considers how some fears are normally subsumed in the course of individual development—such as the fear of heights. Certain factors appear able to reactivate these fears that had previously been subsumed in the development of either the individual or the species. Moreover, it has been observed that individual energy toxins may sometimes reactivate fears that had previously been successfully treated with TFT.

The 'apex problem'

Callahan noticed an intriguing response shown by many clients, regularly observed by any effective TFT practitioner. This is that the client will experience a marked relief of the presenting problem or symptom, but will then appear not to believe this, or will confabulate some explanation so as to dismiss this effect. Sometimes a person will deny that he or she had a problem in the first place, or may assert that it has gone simply because they have been distracted by the tapping. Commonly the client may suggest that he or she cannot feel any of the previous anxiety because it is so relaxing in the therapist's office, or because the therapist has such a calming voice or charisma. It seems that because the client's brain cannot track the process of emotional change, he or she is bewildered by it and resorts to a degraded form of thinking and spurious explanations. In Callahan's terms, the client retreats from the *apex* of his or her thinking—and hence Callahan referred to this as the 'apex effect'.

Heart rate variability

One of Callahan's further innovative developments is his demonstration of how heart rate variability [HRV] may be used as an objective measure of the effects of TFT. HRV is the subtle variation in the heart rate, which can provide important indications of the health of the body, including the autonomic nervous system. In a state of health, the HRV remains within optimal limits, neither too high nor too low. A completely even heart rate is a very dangerous sign—and, indeed, a midwife confirmed to me that this is considered an emergency in a foetal heart rate. A person is not conscious of their HRV. It is difficult to influence. Callahan's attention was drawn to the effects of TFT by a cardiac specialist, Dr Fuller Royal. Dr Royal had been giving some of his patients very simple TFT treatments, basically the algorithm for phobia, and had done HRV testing before and after the TFT. He reported to Dr Callahan as follows: "I can tell you that the effect on the autonomic nervous system is nothing short of phenomenal" and added that "Heart Rate Variability is the only test known that will not respond to a placebo effect" [quoted in Callahan, 2001, p. 57]. HRV measures have now become part of the routine repertoire of many TFT practitioners and Callahan and colleagues have continued to find that Thought Field Therapy helps normalise HRV in a way that other psychological therapies do not. Thus TFT appears, on this objective measure of the body's physiology, to work at a deeper level and more effectively than any other known therapy. The implications of this are clearly immense.

'Voice technology'

This term refers to the capacity to diagnose meridian sequences by hearing the client's voice over the phone, thus enabling many clients to be treated much more easily. I cannot discuss this further because I do not know what it is. No-one has been able to tell me what it consists of. Dr Callahan told me it was a trade secret. Very few people have trained in the use of VT. Thus, whilst I can speculate, there is nothing I can usefully write about it.

Summary of some of Callahan's achievements in developing TFT

- Discovery of an extremely effective and efficient method of treating emotional problems—contrasting starkly with the relative ineffectiveness of earlier talk-based therapies.
- Discovery of the way in which emotional distress is encoded in the energy field of the body.
- Development of an efficient way of diagnosing these encoded perturbations through muscle testing.
- Development of the algorithms of regularly occurring meridian sequences.
- Exploration of psychological reversal and its treatment.
- Exploration of how psychological reversal is manifest in voltage shifts on the surface of the body, measurable with ordinary voltmeters.
- Development of simple and efficient ways of correcting neurological disorganisation through collar bone breathing and the 9 gamut procedure.

- Discovery of the role of energy toxins in psychological disturbance, how their effects can be identified and treated within the
  framework of TFT.
- Exploration of the use of Heart Rate Variability as an objective
  indicator of the effects of TFT.
- Identification of the 'apex problem'.
- Development of a subtle theory of the 'thought field'—and elaboration of the many implications of TFT for understanding the
  mind-body interaction.

The contribution of James Durlacher

Dr James Durlacher, a chiropractor, became involved with Applied
Kinesiology at the very beginning of its emergence in 1964, and was
a Teacher Diplomate of the International College of Applied Kinesiology. Somewhat influenced by Callahan, whom he met in 1985,
as well as others associated with Applied Kinesiology, he published
a book in 1994 called *Freedom From Fear Forever*. Here he described
the use of muscle testing to detect psychological reversal and also
to find the particular meridian most involved in the target problem.
However, the text implies that he generally focused on just the first
meridian point that was found to make the arm strong—and he
would have the client tap on this point until the SUDs dropped substantially. If they did not drop, he would check again for psychological reversal. He considered that where various meridians were
involved these related to different aspects of the trauma or other
problem. A further difference from Callahan's approach is that he
would use the treatment/tapping points (as used by Callahan) also
as the *test points* for 'therapy localisation' to find which meridian
rendered the muscle strong when the client thought of the problem.
Durlacher died in 2006.

Emotional Freedom Technique [EFT]

In 1995, Gary Craig, a personal performance coach who had trained
with Callahan, launched a simplified derivative of TFT, which he
called Emotional Freedom Techniques. One of the major differences

from TFT was that the method relied on a simple standard tapping sequence—basically tapping all the meridian points. Muscle testing was also not involved. Apart from this, most of the ingredients of the algorithm level of TFT were retained. Craig incorporated a routine correction for psychological reversal by having the client tap on the side of the hand whilst making a statement that both referred to the problem and affirmed self-acceptance. The formula for this 'opening statement' was "Even though I have [X problem] I completely accept myself", repeated three times. The client would then tap on all the points whilst uttering a brief 'reminder phrase' at each point. At the end of the sequence the 9 gamut would be performed and then the sequence would be repeated. The TFT 'mini-reversal' would be addressed by having the client tap on the points whilst saying "remaining ...X...", thus instructing the energy system that the rest of the problem is now being targeted.

One of the advantages of this simplification was that the procedure became very widely and easily learned and available worldwide. Craig produced a free manual, downloadable from his website [www.emofree.com], written in simple language for the general public. In addition he prepared an inexpensive 'EFT course' on DVD, which provides quite extensive teaching on many aspects of the application of EFT, much of which is based on TFT—later followed by a number of more advanced teaching series. However, it must be acknowledged that in some of the examples on the 'EFT course', Craig is using TFT algorithms and even Voice Technology, rather than relying on a standard tapping sequence.

Used in a mechanical way, EFT is certainly helpful but appears not as dramatically so as TFT. This is not surprising since the crucial role of sequence of tapping is discarded. Craig argues that sequence seems not important, although in later DVDs [such as Steps Toward Becoming the Ultimate Therapist] he teaches the use of intuition and surrogate muscle testing in determining the best sequences to tap. Of course, simple sequences will be covered within a few rounds of EFT tapping, even though a number of unnecessary points may also have been tapped.

An indication of Craig's stance toward diagnostic sequence is indicated by a few quotes from the transcript of the workshop Steps Toward Becoming the Ultimate Therapist (2002):

"Today is going to deal with diagnostics via muscle testing. But not via muscle testing in the standard way; that is one-on-one muscle testing where the practitioner tests somebody else's arm ... This instead is going to be surrogate muscle testing, where we test ourselves as though we are the other person... [p. 51]

[and, a little later, describing his own intuitive sense of which points need to be tapped] ... I just get an inkling, a notion, and I pay attention to it. This is a very, very important point ... I just had a couple of calls from people in the last seminar asking me how to do that. It's like they were looking for a GONG, like a voice from God 'Under the eye, stupid'. And it doesn't happen that way. Some people get a strong sensation. I don't. I just get a notion, a sort of a knowing. And I pay attention to it. And it's different for different people." [p. 59]

However, Craig has emphasised another aspect of precision and specificity—that of focusing on the many different aspects of a target problem. These aspects might be sensory details of a feared situation, temporal details of a trauma narrative, or different thoughts and emotions linked to the target. He has repeatedly pointed out that EFT does not work if applied too broadly or globally. Each detail of the target must be addressed in turn, and if the presenting problem is inherently global, then the underlying traumas, emotions, and thoughts must be addressed. Craig and other exponents of EFT have developed considerable skill in the use of language to locate and target the issues underlying the presenting problem. A rhythm of 'tapping and talking' develops, often with intense attunement between therapist and client, both tapping at the same time. Thus, where TFT practitioners emphasise the importance of meridian sequence, EFT practitioners make skilful use of language to tune into and evoke the relevant emotional details of the target problem. Whilst EFT is very linguistically oriented, TFT is relatively non-verbal during the specific treatment, since the client is asked simply to think of the problem. EFT is relatively unconcerned with niceties and details of the energy system, but is very concerned with what Craig calls the 'art of delivery', by which he means the skill with which it is targeted on the most relevant aspects of the problem.

A further important difference from TFT is in Craig's theory behind EFT. He states that EFT is like a psychological application of acupuncture and that "the cause of all negative emotions is a disruption in the body's energy system". Whilst this has a certain simple immediate appeal, as an explanation, it is somewhat less subtle that Callahan's account of the thought field, perturbations, and active information. Actually, of course, neither TFT nor EFT are *based* on theory. TFT derived from *observations*, as did the earlier discoveries within Applied Kinesiology. This basis in observation is part of its strength.

EFT has developed considerably since its first launch in 1995 as a sort of simplified TFT. Many practitioners around the world have developed innovative and useful applications with all manner of psychological and physical problems, and in a great variety of settings. Craig has always encouraged creative and imaginative play in the use of EFT. Dr Callahan, perhaps not surprisingly, does not hold EFT in high regard. One of his persuasive criticisms is that, torn from its roots in TFT and muscle testing, EFT gives its practitioners little direct awareness of what exactly is going on in the client's energy system. From this point of view, EFT might seem like using a formula without understanding why or what the formula is based on. Others might feel that both TFT and EFT have their strengths — and that EFT, initially a rebellious breakaway from TFT, has developed its own life and identity.

Further developments in energy psychology

For some years Callahan was working largely alone in developing TFT. We have reason to be grateful for his persistence during those lonely years, which cannot have been easy. During the 1990s others began to use his methods, teach them and modify them. EFT certainly played an important role in this expansion. Then in 1998, the Association for Comprehensive Energy Psychology was launched, providing a network for practitioners to share ideas and observations, undertake research, and organise conferences [www.energypsych.org]. The field is now very lively and vibrant indeed.

CHAPTER FOUR

Some simple beginnings—tapping points and procedures, using EFT as a derivative of Thought Field Therapy

A comment on the differences between EFT and TFT.

I learned EFT before I learned TFT—and found EFT to be the most extraordinarily effective, rapid, and gentle form of emotional healing that I had encountered in 30 years of clinical practice. Later I studied Thought Field Therapy, and other derivatives of Applied Kinesiology, and learned more detail of the human energy system, how it encodes trauma, and how to read the information written in the energy system. Although EFT is a derivative of TFT, it has established its own particular line of enquiry and skill, focused less on the details of how the dysfunctional information is encoded in the energy system and more upon identifying and targeting the content of the core beliefs, emotions, and traumas—the implicit psychosomatic structures lying beneath the client's presenting problems. Whilst often perceived as competing technical and theoretical perspectives, with a certain element of mutual bad feeling, I believe TFT and EFT are complementary.

Where to tap

The following points are mostly either the beginning or ends of the fourteen main meridians—with two exceptions: [1] the collar bone point is K27 on the kidney meridian; [2] the neurolymphatic area on the upper left side of the chest, sometimes termed the 'sore spot' (used sometimes in connection with correcting psychological reversals and in the 'set up' stage of EFT). Dr Roger Callahan discovered that these meridian points can be tapped to clear perturbations from the energy field when the relevant thought field is activated. Since EFT, as developed by Callahan's student, Gary Craig, is an offshoot of TFT, the same tapping points are used.

When I first came across accounts of energy tapping methods, I wondered whether the meridian points would be recognisable to acupuncturists. Further study revealed that they are absolutely the same points used in acupuncture. I have taught energy psychology to acupuncturists, who have not objected to any of the information or principles described, although they were previously unaware of how to use the meridians in this way. There are good pictorial atlases of acupuncture meridians—e.g. Ogal & Stor, 2005. These can be useful for the student who would like to explore the use of other points on the meridians, which can sometimes be helpful.

Both TFT and EFT use the following meridian tapping points. In EFT, no particular sequence is followed, but commonly the order listed below is followed. There are differing views about the importance of sequence—but if a standard sequence is tapped repeatedly, then various embedded sequences will eventually be covered.

1. 'Karate chop', side of hand. Small intestine meridian—used to correct psychological reversal and as part of the 'setup' phase of EFT.

2. The neurolymphatic area on the upper left area of the chest—there is more lymphatic tissue on the left than the right. This area, known as the 'sore spot', because it is usually tender, is rubbed for reversal correction and may be used during the 'setup' phase of EFT. Gentle strokes downwards, following the natural lymphatic flow, may be preferable to circular movements. Dr Callahan no longer uses the 'sore spot'.

3. Eye brow, next to nose. Bladder meridian—particularly important in relation to shock/trauma and sadness.

4. Side of eye. Gall bladder meridian—can be important in states of rage.

5. Under eye. Stomach meridian—important in anxiety.

6. Under nose. Governing vessel—important in states of embarrassment and also used sometimes to correct reversals.

7. Chin, under lower lip. Central vessel—important in shame.

8. Under arm, opposite male nipple and on female bra strap. Spleen meridian—important in relation to feelings of insecurity.

9. Collar bone end. Kidney meridian—very important generally.

10. Under nipple towards base of rib cage. Liver meridian. Not often used, partly because it can be socially awkward for women to access. It can, however, be important in relation to issues of toxicity, including emotions and experiences that are perceived as toxic.

11. Thumb, outside at base of nail. Lung meridian—important in relation to breathing difficulties and early traumas, including birth trauma.

12. First finger/index (thumb side) at base of nail. Large intestine meridian—important in guilt.

13. Middle finger (thumb side), base of nail. Pericardium—heart protector—or circulation-sex meridian. This can be important in relation to protection of 'emotions of the heart'.

14. Little finger (thumb side), base of nail. Heart meridian—important in states of anger.

15. Gamut point—back of hand, between knuckles of little finger and ring finger. Triple heater, or thyroid meridian. This is so called because Dr Callahan devised a gamut of procedures to be performed briefly whilst tapping this point.

In Thought Field Therapy, specific sequences of points are tapped—either the 'off the shelf' algorithms, or sequences that are diagnosed by muscle testing for the particular problem of the particular patient at that particular time. TFT algorithms are listed in various texts, such as Callahan (2001)—and some are indicated at various points in this book. For a thorough understanding of the procedure of TFT, the reader is advised to seek the training workshops and other material available through official websites, such as www.tftrx.com and www. thoughtfieldtherapy.co.uk.

By contrast, in Emotional Freedom Techniques—the simpler derivative of TFT—the procedure is to tap more or less all the points, without regard for sequence. This still works quite well, although perhaps without the laser-like dramatic effects often found when using more specific TFT sequences. The obvious advantage of EFT is that it is very easy to learn the basics, and then to become skilled in what Gary Craig calls 'the art of delivery', which is to do with nuances of the use of language and the way EFT is targeted on the most crucial aspects of a problem. Whilst I would always recommend a potential practitioner of energy psychology to learn Thought Field Therapy, with its clearer focus on what precisely is going on at the interface of the thought and the energy field, I also believe that EFT is valuable, flexible, and fun—and has become highly sophisticated in its manner of accessing and targeting the detailed aspects of an emotional problem. It is also ideal for clients to learn as a self-help tool for affect regulation and relief of distress.

Notes on modifications of the standard EFT sequence:

[a] In practice, a short version of the full EFT sequence is often used: eyebrow; side of eye; under eye; under nose; chin; under arm; collar bone. Other additional tapping points may be used, particularly the top of the head, the insides of the wrists, and the insides of the ankles.

[b] Gary Craig's standard sequence runs from chin, to collar bone, to arm, since it is basically moving down the body. I have modified this slightly in the above list to: chin, arm, collar bone—in order to incorporate one of the most commonly used Thought Field Therapy algorithms for anxiety: under eye; under arm; collar bone.

[c] Other commonly used TFT sequences that may be incorporated:

For anger: little finger; collar bone.
For shame; chin; collar bone
For claustrophobia and fear of spiders: under arm; under eye; collar bone.
For depression and physical pain: 30-50 taps on the gamut point.

The basics of using EFT

Detailed teaching of EFT can be obtained from the DVDs available inexpensively through Gary Craig's website (www.emofree. com) or from a book such as Feinstein, Eden, and Craig (2005). The basic method is described in Gary Craig's free manual available for download from his website. Many different applications of EFT are described on the DVDs—and these remain the best source of information on how to use EFT by its original developer. The one single complete video demonstration of an EFT treatment is 'Dave's fear of water', on Craig's 'EFT Course' (the first of the DVD series). This begins with a period of work addressing the various aspects of Dave's water phobia whilst in a consulting room, proceeding then to an in vivo desensitisation with both client and therapist in the swimming pool, continuing the tapping—thus illustrating how EFT can be construed as a component within a cognitive-behavioural approach. However, when used skilfully, EFT can rapidly lead into deep psychodynamic material.

The simplest and most theory-lean formulation of the nature of the EFT method (as opposed to TFT) is to consider that, in some incompletely understood way, tapping on certain sensitive areas of the body disrupts previously persisting patterns of thought, emotion, and physiology, resulting in sensations of calm and well-being in the body in place of the anxiety or other distress. This appears to bring about a process of desensitisation in relation to anxiety-evoking stimuli. There is no necessary assumption about meridians or energy fields. Craig proposes his 'discovery statement' that 'the cause of all negative emotions is a disruption in the body's energy system'. However, since the link between cognitive-emotional constellations and particular meridians (or meridian sequences) is greatly loosened in the procedure of EFT (compared to TFT), all we are left certain of is that tapping on the body seems to clear or disrupt previous states of distress, and that this effect is often lasting. It may be that different healing components are at work in TFT and EFT, some acting more strongly in one method than the other.

One of Gary Craig's most important points of emphasis is his advice to focus EFT on specific aspects of a problem. If the target is too broad or global, it will not be impacted very strongly by EFT. By addressing one aspect at a time—whether this be a sensory-perceptual detail, a kinaesthetic sensation, or a temporal element (i.e. this happened and then that happened …), or a particular thought—the target problem can be worn away bit by bit. It may also be necessary to unearth the emotions, traumas, and thoughts underneath the presenting problem, just as one would in any psychoanalytically oriented therapy. Fortunately, once tapping begins, it starts to loosen and facilitate the free-associative and intuitive processes in both client and therapist, so that the underlying issues soon come into view.

The basic EFT procedure

1. Take a history in the normal way.

2. Identify issues to target with EFT. These might be recent or past traumas, recurrent anxieties, physical or emotional pain etc. Be aware that the presenting problem may be the surface of a number of complex strands of emotional and psychodynamic problems. Core beliefs can also be targeted, especially if these can be linked to recurrent messages given by caregivers in childhood, or to formative traumatic experiences.

3. If appropriate, ask the client to generate a movie-like mental sequence that captures some representative aspects of formative early experiences that have contributed to the presenting problem. EFT is applied at each point in the sequence where the client experiences any emotional intensity.

4. If a trauma or anxiety, or other distressing event is targeted, ask the client for a Subjective Units of Distress/Disturbance rating (usually 0-10).

5. Provide an explanation of EFT that is appropriate and acceptable to the client—e.g. to say that it is a psychological application of acupressure, or simply that it has been found that tapping on certain areas of the body helps to loosen the fixed patterns of thought and distress that have become established. Clients will often readily accept the statement that talking alone is often insufficiently helpful, since their experience tells them that this is true.

6. Find an appropriate form of words to refer to the problem— using, as far as possible, the client's own words.

7. Begin the 'set-up'—tapping side of hand (or 'sore spot' neurolymphatic reflex) whilst having the client say "Even though I have this problem (name it) ... I completely accept myself". This combines two functions, of correcting any psychoenergetic reversal that might be present, and also activating the relevant thought field.

8. Have the client tap through the EFT sequence, whilst using a short 'reminder phrase' at each point.

9. Proceed through the 'nine gamut' sequence: whilst continually tapping the back of hand on the 'gamut spot' between the knuckles of the little finger and next finger, close eyes, open eyes, look down to right, down to left, eyes roll in a circle, circle other way, hum a few notes, count, hum again (or count, hum, and count again).

10. Repeat EFT sequence.

11. Check SUDs.

12. Repeat until SUDs have dropped to 0.

13. If the SUDs are not dropping, consider the possibility that the client has shifted aspects and is now preoccupied with another thought or emotion or memory. Apply EFT to this new aspect.

14. If the SUDs are not moving, use words that may address other or deeper aspects, voicing thoughts and fears that may relate to the client's deeper anxieties and feelings.

15. If the SUDs seem to be stuck at around 2 or 3 (a *minireversal*), use the phrasing "Even though I still have *some* of (this problem) ..."

16. Or "Even though I have some *remaining* ..."

17. Then have the client tap to "*remaining* ...".

Always test the result. Ask the client to think vividly of the previously troubling situation and to try to locate any distress.

Treatment of complex cases ('personality disorders' etc.) simply involves the application of the EFT (or TFT) method to each of the numerous issues (anxieties, traumas, emotional pains and injuries)—i.e. to the multiple thought fields—that will emerge in the course of psychotherapy. In this way, EFT will be combined with a more conventional psychological therapy (cognitive, psychoanalytic etc.).

However, energy methods can cut through much of the superficial verbal derivatives of the deep energetic structure of the patient's problems, allowing this to be addressed more directly and rapidly than is possible with conventional forms of psychotherapy.

30 strategies for making EFT effective

Although the basic procedure of the Emotional Freedom Technique is almost absurdly simple, applying it effectively requires some skill and artistry. I have found the following strategies to be helpful, most of which are well known amongst practitioners of EFT and are described within the online tutorials and newsletters of the www. emofree.com website.

1. **Be specific**
   Be specific about the target of the tapping round. Gary Craig repeatedly emphasises that EFT works extremely well, but only when applied to specific events, or details of these events. He uses the analogy of cutting down a forest. If the target is too global (e.g. 'my low self-esteem' or 'being rejected by my mother') this may be like trying to cut down a forest with one blow of an axe. Instead, more specific experiences and issues should be targeted. This is then like cutting down individual trees, with the positive result that the effect generalises—so that (to pursue the analogy) the whole forest begins to tumble. Another analogy favoured by Gary Craig is that of the table top and its legs. A global problem, such as low self-esteem, or a general feeling of abandonment or anxiety, is like the table top, but it is held in place by the 'table legs' of the various specific experiences that have given rise to it. However, the specific experiences might themselves contain many aspects and therefore are like further table tops. For example, if one specific event is 'the time my mother left me in the shopping mall when I was 8', this might include aspects such as 'the fear of being all by myself', 'the fear of all the big adults around me', 'the guilt I felt for what I might have done to cause it', 'the don't care look in my mother's eyes when I got home'. Each such element may need to be addressed. http://www.emofree.com/Archives/Archive44.htm

2. **Identify aspects**
   Identify the various important *aspects* of the problem or traumatic experience. Aspects may include sensory-perceptual details of a traumatic experience, the various details of the sequence of a trauma, the different emotions involved, the

significant thoughts (especially the self-related negative cognitions), and the bodily sensations. Gary Craig provides a
tutorial on aspects on his website: http://www.emofree.com/
tutorial/tutordfour.htm

3. **Be alert to shifting aspects**
    If the SUDs do not appear to be dropping, it may be that the
    client has shifted aspects. The first one that was address has
    dropped in intensity, but now another emotional aspect (a
    feeling, thought, or traumatic memory) has come into the fore-
    ground of consciousness. This new aspect must then be tar-
    geted. It is important to enquire what is in the client's mind at
    any particular moment.

4. **Layering of emotions**
    Psychopathology derives from disturbing emotions, against
    which the person has developed various defences. It is impor-
    tant to identify the warded off emotions behind the presenting
    symptom or problem—and then to target these with EFT. There
    may be many layers of emotions and associated thoughts and
    memories. As one layer is cleared, the next may step forward
    in the mental queue.

5. **Finding core issues**
    Gary Craig emphasises the importance of reaching the 'core
    issues' that lie behind the presenting problems. He suggests
    the following questions as often helpful in finding these: 'What
    does this issue remind you of?'; 'When was the first time you
    can remember feeling the same kind of feeling?'; 'If there was
    a deeper emotion underlying this problem, what might it be?';
    Sometimes a client may answer that they do not know. This can
    often effectively be countered with the paradoxical question:
    'If you did know, what would it be?'. Another useful question
    is: 'If you could live your life over again, what person or event
    would be prefer to skip?' http://www.emofree.com/tutorial/
    tutorgseven.htm

6. **'Bottom line' beliefs and fears—'writings on the wall'**
    Core issues may be related to what cognitive therapists think of
    as 'bottom line' thoughts and beliefs. Cognitive therapy strate-

gies of Socratic questioning can be helpful in identifying these. The core troubling cognitions or schemas *and* the traumas behind them can then be targeted with EFT.

Listen to the spontaneous words and phrases that the client uses free-associatively in the work. Every now and then the client will express a distinct thought or perception (e.g. "I was completely helpless" — "nobody cared" — "I am so stupid" — "He was a bastard" etc.). Immediately seize these and target them with EFT.

Gary Craig often refers to the cognitive structures of beliefs, internal messages, and automatic thoughts, as the 'writings on the wall'. These are the inner rules by which we organise our perceptions and expectations in the world. In turn, our thoughts, beliefs, and perceptions influence our physiology.

7. **Use of EMDR**
    Those who are qualified to use EMDR may like to employ bilateral stimulation to facilitate the free-associative process to generate further aspects relevant to the presenting problem — then to tap the perturbations away.

8. **Use of language to fine-tune the thought field**
    Language can be used to deepen, enhance, and fine-tune the emotional aspects of the thought field. Sometimes stronger words, spoken with more emphasis are required. For example, a woman responded with only partial relief when tapping through her thoughts of anger and envy towards a group of colleagues who excluded her in the shop where she works; however, when she was guided to speak with more emphasis along the lines of "I really hate that group; I hate their happy smiling faces; I hate their laughter; I hate their enjoyment; they really make me want to vomit ... etc" she experienced a signifi-cant drop in her anxiety and distress.

9. **Free-association**
    As the rhythm of EFT develops, it can become free-associa-tive — moving rapidly and deeply through many fundamen-tal issues. This is quietly awesome and exhilarating. At such times, I find my own energy shifting to a different level or

dimension—and the experience is of surrendering to a healing process that has its own momentum. This involves a slightly altered state of consciousness, which appears to enhance intuition. When flowing with this process, the therapist may voice phrases and associations for the client that often turn out to be startlingly apt.

10. **Tapping and talking**
Although the standard EFT protocol would normally target a specific aspect, very often it is helpful to engage in a process of 'tapping and talking', following whatever cognitive and emotional content emerges. Emotions and insight seem to flow much more rapidly when this is done. Gary Craig often dwells a great deal in a process of linguistically mirroring the client's initial state of mind, then gradually leading, through tapping and talking, taking the client through a range of potential insights and reframes of the problem. Tapping somehow seems to facilitate this process much more easily than if the two were simply talking.

11. **Addressing fundamental anxieties**
One of the delights of EFT is that even the most fundamental anxieties and self-perceptions can be drawn up into the EFT net and processed. For example, a man spoke of a recurrent dream in which the foundations of his house were weak and inadequately shored up. After he tapped on "Even though the foundations of my personality are about to collapse ..." he began to laugh and his mood noticeably lightened.

12. **'Tearless trauma technique'**
For many of our patients, their traumatic experiences may be too overwhelming to be processed with full conscious awareness. In such cases, Gary Craig's 'tearless trauma technique' is helpful. The client is asked to think of the trauma but not to enter into it with emotional intensity. Surprisingly, the EFT is still highly effective even though the trauma has not been accessed with affective vividness. By using this method the trauma can be gradually approached and eventually tested directly. When employing this tactic, the client can be asked

to keep their eyes focused externally in order to avoid become immersed in internal memories of trauma.

13. **Code word method**
The code word method. This is my elaboration of the tearless trauma method. The client is told that a neutral word (e.g. 'X' or a colour) is to be used to represent the traumatic experience. I find that it is possible to 'load' the code word with a large number of different emotions and other aspects relating to the trauma. The way it is done is simply to tell the client, carefully and with some emphasis, that all of these are to be represented by the code word, listing them in turn. I then tell the client not to think of the actual emotions or the target experience, but simply to tap with the words 'X'. Not only does this method seem to work extremely well, but also a great deal of psychological ground can be covered very quickly (and painlessly).

14. **"Sneaking up on the problem"**
Another strategy to minimise the potential for the client to feel overwhelmed when thinking of a trauma is what Gary Craig calls 'sneaking up on the problem'. This is the reverse of the usual recommendation to aim for specificity in the use of EFT. With some clients, such specificity in reference to trauma would evoke unmanageable levels of affect. For them, it is safer to begin at a more global level. A starting phrase might be "Even though that terrible thing happened …". Once the emotional intensity of this has been reduced by tapping, more specificity can gradually be introduced. The specificity might involve greater precision of emotional language—e.g. "I was *terrified* by what happened"—or more detail of the actual event—e.g. "I was terrified when I saw the plane hit the tower". In this way, the full detail and emotional qualities of the experience are gradually approached, but in a safe and manageable manner. Patricia Carrington describes a related method of breaking the traumatic event into very small details that are tapped on one at a time (there are related procedures used in EMDR). She describes both these techniques in the following article: http://www.emofree.com/Articles2/sneaking-up-on-problem.htm

Gary Craig writes more about 'sneaking up on the issue' in his discussion of major traumas that are experienced by the client as 'the big one', the constellation of memories and emotions that he or she simply cannot face, and which they dread the therapist leading them towards. He advises that in such cases the EFT is first targeted on the emotions and physiological reactions experienced on simply thinking of the problem: e.g. "Even though my heart is pounding thinking of this thing … Even though this thing seems too big to deal with …". Then, as the intensity begins to fall, the client might be asked if there is any aspect of the problem that they might be able to speak of. If so, then this aspect is tapped. Craig describes it as being like opening a door, whereby the intensity can gradually be worn away and the door opened more and more—all the time avoiding exposing the client to extreme levels of distress. http://www.emofree.com/FAQ/bigone.htm

15. When there is no emotional intensity

Sometimes the difficulty is the opposite of feeling overwhelmed and instead the client is unable to locate emotional intensity. This can make it difficult to identify the most relevant target for tapping. Gary Craig recommends asking the client what experience and memory he or she would most wish to have avoided. This is then targeted for EFT, focusing on whatever aspects the therapist intuits might be relevant. Although the client may not consciously register much change, if they are asked next time what memory they would wish to avoid, it is most likely they would choose a different one; this can be taken as an indication that the emotional aspects of the target memory have been addressed without conscious awareness. http://www.emofree.com/FAQ/nonfeeling.htm

16. Emphasis upon elimination of toxic emotions.

The two tapping points that can be used in the 'setup' as the treatments for 'psychological reversal'—the small intestine point on the side of the hand and the 'sore spot' lymphatic node on the chest—are both concerned with elimination of toxic material. To some extent, old emotions that have become stored within the body-mind tissues can be viewed as analogous to toxins (emotional toxins) and the system may need help and encouragement in clearing these. Where there is a particularly major or difficult issue to address, I like to have the client spend some time tapping on these points, with a statement about 'eliminating' the emotion or other aspect. The liver point, concerned with detoxification, can also be included in this way. This seems to combine particularly well with the code word method.

17. **'Chasing the pain'**
When using EFT in relation to physical discomforts, the location and nature of the pain may change. The strategy then is just to keep following the evolving discomfort, modifying the tapping statements appropriately, until it eventually collapses to a SUD of zero. Gary Craig calls this 'chasing the pain'. http://www.emofree.com/tutorial/tutorpsixteen.htm

18. **'Writings on the wall' and positive choices**
Gary Craig has likened EFT to an eraser—removing unwanted disturbances in the energy system. He has argued that this function can be complemented with affirmations of a positive nature. The affirmations work when the negative beliefs and anxieties (which Gary Craig calls the 'tail-enders'—see his *Palace of Possibilities* DVD) are neutralised with EFT; he also describes the negative beliefs as the 'writings on the wall', written by our significant caregivers and childhood attachment figures. Affirmations, the alternative positive information or 'writings' can easily be incorporated into the tapping sequence. Patricia Carrington calls this the 'choices method' (Carrington, 2001). This simply involves introducing the phrase "I choose now to ..." after the negative emotions and beliefs have been eliminated with EFT—or the 'choice' can be stated in place of the usual phrase of self-acceptance. The 'choice' must relate to the target problem and be congruent with the client's perceived reality. For example, this might be: "Even though I am anxious about this interview I choose to become calm and do the best I can". As with EMDR, positive ideas can be 'installed' just as negative ones can be processed or eliminated. The mind-body system appears naturally to move in the direction of health and a positive emotional state if the energetic blocks are released.

19. **Morphing the language, from negative to positive**
It is now common for EFT to build upon Carrington's modification by using a gradual morphing of language phrasing to lead
the client from a state of negativity into a more positive state of
mind. This is done by beginning with phrases and statements that
accurately mirror the person's anxiety or other negative emotion,
then, as tapping continues, alternative positive possibilities are
introduced. A particularly skilful practitioner of this approach is
Carol Look, who has developed many innovative forms of EFT,
including tapping whilst stating contrasting sides of an internal
argument, or whilst stating various versions of a refusal to relinquish a problem, before moving on to positive solutions. http://
www.emofree.com/Articles/top-10-tapping-tips.htm

An example of morphing the tapping statements and reframing the problem, from my own recent practice, is as follows. A
young woman had made progress, using energy methods, in
addressing various aspects of early trauma and their impact
on her life. Partly as a result, she had become more aware of
her husband's abusive behaviour towards her. This involved
constant insults and demeaning remarks, including saying
she was grumpy, a 'moody cow', that she had 'an attitude
problem', and providing no help with the housework and
criticising her for objecting to his tramping mud through the
house. His behaviour had reminded her of the years of abuse
from a stepmother, who would make her do all the housework,
say she was grumpy and had an attitude problem "before she
hit me". At the beginning of this session, she was feeling very
low and full of self-blame. We started tapping, and I offered
her the following evolving statements:

"Even though I am grumpy—and a moody cow—and I
have an attitude problem—and I'm useless—and I make
a fuss about mud in the house—and my stepmother used
to hit me—I accept myself anyway … I'm grumpy … I'm
a moody cow … I have an attitude problem … and I like
being grumpy … anyone would be grumpy if they had
to do all the housework … I've a right to be grumpy …
I'll be a moody cow if I want to be … I'd like to go back
in time and make my stepmother do the housework …

and hit her if she didn't do it right … and hit her if she complained … and tell her she had an attitude problem … (continuing along these lines for a minute or so, then shifting tack again as the mood began to change) … I'm so bored in thinking about my stepmother … she's not even worth thinking about anymore … I can't even be bothered to feel anything about her anymore …"

Following this she looked quite transformed—smiling and laughing, and expressing amazement at the rapid emancipation from her despondent mood. The morphing of the tapping statements does not seem to me to be an imposition of some external manipulation, but rather is an articulation of the underlying psychodynamics (of a rather obvious nature) and a response to the therapist's reading of the client's mood as it begins to shift during the tapping.

Another example is from work with a woman who talked of her self-blame following the ending of a relationship. Her ex-boyfriend criticised her, saying that his abusive behaviour was her fault, and she appeared to accept and identify with this view. I took her tapping through the following statements:

"Even though the ending of the relationship with X is all my fault … it must be my fault because X says it is … and this must be true … because he is perfect … whatever he says is completely true … everything is my fault … I am entirely to blame … X is blameless … X is completely free of fault … X is perfection personified … X is incapable of being anything other than a wonderful human being … I am utterly unworthy to be in his presence … all that is bad and unworthy is within me … (and so on)".

By the end of a minute or so of this, she was laughing and her perspective had shifted significantly towards what appeared to be a more realistic view of the relationship. All that I did here was to offer statements that mirrored and amplified what she had been saying.

20. 'Golden gate technique'
EFT Masters, Lindsay Kenny and Zoe Walton, have developed a useful framework strategy that they call the Golden

Gate Technique, a metaphor referring to three sections of the bridge. In the first set of tapping, where the SUDs are between 8 and 10, the client is asked to use phrases that simply express the various negative aspects of the problem. Then, in the second stage, when the SUDs are between 4 and 7, the client is encouraged to engage in "a stream of consciousness venting", voicing all the spontaneous thoughts and feelings that emerge when focusing on the problem. In the third stage, when the SUDs are at 3 or lower, the client is asked to use the phrase 'remaining [problem]'. http://www.emofree.com/Articles2/golden-gate-technique-lindsay.htm

21. **The body as feedback and as container of emotions**
    Use the body for feedback. EFT, like EMDR, can be very focused on the client's bodily experience. Emotion is a bodily event. It is often helpful to enquire what the client is experiencing in his or her body. The states of bodily tension can then be targeted with EFT (or other energy methods, such as EmoTrance). Conventional talk-based therapy often ignores bodily feedback—rather surprisingly since emotions are bodily events.
    Where the body is itself the target problem, as in physical pain or illness, a helpful focus is often upon the 'emotions in the body'. Thus tapping phrases might draw upon likely sources of emotions on the basis of clues the client has provided: e.g. "anger with my father in my back"; "my boss insulting me in my shoulder"; "wanting to punch my brother in my stomach"; "my mother walking out when I was three in my lungs". Whilst seemingly strange, such phrasings do capture the way that emotional aspects do find somatic expression—much as Freud discovered in the 19th century in his studies in hysteria.

22. **Difficulties with the self-acceptance statement**
    Sometimes the client's beliefs or inaccurate perceptions may interfere with the process. A common misunderstanding is when the client thinks that the "... I deeply and completely accept myself" statement must be believed, or that it is a kind of hypnosis. This misperception can engender resistance because self-acceptance may appear quite unrealistic. It may be important to explain that the statement simply has to be said, but

not necessarily believed. This can humorously and paradoxically be expressed by having the client tap on 'Even though
I believe I can never accept myself, I deeply and completely
accept myself'. Another common fear is that tapping along to
the statement of the problem will somehow make it worse—as
if it were a negative affirmation.

The meaning of the 'I accept myself' phrasing is often more
along the lines of 'Even though I have this problem, and I am
pathetic and useless, and doubt that anything will help, and
this tapping is clearly a lot of nonsense, well, what the hell, I'll
do this tapping anyway!' By voicing the negative evaluations of
the self, the future, and the therapeutic method, the obstructive
power of these is temporarily neutralised. This is also similar
to the teaching of acceptance of emotions and self-images that
is part of cognitive therapy (e.g. Beck & Emery, 2005).

23. Targeting unknown issues—dream meanings

EFT can be used to target unknown issues—such as those
expressed in dreams. Dr Shoshana Garfield has described
how to apply EFT to dreams, even when these are remembered only partially and with little conscious understanding
of their meaning. For example, the set-up phrasing can be:
"Even though I have these unresolved dream issues, I fully and
completely love and accept myself, including the parts with
the unresolved issues." http://www.emofree.com/Articles2/
dream-issues.htm

24. Metabeliefs and reversals

If the target problem is not clearing—or if it has reduced
somewhat but has reached a plateau—it is important to
consider why this might be. EFT is inherently very effective,
so when it is not, we must wonder about the reason. Often this
will reveal a metabelief or motive that acts to resist full resolution of the problem. For example, a person might believe that
it is not safe to be free of their anxiety because then they would
not be on guard against danger. One woman, being treated for
PTSD following an RTA, was troubled by an intrusive image
of her partner smashing into the windscreen—which was an
imagined rather than actual event. Although the emotional

intensity of this image reduced after two or three rounds of tapping, it still persisted. We were able to identify that she feared that if she did not have this alarming intrusive image she might become careless in her driving and have another accident. Once these underlying beliefs and motivations are identified, they can themselves be targeted with EFT.

These blocking metabeliefs form components of psychological reversals. Sometimes the precise nature of the content of the reversal is not easily identified. At such times it can be useful to have the client tap the side of the hand whilst articulating a variety of possible reversal statements, such as: "Even though I feel I do not deserve to be over this problem ... Even though I may feel it is not safe to be over this problem ... Even though I feel I won't be me if I get over this problem ... Even though some terrible unknown thing might happen if I get over this problem ... Even though it may feel like trivialising my experience if I get over this problem ...". Sometimes the reversal and set-up statements may need to be vocalised with emotional emphasis. http://www.emofree.com/faq/whenit.htm

25. **Massive psychological reversal**
Many of our patients, particularly those with more severe disturbance, including depression, suffer from major or 'massive' forms of 'psychological reversal'. This reversal constitutes a substantial obstacle to recovery. Whilst at an energetic level this can be understood as reversal of the optimum flow, at a psychological or emotional level, factors such as profound guilt and need to suffer or be punished (consciously or unconsciously) can be identified. These problems may require extensive corrections for reversal, involving tapping on opening statements such as "Even though I believe I will never recover ..." or "Even though I believe I do not deserve to feel better ..." or "Even though I am terrified of change ...". Another helpful opening statement may be "I accept myself with all my failings and inadequacies and problems ...". However, massive forms of psychological reversal are often caused or exacerbated by energy toxins (identifying and dealing with these are taught on TFT trainings).

26. **Sluggish energy systems**

Although there are many patients who respond rapidly and positively to energy tapping methods—and who generate an energised feeling in response in the therapist—there are others whose energy systems appear distinctly sticky or sluggish and unresponsive. This is often associated with a rather intractable depression. They may show signs of massive reversal, and also may fail to display any differentiation in muscle testing. Such features may not initially be apparent on first meeting. In addition to the need to address the psychological reversals, these problems may require much more persistent EFT, including tapping at home, and perhaps also corrections for neurological disorganisation (such as 'collar bone breathing', Cooks' hookups etc). Energy toxins may also be a factor to address. Working with people with .heavy. energy systems can be extremely wearing and draining for the therapist—and, in the long run, potentially very toxic. Attention to one's own energy 'hygiene' may be important. Sometimes I like to stand up and ask the patient to stand up when doing energy work. The energy really does seem to flow better then—and really there is no inherently necessary reason why psychological therapy should take place sitting!

27. **Persistence**

Although EFT can often resolve problems permanently in a few minutes, in other cases more persistence is required. Trial and error, combined with careful listening and observation over a period of time may give rise to good results eventually.

28. **Individual energy toxins**

In cases where problems are very resistant to change, or when a problem that has appeared successfully treated (i.e. to a SUD or 0) repeatedly recurs, the role of individual energy toxins has been considered. It has been found that people may be sensitive to foods or common environmental substances, perfumes etc., that somehow interfere with the energy system. This has been emphasised greatly within TFT in recent years, and, to a lesser extent within EFT. The mode of action of energy toxins is unknown. Gary Craig draws attention to instances in which chemical sensitivities subside as EFT is used to address both the symptom and possible emotional associations linked with it (DVD. *Using EFT for Serious Diseases*.1). Methods of detecting and dealing with energy toxins are taught in TFT trainings.

29. **Human touch (and some cautions)**
Gary Craig reports that occasionally when EFT appears not to be working, a breakthrough occurs when the therapist taps on the client's body (as opposed to the usual practice of the client tapping his or her own body. Obviously considerable caution and discretion must be observed if this form of physical touch by the therapist is to be considered. It is probably best avoided unless there are particular circumstances in which it appears appropriate. [Note that it is one thing for a teacher of EFT to tap on a client's body within the safety and boundaries of a public workshop, but such activity may take on different emotional meanings in a private consulting room]. http://www.emofree. com/faq/whenit.htm

30. **Remaining open to the unknown**
One of Gary Craig's most valuable contributions is his emphasis on how much is unknown in the scope and applications of EFT. His frequent advice to 'try it on everything' helps to encourage an attitude of enquiry and receptivity that facilitates discovery.

Drawing out and elaborating the thought field

There are subtle nuances in using EFT (and other methods). Although it is important, as Craig advises, to target *aspects* rather than the global problem, it is possible, through the use of language to draw many different aspects into the 'thought field', which can then be targeted more or less all at once. In working in this way, one might listen to the client for some time, gathering themes, conflicts, traumas, core beliefs, and so forth, and then capture all of these in the 'set up' phrasing.

For example, in a session recently the client and I had been talking about his childhood situation in which he had warded off his rage against his mother because he loved her and perceived her as vulnerable; we had begun to understand how he had channelled his rage into his body, causing a variety of somatic disturbances, and also how he had inhibited his own intelligence in order not to reveal her stupidity. When we got around to addressing the energy dimension, towards the end of the session, I offered him the following words as he tapped initially on the side of the hand:

"Even though, out of love for my mother, I protected her from my aggression—and protected her from others—I fiercely protected my mother—I was a brave little boy—defending her—and so I hid my aggression, my rage, my criticism of her—hid it in my body, hid it in my bones, where it made me ill—attacked my own body to protect my mother—I sacrificed my body because I loved my mother—I felt it was better to attack my own body than to attack my mother—my illness is my sacrifice to my mother—and I made myself appear stupid so as to conceal her stupidity—I did not want to shame her by being intelligent—I had to hide my perceptions of her—I could not bear to see my mother was stupid—I could not bear to know that the woman I loved was stupid—in acknowledging this, I can let go of my illness—I can acknowledge that I loved my mother—and I can be grateful for my own intelligence—and I can love myself as well as my mother—and I can allow myself to be well."

In tapping on complex thought fields of this kind, therapist and client may articulate further aspects as the tapping continues, the emerging words functioning to focus and highlight these.

Whilst some applications of energy psychology methods address rather specific anxieties, phobias, or traumas, in other cases the psychotherapeutically trained practitioner can draw out pervasive themes and patterns that are woven deeply within the client's personality.

Example 1:[1] Clearing deep patterns of insecurity and self-loathing

A woman talked for some time of her struggles to extricate herself from her addictive attachment to her abusive husband, from whom she was separated. She spoke of his systematic undermining of her self-esteem over a period of years. Then she reflected on her state of depression prior to meeting him, describing various events and circumstances that had rendered her insecure and traumatised. Her husband had seemed like a knight in shining armour—"perfect—everything I had dreamed of"—but gradually the relationship had turned sour and she experienced him as wanting complete control over the way she thought, making her into a 'performing puppet'. She then went on to speak of her childhood, characterised by a lack of basic security and feeling that she was a burden to her mother, describing her father as moody and critical. The family ran a pub and in her early teens she "went wild", having her first intercourse at 13, and generally offering herself sexually in return for male attention. Her gradual realisation that making herself sexually available did not lead to her being valued and loved for herself contributed further to the plummeting of her self-esteem. She concluded that a core feeling was that nobody had time for her and that she was not worth spending time with.

As we began tapping, I offered opening phrases along the following lines:

"Even though I lacked basic security—and felt I was a burden to my mother—and my father was moody and critical—and I looked for male attention by offering sex—but this made me feel worse about myself—I felt used and discarded—and I feel nobody has time for me..."

In this way the general themes of her development were succinctly outlined.

After a few moments of tapping she reported that she had just remembered a dream. In the dream her husband was heavily pregnant and breast feeding a baby; she took a drink from his other breast and asked if she was still his baby. Continuing to tap, she reflected on how this represented her wish to seek nurturance from her husband that she had felt missing in her childhood, the dream image also expressing her feeling that this might be given to rival babies. With further tapping she then recalled another recent dream: she had been in bed with her husband and had turned to talk to him but he threw up because her breath smelt so bad—a dream she saw as clearly representing her feeling of being disgusting and unwanted.

Still tapping, she spoke of how people sometimes say she is like a man in some of her attitudes, appearing confident and even dominant. She talked of seeing women as emotional and irrational—linking this to the way her father treated her mother. She then remarked that she wanted to be special, to be like somebody's princess. I commented that she had wanted to be her father's princess. She returned to reflecting on the early stages of her relationship with her husband, an Indian man, and how she had felt pleased that she would stand out with her white skin amongst his family and associates. Continuing to tap, she talked more of her realisation of her many behaviours motivated by the search for attention. She remarked: "I can understand how some people develop Munchausens for attention!"

At this point, having guided her tapping extensively through the meridians, I felt it was time to clear the relevant patterns from her chakra system. I suggested she hold the heart and brow chakras whilst she continued to reflect on what she had been speaking of. I knew from previous work with her that she tended to become deeply immersed in her internal processing when engaging the chakra system. With her eyes closed, she spoke of an inner sensation of sobbing and crying, of wanting a cuddle, and of feeling in a place of darkness and loneliness—"there's no-one there and no-one can hear me". She then went on to describe an image of her brain with a red lesion at the front. Elaborating on this train of thought, she remarked: "I'm frightened of my brain—it can be so self-destructive—like it is my enemy—always putting me down—telling me negative things—it frightens me—it can hurt me so much—nothing external can hurt me in this way, its how I process it—I want to like my brain again—I want it to look after me—well I suppose it does look after me—it keeps my body functioning—but does it keep me alive just in order to torment me?—it's bizarre what I am saying—why do I see my brain as separate?—it wants to be in control—my biggest fear is mental illness—I hate my body—as if it is separate." I commented "you want to love your brain and your body". She replied (still with her eyes closed and holding the heart and brow chakras) "Yes I want to be all the same team—to be loved by them"—then adding "this is powerful stuff!". Finally she commented "my brain hurts—like the feeling after exercise, growing new muscles—like growing new neurons!". At this point she indicated that she felt she had finished processing that particular constellation and opened her eyes.

This was deep processing of material, at energetic, psychic, and somatic levels. As perturbations began to be cleared, she proceeded to access further and deeper thought fields, including dreams. Her thoughts about her brain being her 'enemy' expressed her sense of being divided within herself. Her final comments as she finished her session implied some degree of healing of these splits.

Example 2. Recovery from the layers of depression

A severely depressed woman talked of the anguish of her child-hood in which she had felt responsible for looking after her disabled mother, her father having left during her first year of life. She had missed out greatly on many aspects of normal adolescence and clearly felt furious with her mother, who had often been critical of her, whilst also feeling guilty over her resentment. In addition she had experienced sexual abuse. Thus there had been much for her to be depressed about in her childhood and adolescence, and some current events had resonated with these early circumstances. I felt quite daunted by the obvious depth of this lady's depression. Despite my misgivings, after listening for half an hour or so, I asked her to state aloud a series of statements succinctly summarising what she had been saying, whilst she tapped the side of her hand, and then took her through a lengthy tapping sequence. At the end of this sequence she reported feeling calmer and more relaxed. Following a second long sequence, she said she was now feeling *much* better (but with an implication that she still felt quite troubled).

I tested her meridians using the John Diamond method (Diamond, 1985). The lung meridian tested weak. I invited her to tap the side of her thumb whilst affirming that she could breathe easily and deeply. She asked in surprise why I had referred to breathing and told me that one of her recurrent childhood terrors was of not being able to breathe. We applied a tapping sequence specifically to her terrors and traumas about not being able to breathe. Following this, she remarked that she felt "a lot stronger and more normal than I have for a long time". I tested her meridians again. The gall bladder tested weak, suggesting a problem with persisting rage and lack of forgive-ness. We applied a tapping sequence to this, following which she reported feeling *very* much better and her meridians all tested strong (using the Diamond method of testing).

Working through the layers of thought fields

In the course of a successful session with TFT or EFT, it is very common for a client to start from some presenting problem, and then to work through various layers of thought and emotion underneath as these are progressively cleared. Sometimes, by starting with a relatively global issue, the more specific experiences, phantasies, and conflicts that have contributed to this will become apparent once the tapping begins.

For example, it was possible to discern in the discourse of a chronically anxious woman the basic themes that the world is a dangerous place and that she wished to isolate herself and avoid contact and communication from others. This fundamental stance of distrust supported her tendency towards obsessive compulsive anxieties, with fears of contamination.

As we proceeded with TFT in relation to her fear that the world is a dangerous place, she reported feeling calmer. However, she then went on to speak of anxiety about blushing—something she had not mentioned before, although we had met several times. Her response to TFT focussed on her worry about blushing led her to remark that she could not imagine ever being without this anxiety since she had always had it. I asked her to tap for this reversal, based implicitly on her sense of identity (I wouldn't be me without this anxiety)—followed by tapping again in relation to the anxiety itself.

She then remarked that she was feeling "annoyed at how many fools I have had to put up with during my life". I commented that perhaps she was feeling some anger—and she agreed that perhaps she was. We applied TFT to her feelings of anger. She responded with thoughts about "bloody fools—there have been so many". I asked who she thought had been the first fools. She replied that they had been boys at her school—at age 7 all the boys had been kissing another girl, who was blonde with long legs—and "they didn't want to kiss me!". We continued tapping in relation to this experience, but combined this with discussion about the boys' behaviour. I pointed out that boys behave as pack animals, so that if a dominant boy started kissing the girl, the others may follow simply because that had become the group behaviour at that moment. Following this sequence of tapping, she remarked "that feels better—I had been carrying it around ever since—feeling that I was no good—I remember a boy told me I was ugly".

We then applied TFT to the experience of the boy telling her she was ugly. She responded by saying "I was just remembering when I was older—I went around with another girl—and she was pretty and blonde, with long legs—she was beautiful—and all the boys wanted to be with her rather than with me—and then I just remembered that at ballet class an older girl was going to partner me but then she went off with another girl with blonde hair!". We applied TFT to her understandable hatred of blonde girls! Following this, she remarked: "the thing is … I know its pathetic … but I've always wanted to be like the blonde girls with long legs—I've always wanted men to look at me!".

We tapped through her feeling that she wanted men to look at her, to admire her, to fall in love with her, and so on. In response she remarked: "I think men will like me until they see my teeth". She then talked of her unhappiness with the appearance of her teeth.

Thus, in this sequence which took only a few minutes to emerge, she moved from the initially rather global idea of the world being a dangerous place, to social anxieties and fears of blushing, and then to various narcissistically injurious experiences that had contributed to these anxieties. She spoke of anger with the 'bloody fools', the boys who preferred the blonde girls, describing three specific groups of episodes. She then revealed her narcissistic desire to be looked at and admired—a desire previously concealed, presumably because of shame. Finally, she disclosed her worries about the appearance of her teeth.

What EFT teaches us

The feature of EFT that attracts criticism from practitioners of TFT—its abandonment of Dr Callahan's emphasis upon information sequentially encoded as perturbations in the energy field—has, paradoxically, enabled it to pursue its own journey of exploration into the core issues and layers of cognitive-emotional and psychodynamic material that lie behind presenting clinical problems. Somehow 'tapping and talking' form a synergy that makes the psycho-somatic-energy system more plastic, allowing insight and shifts of cognition and emotion, as well as new levels of integration and resolution of conflict, to occur much faster and more easily. This does not in any way mean that EFT supplants TFT—absolutely not. They are different, but complementary.

From a purely TFT theoretical perspective, EFT should be just an inefficient form of TFT—and, when used mechanically, it probably is. Yet skilled EFT practitioners bring about results far in advance of that. How can this be? One hypothesis might be that skilled EFT practitioners, with pronounced capacities for energetic as well as emotional rapport with the client, form a temporary engagement with the client's energy system, in a way that catalyses, through intention, talking and tapping, a broader facilitation of healing despite the lack of attention to the more precise encodings addressed within TFT. From this kind of perspective, EFT and TFT might be related, but are operating in somewhat different ways.

The implicit model of psychological disturbance in Gary Craig's EFT

Implicit within Gary Craig's rather folksy style of speaking and writing—including, for example, his frequent descriptions of his skilful use of language during the 'setup' phase as his 'rambling'—is a rather sophisticated account of psychological disturbance. Basically, he says that clients present with difficulties as a result of [a] traumas and other adverse or injurious experiences of various kinds, [b] the beliefs and expectations deriving from these experiences, and [c] the maladaptive messages imbibed from within our family of origin (the 'writings on our walls'). There are many details (aspects) of adverse experiences that trouble us, including sensory, emotional, cognitive, and temporal elements. Presenting problems, symptoms and so forth, are often the result of multiple adverse experiences, maladaptive beliefs, and emotional distress (i.e. the symptom is multipli determined). Global problems, such as depression or low self-esteem, are the surface presentation that is held in place by a number of underlying core issues or adverse experiences (the table top metaphor). Psychological problems also have an expression within the body—and are associated with a disturbance in the body's energy system. By tapping on the energy system at the same time as directing attention to the psychological components, the trapped patterns of mind-body dysfunction begin to dissolve—thereby freeing the person to function more fully in the present. The human psychosomatic system is highly organised by language and belief. By using language that mirrors the existing cognitively imprisoned state of the client's system, and gradually morphing this towards more constructive and positive language, combined with rhythmic sensory-energetic stimulation, it is possible to release the client into a more benign psycho-somatic space.

Notes

1. In the following two examples, TFT sequences were at times used. However, the basic principles of exploring the depths and ramifications of the thought fields apply also in EFT.

CHAPTER FIVE

Basic procedures in an energy psychology session

Despite differences between the various energy psychology approaches, it is possible to outline some general principles and procedures that may guide the energy psychology practitioner. The account provided here is not intended as a substitute for training in appropriate workshops and supervised practice. Instead, the purpose is to help broaden the perspective of those who have already begun some degree of training and practice in an energy psychology approach.

Initial listening

The first step is to listen in the normal way—to listen to the history and nuances of the client's discourse, allowing the recurrent themes, conflicts, significant traumas, and childhood interpersonal patterns to emerge. Whilst listening on many levels, it is possible to identify potential targets for TFT or other energy treatment. Such targets might include: a specific recent trauma; a specific childhood trauma; a pattern of traumas; a particular anxiety; a dynamic conflict; a core belief deriving from traumas or other profoundly discouraging experiences. Any of these may also need to be broken down into various constituent elements or aspects.

Locating the target issue

Sometimes the target problem is obvious—e.g. a known recent trauma, or a specific anxiety or phobia. However, in more complex cases, especially where the disturbance is woven deeply within the personality, it will not be immediately clear where to focus the energy treatment. There are some commonly used strategies for eliciting core traumas to target. One is to ask the person what he or she feels is the worst event they have ever experienced. Another is to ask what events he or she would choose to omit if given the opportunity to live their life over again. Of course the person may not be aware of the important traumas, either because these occurred too early, before normal autobiographical memory is established, or because they have been repressed or dissociated. Nevertheless, such forms of enquiry can provide useful clues. Muscle testing may also be used as a means of locating the most relevant experiences behind a problem—for example, asking whether there is a trauma underpinning the presenting issue, and then, if the response is 'yes', to ask whether it was in childhood or adulthood. By enquiring about ages and years, it is possible to identify more precisely the nature of the most relevant trauma and when it occurred.

Not all psychological problems are rooted in trauma, however, and kinesiology muscle testing should not be regarded as a foolproof means of identifying hidden traumas behind a symptom; to do so would run the risk of generating false beliefs or 'false memories' [Brand, 2007; Mollon, 2002]. Moreover, as Dr Callahan has shown, seemingly psychological problems may sometimes be a result of energy toxins, which may exacerbate problems of anxiety and depression, or even be the prime cause of these. A state of chronic and pervasive depression, rooted primarily in biological or energy toxic factors, could function as a "mood in search of a reason", darkly colouring a person's perception of their life and generating a misleading focus on assumed traumas or other adverse early experiences within the family.

Informed consent

If an energy psychology approach is considered, then the client's informed consent is required (see Hover-Kramer, 2006 for an extensive discussion of this and related issues). Some simple yet truthful means of explaining the energy psychology method and its rationale should be offered to the client. When I see clients who present with problems relating to specific anxieties or traumas, I may put to them that I have found that whilst purely talk-based therapies can be somewhat helpful, they often fail to clear away the underlying pattern of distress. Clients are often startled and relieved to hear this said—startled because they may have been expecting endless talk-therapy because that is what they have been told to expect (by the GP, or by the popular media), and relieved because they know that talking has not helped them so far.

Tests for polarity and organisation of the energy system

Having obtained the client's informed consent for energy psychology methods, and also having identified likely targets for such interventions, the next step is to test the person's energy system for its polarity and readiness for treatment. A non-polarised or disorganised energy system will not respond efficiently to meridian or chakra based desensitisation. Two main tests can be used, both of which take only seconds. One is the palm over head test. Muscle testing should indicate a strong muscle to palm down over top of head ('palm is power'), and weak to back of hand held over head ('back is slack'). This is because the normal polarity is for the palm of the hand to be negative, whilst the top of the head is positive— and back of hand is positive. If the result is reversed, this suggests general psycho-energetic reversal. If there is no difference between the two, this suggests disorganisation or non-polarisation. Energy toxins could be playing a part in either case. These can include smoking and excess consumption of alcoholic drink.

The second test is to check for a clear differentiation between muscle test responses to true and false statements. True statements, such as 2+2=4, or the person's name, should test as muscle strong, whilst false statements should test as muscle weak. If this is reversed, such that false statements test strong and true statements test as weak, the person is in a state of general or massive reversal. If there is no difference, this suggests a state of energetic (or neurological) disorganisation.

To correct disorganisation, the client may be asked to perform a basic 'unswitching' procedure of holding the navel whilst rubbing the ends of the collar bones K27 points, then tapping chin, then under nose, then tailbone—then repeating with the other hand. Alternatively, a minute or two of 'cross crawl'—raising a knee and tapping it with opposite hand, then raising the other knee and tapping that with the opposite hand, in a 'marching on the spot' movement (this can also be done sitting down).

To correct general energetic reversal, tapping the side of the hand for half a minute will often suffice. This can be combined with asking the client to say "Even though my energy system is in reverse I completely accept myself".

After these corrections, further muscle testing will indicate whether the client is still in a state of disorganisation or reversal.

Testing for reversals

So far the testing has ascertained whether the client's system is in a general state of organisation and correct polarity and is not in a state of general reversal. Corrections for these have been made if required. It is now necessary to test for specific reversals in relation to the target problem (anxiety, trauma, or other form of distress or behavioural symptom). Typically the muscle testing might proceed through the issues of [a] wanting to be over the problem; [b] all parts wanting this; [c] safety; [d] guilt/deservedness; [e] shame; [f] identity—and so on, according to the therapist's intuition and the clues provided by the client. Corrections for any reversals are carried out by asking the client to think of them, perhaps also putting the reversal into words aloud, whilst tapping the small intestine point on the side of the hand.

Tuning the thought field

When the client's system is in a state of energetic readiness and willingness to respond to treatment, the tapping or holding of acupressure points can begin. At this point it is necessary to elicit and activate the relevant thought field, or constellation of thought fields containing the perturbations that generate the distress. Is it necessary for the thought fields and their various aspects to be fully in consciousness? Perhaps sometimes it is. However, I have found that often it is not. All that is required is that the client's system is accessing the relevant areas, but not necessarily consciously.

Conscious accessing of the thought field

The client may be asked to think directly of the target distress (a trauma, or anxiety, or other disturbing event, or thought or emotion), whilst a tapping sequence is carried out. Some practitioners will break the target into its various aspects. These aspects may include many different elements in a time sequence. For example, if the target is a traumatic event, each temporal stage of the event may be targeted: i.e. "first this happened, then that happened, then this next bit happened", etc. Gary Craig calls this the 'movie technique', in which he asks the client to narrate the event as if it were a short movie, and tapping is applied at each point when the client experiences distress. There may be many sensory details associated with the event, and these too can be targeted. Another form of aspects is the variety of thoughts linked to the target, including the self-related cognitions and beliefs about the self that may have arisen from the trauma: e.g. 'I am stupid'; 'I am helpless'; 'I am disgusting' etc. Thus aspects may involve *temporal*, *sensory*, and *cognitive* elements of an experience.

Practitioners of EFT tend to emphasise particularly the importance of focusing on aspects. Gary Craig provides the metaphor of trees and the forest. If a person were to try to take an axe to cut down an entire forest in one go, this would be unlikely to succeed because the target is too large and global. However, if the axe were aimed at one tree at a time, some steady progress could be made. Fortunately, after a few central trees have been cut down, the effect tends to generalise so that the entire forest of problems begins to collapse.

On the other hand, the focus on aspects has traditionally been given less emphasis within TFT. The person is simply asked to think of the target and to tap the appropriate sequence of acupoints. Unless there are reversals or disorganisation blocking the process, this normally seems to work very well and the subjective units of disturbance rapidly fall away. It seems rather as if the focus on details of aspects in EFT takes the place of the emphasis on details of tapping sequence in TFT. What often seems to happen during TFT tapping is that various aspects of the target situation and related thoughts and memories and emotions are passing through the person's mind and are being cleared as they arise. During this process there is no need for every detail of thought, memory and emotion to be voiced. Indeed there may be much that the therapist does not get to hear about, and this does not matter since it is the process within the client that is important rather than the interpersonal communication between client and therapist.

The lack of necessity for the therapist to know the content of the client's distress is illustrated clearly in certain demonstrations I like to provide in some of my workshops, of clearing the person's perturbations through the guidance of muscle testing alone. In this procedure the person is asked to think of a troubling event or situation, without telling the practitioner what it is—reversals are identified by muscle testing, are then corrected, and a sequence of tapping is found through muscle testing. Usually the person's SUDs drop near to zero through this process in which the 'therapist" is blind to the content. The client's troubling issue is thus treated purely at the energetic level. Probably many different cognitive and emotional aspects of the situation pass through the client's mind during this.

Non-conscious accessing of the target thought field

It is also not always necessary for the client consciously to be aware of the target issue and the associated thought field. Thus the target can be a trauma or other experience that is not consciously known. The crucial requirement seems to be that the psycho-somatic-energy system knows what event it is searching for. Again, the system seems to function like a bio-computer with a search facility. If given the search field "the most important trauma behind this symptom", or "all the roots and causes of this problem", the system will identify and target the required area. It is as if the relevant information is 'downloaded' and activated so that the perturbations can then be cleared through tapping on the energy system—but the downloading is not necessarily into the conscious mind. Another way of thinking of this is that it is a function of intention—the intention to target a particular event or issue. Some methods within energy psychology rely particularly on intention—notably Larry Nims' BeSetFreeFast [BSFF], but also Tapas Fleming's Tapas Acupressure Technique [TAT]—are commonly used to target areas that are not consciously known, relying on the inherent intelligence of the system to locate and clear the relevant information and perturbations.

However, this accessing of targets that are not consciously known may still depend on identifying and clearing any relevant reversals. The usual set of statements may be used, even though the precise nature or details of the target are not known consciously. Similarly the reversals can be cleared in the normal way, by articulating their existence and tapping the side of the hand, without knowing their precise content—other than that revealed by muscle testing. Another factor that may have a bearing on whether or not the target issue can be accessed and the perturbations cleared is the extent to which it is stored in a dissociated state. Active dissociation may mean that the target cannot be 'downloaded' and thus does not become available for clearing its perturbations. Sometimes it is possible to approach deeply guarded targets only after other more surface issues have been addressed and the perturbations cleared. Practitioners who are accredited in EMDR may use this to download more of the relevant cognitive-emotional targets. EMDR can indeed be very helpful in eliciting emotional material and enabling the client to become more in touch with this. One procedure that often works quite well is to alternate a set of eye movements with a sequence of tapping, proceeding directly from one to the other, checking in with the client's verbal reports only from time to time but gauging his or her emotional state from observable cues. In this process it is rather as if the eye movements download more emotional information and the accompanying perturbations are then cleared with tapping, before further information is downloaded with the next set of eye movements.

Further typical reversals to be tested and corrected

Although the subject of reversals and their many variations is discussed at length in another chapter, a brief summary here may be helpful. It is not always necessary to work through the entire list, and the clinician will be guided by the client's clues as to what additional reversals are worth investigating. Often muscle testing the simple statement "I want to be over this problem" will be sufficient, since the other potential motives for reversal (anxieties about safety, identity, guilt etc.) form part of the target thought field and are cleared in the process of the subsequent tapping.

Test for global reversals:
I want to be well/I want to be sick.
I want to be happy/I want to be miserable

Test for specific reversals:
I want to be over this problem/I want to keep this problem.

Then test for 'parts':
All parts of me want to be over this problem/some parts want to keep the problem.

Test for layers:
All layers of me want to be over this problem/some want to keep this problem.

Test for safety:
All parts of me think it is safe for me to be over this problem/not safe.

Test for guilt/deservedness:
All parts of me think I deserve to be over this problem/do not deserve.

Test for shame:
I have feelings of shame that interfere with becoming free of this problem.

Test for identity:
I will still be me if I am over this problem.

Test for intergenerational reversal:
I can still be lovingly connected to my mother/father/family/ancestors if I am over this problem/cannot remain lovingly connected.

Test for programmes/bio-software:
All programmes in my mind that have a bearing on this problem are permitted to be removed or modified in order to allow me to be over this problem/are not permitted. [in effect, some programmes may be 'write protected'—but this feature itself can be modified.]

Test for (intervening) mini-reversal:
If the treatment progresses and the client experiences a reduction in distress, but further reduction seems to be stalled, testing for mini-reversal may be appropriate:
I want to be completely over this problem/want to keep some of this problem.

Test for level 2 reversal:
When the client is no longer experiencing distress in the present, it may be appropriate to test for what Dr Callahan called 'level 2' reversal, which relates to the future.
I will be completely over this problem/will not.

Test for level 3 reversal:
A further level identified by Dr Callahan relates to becoming or feeling even better. It seems likely that this, in turn, relates to feelings of guilt or lack of deservedness, or inhibitions against success based on intergenerational reversals.
I want to be even better/do not want.

Note that some of the emotions or beliefs that can function as the basis of reversals, such as guilt, shame etc., can also be part of the target constellation. For example, a man presented with a desire for a better relationship with his sister. Muscle testing indicated a reversal based on safety. This did not clear with tapping side of hand. When invited to speak more of his sense of danger, what emerged was his profound fear that his sister had hated him so much that she wanted to murder him and had indeed attacked him when he was very young. This then became the obvious target for tapping.

'Software programmes" may be very similar to core beliefs. These normally do respond to the usual reversal corrections, by focussing on their apparent immutability whilst tapping the side of the hand. This will "loosen" them sufficiently to allow deletion or modification from the biocomputer's software. What often then works well is for the client to continue tapping side of hand while saying "I ask the software engineer within my system to review or delete the programmes that prevent me being free of this problem". Muscle testing can then be used to check whether the programmes are still present or have been modified.

Taking SUD and VOC ratings:

Subjective units of distress/disturbance ratings—abbreviated to SUD—(e.g. 0-10, where 10 represents maximum distress and 0 indicates no distress) are useful in giving a guide to the person's shifting experience as the tapping proceeds. These should not be used slavishly, however. Sometimes a person's level of distress is perfectly obvious. In other instances the target is not fully in conscious awareness so that SUDs cannot be obtained. Under these circumstances muscle testing may be used in order for the deeper system to provide the rating. This may be done by muscle testing and asking "the distress is at 10/9/8 etc.?", progressively reducing the numbers until the arm tests strong.

Validity of cognition scales (VOC) are used to gauge the person's strength of belief in either a dysfunctional cognition that the therapy is intended to modify or a positive one that is to be installed. Again the ratings may be from 0 (meaning the cognition is perceived as having no validity) to 10 (meaning that it is perceived as having maximum validity or truth)—or some may use a scale of 0-7. The precise range of the scales of SUD or VOC is unimportant since they are just a means for the client to convey shifts in subjective experience. Both scales have been used extensively in EMDR for many years.

Selecting a tapping sequence
—*universal sequence, specific algorithms, or diagnosed sequences?*
The practitioner has various choices. One option is to opt for the simple EFT sequence, which is a universal algorithm covering all fourteen major meridians. Gary Craig, developer of EFT as a simplification and modification of TFT, argues that sequence is unimportant—although in some of his DVDs he teaches ways of using intuition systematically as a guide to selecting particular sequences of acupoints. This lack of concern for sequence certainly makes the procedure technically simple—and commonly only some of the meridian points are used, such as those around the face, collar bone and under the arm. The implicit assumption seems to be that tapping anywhere on the energy system seems to make it more malleable so that shifts in emotional information occur more easily. EFT practitioners seem to make up for lack of attention to meridian detail by a greater preoccupation with ways of homing in on the core of the

psychological problem and the use of language to access this. On the other hand, those who have trained in TFT do in general find that sequence is important. Personally I feel convinced from my experience that, most of the time, the sequence of tapping is important. When I used to use the EFT procedure without concern for sequence I did obtain good results in many cases—but after learning TFT my results were even better, with SUDs often dropping dramatically in a single round of treatment. The only disadvantage of this is that the 'apex effect' of client bewilderment and disbelief at the substantial and rapid shifts in their experience became more pronounced! My overall impression is that although precision of tapping sequence is important, tapping more or less anywhere on the body (and therefore on the energy system) makes the system somehow more plastic, allowing easier shifts in emotion and cognition.

One paradox is that although sequence of tapping does appear to be important, it does not seem to be fixed. There is something elusive here. It is possible that the sequence of meridian points corresponds in some way to the sequence of layers of emotion associated with the target problem. The different meridians correspond to some extent to different emotions. It may be that one emotion has to be addressed before the next one can be, with potentially many layers of emotions, just as can be apparent more slowly in conventional verbal psychotherapy. In this way the sequencing of meridians in TFT may correspond rather closely to the sequence of emotional aspects addressed in EFT. However, in a queue of emotions—A, B. C, D, E etc.—although there may be some inherent need for emotion A to be addressed before emotion E, for example, it may be that emotions A and B are both close to the surface and that either could viably be addressed first.

Another alternative is to use the TFT algorithms that have been found to occur regularly in relation to particular emotional issues—e.g. different sequences for anxiety, panic, anger, guilt, shame, trauma, addiction etc. These have been published—for example, in Dr Callahan's *Tapping the Healer Within* (2001).

Some TFT algorithms

The basic TFT algorithm for trauma and anxiety is:
Eye brow; under eye; under arm; collar bone.

For claustrophobic anxiety:
Under arm; under eye; collar bone.

For obsessional anxiety:
Collar bone; under eye; collar bone.

For anger, add:
Little finger; collar bone.

For rage, add:
Outside eye; collar bone.

For shame, add:
Chin; collar bone. Often this may usefully be combined with little finger and outside of eye [shame-rage against self].

For embarrassment, add:
Under nose; collar bone.

For guilt, add:
Index finger; collar bone.

Note: the collarbone often functions as a kind of punctuation in the code.

Summary:
Under eye; under arm; collar bone [anxiety]
Under arm; under eye; collar bone [claustrophobia].
Under nose [embarrassment]
Chin [shame]
Little finger [anger and frustration, including anger towards self]
Outside of eye [rage].
Index finger [guilt]
Eye brow [shock/trauma; sadness; depression]
Gamut point [depression].

Further algorithms are provided on TFT algorithm trainings [see www.thoughtfieldtherapy.co.uk]. A useful book describing TFT with algorithms applied to a variety of common problems is Connolly [2004].

An even better option is to use diagnostic muscle testing to find individual sequences for the specific problem experienced by the individual client at that moment. This process allows the encoding of the distress or symptom to be felt and observed directly in the energy system. By enquiring in this way, the reality of the energetic code is revealed vividly, and confirmed by the way that tapping through the resulting sequence leads to a rapid drop in SUD. Diagnostic muscle testing will often unveil meridian sequences that are somewhat different from those of the algorithms—and may be longer.

Muscle testing for sequence

The essential process of muscle testing for sequence is simple enough. Normally, when a person thinks of an anxiety or other emotional problem their test muscle will become slightly weak (unless they are in a state of reversal or disorganisation). The task then is to find a meridian point that when touched by the client's other hand makes the arm register strong (the test points—or 'alarm' points, as they are termed in traditional acupuncture [Stux et al. 2003] and Applied Kinesiology [Walther, 1988]—are not always the same as the tapping treatment points). That point reveals the first meridian in the sequence, which can then be tapped. Then the procedure is repeated in order to find the next point that will make the arm strong. Normally the previous point will now no longer make the arm strong since its associated meridian has been treated with tapping and is no longer registering as needing to be treated. Usually there is only one of the fourteen main meridians that will make the arm strong at any one moment—and thus there does seem to be an inherent sequence encoded in the energy system. The coding appears to be layered, so that only one meridian and associated emotion can be addressed at a time. By working systematically through the encoded perturbation, with muscle testing and tapping, a point will then be reached when the arm remains strong as the person thinks of the problem. This would usually also correlate with a substantial collapse in the client's SUD. Checks may then be made for whether the 9 gamut procedure is required—by testing whether the arm goes weak when the person closes their eyes, or moves the eyes down to the right or left or in a circle in either direction. Alternatively, the 9 gamut may be performed without testing since it is quicker to do it than to test for it. Further muscle testing enquiries may be made to check for any remaining distress: e.g. muscle testing the statement "the amount of distress in my system regarding X is zero". However, since it is common for some phobic people to experience a complete collapse of their SUD during the session, only to experience a partial recurrence when in the phobic situation, a useful further muscle test may be to the statement "I will remain free of anxiety when I an in the situation of X".

Although I have described here a basic outline of muscle testing for sequence, this cannot adequately be learned from a book. Moreover, people often seem to become confused about the procedure. Therefore I strongly advise the interested reader to attend a Callahan Techniques diagnostic level training or other training workshop run by a knowledgeable and experienced practitioner.

Some practitioners may be able to refine their self muscle testing, or other forms of systematic intuition, or even dowsing with a pendulum, to diagnose sequences. This takes some practice, but is not inherently difficult. Some partial hints at how to do this can be found in training material from Quantum Techniques [www.quantumtechniques.com]. It appears that one person's energy system can read that of another person. Such work can also take place over the phone. I do not recommend this method unless the practitioner has worked over a considerable time to refine and validate the reliability of his or her means of accessing the information. For example, the practitioner may cross-validate his or her own means of accessing information by checking against direct muscle testing of the client. Ultimately the validity of the method is determined by the results obtained by sequences and therapeutic strategies that are based on the information produced. If the tapping sequence does not lead immediately to a substantial drop in subjective distress, or other signs of positive change, then either the sequence is incorrect, or there is a reversal blocking the process, or the client's energy system is disorganised.

Although it is possible to ascertain a tapping sequence by various means, including strategies of structured intuition, I have the impression that the 'hands on' muscle testing method of diagnosis and treatment is particularly effective. This may have something to do with the way in which the client can feel and see the shifting pattern of information encoded in their energy system. The process of working systematically from a position where the muscle tests weak when the person thinks of the problem to the point when the arm remains strong has its own persuasive inherent validity—demonstrating tactilely and visually that something has changed.

Is it necessary for the client actually to tap?

Whilst it is probably necessary for the client to tap (or press) on the acupoints initially, once his or her system is used to the procedure the same result may be obtained just by thinking of the points. Indeed the process of closing the eyes whilst the practitioner narrates a long sequence of acupoints can be a deeply meditative and calming process of healing. The profound involvement in the internal process is not intruded upon by physical tapping. This method of just thinking of the points is used extensively by Dr Stephen Daniel and other developers of Quantum Techniques [www.quantumtechniques. com], which derived from Thought Field Therapy. These practitioners work exclusively over the phone and provide often rather long sequences, derived by discernment of information encoded in the voice. Thus they do not read the code to the client during the treatment but leave the client to do this alone. I find that speaking a sequence code aloud to the client who has his or her eyes shut can often be deeply effective.

Networks and layers of aspects revealed as the tapping continues

As the initial target issue begins to clear through the tapping sequence, other aspects often emerge. These may be further aspects of the particular problem or traumatic experience, or thematically related further memories, or other psychodynamic conflicts that are linked to the original target, or other anxieties that inherently follow as the original anxiety is cleared. For example, in a workshop demonstration a woman was tapping a sequence to relieve her feelings of helplessness about a particular situation; as her sense of helplessness began to fade, she then became aware of anxieties about the course of action she now believed she should take. This is a simple instance of the general point that as one issue or thought field is cleared of its perturbations, another one will often step into its place. It is as if the layers of anxieties and other forms of distress are organised in a queue, rather like napkins in a spring-loaded dispenser; as one is removed, another is immediately in its place at the front.

Dr Callahan has a colourful metaphor for the emergence of less intense pain after the more intense has subsided as a result of TFT. He calls this the 'tooth-shoe-lump' phenomenon. One day Dr Callahan was suffering from an severe tooth ache. On obtaining an emergency appointment with his dentist and receiving an anaesthetic injection his tooth pain subsided. He then realised that his shoes were too tight and were causing discomfort. After removing his shoes, he noticed that the couch he was sitting on in the waiting room was lumpy and uncomfortable. This illustrates how layers of distress emerge in a kind of queue according to their levels of intensity.

Sometimes a client will move to another preoccupation before the distress associated with the initial one is fully collapsed. The practitioner has a choice at such times: whether to move on to clear the now emerging thought field of its perturbations, or whether to shift the client's attention back to the original target and continue to clear the perturbations until no trace of distress is left. Sometimes one choice may seem best, and sometimes the other may appear more appropriate.

Sometimes words may be used to help keep the client focused on the target—and thus a short 'reminder phrase' is used in classic EFT as the client taps each point. This is not normally used within TFT, where the client is simply asked to think of the problem. In general, fewer words are used in TFT than in EFT. This may be a particular advantage when working with severely traumatised clients, who may find speaking any words relating to the trauma evokes an unmanageable level of distress. I find that when I am able to keep generating an ongoing sequence of points whilst allowing the client just to think of the target problem, he or she will be experiencing various cognitive and emotional aspects as these are "downloaded" and pass through consciousness in the process of clearing the perturbations. At the end of the long sequence (lasting perhaps two or three minutes) the distress may have largely cleared and the client will have worked through a range of thoughts, emotions, memories etc. without these being articulated explicitly. These various cognitive-emotional aspects will have corresponded in part to the sequence of acupoints.

For thorough treatment of an issue it will often be necessary to continue the work (within the session or over several sessions) until all the associated issues and perturbations are cleared from the field. The return of a problem after it had appeared to be cleared is often due to hidden aspects or related thought fields that have not been cleared of perturbations. With complex problems that pervade the personality, there may be many issues and layers to be addressed.

Example of rapid shift in aspects of emotions and cognitions

A woman was speaking of her aversion to sex with her husband. She disclosed that she had never particularly liked sex, although she had allowed boys to have sex with her from an early adolescent age because she thought this would please them. She felt that sex was dirty and disgusting—animal lust—and she hated people speaking of "making love" because she could not feel that sex was anything to do with love. Partly these feelings were linked to having discovered her father's pornographic magazines when she was age 11. She acknowledged that she had found them exciting. Another contributory experience had been sexual harassment from a relative during her teenage years.

Muscle testing indicated a reversal based on safety—and she recognised a fear of enjoying sex with her husband. This was to do with her perception that they had little in common other than initial lust for each other. She felt that sex was a trap since it could enhance attachment and potentially bind her further to her husband, from whom she felt she should eventually separate. We began TFT, focussed on these issues. As she began tapping, she verbalised more vividly her disgust, clearly experiencing strong emotions as she did so. She suddenly remarked that she used to have fantasies of being raped because then she could have sex without feeling responsible—and then expressed extreme shock and shame that she had disclosed this to the therapist. She spoke of self-loathing in connection with this fantasy—regarding herself as "dirty".

As she continued tapping, she began to look calmer. I mirrored back to her some of her words and phrases, at times amplifying and exaggerating their meaning—about sex being disgusting, that she was disgusting for having wanted sex, that sex should be banned, that sex was dangerous and dirty etc. Gradually she relaxed, showing some amusement at the phrases mirrored back to her. Then, still tapping, she remarked that she was no longer feeling dirty, but now saw that it was other people in her past who were dirty and had made her feel this way. She spoke of realising now that sex could be part of an expression of love—and that she would like to be able to make love with a person she loved. This was a startling transformation in her feelings and thoughts in relation to sex, taking place over a period of just a few minutes of tapping.

Testing the result

After any energy psychology treatment is important to test the result. This may be done by asking the person to think of the issue or situation that had previously troubled him or her and to report whether any distress remains. Often some reduced level of disturbance will still be noted. This would be a time to test for mini-reversal, the resistance to being *completely* free of the problem. When found, this normally clears easily enough with tapping the side of the hand. Further treatment sequences will usually then clear the remaining distress.

If the client reports no remaining distress, he or she may be encouraged to think more vividly about the previous target—perhaps to imagine how the situation would look, sound, smell, and the kinaesthetic sensations involved. If further traces of distress are noticed, additional tapping may be carried out—often only briefly. The absence of distress may mean that the client's system is indeed now completely free of perturbations in relation to the original target. Another possibility is that he or she is dissociated from the distress. This can happen with people who have employed dissociative defences in relation to trauma, and also with those who are generally avoidant in relation to anxiety. A helpful check here is to muscle test the person while they say "I am in my body/not in my body". If dissociated, the muscle will often register weak to being in the body. A related question can be "I am alive". This can be corrected by tapping the side of the hand and stating "Even though not all parts of me are in my body, I completely accept myself"—or "Even though not all parts of me are alive …". Following such corrections, the tapping will usually proceed to an adequate conclusion.

Sometimes phobic people will not be completely free of perturbations about the target situation until they have cleared these *in vivo*, actually in the feared condition. The client may be asked how he or she would know whether the problem had gone, and then the test deriving from this may be applied.

A check for level two reversal may be carried out, by muscle testing to the statement "I *will* be free (or will remain free) of this problem". If this registers negative, it can be cleared either by tapping side of hand, or by tapping under the nose (the latter is recommended by Dr Callahan).

Further future-pacing can involve having the client imagine future circumstances in which his or her behaviour and emotional reactions will be different. Muscle testing may be carried out whilst imagining this. If the muscle goes weak, further tapping may be done whilst imagining these future situations.

Working with the chakras

Some energy psychology practitioners work partially or predominantly with the chakras, which are energy centres along the midline of the body. The meridian and the chakra systems can easily be combined. Some practitioners have the impression that the meridian system is the more appropriate focus for specific traumas, whilst the chakra system may be more important in relation to deep patterns, 'software' programmes, core beliefs, and so on. In practice, both systems can be used for both specific events and wider patterns. One possibility that has occurred to me is that deletion of perturbations from the meridian system is analogous to deleting files from the desktop of a computer—so that they are still potentially able to be restored because they remain on the hard drive—whereas removing them from the chakras is more like permanent deletion from the hard drive.

Asha Clinton's Seemorg Matrix is a method which works exclusively with the chakra system, whilst also combining the energetic, the cognitive and the psychodynamic. It is used to clear trauma, patterns of traumatic reaction, addictions, dysfunctional cognitions, energetic signatures of toxins and many other problems. Positive cognitions can also be installed. The approach is deep and comprehensive, consistent with Asha Clinton's background as a Jungian psychotherapist. She is one of the few in the energy psychology field to have developed an approach specifically for personality disorders.

Tapas Fleming's Tapas Acupressure Technique [TAT] works with the third eye forehead chakra, the two bladder 1 points either side of the nose in the corner with the eye brow, and the occipital region at the back of the skull. The client holds these whilst proceeding through a series of meditative steps. These steps are not fixed and there is great flexibility in the procedure, but usually something like the following steps are followed: [1] to acknowledge the problem, or to accept that the traumatic event happened; [2] to consider a state of being without the problem, or simply to acknowledge "I am here, I survived"; [3] then to entertain the thought that "all the roots and origins of the problem are healing now"; [4] to allow the thought that "all the places in my mind, body, and life, where this problem has been stored are healing now"; [5] to allow the thought that any part of the person that has benefited from, or got something out of the problem, is healing now; [6] to allow the thought that anyone whom the person has blamed for the problem, including the self, can be forgiven; [7] to allow the thought that anyone who has been hurt as a result of the person having the problem can be asked (inwardly) for forgiveness; [8] any other aspect of the problem, from any time or place, is healing now.

The point of the series of thoughts in TAT is not to convince the person that they are true, but simply to allow them to have a space as an alternative to the fixed position or attitude that traumatised or hurt people often have. By shifting from the usual fixed attitude a space is allowed, and a moment of stillness, within which the light of healing love can shine. There is a very gentle and awesome quality in the process of TAT—qualities which many have noted to be characteristic of Tapas Fleming herself [www.tatlife.com].

There are certain commonly used principles and procedures in working with the chakras either to delete or install cognitions or emotional qualities. Sequences of chakras can be diagnosed for a particular target problem, in just the same way as meridian points. Then the chakras can be touched or held as the issue is focused upon. Muscle testing can be used to discern how long each chakra needs to be held. Often this may be proxy self muscle testing by the therapist. Deleting cognitions, emotions, or programmes may be done by proceeding down the chakra system from the crown to the root. Installing positive qualities may be done by moving up the chakras from the root to the crown. An additional strategy is to 'spin' the chakras, by making a movement with the hand. To delete a quality, the chakra is spun counterclockwise, where the front of the body is taken as the face of the clock—i.e. as counterclockwise would look to an observer facing the clock on the front of the client's body. To install a positive quality or cognition, the chakra is spun clockwise, starting at the root and moving up to the crown. Asha Clinton recommends an exclamation of exultation (e.g. Hallelujah!, or any exuberant shout) as a means of sealing the shift and of bringing in new fresh energy.

Particular applications of energy methods

Using energy methods with addictions

Roger Callahan was the first energy psychologist to propose the view that the most crucial cause of addictive behaviour is anxiety. The addictive substance or behaviour is used to mask or tranquillise the underlying anxiety. Therefore, in working with addictions, it is important to discern the nature of the anxiety that is warded off. Often this anxiety relates to another emotion that the person is afraid to experience (such as sadness, or anger, or loneliness—or other emotions related to trauma). However, another obvious factor in relation to addictive substances is the craving, which may in itself create anxiety, continually relieved by recourse to the addictive substance. A third factor is that of psychological reversal. Roger Callahan has emphasised that the addict is not reversed against relief from the cravings for the addiction, but is usually reversed against recovery from the addiction itself. For this reason, it is recommended that the addict tap the side of hand (correction for reversal) frequently throughout the day (perhaps each hour). Another form of reversal may relate to a lack of belief that it is possible to give up the addiction—perhaps with links to self-image (e.g. 'I am a smoker').

In summary, the energy treatment of addiction involves the following elements:

1. Addressing the underlying anxiety and the emotions giving rise to it.
2. Addressing trauma that has given rise to anxiety.
3. Addressing cravings.
4. Addressing psychological reversal (including belief and self-image components of this, as well as anticipated feelings of loss or deprivation on giving up the addiction).

Treatment of trauma and PTSD

Increasingly, most forms of psychological disorder that do not have a clear genetic-biological basis are seen as expressions of trauma, including traumatic events and patterns in childhood. This perspective was developed particularly within the framework of EMDR (many practitioners of which have become drawn to energy methods—Galvin & Hartung, 2003). The general awareness of the significance of psychological trauma did not develop until the late 1980s—and even today is not universally appreciated within psychiatric circles.

Energy methods, including EFT, can be extremely effective in reducing or eliminating the effects of trauma and post traumatic stress disorder (PTSD). However, practitioners of energy methods should obviously not attempt to treat PTSD (resulting from serious accidents, assault, disasters etc.) unless already knowledgeable and experienced in doing so.

The general approach, using EFT, TFT, or any other energy method, would be to address each aspect of the traumatic situation until all distress is eliminated. The various aspects may include:

1. The different points in the sequence of events—the 'movie technique'.
2. The different emotions (often in layers).
3. The different sensory qualities of the experience.
4. The negative beliefs—or self-related cognitions—that have resulted from the trauma.
5. The connecting links between the trauma and subsequent behaviour ('Because X happened, I must do Y').

Traumas are often connected in a web or matrix. Thus a more recent trauma may carry some of its power to disturb through its resonance with an earlier trauma, perhaps from childhood.

The Movie Technique

The client is asked to recount the trauma as if it were a short movie sequence. At each point that the client experiences emotional intensity, he or she is asked to tap until the emotion subsides. The aim is to work until the client is able to recount the event coherently without experiencing emotional distress.

Tearless trauma technique

Gary Craig has described a useful method of working with trauma using partial dissociation. He calls this the 'tearless trauma technique' and recommends its use when the person might become overwhelmed if thinking too directly about the trauma. The procedure is as follows:

- The client is asked *not* to think vividly about the trauma, but to guess what the SUD level would be if he or she *were* to recall it with full emotional intensity.
- Then EFT is carried out in the usual way, using a reminder phrase which relates to the trauma. It may be helpful to ask the client to stay focussed externally—e.g. to look at the therapist—so that he or she does not defocus the eyes and become internally immersed in the trauma.
- The EFT is continued until the guessed SUD is low.
- The client may then be invited to think vividly about the trauma and rate the SUD.
- EFT may then be continued until the SUD is low even when the client is trying to recall the experience vividly.

A useful variant of the 'tearless trauma' technique is the use of a code word to refer to the traumas. Thus the person can be told that the particular trauma, or a whole series of traumas, are all to be designated 'X' (for example). Then the usual procedure is followed, beginning with tapping the side of the hand and saying "Even though X I completely accept myself", the tapping the relevant points, saying "X" at each one. This is usually surprisingly effective. After working with the code word, the person can then be invited to think about the traumas directly, in order to test whether the distress has cleared.

Dissociation—parts not in the body

One potential obstacle to successful clearing of trauma may occur if the person has dissociated from it such that the thought field cannot be activated. A useful check for this is to muscle test the statement "I am fully in my body". Clients are sometimes rather startled to discover that, according to their own energy system, they are not. This can be treated as a reversal and cleared in the normal way.

Subsequent tapping sequences will usually then be successful in relation to the trauma.

Tapping 'the traumas I don't want to think about'

In working with a man on his difficulties in his experiences with his mother, we had cleared certain areas of his distress, but there were some remaining traumas to do with her abusive expressions of anger when he was young. When I asked him to think about these to test for residual emotional distress, he remarked that he felt a barrier coming down and a sense of not wanting to think of them. Therefore I used a TFT sequence using the phrase 'the traumas I do not want to think about'—working through a diagnosed sequence until this muscle tested strong. I then asked him to try thinking of the traumatic experiences with his mother now—and this time he said he no longer felt the resistance to thinking of them. He reported an absence of emotion. Moreover, he elaborated an image of opening doors in his mind, looking inside and surveying his memories. He experienced no distress in doing so, whilst previously he would have felt afraid to look at all. Now these memories just appeared like still photographs of past events, without any emotional charge.

When trauma does not clear, check for shame and denial of shame

Shame is an extremely potent and painful emotion (Mollon, 2002). Moreover, it is so painful and threatening that it may be hidden from the conscious self as well as from others. Shame will block access to emotional information. Because of this it can sometimes be a factor blocking the activation of a thought field and the clearing of the perturbations. It is inherent in the nature of shame that this will not be obvious. Thus shame can be denied—and a further step is 'denial of denial', rendering it even more hidden. Fortunately, muscle testing will still reveal this.

I became aware of this more clearly one day when working with a man to clear the distress associated with an experience with a previous therapist. We continually encountered reversals based on safety. Then it appeared that an earlier trauma was blocking the processing and clearing of this one—so we shifted the focus to 'the trauma behind the trauma with X'. Some partial progress was made, but then the process again seemed to become blocked, with no indications arising as to which meridians needed to be tapped. Prompted by a sudden intuition, I muscle tested him to the statement "there is shame blocking this process", resulting in an ambiguous 'yes'. I then tested the statement "there is shame and denial of shame blocking this process", which resulted in a clear affirmative. After treating this as a reversal and correcting it, we then proceeded rather easily to clear the remaining distress about the situation with the previous therapist. The man then arrived at the insight that he had not previously felt it safe to be over the anger regarding the previous therapist because he might then have to face his deeper feelings of toxic shame rooted in earlier situations in childhood.

Treatment of phobias

This is very similar to the treatment of trauma. EFT or other energy method is applied to the various aspects of the phobia. There may be progressive approaches to a vivid imagining or actual behavioural contact with the phobic situation or object. Sometimes trauma may lie behind the phobia. However, Roger Callahan considers that often phobias do not have a basis in personal trauma but are energetically inherited through the thought fields of family and the wider culture.

Treatment of allergies and sensitivities

Many energy methods, including EFT, are used to reduce allergies and sensitivities. Good results are often reported. Tapas Fleming's Tapas Acupressure Technique (TAT) was originally developed to treat allergies. Sandi Radomski is one of the main practitioners of energy methods for treating trauma—see www.allergyantidotes.com. Roger Callahan places emphasis on 'energy toxins' and teaches a 'seven second toxin treatment'. However, he believes that energy treatments for toxins and allergies are often not permanent in their effects. This is a rather specialised area of energy work and practitioners are advised to explore this with caution and to seek further training.

Warning. It could be extremely dangerous to assume that a severe allergy had been successfully treated with an energy method. Anaphylactic shock is a life-threatening medical crisis.

In the case of milder sensitivities and allergies, it may well be worthwhile to explore whether an energy method is able to help.

Treatment of generational-ancestral trauma

Sometimes I have found that muscle testing will indicate the presence of intergenerational or ancestral trauma that is present in the client's energy field. The muscle testing statement can be "there is trauma and pain from my mother's/father's ancestral line in my energy field". For example, a client reported no clear and obvious trauma from her childhood, but she seemed overwhelmed with anxiety and somatic problems, and to have a core belief that the world is profoundly dangerous and that any developmental initiative by her would be disastrous. On listening to her, I gained an impression of her energy field having been overwhelmed by trauma and pain from both parent's family lines. The image that occurred to me was of her energy field having become the depository of pain cascading down from both ancestral lines. Muscle testing confirmed this and also indicated that the distress from her father's line needed to be cleared first. This was done fairly easily. Clearing the trauma from her mother's line was more problematic—with various psychological reversals appearing along the way (based on fears of abandoning her mother, guilt if she were free of the pain, and so on). Once these reversals were corrected, the distress from the maternal line was easily cleared. The client expressed surprise at the comparative difficulty in clearing the perturbations from her mother's side of the family since she had always thought of her father as having been the more troubling figure, with his volatile temperament and overt personality disorder. By contrast she described her mother as more withdrawn and schizoid. The work indicated that her awareness of distress inherited from her father was more conscious, but that from her mother was more hidden and insidious.

With another client, we were encountering some issues of internal objection to being happy, which were not clearing with the usual corrections for reversal. After unsuccessfully attempting to clear this with a focus on beliefs, parts, and programmes, I tried the muscle testing statement "I cannot allow myself to be happy because I am carrying the pain and trauma from my parents' family lines". Immediately she was convulsed with distress and anxiety, the content of which remained unclear. We tapped through a long sequence and five minutes later she became calm. She then reported feeling a deep peace—and did indeed look profoundly calm and peaceful. Presumably this was the first time in her life that she had been free of the inherited trauma in her energy field. Although the clearing of inherited perturbations of trauma may on occasion give rise to conscious distress, as in this case, often the client feels little other than an enhanced sense of well-being following the tapping sequence.

A further aspect of inherited trauma is that a part (or parts) of the person appears to be attached to it—often as if oriented entirely in relation to this pain. Without it, that part feels lost and disoriented. The part that is attached to the pain may form the basis of a reversal (or commonly a mini-reversal) blocking the complete release of the inherited perturbations. This reversal can be corrected in the normal way.

At the time of writing, I have the impression that attachment to inherited trauma and pain may give rise to persisting feelings of guilt and patterns of self-sabotage. It is as if the person feels that he or she must share in the burden of inherited pain and suffering—and that to be happy or successful is like abandoning the parents, or even like pushing the pain back into them. Sometimes, but not always, it can appear that one or both parents have also attempted to induce feelings of guilt and difficulties for the child in pursuing his or her independent strivings, or may have used the child as a container for their own pain. This latter kind of interpersonal dynamic corresponds to familiar psychoanalytic concepts of projective identification, but inherited pain and trauma seem to be transmitted down the generational energy fields without the mediation of a psychodynamic fantasy or mechanism of defence.

My experience of exploring inherited trauma is fairly recent, but so far my impression is that this is transmitted particularly (but not exclusively) down the maternal line. Perhaps this is not surprising since we are all conceived within our mother's energy field—our own system thereby becoming imprinted with the information in hers.

A useful statement to muscle test for inherited trauma and pain is "There is someone else's pain and trauma in my system/energy field". If positive, this can be followed with "There is pain and trauma in my system/energy field from my mother's/father's family line". It may then be necessary to muscle test "We have permission to clear this pain and trauma"—treating this as a reversal—and then to ask if it can all be cleared in one go or whether the two family lines need to be dealt with separately. After clearing it with tapping, the same original statements can be muscle tested again. Check for its complete clearance from all parts and all layers. Although the clearing of inherited perturbations of trauma may on occasion give rise to conscious distress, often the client feels little other than an enhanced sense of well-being following the tapping sequence.

If there is a negative muscle response to statements about the presence of inherited trauma and pain, it can be worth trying the following statement: "there is *denied* inherited trauma and pain in my system". This may register positive. It is an example of how a muscle test may fail to indicate the presence of particular information in the energy field if this has been rendered 'denied'. Once the denied inherited trauma and pain has been detected, it can be cleared in the normal way.

It is not necessary—and usually not possible—to know consciously the content of the inherited trauma and pain. Brief slight emotional reactions may occur as it is cleared.

After clearing inherited trauma, it is a good idea to muscle test "I want the trauma back". If the answer is yes, then this can be treated like any other reversal.

Application to other problems, including physical conditions

The great feature of the TFT muscle testing diagnostic method is that it can be applied to any mental or physical problem. There is no requirement that the practitioner understand the full nature or cause of the problem. All that is required is that the client think of the problem, or perhaps touch the troubling part of the body if the problem is physical, or simply focus on how he or she is feeling right now. Then the muscle testing procedure is followed, establishing the correct tapping sequence for that problem through seeking the meridian points that make the muscle lock strong. In this way, the layers of emotion and stress in the psychosomatic system are systematically cleared. The client experiences a tangible shift in the feedback provided by his or her own energy system. If targeting an emotional state of mind, this energy shift will be accompanied by a distinct improvement in mood, usually with an increased sense of calm and peace. If the target is a chronic physical problem, then the tapping sequence has been provided by the client's own energy system and is therefore likely to help the condition if carried out regularly. So long as it is possible to start from a mental focus that makes the arm weak, the muscle testing diagnostic method can be used to seek the sequence that will make the arm strong. Thus there can be diagnosis and treatment of anything that makes the system weak when the person thinks of it.

Mindful energy scan

I have developed a simple method derived from the intriguing work of William Redpath (1995) on 'held-energy systems'. Redpath, a practitioner with a background in bioenergetic and psychoanalytic perspectives, has written of the ways in which traumatic experience becomes frozen or 'held' in the body, sealed off from conscious access and yet continually influencing our reactions and behaviours:

"As a passenger in the front seat of an automobile, we forget to fasten our safety belt, and our car hits a wall. Heading in prewindshield chaos toward the windshield, our mindbody rigidifies in some energetically essential place in primitive brain, objectifying itself, becoming molecularly fixed, like, perhaps, the object it is about to hit. Our life energies, including the auric, appear to immobilise prior to and within the moment of contact with the windshield ... The energy within our primitive brain seems not to know what to do with this neurochemical traffic bump and detours around it ... The gates to this stored memory phenomenon, now a held-energy system, with all of its kinaesthetic network of total body and mind involvement, are as if closed. The brain cannot enter its own ... closet, and as with a taboo, the remaining life energies appear forbidden to enter the room of encapsulated memory. Behind its door is some sense of chaos or pain which the mindbody cannot deal with. Our inner emotional sense is that without this neurochemical gateway to past overwhelm sealed, our circuits will burn out or we will go crazy, go over the edge, or 'lose it'." [Redpath, 1995, 77–78]

This situation then gives rise to denial, and denial of denial, and the area of trauma becomes ever more hidden. Redpath provides the following analogy:

"The first time the mindbody scans, the chemical door to trauma-held memory is shut, the second time it is sealed. The third time, our erotic, scanning energy asks, 'Where is the door? It was here just a moment ago.' And the neurochemical doorkeeper replies, "What door? What are you talking about?". [Redpath, 1995, p. 79]

Redpath's therapeutic method is to provide energetic support by physical holding the back of the client's head and neck (although this is not essential), whilst the client, lying down and in a meditative state, is asked to notice and report the visual shapes and colours apparent in his or her subjective field. The brain appears able to represent and focus upon its own areas of held-energy. Patterns of black seem to express areas of loss of energetic movement resulting from trauma. Whilst avoiding providing any content, which would disrupt the focus on the purely energetic level, the therapist facilitates the client's processing of the held-energetic patterns.

My adaptation of this, which also has some similarities to Hartmann's (2003) EmoTrance and Jaffe's Awareness Release Technique (Stux, 2003), is as follows. The client is asked to think of the target problem, and then, with eyes closed, to scan their own energy field by 'looking' in all directions, up and down, front and back, sides, above and below, and to report on any areas that appear black or dark. Then, having identified these, the client is guided simply to observe these and also to observe their own breathing concurrently. It is important that the client is not instructed to 'do' anything with either their black/dark areas or their breathing, but simply to notice them. When the client's attention is directed in this way—a form of mindfulness—the patterns change spontaneously, black areas fading and breathing becoming calmer. This shift at the purely energetic level is associated with a diminution of distress when the target problem is again accessed. There is much more to say about Mindful Energy Scanning, but this would require a further book.

When nothing seems to work

Although energy psychology methods mostly work very well and rapidly, with clearly observable results, especially when used by skilled and experienced practitioners alert to the many complexities and nuances involved, there are occasions when progress appears slow or non-existent. Few situations are more likely to lead a practitioner to appear and feel utterly foolish than to be attempting to engage the client in a variety of seemingly strange energy procedures that are clearly failing to have any effect whatsoever! Sometimes, albeit rarely, despite all my best efforts, I find that energy psychology methods simply do not work and I cannot figure out why. However, I have found the following principles often provide a way forward.

- Check for every conceivable psychological reversal (including permission to treat the problem).
- Check for neurological disorganisation.
- Check for energy toxins.
- Check for "all parts of me are in my body/are alive".
- Check for "my brain/mind is connected to my body".
- Check for some basic distrust felt by the client towards the therapist.
- Check for the correct thought field (the most relevant thought relating to the problem).
- Check that the thought field is actually activated. Some (rare) individuals need to focus with particular conscious concentration upon the target issue before the thought field is effectively activated.
- Check for dehydration (tugging a strand of hair or pinching skin around the head or face will muscle test weak if dehydrated).
- Check for perturbations in various levels and realms—such as: unconscious mind; body; chakras; 'all parts of me'; 'all compartments of me'. Muscule test by stating the level/realm followed by the target problem. [inspired by the intentions of Dr Judith Swack www.jaswack.com]

If none of these leads to any shift, then sit back and just listen and observe—listen to the client's communications and also to one's own inner stirrings and intuition. Often, the deeper issues that need to be addressed may become apparent.

Since each person is an individual, there is no limit to the subtle variations and adaptations that may need to be found in order to accommodate the particular psychological and energetic situation.

Failing this, the situation is best taken as a further lesson in humility and the current limits of one's skill and knowledge.

CHAPTER SIX

Neurological (energetic) disorganisation

W hilst psychological reversal acts as a clear and coherent prohibition on therapeutic progress, the phenomenon known as 'neurological disorganisation' acts to make the process fuzzy and inefficient. Clients who do not respond easily to TFT and related methods, or who show a return of a previously successfully treated problem, or who repeatedly regenerate psychological reversals after they have been corrected, often show this disorganisation. It can result from environmental or endogenous 'energy toxins', as well as constitutional and nutritional factors or subtle structural damage. In certain ways the disorganisation does appear to be *neurological*, since it can be associated with some of the subtle disturbances of brain function, such as dyslexia, ADHD, clumsiness, right-left confusions etc. However, it also seems to involve an *energetic* disorganisation. For example, muscle tests may be inconclusive, giving little distinction between strong and weak responses, or between the polarities of palm down and palm up over head. The person suffering such disorganisation is in a state of inherent confusion, lacking a clear sense of goal or purpose, and experiencing chronic underlying frustration over an inability to think coherently. If one listens to such patients psychoanalytically, there will often be

123

a lack of coherent themes emerging, and a difficulty will be experienced in penetrating to any depth in the free-associative material. Instead, there will be a repetitive and affectively shallow discourse that seems to lead nowhere and does not deepen. Messages appear to be scrambled. The client may experience anxiety and feel spaced out or disoriented, with depersonalisation or derealisation.

Disorganisation and overarousal

Such a condition expresses a kind of mistunement or disorganisation in the energy system. A related state is that of general overarousal. This is commonly found in people who are very anxious, or who suffer panic attacks. Feinstein (2004) describes this as a state of 'triple warmer in overwhelm'—in which the triple warmer meridian, responsible for fight-flight reactions, is in chronic high arousal, and is recruiting energy from other meridians for these emergency functions. The result is not only high anxiety but also exhaustion and potentially chronic fatigue. When there is energetic disorganisation or triple warmer in overarousal the energy system is not able to respond optimally to energy tapping treatments. The overall system is in an abnormal state, so that addressing the particular target problem will have only partial success. If disorganisation and overarousal are reduced, so that the resting system is organised and calm, then targeting the problem is much more likely to be successful.

The arousal associated with anxiety is not in itself a state of disorganisation. It is not in itself a *disturbance* in the meridian system. Dr Callahan often points out that states of anxiety are highly organised, many different physiological and biochemical processes intricately choreographed for the purposes of fight or flight. The problem arises when the fight-flight arousal is not dissipated by appropriate physical action, and when the anxiety has become linked to situations that are not actually dangerous.

However, high levels of neurological disorganisation, *combined* with high levels of physiological stress arousal, can lead to states of overwhelming anxiety and confusion. The intensified scrambling of information processing can lead both to fears of going mad and to momentary states of psychotic cognition, involving misperceptions, misunderstandings, and faulty inferences. Walther (1988), following earlier observations by Goodheart, discusses the role of neurological disorganisation in schizophrenia.

The phenomenon of Attention Deficit Hyperactivity Disorder, a condition that appears to be exacerbated by the current prevalence of 'energy toxins' in processed foods and drinks, illustrates some of the difficulties arising from neurological disorganisation. ADHD is thought to involve a deficiency in the executive functioning of the frontal lobes, resulting in difficulties in regulating emotion, maintaining attention, planning, and pursuing goals. The ADHD sufferer experiences his or her mind as often like a storm of unco-ordinated and unregulated thoughts and feelings. Fonagy and colleagues (Fonagy et al. 2002; Bateman & Fonagy, 2004) have referred to 'hyperactive mentalisation', a condition in which a frantic kind of quasi-thinking takes place which is not rooted in a clear problem-focused task. Deep cognitive structures, such as self-concept and self-image, tend to be unstable in the person with ADHD, resulting in a sense of identity confusion, generating further anxiety and a hyperactive search for meaning. This is the opposite of a coherent and integrated energy system. Moreover, because of a deficit in the normal capacity to decentre from his or her own perspective, the person with ADHD may encounter repeated and, to them, bewildering frustrations in their interactions with others—paradoxically, the person with ADHD will tend to perceive *others* as egocentric and lacking empathy. Because of the anxiety and stress that is inherent in the ADHD condition, the sufferer is likely to be in a physiologically overaroused state much of the time, generating fight-flight hormones, and hyperventilating. At times the spiralling neurological and energetic disorganisation may intensify to panic levels, accompanied by increasingly abnormal thought processes. Dr Callahan's work with TFT has developed further the understanding of energy toxins in ADHD and related conditions, as outlined originally by pioneers such as Doris Rapp (1991).

Hyperventilation—effects and correction

Hyperventilation is a common accompaniment of triple warmer overarousal, resulting in a variety of symptoms, such as palpitations, anxiety, pains or tingling, and a sensation of breathing difficulties

(Bradley, 1998; Fried, 1999). Some of the symptoms of hyperventilation are identical to those of neurological disorganisation—such as
confusion, feeling spaced out, and being uncoordinated. This is often
a hidden problem. Whilst many mental health practitioners are aware
of the phenomenon of acute hyperventilation occurring in relation to
panic attacks, the more hidden chronic form of hyperventilation is
frequently overlooked. Since routinely screening for hyperventilation amongst my NHS patients, using a standard questionnaire, I
have found that a high proportion of those presenting with anxiety,
phobia, or panic, are suffering symptoms of hyperventilation whilst
having no idea that this is the case. Hyperventilation can be part of
the response to anxiety, since drawing in more air is a component of
the fight-flight reaction to perceived danger, but can in turn *generate
anxiety* and other alarming symptoms.

What happens in hyperventilation is that the blood becomes
essentially toxic (the wrong pH—too alkaline), disturbing and disorganising all systems of the body and brain. In this state, TFT and
related methods are much less efficient. Here is how it happens
(with thanks to Ian Graham, leading TFT practitioner in the UK, for
explaining this to me). In normal conditions the blood is more or less
completely saturated with oxygen, carried as oxyhaemoglobin in the
red cells. Carbon dioxide is carried in the blood plasma (in the form
of hydrogencarbonate ions). The presence of carbon dioxide keeps
the pH (acid-alkaline balance) of the blood at the normal optimal
level for the body's cellular enzyme systems. When a person perceives danger and the fight-flight mechanism is triggered, he or she
may begin to breathe too much or too rapidly. This would not be
a problem in primordial times when danger meant a need literally
to fight or take flight, actions which would generate high levels of
carbon dioxide as products of metabolism. In modern circumstances
of stress—which might, for example be the result of a bill in the
post, a piece of paper rather than a snake or tiger—carbon dioxide
production is not increased by physical activity, but the excessive
breathing drives off too much carbon dioxide. This makes the blood
too alkaline. There are many effects of this: the sodium/potassium
balance in the nerve fibres is disturbed, resulting, for example, in the
'tingling fingers' symptom, the balance between the sympathetic and
parasympathetic nervous system is disrupted, creating anxiety and
palpitations, delivery of oxygen to the tissues is impaired, causing

tiredness and the build up of lactic acid, resulting in muscular pain; the ventilatory centre in the medulla responds by inhibiting contraction of the diaphragm and intercostals muscles, resulting in a sensation of being unable to breath. If the sufferer, in this acute state of hyperventilation, continues to try forcefully to breathe—often in reaction to panic at feeling unable to breathe—the toxicity in the blood rises further, with an eventual loss of consciousness, which then allows the body to restore its balance.

In the more chronic pattern of hyperventilation, it appears that the brain may have become set to respond to the wrong threshold of carbon dioxide, triggering urges to breathe when in fact there is already too little carbon dioxide in the blood. This pattern is less obvious, but presents a backdrop of continual anxiety, often leaving the person feeling constantly on the edge of panic. The content of the anxiety is not psychological but physiological. When faced with any further stress, the person's system may be precipitated into a toxic emergency state, resulting in feelings of full blown panic, confusion, and helplessness. It may be that this is one factor behind the common phenomenon of self-harm, such as cutting, as a means of stress relief. The act of cutting the body, and the sight of the blood induces a shock reaction of lowered blood pressure and metabolic rate (to conserve blood and biochemical resources).

Hyperventilation can often be confirmed through muscle testing. The client is asked to say 'breathing' whilst the indicator muscle is pressed, and then to say 'holding my breath'. In the case of the hyperventilating person, the indicator muscle is likely to go weak to 'breathing' and strong to 'holding my breath', showing that at that point breathing is acting as a source of toxin.

It is often important to break this cycle of chronic hyperventilation in order for the person to benefit from a method such as TFT. Without such correction, the toxic internal environment is continually generating neurological/energetic disorganisation. The emergency treatment for acute hyperventilation is to breathe into a paper bag, thereby recycling the carbon dioxide rich air and rapidly restoring the optimal level in the blood. Another strategy is to hold one's breath. Physical exercise will also relieve the symptoms by generating more carbon dioxide. Physiotherapists can teach methods of deeper and slower breathing. The collar bone breathing exercise, developed by Dr Callahan, combines a correction for neurological disorganisation with a regulation and slowing of the breath that probably acts to counter hyperventilation. Tapping on the 'gamut point', in the Callahan version of collar bone breathing, also helps to soothe the triple warmer/thyroid meridian that is overactive when fight-flight arousal is in place but is not actually required for immediate survival.

Walther, in his substantial 1988 text Applied Kinesiology, suggests that neurological disorganisation is often related to problems in the 'cranial-sacral primary respiratory mechanism'. This is a subtle wavelike oscillation in the material covering the surface of the brain and the spinal cord, which is also related to the breathing of air. Whilst structural damage or distortions in the cranial bones may give rise to these problems, it seems likely that disturbed or abnormal breathing may also contribute.

Dr Callahan's work with Thought Field Therapy has shown how neurological disorganisation is often caused by individual energy toxins. He has developed an energy toxin neutralisation procedure (the seven second toxin treatment[1]) that involves pressing lightly on the cranial bones on the forehead on either the in-breath or out-breath (depending on the particular toxin)—again illustrating the significance of breathing in relation to energy organisation and disorganisation. The importance of correct breathing—balanced, deep, and slow—is emphasised in yoga traditions, as well as in many modern forms of complementary medicine.

In addition to the collar bone breathing technique, developed by Dr Callahan, gentle breathing whilst in the Tapas Acupressure pose, or the Over-Energy Correction, will also correct hyperventilation (all described below).

A simple method of tapping and visualisation to reduce overarousal

I have found the following method helpful with a number of clients after the problem of overarousal has been explained.

Tap the triple warmer 'gamut' point on the back of the hand. Whilst doing so, close the eyes and imagine a control panel with a dial representing physiological arousal level. Notice that it is turned up too high—the pointer over into the red 'danger' zone. Find the adjustment control and turn it right down. Then press the button labelled 'set new default'. Then open the eyes and exit the control panel.

Energetic underarousal, also known as 'blow out'

In this condition, the person muscle tests weak whatever the question or statement. It is a form of general energetic depletion, which can accompany or follow illness. The person may be in a state of exhaustion. Treatment of deeply rooted traumas or conflicts probably is best not attempted when the person is depleted in this way. Rest, good nutrition, and water may be required. The 'thymus thump', along with gentle tapping on the side of the hand accompanied by the statement "Even though I am exhausted, I accept myself" may help to restore the person's energy. Simple corrections for disorganisation, outlined below, may also be effective in some cases.

Testing for neurological/energetic disorganisation

There are common indicators of neurological/energetic disorganisation: a history of clumsiness, dyslexia, dyspraxia, ADHD, left-right confusion, spatial disorientation, homolateral arm-leg movements (left arm swings with left leg and vice versa) faltering when attempting to communicate—and sometimes a certain subtle facial look of confusion or perplexity. I have also noticed, particularly with certain mental health patients, that some neurologically disorganised people will appear to feel that others do not understand them—e.g. he or she will be speaking and will interrupt their own speech with a comment such as "you don't understand"—as if the sense of internal disruption of meaning spills over into the speaker's perception of the receptive comprehension of the listener.

However, there are also simple and rapid muscle tests to identify neurological disorganisation. It takes only moments to carry out these tests, and the first three are the most common and routine. Tests 1 and 2 are actually inherent in any muscle testing procedure. If the client passes test 3, there would often be no need to perform the additional tests, unless particular difficulties arose in the subsequent treatment.

1. Lack of differentiation between 'yes' and 'no' muscle responses. The normally skilled tester detects no difference between the muscle responses to true and false statements.
2. Rapidly altering, inconsistent, or confusing muscle responses.

3. Lack of differentiation, or reverse of the normal response, between palm down and palm up on top of the head—a phenomenon sometimes called 'non-polarisation'. To test this, the tester presses on the client's outstretched arm whilst the client's other hand is held, first palm down, and then palm up above the head. The normal response is the muscle is stronger to palm down (easily remembered by the phrase 'palm is power; back is slack'). In neurologically/energetically disorganised states there may be either a lack of differentiation or a reversal of the normal response, so that palm down is weaker than palm up. This latter response may also indicate a state of general or massive reversal in the energy system—thereby illustrating links between neurological disorganisation and psychological reversal, two phenomena that are somewhat different but also related.

4. Ocular lock—jerky movements if the client is asked to roll the eyes in a circle (check both directions). People with this problem may experience particular tiredness when reading. A further indication of ocular lock is shown if the indicator test muscle becomes weak after the eye movement. A correction for this is routinely incorporated into TFT and EFT in the form of the '9 gamut' sequence. This came about because Dr Callahan noticed that sometimes a client may have largely eliminated the target problem but will still show some residue of it when asked to make certain eye movements. The '9 gamut" eliminates the ocular lock by tapping on the triple heater 'gamut point' whilst making the eye movements.

Three further, less commonly used, tests for energetic disorganisation (described by Feinstein, 2004):

5. Overwhelmed triple warmer—the meridian system governing fight-flight, the immune system, and survival responses. The test is for the client to hold a cupped hand around one of the ears, the fingers touching the head a couple of inches above the ear. If the indicator muscle goes weak, this is thought to suggest triple warmer in an overwhelmed state.

6. Meridians running backwards. This may relate also to the general state of massive reversal. Normally, the movements

of ordinary walking vitalise the energy system. When the meridians are in reverse, the action of taking a few steps forward will weaken the indicator muscle; this will be confirmed if the muscle is strengthened by the action of walking backwards.

7. Homolateral energy flow. The body's energies are meant to cross the left and right sides of the brain and body. Looking at an 'X', made either by the therapist's fingers, or drawn on paper, should produce a strong indicator muscle response; two parallel lines should produce a weakening of the indicator muscles. If the muscle response is the reverse of this pattern, homolateral energy flow is indicated.

Corrections for neurological/energetic disorganisation and overarousal

The following tend to be used in various slightly different ways, and have different names according to the author. Most are derivatives of methods used in Applied Kinesiology, adapted by innovators such as Callahan (1999), Gallo (1998) Feinstein (2004) and Diepold, Britt & Bender (2004). Many further examples can be found in Dennison's 'Brain Gym' (Dennison & Dennison, 1989) and the field of educational kinesiology. The Dennisons' book provides interesting notes on the history and origins of each exercise.

1. **Brief generic correction for neurological/energetic disorganisation.** The finger tips of one hand are placed on the navel/ umbilicus. With the other hand, the fist is lightly tapped on the upper chest, then the two K27 collar bone points are tapped or massaged for a few seconds, then the point under the lower lip is tapped or massaged, then the point under the nose, then the 'third eye' point an inch or so above the eye brows in the centre, and finally the base of the spine. Then the hands are swapped and the process is repeated. It takes only a minute or so. Often this will be sufficient to create a clearer and more organised muscle response and to correct non-polarisation. This procedure can often helpfully be combined with tapping the side of the hand (small intestine reversal correction point) for thirty seconds or so.

A simple variation on the above is to tap or hold the start of the governing meridian under the nose, and with the other hand to tap or hold the base of the spine. According to the Dennisons, this stimulation, naturally experienced by the baby when held whilst breast feeding, facilitates increased nourishment to the brain through the blood and cerebrospinal fluid.

Another similar and simple exercise is to hold one hand over the navel, whilst two finger tips of the other hand rest on the point either side of head, just above the indentation where the skull rests on the neck. These points are held for about thirty seconds. Then the hands are switched and the point on the other side of the head is held. According to the Dennisons, this exercise helps to correct disorganisation, or switching, in all three dimensions of top-bottom, left-right, and back-front.

2.   **The 'Cook's Hookups' overenergy correction**. Wayne Cook was an innovative chiropractor with a particular interest in electromagnetic energy, and he developed several 'hookups' that help to correct energetic disturbance. The following one, derived partly from a traditional yogic posture, is highly recommended. It is comforting, deeply relaxing as well as neurologically and energetically organising, counters hyperventilation, and is of particular benefit to those with significant levels of general disorganisation and overarousal, such as in conditions like ADHD. To do this, the client first sits with the left ankle over the right one. Then he or she stretches out the arms, with the thumbs turned facing downwards. The right hand is placed over the left hand (the important point is that feet and hands are crossed in opposite directions). Then the fingers are entwined. The entwined hands are brought up and under (this movement may feel slightly awkward to begin with), to rest on the chest (on the heart chakra area). The chin may rest on the hands, the tongue naturally tending to rest on the roof of the mouth behind the teeth. Whilst sitting calmly in this position for one or two minutes (or longer if desired), the client may breathe gently.

A second part of this exercise can be done. This is to uncross the legs and arms, and to sit with the finger tips touching whilst still breathing gently and deeply.

3. **The triple warmer-Spleen hug** (Feinstein, 2004). This is a further simple exercise that is soothing and helps to reduce triple warmer overarousal. One hand is wrapped around the body, the fingers resting under the arm above the waist. The other hand rests on the other arm, the fingers placed in the indent just above the elbow. This position is maintained for three deep breaths, or longer if desired. Then the arms and hands are switched and the process repeated.

4. **Cross crawl**. This standard and long established method from Applied Kinesiology will help to correct homolateral energy flow and meridians flowing backwards. First the K27 points under the collar bones are stimulated for a few seconds. Then the client marches on the spot, raising opposite limbs (e.g. right leg and left arm). This is done for 30-90 seconds. If this does not correct the disorganisation, the following more complex sequence is followed. This involves first having the client march on the spot in the homolateral pattern (i.e. raising right leg and right arm) for about 12 cycles, whilst breathing deeply. Then the pattern is shifted to the normal cross crawl for a further 12 cycles. Thus the exercise first engages with the abnormal homolateral pattern, before leading the system into a cross crawl.

5. **Collar bone breathing**. This is the classic and very effective method developed by Dr Roger Callahan as a routine feature of Thought Field Therapy. It involves touching the K27 points just underneath the collar bones, with the finger tips, and then with the knuckles (i.e. touching with either side of the hand), whilst proceeding through a sequence of breathing punctuated by pauses. In Callahan's method, the triple warmer 3 point (gamut point) is tapped continuously. There are some variations on the basic idea.

The Callahan procedure (best learned through personal instruction from a Callahan Techniques teacher) is as follows. Placing the finger tips on one collar bone point, whilst using the other hand to tap the gamut point, the client proceeds through the following breathing sequence.

Breathe normally. Then breathe in fully and hold for about 5 seconds.
Breathe out halfway and hold for about 5 seconds.
Breathe out all the way and hold for about 5 seconds.
Breathe in halfway and hold for about 5 seconds.
Breathe normally.
The fingers are then placed on the other collar bone point and the breathing sequence is again followed.
Then the knuckles of the hand are placed on each collar bone point in turn, as the breathing sequence is followed.
Then the hands are swapped and whole process is repeated.
Altogether there are 8 different hand positions, each with 5 different breathing steps (including the breathing normally).

Diepold, Britt & Bender (2004) describe a simplified collar bone breathing, which does not involve tapping the gamut point. In this procedure, the finger tips of both hands (and then both knuckles) are placed on the K27 collar bone points. Then the hands are crossed over (right hand to left collar bone and left hand to right collar bone) and the breathing sequence is repeated for both finger tips and knuckles. Diepold and colleagues follow basically the same breathing sequence as in the Callahan method, but with the addition of further steps of forcing more air in after the pause following the full inhale, and forcing more breath out after the pause following the full exhale. They find these two forced breath positions to be advantageous.

6. **Tapas Acupressure Technique** [TAT]. Although this is a complete energy therapy in itself, the basic procedure is so simple that it can combine very helpfully with other methods and is profoundly calming and organising. To do the TAT pose, the thumb and ring finger of one hand rests gently either side of the corner of the nose and the eye brow (the two Bladder 1 points), whilst the middle finger rests on the 'third eye' point, in the centre of the forehead about an inch above the eyebrows. The other hand cradles the occipital bulge in the back of the skull just above the top of the neck. This pose can be held for a minute or two (but should not be maintained for long periods).

7. **Neurovascular holding points**. There are two points, sometimes called the frontal eminences, on the forehead, above each
   eye, halfway between the hairline and the eyebrows. Fingertips
   of each hand can be lightly rested on these points for a minute
   or two. Like the TAT pose, this is deeply relaxing. These neurovascular points are related to the stomach meridian and can
   help release stress manifest in stomach disturbance. The Dennisons suggest that holding these points helps to bring blood
   flow from the hypothalamus to the frontal lobes, thus reducing
   the fight-flight response and facilitating rational thought.

8. **Drinking water**. Often energetic problems are due to inadequate hydration. A test for this is to tug a strand of hair or pinch
   the skin around the head or face—if an indicator muscle tests
   weak to this, dehydration is indicated. After drinking some
   plain water, the muscle will usually immediately test strong.
   This immediate effect does not allow time for the water to be
   absorbed through the gut, but somehow the system appears to
   register that water has been taken in.

9. **Removal of energy toxins**. Dr Callahan's observations have
   highlighted the common involvement of 'individual energy
   toxins' in many seemingly psychological problems. It can
   happen that a person shows a state of disorganisation, or a
   reversal that fails to clear with tapping the side of the hand,
   or a meridian tapping treatment fails to hold, but then, if an
   energy toxin is identified and removed, the person responds
   easily to the treatment and the problem is resolved.

   For example, one person gave confusing muscle test responses, generating reversals which appeared to recur seconds after
   they were corrected; after she removed a scarf on which there
   were residues of a particular perfume, this erratic response
   ceased.

   In another case, a woman who was being treated for anxiety
   when travelling in a car, following a road traffic accident, showed
   some partial reduction in SUDs during the initial session, but
   when seen a week later reported that the anxiety was as bad as
   ever. Moreover, muscle testing at this point revealed massive

reversal (testing weak to wanting to be well and wanting to be happy, and strong to wanting to be sick/miserable). This reversal did not clear with tapping the small intestine karate chop point. Therefore, she was asked whether she could think of any food that she was addicted to. She immediately answered 'chocolate', and said she had eaten some that day. Muscle testing to chocolate indicated a massive weakening. The '7 second' toxin treatment was applied and then muscle testing was repeated. Now the general/massive reversal was shown to be corrected. TFT was applied again to her anxieties—and this time her SUDs rapidly fell away to zero. A subsequent drive in her car elicited no anxiety. This kind of effect could be categorised both as psychological reversal and as neurological/energetic disorganisation. Although its effect was a massive reversal in the energy system, its persistence and its origins in an energy toxin link it to the phenomena of neurological and energetic disorganisation.

Massive reversal that fails to correct in response to tapping the small intestine point on the side of the hand may indicate the presence of toxins. One woman who had experienced a general decline in her functioning, both emotionally and cognitively, showed a massive reversal, muscle testing weak to "I want to be well", strong to "I want to be sick" and also in reverse to neutral true/false statements (such as day of week, 2 & 2 is 4, etc). This general reversal failed to correct in response to the normal method. Therefore I commented that this led me to wonder whether any toxins might be interfering. She immediately replied that a holistic doctor had carried out hair analysis tests indicating that she suffered from heavy metal toxins. We used the TFT '7 second' toxin treatment as a temporary neutralisation of these. Following this, the massive reversal was found to be corrected. It was then possible to proceed with TFT for the emotional traumas.

Recurrent massive reversal may also indicate the influence of energy toxins. For example, a woman was found to be massively reversed each time she came for her session, although this was easily corrected each time. Muscle testing was used to identify the cause of the problem—asking if the reversal was due to emotional factors or toxins (the latter was indicated) and then asking if the toxin was a food (no) or something inhaled (yes), a grooming product (yes), a perfume (yes). The client then revealed that she had used the same perfume for twenty years. Muscle testing revealed that this perfume caused a reversal—she tested strong to the name of the perfume, but then weak to "name of perfume—I want to be well". Following the TFT '7 second' toxin treatment, this effect was neutralised. Subsequent TFT work proceeded easily and rapidly.

Energy toxins are very 'individual', varying greatly from person to person—hence the TFT term 'individual energy toxin'. A perfume or food that is fine for one person may be an energy toxin for another. Food that is healthy for most people may be an energy toxin for a particular individual. For example, garlic is generally considered a healthy food, but for this writer it not only tastes and smells very unpleasant but makes him argumentative and aggressive (which are amongst the frequent effects of energy toxins). Common forms of individual energy toxins include: foods; perfumes and other grooming products; cleansing substances used around the home; industrial fumes; insecticides; washing powder fragrance.

Electromagnetic pollution, from computers, cell phones, and other equipment, is now widely recognised. Sometimes other people's energies, or the energies of a particular room or building, appear to be toxic. Some people are particularly sensitive to these phenomena.

The standard Callahan test for individual energy toxins is to muscle test the person whilst he or she holds or thinks of the suspect substance, perhaps saying "this (substance)". If the muscle goes weak, the substance may be an energy toxin for that person. A second level of testing is for the person to say "this (substance)—I want to be well". If the muscle then goes weak, it may be an energy toxin that produces a reversal. This effect is hidden at the first level of testing. For example, smokers will usually muscle test strong to "tobacco", superficially suggesting that it is good for the person. However, they will usually test weak to "tobacco—I want to be well"—indicating that the substance effectively disguises its toxic effect by creating a reversal (analogous to switching the wiring of the signalling). If the person tests strong to "substance—I want to be sick", this may indicate that both tester and client experience a reversal in relation to the particular substance (there is no obvious logic to this phenomenon, which is just an empirical observation). Details of how to test and treat for individual energy toxins can be learned through the 'toxin pack' produced by Callahan Techniques [www.tftrx.com]. There are also many other energy approaches that claim some success in identifying and neutralising energy toxins.

The relationship between neurological/energetic disorganisation and psychological reversal

Whilst disorganisation and reversal can appear clearly distinct concepts—the first referring to chaos in the system and the second indicating an organised system working against healing—there are ways in which they overlap. For example, massive or general reversal—the person testing strong to "I want to be well" and to palm up over head—is sometimes considered a form of neurological disorganisation. Such a state may result from physical illness, including viral infections, or from exposure to toxins, including heavy use of alcohol. This kind of seeming death wish can also result from extensive experiences of rejection and interpersonal trauma in childhood. Confusing muscle responses may also express a person's wish not to be known—thus the disorganisation may function as a defensive shield, sometimes arising when the early relationship with the mother has been experienced as malevolent. The presence of multiple parts within the personality, with divergent goals in relation to the treatment agenda, may also create an impression of disorganisation.

Why do energy toxins and neurological/energetic disorganisation sometimes cause problems to return?

One of the consistent and intriguing findings of Dr Callahan's TFT is that problems (e.g. an anxiety) that appear to have been successfully eliminated with a meridian tapping method may sometimes recur in response to an individual energy toxin. If the energy toxin is one that the person is exposed to very regularly—tobacco smoke, or certain washing powder residues, for example—the TFT treatment may be continually undermined. On other occasions, a person may be symptom-free for months or years and then, in response to exposure to a particular toxin, the problem suddenly returns. Although it is rightly assumed that the re-emergence of a seemingly resolved issue often reflects the presence of an untreated additional aspect of the problem (another related trauma or psychodynamic conflict), the experienced practitioner will find, on occasion, that the return of the problem is not driven by any psychological content and that an individual energy toxin is the culprit.

The phenomenon suggests that treatment with TFT is analogous to the deleting of a file from a computer; the deleted information (perturbation) remains generally inaccessible, but still exists on the hard drive, and can, under certain circumstances, be 'reinstalled' when triggered by an energy toxin—just as a deleted file can be recovered by special software. This analogy also raises the possibility that energy toxins may have effects somewhat like a computer virus.

Dr Callahan has described how certain universal early anxieties, such as fear of heights, are normally 'subsumed' in the course of development. He uses a video of the first few days of life of the hornbill bird to illustrate this; intense anxiety at leaving the nest at one point in development is no longer present just a short time later. Many common phobic anxieties are normal and understandable in earlier developmental or evolutionary contexts. Intense separation anxiety, or stranger anxiety, is expected when a young child feels lost and parted from his or her mother. Snake phobias are helpful for survival in contexts where deadly snakes are prevalent. It appears that, for some people, the normal subsuming of developmentally early anxieties does not take place, or that a previously subsumed anxiety can, under certain circumstances re-emerge. Exposure to energy toxins appears to be one such condition that may cause regression to an earlier developmental position—just as brain damage may do. Indeed, energy toxins may be viewed as causing a kind of temporary brain disorder. Another circumstance appears to be extreme or prolonged stress and trauma which eventually has a debilitating effect on a person's overall mind-body-energy system. Previously high-functioning people may, in the wake of such stress, undergo a *regression* to a state of intense childlike separation anxiety. This may be deeply humiliating for the person because he or she knows that the anxiety is not rational and is not congruent with an adult perspective, but the terror is completely compelling and resistant to reason.

Note

1.   Instructions for the Callahan Techniques toxin neutralisation procedure can be found by obtaining the 'toxin pack' from www.tftrx.com.

CHAPTER SEVEN

Psychological reversal and associated resistances

"I found to my chagrin that a large number of my clients got weak when they thought of getting better and stronger when they thought of getting worse. No wonder psychotherapy is so difficult!" (Callahan, 1985, p. 49).

A s in the case of the psychoanalytic emphasis upon 'resistance', often the crucial work of energy psychotherapy is to address psychological reversal. If this is active and uncorrected, the therapy will be completely unsuccessful. It is not a matter of slowing the work down, but of a complete block on any energetic movement. This vividly observable difference between a state in which change is permitted and one in which it is internally forbidden is rather interesting—one which would be largely obscured if working with less efficient methods. Often reversals are very specific, and correction requires rather precise wording—somewhat akin to unlocking a computer code. Reversals seem to have both an energetic and a mental cognitive-emotional dimension, as well as often expressing psychodynamic conflict. The energetic level is readily apparent through muscle testing—strong to "I want to keep this problem" and weak to "I want to be over this problem". Thus the resistance can be literally palpated and seen in the energy system.

Once the identification and correction of reversals are done, the energetic collapse of the issue usually clears rapidly and easily as the appropriate meridian or chakra points are stimulated. The identification of reversals is most easily done using muscle testing. Typically the client can be rapidly tested with the following statements: [1] "I want to be well/I want to be sick" or "I want to be happy/I want to be miserable" to check for massive/generalised reversal; muscle should test strong to the positive emotions; [2] "I want to be over/be free of this problem"; [3] "it is safe for me to be over this problem"; [4] "I deserve to be over this problem"; [5] "it is permitted for me to be over this problem" (this can be useful in checking for some as yet unidentified reversal). Commonly the cognitive-emotional content of the main reversals revolve around anxiety (safety) and guilt (need to suffer). These do, of course, correspond to the motives for resistance and negative therapeutic reaction originally identified by Freud (1920g); for a contemporary psychoanalytic perspective, see Waska (2006).

If a reversal based around safety or guilt is identified, it may be helpful to invite the client to consider why this might be. Muscle testing can be used to explore the precise cognitive-emotional content of the reversal.

If the practitioner is working without muscle testing—for example, using standard EFT, or the algorithm level of TFT—the identification of reversals is by inference and is much more 'hit and miss'. In some settings it may not be considered appropriate to engage in physical contact with the client during muscle testing. An alternative then is the use of proxy muscle testing—the practitioner discretely employing his or her own muscle response as an indicator as the client makes the statements above. Proxy muscle testing requires skill and practice.

Correcting reversals

Tapping the side of the hand will often correct the reversal. Originally, Dr Callahan found three treatments for psychological reversal following his original discovery of this phenomenon in 1979: [1] tapping the side of the hand (small intestine point); [2] the homeopathic 'Bach Rescue Remedy'; [3] an affirmation of self-acceptance derived from the work of Carl Rogers (Callahan, 2001d). At one time he recommended combining the affirmation of self-acceptance with the tapping on the small intestine point on the side of the hand—and this strategy was incorporated into EFT. However, keen to pare his method to its essentials, Dr Callahan no longer makes use of what he calls the 'verbiage' and just has the client tap the side of the hand. He found that quite often a client will be able to release a considerable amount of distress or anxiety, but then the process will seem to freeze. This is a 'mini-reversal'—revealed by the muscle testing weak to 'I want to be completely over this problem'. Tapping the side of the hand, whilst thinking of the remainder of the problem will usually clear this. The concept of mini-reversal was incorporated into EFT in Gary Craig's emphasis on the 'remainder' phrasing—as in the reminder phrase 'remaining anxiety', whilst tapping each point, and set-up phrasing such as "Even though there is some remaining anxiety … [or] even though my anxiety is still at 4 … I completely accept myself."

Sometimes reversals do not clear easily just by tapping the side of the hand, even when using the affirmation of self-acceptance. Prolonged tapping the side of the hand may be required in some cases (e.g. a minute or so). Very often an explicit statement of the reversal may also be necessary—e.g. "Even though I want this anxiety to get worse … want to keep some of this anxiety … even though I want to hang on to this anxiety … I completely accept myself." The underlying content of the anxiety, or blocking belief, may need to be made explicit. Sometimes the client will voice this spontaneously. For example, a woman who was tapping through her early experiences of childhood abuse, suddenly remarked "I think there is something in me that is resistant to this—I think I am afraid of losing my identity as an abuse survivor". Once this reversal was tapped, she then easily released the remaining disturbance linked to the childhood trauma. However, until this particular anxiety was put into words, accompanied by tapping the reversal point, the resistance did not shift.

The anxieties and meta-anxieties behind reversals

There are certain common contents to the anxieties (or 'meta-anxieties') associated with reversals: the fear that it is not safe, that it is dangerous to self or other if the problem is overcome; the fear that overcoming the problem will involve a loss of identity (I don't know who I will be if I do not have this problem); the fear of disintegration (my whole mental world is structured around this problem—if it changes, my mental world may disintegrate); guilt (I do not deserve to be free of this problem—or, it would be a betrayal of 'someone' if I am free of this problem). These, and many other such concerns which drive reversals, may be considered meta-anxieties because they are anxieties that hold other anxieties in place.

One very obvious and simple kind of meta-anxiety that maintains a lower level anxiety is often shown by people who are on sick leave as a result of stress in the workplace. The fear may be that if the lower level anxiety and stress symptoms are cleared, there may be an expectation that he or she return to work. Return to work, where there has been traumatic stress, or bullying and humiliation, may be perceived as dangerous and unsustainable. This is not always the case with people who have experienced work-related stress. It seems to reflect a blocking belief, which has become entrenched, that it will never be safe to return to that particular employment.

Sometimes reversals can be very specific and idiosyncratic. Identifying the psychological content behind them can be crucial. For example, a young woman presented with a difficulty in falling asleep at night, although she could sleep during the day. Muscle testing indicated no reversal against wanting to be free of the problem, but a reversal around feeling that it would not be safe to do so. I asked her if she had any idea why she might feel it was not safe to overcome the problem. She immediately associated to her childhood in another country where there had been attempted break-ins during the night by marauding gangs. Her childhood bedroom had been on the side of the house where such a gang might be most likely to try to enter. Once this information came to light, it was obvious that part of her felt that she must stay awake all night in order to listen out for gangs who might break in and attack or murder the family. After this reversal was corrected and the fear tapped, the problem was rapidly eliminated. She then tested strong to it being safe to sleep at night and subsequently was indeed able to sleep without problems. This work took just a few minutes.

Whilst reversals can, to some extent, be cleared just by tapping on the small intestine side of hand point—i.e. just by working at the energetic level—it does seem to help sometimes to be able to use the language of the anxiety associated with the reversal. Many practitioners find that once tapping starts, and the therapist begins to offer words for the reversal, further words and phrases spontaneously emerge. The tapping seems to facilitate an attunement between the two participants, consciously and unconsciously, so that the required ideas just seem to emerge in speech. In effect, the phrasing may amount to playing 'devil's advocate' for the reversal, stating the case for the good sense in blocking change. For example, to take the relatively trivial case of cigarette addiction, the language of the reversal might be articulated as follows: "… why would I want to give up cigarettes? … they are reliable, always there, you're never lonely with a cigarette, they've kept me company for years .. what would I do with myself if I did not smoke? .. I would be lost without a cigarette … and anyway all those healthy non-smokers are boring." The humour in such phrasing, exaggerating and caricaturing the case against the consciously desired change, also seems to help.

Low self-esteem and a general lack of confidence may be held in place by reversals associated with anxieties about what may happen if the person becomes more confident. A patient spoke of her tendency to avoid following through on whatever plans or intentions she might form. For example, she sometimes thought of pursuing the idea of starting her own business—a perfectly feasibly project since she was offered assistance through a government scheme—but she would continually avoid taking further steps, explaining this in terms of having no confidence. As we tapped on this problem there was no shift in her feelings and perception until I introduced reversal formulations along the lines of "it is not safe for me to have confidence—if I had confidence I might do more and take risks and everything might go wrong—it is much safer to have no confidence—then I cannot fail—I can always succeed in never trying anything—it has always worked well for me". Following this the reversal cleared and her perception shifted. She felt a renewed enthusiasm for exploring the possibilities of her own business.

One example of situations where powerful forms of reversal may be at work is that of complex grief. The surviving person feels that it would be a betrayal of the memory of the dead person to feel better and to move on in life. One woman was particularly mired in such a reversal as a result of her twin sister dying by suicide; in their childhood it had been the two of them against an abusive and neglectful world, with an implicit pact that they would always be there for each other. The sister's death functioned as a tremendous reproach to the one left behind—and any potential progress tended to crash into the guilt about betrayal by going on living. This reversal, manifest also through muscle testing, had to be continually addressed emotionally and corrected energetically.

Reversals based on guilt

Sometimes a client will test strong to "I want to be over this problem" but weak to "I deserve to be over this problem". If this occurs, it can be useful to invite the client to consider why this might be. For example, a woman presented with persisting anxieties associated with the death of her husband some years previously. She tested weak to deserving to be over this trauma, and strong to "I want to keep punishing myself". When asked why this might be the case, she remarked "because I couldn't keep any of them alive". This rather startlingly stark comment referred to the fact that her mother and father had both died within a year of each other when she was age around twelve or thirteen. Her statement clearly revealed the phantasy that she was in some way to blame for their deaths, as well as that of her husband. Following the correction of this reversal the TFT sequence was able to proceed successfully. Guilt was still a feature of the emotional constellation requiring release through tapping (being relieved particularly through tapping the index finger) but it was no longer functioning as the basis for a reversal.

Guilt can be the fuel driving other problems. A man whose wife had died in an accident several years previously tended to worry all the time about various issues in his life. He tested strong to a deep feeling of guilt because he was alive and wife was not—and to wanting to punish himself with worry because of this feeling of guilt. The large intestine meridian, often associated with guilt, featured significantly in the tapping sequences. His sense of worry diminished substantially when this reversal was identified—and particularly when the whole large intestine meridian was tapped along, from thumb and up the arm to the neck and under the nose. Presenting symptoms are often employed unconsciously in the service of guilt and self-punishment—as Freud (1920) originally noted.

Reversals based on an absolute 'blocking belief'

The beliefs and anxieties behind reversals vary in the intensity and rigidity with which they are held. Some have a more absolute quality, akin to a kind of internal law. A common one of these is the belief that it is profoundly dangerous, and internally forbidden, to trust deeply another human being. In an earlier work (Mollon, 2002), I described a pattern of deep distrust which I called 'psychic murder syndrome'—whereby the person is compelled repeatedly to destroy the internal and external components of intimate relationships once they develop beyond a certain threshold of trust. This pattern is based on experiences in early relationships. The deep blocking beliefs associated with this core conflict in relationships—between wanting to trust and feeling that it is profoundly dangerous to do so—are not as easily modified as more superficial reversals. For example, a woman presented with recurrent problems of distrust in her relationships. She loved her current partner very much and consciously wanted to be able to trust her but could not. Muscle testing indicated that her system did not want to trust her partner and held the belief that trusting anyone was profoundly unsafe. To shift this belief required extensive tapping on the side of the hand, accompanied by voicing various aspects of the rationale behind the belief—e.g. "Even though I do not want to be over this problem with trust ... even though I want to keep distrusting my partner ... even though I do not believe it is safe to trust anyone ... even though I believe it would be utter madness to trust anyone ... even though it is internally forbidden to trust anyone ... even though all my early experiences tell me I must not trust anyone ..." etc. Still tapping, she was then led into a revised perspective that offered a way forward: "Even though my judgement in the present is coloured by my experiences in the past ... I want to be able to see clearly in the present ... I want a better judgement of whom I can trust and whom I cannot ...". Gradually her muscle response changed—not suddenly switching the reversal but a gradual weakening of the previous pattern and eventually a shift to strong to "I want to be over this problem about trust" and to "I want to be able to trust my partner". Once this correction of the reversal had been achieved, the TFT treatment of traumas behind it proceeded rather easily.

Resistance to energetic change

The fact that energy methods can work quickly and effectively, sometimes clearing the negative affect from a wide area of traumatic experience in a single session, may on occasion evoke resistances and reversals through the sheer volume of change. For example, a young woman who presented a background of childhood abuse, involving several perpetrators, including her father, suddenly remarked, during TFT, "I think some part of me is blocking this—I think it is that I don't know what I will be if I give up all this". This comment emerged at a point where the process seemed to be sticking—the SUDs not dropping below 5. After the energy correction for this, the process proceeded rapidly and easily. Subsequently she reported an upsurge of anxiety the day after this session. As this was explored, with additional energy work, she reported feeling a mixture of "part of me is better and part of me is feeling full of grief". Further energy tapping led her to remark "I think I might be trying to stop this—it just seems such a lot to give up, painful though it is". Again, this required extensive energy correction, along with voicing the 'logic of the reversal': "Even though I want to hold on to this grief and trauma—its what I am made of—I might not exist without it—its what I've always known—the fabric of my being—I want to be full of more and more grief and trauma—I completely accept myself." When asking the client to voice such reversals, it is important to explain that it is not assumed that this is what the client actually believes in her mind—it is simply an expression *in words* of the energetic reversal in the system. Sometimes this combination of vivid voicing of the reversal combined with tapping the side of hand point for a minute or so, may be necessary in the case of deeply entrenched problems.

Related to this resistance or reversal linked to the volume of change, a person's energy system may sometimes reveal a need for *gradual* relinquishment of anxiety or distress. The muscle may be strong to "I want to be completely over this anxiety", but weak to "I want to be completely over this anxiety now"—and strong to "I want gradually to be completely over this anxiety". This inherent preference for gradual change seems quite reasonable since any major internal shift of an economic or dynamic nature may require time for adjustment.

Belief that rapid resolution of long-standing problems is not possible

Some clients will show evidence of rapid change, as evidenced, for example, in muscle testing, but will give the impression of some internal resistance or inertia that delay the consolidation of the improvement. One such client spoke very clearly about this. He suddenly remarked that although we brought about deep and rapid changes during the sessions, which often astonished him, he had difficulty believing that long-standing problems, which had perhaps been in place for years, could be resolved quickly. In addition to tapping on the side of the hand whilst talking about this, he was helped to resolve this resistance by an analogy with a fault in a computer software. I put to him that if there is a problem in a computer programme this problem would remain indefinitely, potentially for years, if it were not fixed; but if a computer engineer were asked to look at it, quite possibly the engineer would be able to resolve the problem in a few minutes—so why should a problem in the human software be any different?

Fears of leaving the 'tribe'—intergenerational reversals

A rather global kind of reversal can be associated with the fear that if the person follows his or her developmental path they will be alone. This can take the form of fear of moving on from one's current peer group—essentially a fear of leaving the group, the family, or the tribe. It may reflect a feeling or belief, in relation to the family or cultural line, "We are/are not the kind of people who ...". Muscle testing may reveal reversals (weakness) to "I can stay lovingly connected to my mother/father/family/group/tribe if I allow myself to follow my developmental path". However, even these global reversals can be corrected in the usual way, by tapping on the side of hand and voicing appropriate words. Often the client's thoughts about the issue behind the reversal will shift as a result of the tapping. After tapping for a minute or so, a client who had expressed fears of the loneliness inherent in pursuing her own particular spiritual path reported that she no longer felt this anxiety because she would be with Jesus.

Other forms of intergenerational reversals may relate to an internal prohibition against being happier or more successful than one's parents. As well as reflecting a kind of loyalty to the status of the parents ("I must be the same as them"), it can also involve unconscious guilt over hostile competitive Oedipal strivings in childhood.

Reluctance to feel content or better

Sometimes a person can be reversed against feeling better about a situation because they feel that would mean accepting their circumstances and ceasing to seek something better. For example, a woman muscle tested weak to wanting to feel better about her unhappy marriage, a situation that was causing her much distress. Having identified the reversal at an energetic level, she was invited to consider why this might be the case at the psychological level. After a moment's thought, it occurred to her that feeling better would be like settling for what she had, rather than hoping and striving for a better relationship. She also thought that feeling more content would be 'boring'. Muscle testing confirmed that she liked her emotional roller coaster experience, where she would dip into despair and then rise to intense pleasure. However, she was able to feel congruent and give a positive (strong) muscle response to the statement "I want to find something better than my present circumstances".

Mini-reversal, recurrent reversal, and level 2 reversal

If the collapsing of perturbations and the experience of distress appears to proceed to a certain level but then become stuck, it may be necessary to test for reversals again. There may be what Callahan calls a mini-reversal (and Feinstein [2004] calls an 'intervening reversal') against being fully/100% over the problem. This can be corrected in the normal way.

Often the cognitive-emotional rationale for a mini-reversal can be quite clear. A person may desire relief from the level of anxiety experienced, but not feel it is safe to be *completely* free of anxiety. For example, in working with a woman with a needle phobia, the SUDs dropped easily enough from 9 to 4 with TFT tapping, but then seemed to stick at that level. The sticking continued until the therapist intuitively invited her to say (whilst tapping the side of the hand) "Even though it is not safe to trust these doctors—it might be the first time they've given an injection—they might not know what to do—I might get the worst doctor in the hospital … (etc. elaborating on the possible anxieties)". With this the client began to laugh and the SUDs soon dropped away to zero. She said that these words had indeed captured her anxiety, with the resulting collapse of the perturbation.

Level 2 reversal is revealed by testing the statement "I *will* be over this problem"—i.e. a future tense phrasing.

Recurrent reversal is apparent when a reversal is corrected but it reappears in a few moments or minutes later. When this occurs it is very likely to indicate a role of energy toxins (perfume, toiletries, food, fumes etc.). For example, a man presented with physical pain which was proving difficult to relieve with TFT, although he had benefited in various other ways from the work. Initial muscle testing indicated a reversal to "I want to be free of this pain". This was corrected and a subsequent round of tapping resulted in a significant decrease in SUD—but I had the impression that the process was still sticking. A further muscle test indicated that the reversal had returned. Knowing that he smoked and that cigarettes can cause reversals, I asked if he had been smoking more, or a different brand. He replied that he had indeed been smoking both more and a heavier brand, one that he had bought on holiday abroad. I asked him to carry out the '7 second toxin treatment' (that can be learned from the 'toxin pack' available from Callahan Techniques Ltd.) for cigarettes. Following this, a further set of tapping completely eliminated his pain.

Massive reversal

The patients with the most complex, chronic, and pervasive mental health problems—such as moderate to severe persistent depression, multiple anxieties, extreme avoidance etc.—are likely to demonstrate massive or generalised reversal. This will be revealed by asking the person to make a global statement such as "I want to be well" or "I want to be happy"; often the muscle will test weak, but will be strong to "I want to be sick/miserable". In addition, such people may display neurological disorganisation, necessitating regular corrections for this. People may sometimes be alarmed on noticing their own strong muscle response to "I want to be sick/miserable". It should be explained that this is not their conscious desire, but reflects how their system has fallen into a state of self-sabotage, working against itself—perhaps analogous to a degenerative or autoimmune disease. Energy toxins often seem to play a part in these chronic states of general psychological reversal and neurological disorganisation— and muscle testing can be used to enquire about this possibility. However, they are rarely the sole or major factor, but one amongst the many contributors to the matrix of energetic, somatic, and psychological disturbance. The contrast between the often rapidly responsive energy systems of relatively healthy and well-functioning people and those of people who present with serious psychiatric disorders is often very marked. Although energy methods work well in both of these broad categories, the difference can be between work that is done in a few minutes and that which takes many months. Psychiatric medications may themselves function as energy toxins for some people—thus further impeding progress with psychological and energy methods.

Sometimes massive reversal seems to arise from some early trauma, or accumulation of traumas, that has had the effect of creating a profound sense of discouragement in the person. Muscle testing can be used to ascertain whether this is the case. If the indication is indeed that trauma is a factor in the massive reversal, this effect can sometimes be eliminated by having the person tap on the side of the hand whilst saying "Even though some trauma—perhaps one that I have no conscious awareness of—may have thrown my energy into reverse. I completely accept myself". In this and many other cases, it is not always necessary for the person to know consciously the nature of the trauma.

Need for control

Another factor that can at times completely block the effect of energy methods is a particularly pronounced and entrenched need for control. People with this characteristic will often flatly state that they do not wish to use such a method. The reversal becomes apparent when this attitude is stated *after* experiencing relief using such a method. It seems that the features of energy methods that give rise to the apex effect—the somewhat perplexing experiencing of successful treatment—will, in those who have a particularly strong need to understand and control, give rise to a powerful resistance. Such a need for control is likely to interfere with the work of any psychological therapy, as well as impeding the person in many areas of life. The same attitude will prevent access to deeper emotions, generating a relatively sterile discourse in psychotherapy. Such individuals may correspond to what Langs (1978) called 'type C' communicators, whose mode of discourse is characterised by repetition and cliché and a lack of emotional depth, and is organised against disclosure of the core anxieties. Lesser degrees of this need for control may result in progress that is slow. One woman who displayed these characteristics, a very intelligent, 'left-brained' mathematician, remarked, after experiencing relief with TFT, "Somehow I feel I don't *want* this to work because I don't feel it *should* work!" She meant, of course, that whilst appreciating the positive effect of TFT she felt that it violated her assumptions about how the world is. Such people very often feel particularly comfortable with cognitive-behavioural therapy (without energetic components) because superficially it has a high congruence with common assumptions about the mind, mood and behaviour.

With some people, it is not so much a need for control as a need to understand that becomes an obstacle. This may be particularly the case with people who have an 'engineering' sort of mind. For example, after an initial session in which he had experienced some relief (to his astonishment) through TFT, an engineer brought a written list of his thoughts and questions. These were all, in one way or another, to do with the apex effect and reversals. For example, he wondered whether the mind could obstruct progress, whether he might manage to undermine his therapy, and he quoted his wife as commenting that he tends to be very 'negative'. In fact, it was apparent that he was feeling rather better and clearly more cheerful — but he was 'apexing' frantically. He had looked at websites relating to TFT, but these had increased rather than lessened his perplexity! These resistances were not a substantial problem, however, and he was able to comment with amusement that this was a rare occasion in which he had allowed himself to participate in something he did not understand.

Sometimes a need for control may lie behind a resurgence of anxiety following an initial diminishment. For example, a woman experienced a marked lessening of her phobia of flying after treatment with TFT. She enjoyed a pleasant flight to her holiday destination, not even noticing the landing because she had been engrossed in conversation. On the return flight she felt some resurgence of anxiety, although not as much as originally. As this was explored it became clear that she felt a general need for control in her life generally—and that flying, with the necessity of putting her trust in the airline staff, represented an intense challenge to this desire for control. Moreover, the first, relatively anxiety-free, flight had evoked delayed alarm, in parts of her mind, that she had allowed herself to surrender trust to the flight crew. After these anxieties were voiced and tapped, the remainder of her anxiety rapidly cleared completely.

The conscious mind feels left out

A feeling expressed by some clients is that of a mild resentment and sense of confusion evoked by the diagnostic and treatment methods of Thought Field Therapy and its derivatives. One woman remarked "I think I feel a bit left out". She felt that she should be more involved in a process of active exploration of present and past aspects of her mind and experience that may have contributed to her problems. However, she acknowledged that conventional therapy along those lines, with various practitioners, had not helped her—and she did not dispute that TFT was helping her. I put to her that what she was feeling was that her conscious mind was partly left out—inevitably so, since the work partly took place in a realm that was not inherent in her consciousness. The conscious mind cannot access the energy system through direct awareness—but muscle testing allows the deeper system to "talk" to the conscious mind. I pointed out to this lady that we did engage in ordinary verbal explorations of her mind and experience, but in addition we used muscle testing to access deeper feelings, beliefs, and motivations inherent in her mind-body-energy system. When this was explained to her, she exclaimed: "So really there is *more* of me involved in this kind of therapy—I am more fully involved!" The use of muscle testing, and the results created through meridian tapping, are so far outside most people's expectations and beliefs about how the world is that the work can seem utterly bewildering, evoking a sense of perplexity and deterioration in thought quality. All such reactions can often be alleviated by simple acknowledgement and explanation. In this way, clients begin to learn the 'language' of their own energy system.

Sluggish energy

Sometimes progress is slow and difficult but this does not appear to be due entirely to reversals. It may result from the depth and intensity of emotion involved. The impression may be of dense, stale and stagnant energy blocks—a kind of energetic constipation resulting from huge amounts of indigestible traumatic experience, perhaps exacerbated by dysfunctional coping strategies, such as excessive consumption of alcohol. A man who had suffered a severe emotional trauma reported that the effects of our energy work were increasingly dramatic. He explained that it was as if at the beginning we had been trying to shift a huge mass that did not easily move, but having chipped away at it over a period of several sessions, it was now moving much more easily and further when we targeted it. His sense of tangible energetic shifts within his system had become much more pronounced. This also coincided with his having become able to reduce his alcohol consumption.

Seemingly sluggish energy systems may also reflect 'neurological disorganisation'—which is actually both neurological and energetic. This is often indicated also in relatively unclear muscle test responses. The following quick correction for disorganisation often works well: have the client hold the fingers of one hand on the navel; then with the other hand thump the centre of the chest (thymus); then rub or tap the collar bone points; then tap or hold the chin; then tap or hold under the nose; then the 'third eye' on the forehead; then hold or tap the base of the tail bone behind. This only takes a few seconds. If the energy response is still sluggish, collar bone breathing may be required. Some clients may need to do collar bone breathing on a daily basis.

Deep roots in the cognitive-emotional-energy system

Some areas of emotional disturbance, or energetic pathology, may be deeply rooted. This metaphor of roots often seems very apt. Whilst some problems have shallow roots and are removed easily, others are like trees with deep and widely spread roots, or like the kind of shrub that may appear small on the surface but has a much larger body under the soil. Repeated targeting with energy methods serves gradually to loosen the roots, allowing them eventually to be lifted right away. We can think of emotional problems as sometimes pervading the personality, penetrating and entwining in many different areas, whilst others may be relatively sequestered. Sometimes, more ominously, the metaphor of a tumour seems apt.

Parts reversal

On occasion I have noticed the following phenomenon. My proxy muscle test (using my own finger response) will indicate a reversal when the client says "I want to be over this problem"—but when I check this against the client's own muscle response no reversal is apparent. I used to conclude that my proxy testing was simply wrong, but eventually discovered that when this occurs, it may indicate that a partially dissociated *part* of the client is reversed. Thus the client may test strong to "I want to be over this problem" but weak to "all parts of me want to be over this problem"—and strong to "a part of me does not want to be over this problem". Reversal correction can then occur in the usual way for this part that is reversed: "Even though part of me ... etc". The attention to parts is sometimes crucial with more complex clients. It may often be a factor when results of muscle testing or of the treatment sequence are confusing, or when the work seems to have been carried out successfully but the problem subsequently recurs.

The presence of "parts" does not mean that the person has a dissociative identity disorder. Muscle testing indicates that a division into parts of the mind or personality, which pursue somewhat different, and potentially incompatible, agendas is very common. It would appear that the more striking and overt phenomena of dissociative identity disorder are simply a more extreme variant of a more ordinary pattern of partial division within the mind and personality.

However, checking for parts reversals can sometimes reveal the more malignant and psychotic organisations within the psyche that can exert a hidden control. These can be intensely hostile to the prospect of any change, and may also be opposed to trusting and relating to others. They are like intense concentrated personifications of reversal—functioning like anti-developmental and anti-life saboteurs. Despite their intimidating nature, it is often possible to collapse or reduce these through the normal way of healing reversals.

Layers reversals

This can be similar to parts reversals—and can be similarly hidden. If results of muscle tests and tapping treatments are inconclusive or confusing, and if parts reversal does not seem to be the answer, it is often worth checking for layers. A statement such as "All parts of me want to be completely over all the layers of this problem" will often smoke out the reversal hidden in the idea of layers. Without this check, a muscle test may appear to indicate that the problem is cleared, when in fact there are other layers that need to be addressed.

Apex effect

A further phenomenon which seems closely related to reversal is the difficulty some people have in accepting the results of TFT or EFT. Callahan called this the 'apex effect', a term derived from Arthur Koestler, referring to a retreat from the highest level of thinking in response to the encounter with the dramatic effect of TFT. Sometimes a person will resort to rather extraordinary forms of confabulation—often denying that there had ever been a problem. For example, a woman reported in her feedback form that she had experienced a complete remission of her symptoms of traumatic stress following a single session of TFT—but rated the therapy as completely unhelpful. When asked for her reason, she explained that she felt she must have been fraudulently pretending she had problems since she felt fine and could not see "what good all that tapping would have done". There seems to be something profoundly unsettling for some people in the idea that tapping on the body can affect emotional distress. Whilst some respond with astonished pleasure and clear relief, others express disbelief or even overt hostility. A common reaction is along the lines of "Well obviously I'm not feeling anxious now because I am feeling very relaxed here in your office and you have a very calming manner" or "I am feeling calm now because you have distracted me" or "I am feeling calmer now because I have been talking to you and have got it off my chest". Extreme versions of the apex effect have been reported, such as denying ever having met the therapist before. Some express an expectation that the problem will soon return. Indeed the return of a previously extinguished problem may itself be regarded as a form of reversal in its own right—a reversal against being permanently free of the problem. In such cases it is as if the system registers something missing—analogous to a missing computer file—and searches for it, seeking to reinstall it. To some extent, the apex effect may reflect a form of cognitive dissonance, whereby the person experiences a tension between experience and assumptions about the way the world is. However, it also seems to express a resistance to change, as if the psycho-somatic-energy system attempts to preserve its integrity, even though there may have been a conscious desire to be free of the target problem.

The effect of TFT seems often to create a genuine, albeit subtle, state of confusion for the brain. It seems that the brain scans the internal emotional state in relation to what had previously been a problem and registers no disturbance—thus causing a mismatch with previous scans. The brain may then oscillate between two alternatives (analogous to the Gestalt drawings which permit two alternating but incompatible visual constructions); one is that there never was much of a problem, and the other is that the current absence of the problem is a misperception and that it is really still there. This kind of perplexity may be particularly apparent in those cases where a client's deep emotional trauma is processed or collapsed in a single session. On such occasions there is a sense in which the client comes in as one person and leaves as a different person, insofar as a life-patterning traumatic experience has been resolved. The apex dilemma can be alleviated with explanation of its nature.

A client presented with anxiety and depression relating to childhood sexual abuse over several years. Previous talking therapies had not modified this. When she began to speak of it she experienced intense terror that the childhood abuser would know that she had talked and would come and find her and kill her. This terror was not susceptible to reason. Two sessions of Thought Field Therapy cleared the distress about the abuse and also the terror that the abuser would find her and kill her. Regarding the latter, she remarked "It seems a bit silly now". However, at the next session, she reported having felt strangely preoccupied and distracted—for example, she had been staring out of the window whilst at college and not concentrating on the lecture. As we explored this, what emerged was that she had felt bewildered by the effect of the TFT, particularly since she had been convinced that it would not work. She realised that when she had appeared distracted she had been engaged in a process of repeatedly testing the memories of abuse, searching the missing affect, scarcely able to believe that the distress was truly gone. She found discussion and explanation of this effect very helpful—enabling her to accept and enjoy her new freedom from the childhood abuse.

Related to the apex effect is the feeling experienced by some people that if an energy method were to eliminate a problem too easily it would invalidate the previous state of intense distress—perhaps seeming to make the person appear foolish, or as if he or she had been "making a fuss about nothing". The underlying thought is "if it is that easy to cure, it can't have been much of a problem in the first place!". A similar thought is that if the therapist appears to think the problem can be eliminated easily and quickly, it just shows that he or she does not understand how bad/deep/incurable it is. Yet another related idea is that relief of the problem must entail much suffering—'no gain without pain'. These 'blocking beliefs' often contribute to reversals and resistances to energy work.

Wanting the problem back

This can appear similar to the apex effect. After a problem has apparently been successfully cleared, the person may return and speak as if it has not been modified. Muscle testing may then reveal a desire to have the problem back. Powerful anxieties, regarding the implications of being free of the presenting problem, may lie behind this effect.

For example, a woman presented with depression linked to various losses during her life, beginning with the death of her mother in adolescence. These were cleared and she left the session feeling liberated. Subsequently she reported a drop in her mood, and talked as if expecting her problems to remain chronic and ongoing. Muscle testing revealed her to be strong to "I want to be miserable" and also to "I want the problem back". As these reversals were tapped, she began to experience intense anxiety, bordering on panic and terror. I suggested she tap the side of her hand to the statement "I don't know who I will be or what I will do if I am free of these problems of loss and depression". This led rapidly to her awareness that she was afraid that if she were not depressed she would leave her husband. A fruitful discussion of her marital difficulties then ensued. It became apparent that she had responded to her mother's death by developing personality traits of always trying to please others and take care of others' needs, taking over the caregiving role in the family. She had carried this personality pattern into her marriage, and now felt resentful of feeling trapped in this, yet also guilty and fearful of change.

Reversals due to a desire to punish others

A very common resistance to recovery which can cause energetic reversals is the desire to punish others with a chronic display of suffering. For example, a man muscle tested weak to "I want to be well" and to "I want to be free of this pain" and strong to "I want to be sick" and "I want to keep this pain". After some tapping for reversals and for neurological disorganisation, he tested strong to "I want to be well". He also tested strong to I want to be free of this pain, but weak to "I want to be completely free of this pain". We were able to identify a core conflict in which, on the one hand, he wanted to be free of his emotional pain, but, on the other hand, he felt that to do so would be to let his family off too lightly. He believed that to recover would be to invite minimisation of his childhood suffering. In his rage with his family he wanted to hang on to his distress, as if it were a display and a continual reproach to his mother and other family members whom he felt had let him down. After tapping on both sides of the conflict, he arrived at the thought that if he could find a way of explaining to his family the depth and severity of his emotional problems stemming from adverse circumstances of his childhood, then perhaps he could allow himself to begin to move on and to release his pain.

Reversals based on fears of what others might think if the problem is resolved

A woman experienced some relief through TFT in relation to her distress about the death of her partner a year previously. She then reported feelings of deep sadness. Muscle testing indicated that she did not wish to be free of sadness. She was asked why. One reason was that she valued her feelings (a normal and healthy response)— but another reason was that she feared other people's reactions if she appeared too happy. She felt that others who had known her partner would condemn her if they perceived her as moving on too easily.

Systemic reversals—based on other people's actual reactions

It sometimes happens that a person will experience significant relief through work with TFT and related methods, only to find that their partner or family reacts in such a way as to undermine this. The damaging response may take the form of casting doubt on the improvement, or subtle rejection, provoking a row, or insisting on relating to the person as if he or she still had the problem. Resistances within the internal psychic ecology can be substantial—but those within the immediate systemic environment must also at times be reckoned with. These can be difficult to address since the people in the rest of the system are not the designated client. The best that can be done is often to use TFT to help the client be less troubled by these adverse reactions from the environment, and to be able to move on if necessary.

Reversals based on addiction to suffering

A person may muscle test positively to wanting to be over a specific problem—but negatively to wanting to be over the whole constellation of problems. It can be helpful sometimes to test the statement "I am addicted to suffering". Behind this may be a fear of emptiness without the suffering, or boredom, in addition to feelings of guilt that give rise to a belief that suffering is required. With some patients it may be revealing to muscle test the statement "I am addicted to addiction"—which may reveal a pattern in which he or she feels there must always be some addiction although its content may vary. The varying addictions may all function to ward off a fundamental sense of early deprivation, loss, or lack of connection with mother. This underlying deprivation, along with the perceived need for addiction, and the addiction itself, must all be addressed through appropriate energy tapping.

Reversals against abandoning the previous self

A man had made very good progress addressing a complex of deeply rooted problems and was experiencing great benefit from

TFT. He felt profoundly liberated. Then, after one session which had left him feeling particularly happy, he woke the next morning feeling depressed, and continued in this state until his next session three weeks later. He was unable to identify any reason or trigger for his depression. Nothing particularly upsetting had happened that evening and he had not consumed drugs or alcohol or any unusual food. Muscle testing indicated a state of general reversal, which was easily corrected. Further muscle testing did not reveal any basis for the reversal and depression, until he was tested with the statement "I can be happy and remain connected to my previous self" — which gave a negative response. This clue readily elaborated into an understanding that he felt that to be well and happy and liberated from his past also meant an abandonment of his previous self. This radical breach with the past and with his past self was intolerable for him. However, this reversal was easily corrected in the normal way. A further related component was his thought that although it was great to be set free from his previous problems, it was enraging to think that he had had to wait until now and had suffered all these years. One effect of the rapid, and seemingly easy, results of TFT can be the feeling that it should have been possible to be relieved of the years of anguish much earlier. This kind of reversal can also indicate the common tendency for previous and familiar psychic structures to be clung to, or reinstated.

Reversals due to a developmentally and energetically toxic relationship

Sometimes a significant person in the client's life may function as an energy toxin. This will be a person with whom the client has a damaging or depleting relationship — typically someone who undermines the client's development, autonomy, or independence. Mother, or father, or sexual partner, are common instances. Muscle testing to the phrase "[this person] I want to be well" may reveal the reversal.

A woman who was talented in a performing arts field, and who had been the child protégé taken under the wing of a teacher of the art as a young child through to adulthood, presented with chronic tiredness and low level depression. Muscle testing revealed massive reversal — consistent with her generally depleted state. After this was corrected, she was tested to the name of her teacher and she showed weak—indicating that the thought of this person did have a debilitating effect on her. Moreover, when tested to "[name of teacher] I want to be well" she was weak. This observation caused her some momentary agitation. She loved her teacher, whilst at the same time was aware of considerable conflict in her relationship with this woman who had both encouraged her talent and repeatedly undermined her attempts at independence from her. The psychodynamics of this relationship and associated conflicts were already understood, but their manifestation in the energy system was a new and important observation. Correction of this reversal led to a new surge of energy and lifting of mood.

Resistance due to the desire for a therapeutic attachment relationship

The often startling effectiveness of methods such as TFT reveal resistances to change that are not apparent when less effective techniques are used. One form of this occurs when the client declines the use of energy methods, particularly if it is indicated that these might work relatively quickly. What may be revealed then is that the person is seeking a long term therapeutic relationship rather than a resolution of difficulties per se. The prospect of psychotherapy is seen as meeting an attachment need. This point is in one way so obvious that its significance becomes subtly lost: a person may seek psychotherapy in order to gratify a need for a relationship, for intimacy, for a life companion, and so on. Of course the idea may be that a therapeutic attachment relationship is intended to be a temporary bridge to meeting such needs legitimately in the ordinary world. However, the unconscious agenda may be to seek the fulfilment of infantile wishes and needs—a process that might be thought of as a *misuse* of the transference in seeking a 'corrective' emotional experience that will compensate for the suffering and neglect of childhood. Instead of taking the transference as an indication of internally located memory traces of problematic infantile relationships that require resolution within, the person may seek to compensate for the problems of the past by seeking a better experience with the therapist in the present. This is a recipe for a relatively interminable therapeutic process. The person caught in this agenda is not interested in resolving the internal disturbance quickly but in having a fresh developmental start in a new attachment relationship with the therapist. Whilst it is possible to help patients in such a process of psychotherapy, this may not be the most effective or efficient form of help. Although the transference can provide important clues as to the nature of a person's difficulties, to attempt to resolve those difficulties through the transference is a very long-winded way of going about the therapeutic process (although it is commonly assumed to be the most appropriate way). As Freud originally noted (e.g. 1920), transference can be a *resistance* to the work of resolving the traumas and conflicts of the childhood past.

A person who is reversed against resolving their psychological problems in the most effective and efficient way, because of a more fundamental desire for a therapeutic attachment relationship, will muscle test weak to "I want to resolve my difficulties as quickly and efficiently as possible" but strong to "I want to engage in psychotherapy". What is revealed here is the gratification inherent in the attachment relationship of psychotherapy. Some of the gratifying qualities of the psychotherapeutic relationship—such as attention and attunement from an interested and sometimes empathic listener, regularity and predictability of human contact, assistance with affect regulation, lack of harsh criticism or rejection (in response to behaviour or emotional expression that might evoke negative reactions from others)—can be powerfully appealing and addictive. They may contribute to a gradual therapeutic effect whereby emotional and behavioural change comes about—but they may also have inherently rewarding characteristics of their own. To put the point most simply and starkly, it seems likely that some people would desire and engage in psychotherapy even if it had no genuinely therapeutic, or mutative, effects whatsoever. Although the methods of energy psychology can produce rapid resolution of the presenting problem, the engagement in such methods of healing is probably not inherently gratifying in the way that talking and being listened to can be. The latter may be rewarding but not effective, whilst the former can be effective but not rewarding.

Reversals due to 'energy toxins'—further comments

Reversals brought about by chemical sensitivities, or 'energy toxins' are common. If a reversal appears recurrent—for example, if the person is reversed in relation to resolving a particular issue, the reversal is cleared, but then a matter of minutes, or even seconds, later, it returns—then this suggests the presence of a recurrent reversal that is a response to an environmental (ingested or inhaled) energy toxin. The same applies if a reversal fails to correct in response to tapping the karate chop point. Typically this energy toxin might be a perfume or other grooming product, some other airborne pollutant, or something the person has recently eaten. Cigarettes may act as an energy toxin causing reversal—which can cause problems when treating smokers. Alcohol, and other addictive substances, may also have this effect. Often, if the energy toxin is removed (e.g. perfume washed off, or a garment imbued with the perfume is taken off), the reversal is easily and lastingly corrected. The effect can be tested by bringing the person again into contact with the energy toxin—usually this will reinstate the reversal.

Because some energy toxins, particularly addictive substances (cigarettes, alcohol etc) can bring about reversal, their toxic effect can be concealed at the initial level of muscle testing. Thus a smoker will often muscle test strong to "cigarettes"—giving the superficial impression that cigarettes are of no harm to the system. However, when the person is asked to say "cigarettes—I want to be well", the muscle goes weak, thereby revealing the reversal. When the person says "I want to be well", without the prefix of "cigarettes", the muscle is strong (unless the person is massively reversed across all areas).

When I first heard of the idea of energy toxins and their role in bringing about reversals, it seemed a rather strange idea. Since then I have encountered the phenomenon very frequently, once I knew how to detect it. Whilst I can remember the initial sense of surprise, I no longer feel it. It seems to me now eminently reasonable to propose that the mind-body-energy system may react to both chemical and emotional toxins in a similar way. The idea of toxic relationships, or energy toxic people, also seems fruitful. We can probably all think of particular people who have a disturbing effect on our system. A muscle test would often indicate a weakening effect, or even a reversal [e.g. to "Jo Bloggs—I want to be well"]. Often, the thought of a person's mother will have this effect [e.g. weak to "my mother—I want to be well"]. This may also indicate one aspect of how toxic relationships can be addictive. Just as a toxic substance achieves its hold by triggering a reversal in the internal signalling, such that bad is registered as good, a similar process may take place in relation to toxic people and relationships. Once the reversal has occurred, the person's system reacts as if the toxic substance or relationship is highly desirable.

Why reversals?

Why are there reversals? It is an obvious enough question—but the answer, if there is one, seems obscure. Some degree of resistance to change is perhaps adaptive, a degree of inertia being a feature of systems with persisting structures and internal organisation. A tendency toward change that occurs too easily or rapidly may not, in the long term, be adaptive. Some reversals are expressions of understandable anxieties and psychodynamic conflicts. On the other hand, the phenomenon of massive or generalised reversal—such that the person's system appears to be seeking death, illness, or unhappiness—seems much more difficult to comprehend. Similarly the reversals and self-sabotage of everyday life present a puzzle. Why are human beings so destructive, and frequently self-destructive? Why do people so often display features of perversion, a twisting of what is intuited to be 'natural', not just in the arena of sexuality but in life generally. Is it an evolutionary 'design fault', a genetic error that has become pervasive—or just another of the myriad ways in which human beings can become ill or defective? Or is there some hidden adaptive advantage in the human capacity for reversal?

These puzzles are ones that greatly preoccupied Freud (1920) in his considerations of the death instinct and the compulsion to repeat traumatic experience. Freud was struck by the phenomenon of repetition of trauma in dreams, perceiving this as seemingly incompatible with his theory of the wish-fulfilling nature of dreams. In a previous discussion of this issue (Mollon, 2005), I have pointed out that it is as if trauma hijacks the mind, bringing about a reversal of the normal response, such that trauma is treated as if it were a fulfilment of a wish. Thus the traumatised person compulsively, yet unconsciously, seeks out situations that mirror or repeat the original trauma. Those abused in childhood tend to become abused as adults.

Evolutionary psychology (e.g. Stevens & Price, 2000) teaches that biological and behavioural characteristics may have conveyed subtle adaptive and reproductive advantage at times in the past, even though the nature of this may not be immediately obvious. What evolutionary advantage could there be in the capacity for reversal of the 'normal' response to trauma? Reversal could be seen as form of submission and adaptation to a noxious environment which is experienced as overwhelming and from which there is seen to be no escape. Perhaps a continued 'fight' against overwhelming, or repeated and inescapable trauma would be disadvantageous— perhaps consuming energy fruitlessly. An example of repeated and inescapable trauma might be the child's experience of chronically abusive or psychotic parenting. To become 'reversed' in relation to such trauma might be regarded as a form of identification with the aggressor; instead of fighting the inescapable trauma, the person's energy system embraces it and behaves as if desiring it. This response to psychological toxins can easily be linked to the reversals that are sometimes displayed in relation to chemical toxins. For example, the novice smoker initially responds with a normal 'poisoned' reaction to cigarette smoke, but with repeated exposure develops a reversal which spares the body the continual response of illness (nausea etc.) but at the expense of no longer generating appropriate signals of toxin ingestion. The experienced smoker, now in a state of reversal, will react with a strong muscle response to 'cigarettes', giving the superficial impression that these are good for the body—the reversal being revealed only when the muscle goes weak in response to "cigarettes—I want to be healthy/happy" and weak to "cigarettes—I want to be sick/miserable".

'Perversion'—the realm of reversals

Many phenomena that present puzzles within psychoanalysis become rather simple to understand from an energetic perspective. For example, all of what are commonly viewed as perversions and perverse states of mind (Meltzer, 1973) can be framed as reversals. A major component of the meaning of 'perversion' is that it is a reversal of the normal action or attitude. In a state of massive reversal, a person's energy system will give 'perverse' muscle test results—for example indicating a wish to be ill, or registering good as bad or pain as pleasure. If we think of Freud's original formulation of sexuality in the 1905d Three Essays, it is apparent that he held an implicit energy model, in which the flow of libido follows a certain developmental path unless blocked by anxiety or other interference. When the forward flow is blocked then regression may occur—a retreat to earlier libidinal positions—as the energy literally flows backwards. Thus an implicit concept of energy reversal can be discerned in Freud's original thinking.

Once the normal energetic flow is blocked, resulting in a literal backward flow—indeed like a kind of energy constipation, then all manner of seemingly strange desires and attitudes may emerge. Infantile desires and bodily preoccupations may be cathected and eroticised. Love may be transformed into its opposite. Anti-life orientations may become prominent in the person's character. Taken to an extreme, the realm of reversals becomes truly 'satanic' in its pervasive inversion of normal human values.

Identifying reversals overview—suggested phrasings for testing

First, test the following:

[phrasing for massive or generalised reversal]
I want to be well/want to be sick.
[and/or] I want to be happy/want to be miserable.

[phrasing for reversals specific to the target problem]
I want to be over this problem/want to keep this problem.
I want to be completely over this problem.
I want to be 100% over this problem (this wording is helpful as an additional check).
I can be over this problem.

[Usually, if the above test positive (muscle strong), there are no reversals]

If reversals are indicated, go on to test the following (or other phrasings that seem likely in view of the client's presentation):

[phrasings for safety]
It is safe for me to be over this problem.
I will suffer some harm or disadvantage if I am over this problem.
Someone else will suffer harm or disadvantage if I am over this problem.

[phrasings for guilt]
I deserve to be over this problem.
I give myself permission to be over this problem.
I want to continue suffering (if positive, a reversal is indicated)
I want to punish myself with this problem (if positive, a reversal is indicated).
I can forgive myself for having this problem.
I have some feeling of guilt in relation to this problem that I am not conscious of.

[phrasings for other negative consequences]
I will feel better if I am over this problem/will feel worse.
I won't know who I am if I am over this problem.
I will feel empty without this problem.
I won't know what to do with my life if I am over this problem.
I will behave dangerously or irresponsibly if I am over this problem.
I fear that something terrible will happen if I resolve this problem.
I have some worry about overcoming this problem that I am not conscious of.

[phrasing for shame]
There is something shameful and secret that I will have to address in order to be over this problem.
I am not fit to be a normal happy human being.

[phrasing for punishment of others]
I want to keep this problem in order to punish others.
Resolving this problem would mean 'X' has got away with hurting me.

[phrasing for intergenerational reversals]
I can overcome this problem and remain lovingly connected to mother/father/ancestral line.
I can allow myself to be happier than my parents.
I can allow myself to be more successful than my parents.
I can allow myself to have a better relationship than my parents.

[phrasing for parts]
All parts of me want to be over this problem.

There is at least one part of me that wants to keep this problem.
There is at least one part of me that has benefited from this problem.

[phrasing for layers]
All parts of me want to be completely over all the layers of this problem.

[phrasing for mini/intervening reversal]
I want to be completely/100% over the problem.

[phrasing for level 2 reversal]
I will be completely over this problem.

[phrasing for apex problem]
I want to remain permanently free of the problem.
I want the problem back.
I cannot accept resolution of the problem.
I believe the problem is bound to return.
I believe it is impossible for the problem to be resolved in this way.
I will not accept the resolution of the problem through this method.

A general note on phrasing

These phrasings are only suggestions of how the energy dynamics and psychodynamics might be explored. Nuances of wording are often important—sometimes startlingly so. Where the resolution of the problem seems to be encountering difficulty, it can be very helpful to investigate the underlying block using a variety of different wordings. The unconscious mind and the energy system often appear to operate with a computer-like precision, sometimes responding very literally, without the fuzziness of meaning often employed in conscious interpersonal discourse.

Using language to interpret and reframe the psychodynamic conflicts behind reversals

Reversals, except when derived from energy toxins, express psychodynamic conflict. Tapping the side of the hand, without any vocalisation of words expressing the psychological content of the reversal, may at times be sufficient to clear the reversal enough to allow the problem to be addressed through subsequent meridian tapping. However, often verbalisation of the psychodynamics of the reversal may be necessary, particularly in the more complex cases. This partly involves ordinary interpretation of psychodynamic conflict, much as might be offered in conventional talk-based psychoanalytic therapy. Ideally such interventions are clear, succinct and accurate, and arise from the client's own thoughts and insights. In addition, it may be helpful to engage in a process of some brief discussion and reframing of the issue in order to arrive at a perspective that is acceptable to the ecology of the client's overall system.

For example, a client muscle tested strong to various statements concerning the feasibility of addressing early traumas for which she had no conscious awareness—there were many features of her presentation that suggested severe childhood trauma, but also indications that she would be overwhelmed with unmanageable negative affect if she were to be conscious of these. There were no reversals based on safety, parts, or deservedness. However, she also then tested strong to "There is some remaining internal objection to healing these traumas without my conscious awareness of them". I asked what this might be. Her immediate response was that the thought that just occurred to her was that if such healing took place it might mean there was no justice. She explained that if traumas were healed without her conscious awareness of what those traumas were, and who was responsible for them, it might appear as the traumas did not matter and that the perpetrators got away without justice. Moreover, she was afraid that if she no longer suffered the symptoms that appeared to arise from the traumas, then she might forget that she had been damaged. I invited her to tap on the side of the hand whilst vocalising these thoughts again—but also then, whilst continuing to tap, I talked to her about how she might still remember that she had suffered severe symptoms (anxiety, panic, dissociation, intense reactions to sexual situations) even if she never knew consciously the origins of these. She agreed that this form of remembering her suffering could continue. Following this short process of tapping and discussing, she was muscle tested again to "There is some remaining internal objection to healing these traumas without my conscious awareness of them" and this time tested weak, indicating that the reversal had cleared. Healing the traumas, with a long sequence of tapping, then proceeded easily to a successful conclusion—muscle testing subsequently showing these to be resolved.

However, whilst muscle testing indicated that the original traumas were healed, testing of "all the effects of the traumas" showed these were not yet cleared. These seemed to be linked to various bodily tensions and pains which she was experiencing at that moment. She showed a reversal to "All parts of me think it is safe to be completely over the effects of these traumas". We tapped through various likely reversal contents, such as feeling that there is nowhere in the world that is safe, that no-one can be trusted (including the therapist), that all men will try to hurt her, that anyone whom she trusts will betray her, that it is never safe to let her guard down—and so on. She found all of these articulations relevant, recognising them as anxieties that she could locate somewhere in her mind-body-energy system. It was then possible to put to her the statement "If I heal from the effects of these traumas I can still know when I need to be on my guard against dangers from other people", to which she tested strong. In this way we could validate the protective function of her anxieties, whilst enabling her to become more discerning of when she needed to be on her guard and when she could be more relaxed and open.

Sometimes language can be used to reformulate the dilemma or conflict in a way that is more acceptable to the client. For example, a man complained of his continual worry and anxiety. Muscle testing indicated a persisting reversal to being free of worry and anxiety. This did not clear with tapping the side of hand. On enquiry, it became clear that he felt he needed to worry in order to act responsibly (confirmed with muscle testing), and he feared that without the anxiety he would become irresponsible and apathetic and not take care of his children, in his role as a single parent. However, he tested strong to "I want to act responsibly and be free of anxiety and worry". Using this as a starting statement, he was then able to proceed with tapping a sequence relating to his worry and anxiety, and to experience some relief. This is an example of how some anxieties, that form the basis of a reversal against recovery, are held in place by a further meta-anxiety which does not respond to attempts to clear it with energy tapping. In such cases, a reframing, or reformulation, allows a new perspective which enables the mind-body-energy system to embrace change.

CHAPTER EIGHT

Muscle testing (energy checking or body dowsing)

"With a simple, at-home test of true/false, all the dictators, emperors, demagogues of history would have fallen. If one simply places a picture of Hitler in a manila envelope and has a child hold it over their solar plexus, the child's arm goes weak…

All the slaughters of mankind down through the centuries have been the result of force, to which the only antidote is Power. Force is based on falsehood; power is based solely on truth. 'Evil' loses its hold when it is revealed; that is its vulnerable weak side, its Achilles' heal, which is exposed to everyone. Falsity collapses when it is exposed for what it is. It does not take the U.S. government, the CIA, the FBI, spy satellites, or computers to discern the obvious—the arm of an innocent five-year-old child has the only real might on earth—the power of truth itself is invincible and requires no sacrifice." [David Hawkins, 2001, *The Eye of the I*, pp. 44–45]

T he principles of muscle testing, as developed originally within Applied Kinesiology,[1] adapted by John Diamond in Behavioural Kinesiology, and further developed by Roger Callahan in Thought Field Therapy, form the basis of contemporary energy psychology. All the crucial information was originally derived and validated through muscle testing. Muscle testing provides the ground on which the methods rest. There is indeed a reassuring physicality and immediacy about muscle testing. The information or feedback is provided instantly, so that one can always know whether or not one is on the right track. By contrast, much conventional talk-based psychotherapy is rather vague and woolly as to whether a line of enquiry or interpretation is helpful or not.

Whilst muscle testing is a common feature of many forms of energy psychology, it is not, however, a necessary feature of all methods within the genre. Some procedures, such as TAT or the algorithm level of TFT or the universal algorithm of EFT, do not require muscle testing to diagnose particular meridian sequences. The standard procedure of EFT incorporates a correction for reversal into the 'setup' phase (tapping the side of the hand), so that testing for reversal is not required. In addition, some practitioners, such as Gary Craig, teach the use of intuition—which can include the development of personal ideomotor signals or surrogate muscle self-testing.

Why muscle test?

Muscle testing is used to make enquiries of the mind-body-energy system. Typical questions can relate to the nature and origin of disturbances, the crucial unconscious anxieties, forms of treatment required, acupoints to be used, and so on. The original uses of muscle testing within Thought Field Therapy were primarily twofold: 1. to check the person is not in a state of reversal; 2. to identify the sequence of meridian points that needed to be tapped for the particular problem, and to indicate when this sequence was complete. These remain the most crucial applications of muscle testing, although many other possibilities have been explored since Diamond's original work in the 1970s.

Muscle testing is a route to the unconscious mind—one that is more precise than dreams, which Freud (1900) regarded as the 'royal road' to the unconscious. However, it is actually much more than this, providing access to information entirely beyond the realm of the mind. Whilst the Freudian unconscious contains contents that are repressed from consciousness, muscle testing accesses information that is inherently beyond consciousness.

Is it valid and reliable?

Naturally, this form of interrogation of the mind-body-energy system should not be regarded as foolproof. It is more art than science—a nonverbal mode of conversation between client and practitioner, and is thus open to error and misunderstanding like any other form of communication. For example, muscle testing may be influenced and distorted by factors such as: states of reversal or neurological disorganisation in either the client or practitioner, prior expectations of either client or practitioner, and fluctuations in the thought field whilst the client is being tested, as well as a lack of skill on the part of the tester.

However, the basic principle of muscle testing appears to be sound—for example, Monti et al. [1999] found that computerised measures of muscle strength showed that the response was stronger to true statements than to false statements. Similarly, Wagner and Cousens (1999) report on the use of an electronic muscle tester, finding very consistent results of increase in muscle strength (97.5% of 200 subjects) when tachyonised materials (thought to channel biological energy) were applied to parts of the body, using a blind study. Experienced muscle testers were found to show good inter-examiner agreement (Lawson & Calderon, 1997), but this study also indicated that inaccuracies can arise when groups of muscles are tested at once. A sophisticated 'force transducer' demonstrated differences between muscles perceived by the tester to be strong and those perceived as weak (Caruso & Leisman, 2000a, 2000b). Clear and consistent differences in central nervous system evoked potentials were found during strong and weak muscle test responses (Leisman et al. 1989; Leisman, 1995) and also differences in the electrical activity within the muscles themselves (Perot et al. 1991). A number of studies using the related but more complicated bioresonance method of 'electroacupuncture according to Voll' [EAV], widely used in Germany and other parts of Europe, found this to be highly accurate and more sensitive than conventional diagnostic methods in relation to a variety of forms of illness, subsequently checked against other data (cited in Yurkovsky, 2003).

Criticisms of kinesiology and reports showing negative or inconclusive results are plentiful (e.g. Peterson, 1994; Teuber & Porch-Curren, 2003; Ludtke et al. 2001; Kenny et al. 1988). However, it has been argued that research designs are sometimes used which do not accurately reflect the use of muscle testing within Applied Kinesiology and its neurophysiological correlates (Motya & Yanuck, 1999; Schmitt & Yanuck, 1999).

Psychological (or psychoenergetic) reversal will generate false or misleading muscle test data. This is easy to identify and correct. Those of us schooled in TFT know about reversal, since it was discovered by Dr Callahan around 1979. However, the fact that reversal exists, and is still not known by all who practice forms of kinesiology, raises the question of whether there might be other, as yet undiscovered, factors that can interfere with muscle test data. Muscle testing itself gives indications of factors that can confuse and mislead—for example, the presence of a variety of 'parts' within the personality (even within those who do not have a dissociative identity disorder), who may have different experiences, attitudes, agendas, and perceptions.

The following summary statement expresses my own stance.

Muscle testing is an essentially valid and valuable, *but inherently error-prone*, method of enquiry within the psycho-energetic system.

In most of its applications within energy psychology, muscle testing is used to guide the internal process of the therapy. The 'proof' of its value lies within the 'pudding' of the therapeutic outcome. Mostly we do not need to seek validation of muscle testing outside of the internal framework of the therapy, because it is checked against the outcome of the work and we do not assume it is valid unless it does guide us to a successful outcome. The following analogy may be helpful. Suppose a car mechanic—lets call him Bill—has a personal method of diagnosing the problem within a car engine; he 'scans' the engine with his hand and experiences a particular sensation when near the faulty component. Bill is regarded as eccentric—clearly a sensory-kinaesthetic sort of chap who likes to feel things with his hands and is verbally inarticulate—but his results are good and his customers are satisfied. After fixing each car, Bill runs a conventional diagnostic check to ensure the engine is working well. Probably no-one is going to be too bothered about how exactly Bill's diagnostic system works, so long as he gets the good results. Perhaps, as a result of entreaties from his colleagues, he then tries to teach the skill to other mechanics. Some may get the hang of it—but others may generate errors and misuse it, perhaps claiming that the 'hand scan' method detected problems that conventional equipment can miss. One or two may even decide to advertise their services as 'car kinesiologists', or 'kinesic engineers', claiming to diagnose 'subtle engine faults' with a rapid 'hand scan', which they then 'correct' by tapping the car's energy field—or they may offer advice as to which car to purchase on this same basis. Whereas Bill was operating within his 'scope of practice', checking his hand scan data against conventional criteria for optimum engine function, some of his colleagues who presented the hand scan as an objective and reliable measure, requiring no additional checks, might be going far beyond the realms of their legitimate knowledge and competence.

Therefore, I would like to emphasise the following point:

> Misuse of muscle testing can lead to errors and the risk of discrediting the field. The main form of misuse is to assume that muscle testing is *in itself* a reliable and objective measure—rather than that it provides working hypotheses that are to be tested against other data, such as the outcome of an intervention that is guided by muscle testing.

Muscle testing generates surprise

An indication that muscle testing results are on the right track is the experience of surprise, for both client and practitioner. Early in my explorations with these methods, I was working with a man with very entrenched psychological problems. He was benefiting from energy-based work, but progress was slow. Amongst the many areas of enquiry, I asked him if he had any food addictions. He said he ate vast amounts of chocolate every day—and had done since childhood when his mother used to give him chocolate frequently as a reward. He agreed for me to muscle test him and I asked him to say "I want to be well"—his arm was strong. I then asked him to say "chocolate" and his arm collapsed as if completely devoid of strength. He glared at me in astonishment and declared accusingly "But you pressed harder that time!". I knew I had not, and since he was a large strong man I said I would demonstrate this for him. Asking him to say "broccoli" I pulled on his arm with all my strength (I am a relatively small and feeble fellow) and could not budge it. I then asked him to say "chocolate" and was able to flip his arm down as if he were a rag doll. This was surprising and convincing to him.

Usually people are surprised when they first observe and experience the varying strength of their muscle tone in response to different statements or words—and this can help stimulate their own curiosity about their energy system and what it can tell us. However, I think it is also important that the practitioner be surprised sometimes—and I often am. If not, then the suspicion should arise that he or she is receiving only the feedback that is expected rather than new information that can illuminate the problem and guide its resolution.

When working with complex issues, involving layers, parts, programmes, reversals, and so on, the data provided by muscle testing is often initially perplexing and seemingly contradictory—reflecting the tensions and diverse agendas patterned in the client's system. The clinical task is one of making sense of what emerges and finding one's way to a viable clinical "truth" that leads to a successful resolution of the client's problem. I find that an underlying logic usually emerges behind the surface perplexity if I continue working with a stance that is receptive both to the muscle testing data and my own intuition.

Origins

Muscle testing originated with the explorations of Chiropractor George Goodheart, in the 1960s (Goodheart, 1989). He found that [a] muscle strength and weakness can be correlated with health or sickness in various bodily systems, [b] the making of a true statement is muscle strengthening whilst the making of a false statement is muscle weakening, and [c] muscle strength and weakness is also linked with the acupuncture meridian system and the flow of Chi.

Psychiatrist, John Diamond, further investigated the meridian system in relation to muscle testing, applying this to psychiatric and emotional disturbances. He showed how muscle testing can reveal disturbances in particular meridians, and how the muscle strengthens after the meridian disturbance is corrected through specific affirmations. Another important observation was that muscle testing can reveal a person's deeper responses to almost any phenomenon. Thus, one can muscle test for the effect of a particular person, a photograph, a painting, a cultural object, a belief system, a form of music etc. Certain objects/images will be found to be muscle strengthening and others will be found to be muscle weakening. A smile will make a person test strong, whilst the statement "I hate you" will cause a muscle weakness. Bach music will cause a muscle to test strong, even with people who do not like Bach, whilst heavy metal music will cause the muscle to test weak, even with people who consciously like the music. Statements that are true evoke a strong muscle response, whilst those that are false evoke a weak response—even though the person does not consciously know whether they are true or not. Whalen comments:

> "Is the human brain, at some primal level, a wondrous computer linked with a universal energy field, that knows far more than it knows it knows?" [Whelan, 1995, p. 6]

Muscle testing is now commonly used by many alternative health practitioners, such as kinesiologists, chiropractors—and indeed anyone who wishes to interrogate the mind-body-energy system beyond the level of the person's conscious thinking (Levy & Lehr, 1996). It is enormously valuable, provided its inherent limitations and capacities for error are recognised.[2]

Muscle testing in Applied Kinesiology v contemporary energy psychology

Although muscle testing originated in the field of Applied Kinesiology, its use within contemporary energy psychology is subtly different. The two approaches are outlined below.

Muscle testing in AK

In one form of Applied Kinesiology approach, as outlined by Frost (2002), the patient's muscle is stressed to its maximum. The bones attached to either end of the muscle are positioned so that the muscle is partially contracted. Then the patient is asked to increase the force of the contraction whilst the examiner exerts resistance in the opposite direction. When the examiner senses that the patient has 'locked' the muscle at a state of near maximum strength of contraction, he/she exerts slightly more pressure of around 2-5%. Either the patient can match this extra pressure and the muscle tests strong, or the muscle gives way and tests weak. Thus in this kind of muscle testing, the patient is asked to resist more than he or she normally can, just as might be required in a stress situation. The procedure is testing whether the patient can draw upon extra reserves of energy.

Frost describes the difference between strong and weak testing muscles as follows:

> "It is easy for an experienced examiner to differentiate between weak-testing muscles and normotonic muscles. A normotonic muscle being tested feels like pushing upon a wall. The muscles lock the bones in place without a great sense of effort, and can resist the extra pressure applied after the muscles reach maximal conscious contraction. On the other hand, a weak-testing muscle soon gives way and feels mushy or melting." [Frost, 2002, p. 64]

Note that in this approach the client initiates the test by contracting the muscle, and the strength of the contraction is also determined by the client. The examiner meets this pressure and then exerts a little more. It is not a measure of brute force but a test of how the muscle responds to increased stress.

The body is then subject to a 'challenge' and the muscle is tested again. Goodheart's original meaning of the term 'challenge' referred only to the effect of pushing on the bones attached to the muscle since this was his initial area of interest in his work as a chiropractor. However, gradually the term 'challenge' has become used to refer to any event or stimulus (which can be structural, chemical, mental, or emotional) presented between two muscle tests. If the patient touches a part of the body where there is a problem, the previously strong testing indicator muscle will usually become weak. This procedure is termed 'therapy localisation', which Frost suggests would be better termed a 'touch challenge'.

Frost comments:

> "Much of the magic of AK lies in the fact that most factors that can influence health may be tested using an indicator muscle with challenge or therapy localisation." [Frost, 2002, p. 66]

However, the Applied Kinesiologist is also concerned with links between *particular* muscles and organ/gland systems, meridians, and nutritional indications. Moreover, in chiropractic work and Applied Kinesiology, problems in the muscles themselves may be the focus.

Thus at times the muscle testing of AK may be used for somewhat different purposes than those within energy psychology.

Is therapy localisation electromagnetic?

To some extent, therapy localisation appears to be an electromagnetic phenomenon. Frost (2002) reports that if a metal wire connects the patient's hand and the localisation point on the body, the same muscle effect is found. The insertion of a diode in the wire indicates that the energy flows from the hand to the localisation point (if the latter is making the muscle weak). Muscle test effects of therapy localisation are weakened if the patient is dehydrated—and then can be improved if he or she drinks water or wets the fingertips. Moreover, therapy localisation is blocked by ceramic pottery and certain synthetic materials, just as if electricity. On the other hand, therapy localisation has an effect through substances known to block electricity, such as wood, wool, cotton, or paper—and yet will not work through lead, although this does conduct electricity. Thus, the energy involved in therapy localisation has something in common with electricity and yet is clearly different. The nature of the energy involved remains at present puzzling.

Muscle testing in contemporary energy psychology

In general, muscle testing in the energy psychology field is not concerned with stressing the muscle as in AK, but simply in allowing the mind-body-energy system to provide differentiated responses according to the stimuli presented. In this respect, the principle is closer to the use of ideomotor signalling as used in hypnosis—but not entirely, since we do look for that clear distinction between the 'locked' muscle and the 'spongy' muscle. Unlike the method outlined by Frost in AK, the energy psychologist usually initiates the test by asking the client to meet or resist the light pressure on the wrist (or other area depending on the muscle used). However, it can be valuable to learn the AK method because sometimes it may be more reliable than the approach using tester-initiated pressure.

There are a lot of bad muscle testers around—people pressing too hard, too crudely, and in uncomfortable ways. This can be most unpleasant. In most cases there is no need to press hard. The aim should be to press as lightly as possible in order to obtain differentiated responses. Stating clearly and explicitly that the aim of the collaboration between tester and client is to enable the latter's system to provide the two of them with information and hypotheses to guide their work together can be helpful.

In energy psychology work it is very important to test first for reversals and to ensure accurate responses to statements known to be true or false. Even after this calibration has been done, it is important to be aware that the client's system may become reversed, unpolarised, or disorganised *during* testing and treatment.

Stimuli/challenges to muscle test

Almost any kind of stimulus/challenge can be tested for its effect on the subject. Examples include the following:

- Structural-mechanical challenge—physical movements or pressures (used in AK and chiropractic but not often within energy psychology).
- Emotional challenges—thinking of emotional or stressful situations.
- Sensory challenges (looking, hearing, smelling, tasting etc.)
- Functional-neurological challenges—complex movements (such as the test for ocular lock by circling the eyes), or mental activities drawing on right and left hemispheres.
- Brain areas—holding a hand to various parts of the brain.
- Chemical challenges—foods, drink, drugs, nutritional supplements, healing remedies, toothpastes/mouthwashes, cosmetics and grooming products, perfumes and other fragrant products, household sprays, vapours from carpets and other materials.
- Subtle energy challenges—homeopathy, Bach Flower Remedies etc.
- Physical locations and geopathic energies.
- Music.
- Colour.
- Visual images.
- Particular people.
- Beliefs and religions.
- Cultural or religious symbols.

- Facial expressions
- Statements that may be true or false for that person.
- Meridian points as part of therapy localisation to determine which points need to be tapped and in what order to remove perturbations in the energy field.

Which muscle to use?

Any muscle can be used for energy checking. The arm and deltoid muscle is often used. Partly this is because it is easy to demonstrate in public settings. However, other muscles may be used, particularly if the client becomes tired through holding out the arm. The main muscles used are those of the arms, fingers, or legs. Fortunately, for our purposes in energy psychology it is not necessary to know the technical names, or detailed anatomy and mechanics of the particular muscles. All that is required is the capacity to obtain a differentiated muscle response to a variety of verbal statements or other stimuli.

What are we looking for?

Certain images or objects are inherently muscle strengthening—i.e. they have a positive effect on the energy system—whilst others inherently have a negative or weakening effect. However, we also use muscle response to give us a 'yes' or 'no' answer to specific questions. Usually a strong muscle response is taken as a 'yes', and a weak response is taken as a 'no'. The tester may ask the subject's system to 'give me a yes' and then to 'give me a no'.

In some cases the person may give clearly differentiated responses from the beginning of testing. However, many people require some tuition in order to eliminate factors that may interfere. For example, some people may 'fight' the tester, or may overrule their natural responses by exerting extra force.

If using the arm muscle, the tester may show the person the difference between strong and weak by first squeezing the spindle cells at the top of the arm just below the shoulder [turning the muscle off] to create a weak effect—and the client is told this is a 'no' response—and then stretching the spindle cells to create a strong muscle effect—the client is told this is a 'yes' response. Often this kind of tuition will greatly assist the therapist-client dyad in obtaining useful information.

The tester may need to work further with the subject in order to elicit clearly differentiated responses to true and false statements. Each client's energy and muscular system responds in its own unique way and the tester must attune to this. The best responses to look for are those that feel subtly but unmistakeably 'spongy' or 'locked'.

Initial calibration and checks for reversals

To begin, the client is asked to make a true statement, such as their name, or the correct day of the week, or the geographical location etc, and then the muscle is tested to check that it is strong. The client is then asked to make a false statement and muscle tested again—the muscle should test weak, or spongy. If the strong-weak responses are reversed, the client is asked to tap the side of the hand vigorously for half a minute or more (less may be adequate, but I personally like to give the system a reasonable amount of stimulation to bring about a full correction of the reversal).

Another useful check is to have the client place a hand over the head, palm down, muscle test, and then turn the palm upwards and muscle test again. Palm down should test strong (negative polarity of palm of hand against positive polarity of the top of the head), whilst back of hand should test weak ('palm is power, back is slack'). If these are reversed, there is an massive or pervasive energetic reversal in the system; if there is no difference between the two, there is probably neurological disorganisation in the system (or dehydration).

Further general statements to begin with are: "I want to be well" and "I want to be happy". Both these should test strong, whilst "I want to be sick" and "I want to be miserable" should test weak. If either of these are reversed, it is likely there is a state of massive or general reversal. These massive states of reversal may be precipitated by energy toxins, including quite commonly, excess consumption of alcohol.

Even when reversals and disorganisation have been cleared at the beginning of testing, these may return during the ensuing work. For example, the presence of an energy toxin may trigger *recurrent* reversal, or accessing a severe trauma may activate shock reactions which precipitate reversal or loss of polarisation.

Taking account of psycho-energetic reversals is crucial. Despite the emphasis on this, it is surprisingly easy to forget to do so. Oddly, the whole phenomenon of reversal is not widely known in the kinesiology fields outside of TFT, even though it is so easy to observe.

How to test—a calm and respectful stance

A calm, neutral and receptive stance is necessary—perhaps involving an attitude of respect for the energy system. Somehow it seems that a cynical or irreverent attitude interferes with the response—rather as though the energy system does not reveal its secrets too easily to the casual enquirer.

Laughter or other emotion may interfere with testing. Eye contact may also impede the test.

The tester will explain the way the muscle is to be interrogated. Typical instructions to the testee include 'meet my pressure', or 'hold against my pressure'. It is important to explain that the test is not a competition or arm wrestling match.

The pressure on the arm should be as light as possible whilst being able to differentiate strong and weak responses. Excessive bouncing of the arm should be avoided. A workshop participant once commented that I looked as if I were listening as I was muscle testing. I thought this was a very apt comment—I 'listen' with my finger tips, and I recommend this stance.

It can be helpful to tell the client that once he or she feels the arm giving way, it is ok to let it go.

I believe that the reliability and value of muscle testing is enhanced, paradoxically, by an attitude that does not place too much reliance on the results. This is a subtle state of mind—in which one is trusting the results in the sense of exploring where they lead, whilst at the same time being open to the possibility of being in error. If the tester is quite often surprised by the muscle test data, this suggests an appropriately open, receptive, and non-certain attitude.

Enhancing reliability—hand above the navel

John Diamond found that the reliability of testing can be enhanced if the person being tested places the fingers of the other hand just above the navel. Stephen and Beth Daniel, of Quantum Techniques, also recommend this. It is not known why this improves reliability.

How to test when a statement is used

When testing for the energy system's response to a statement, it is important to wait a fraction of a second before pressing on the arm. A common error among beginners is to test the muscle concurrently with the statement being made. The system needs a moment to register the meaning of the statement before it can give a response—it processes information fast, but not infinitely fast.[3]

The clear phrasing of a statement is crucial. It must be in a form that permits a clear yes/no answer. This is because the biocomputer is digital—also like a nerve synapse that is 'on' or 'off'. It is best if the 'question' is presented as a declarative statement, rather than in the form of a question; the muscle test then indicates whether the statement is true or false.

Again, it is important not to be too invested in the objective truth of a muscle test response, but to regard it as providing possible indications and data on which to base hypotheses. If a therapeutic step, based on the muscle test data, is helpful, then the test has served a useful purpose. An analogy may be made with a psychoanalytic hypothesis or interpretation of a client's communication: this construction may be correct and helpful, or it may be in error. The crucial question is whether it leads to some positive development and lessening of symptoms.

Enquiries about past events and traumas should be treated with particular caution in relation to content (Mollon, 2002). Muscle testing is not meant to form the basis of any form of 'recovered memory therapy'—particularly since it is usually not necessary to know the specific content of traumas in order to resolve the energetic perturbations using the methods outlined here. Hyman (2003) provides a disturbing account of how a form of ideomotor action known as 'facilitated communication' with autistic children led to false reports of sexual abuse, with devastating results for those falsely accused. Muscle testing, in which the relative tone and strength of the muscle is sensed, can be distinguished from ideomotor signalling, in which a muscle movement is observed; nevertheless similar cautions are relevant.

It can be interesting to experiment with a double blind procedure. To do this, write contrasting statements on identical pieces of paper, fold them, and have one person muscle test the other who holds the paper in their energy field and says "the statement on this paper is true".

How to test when a substance is used

Often muscle testing is used in relation to substances, whether these be foods, medicines, household products, perfumes, personal grooming products etc. One way of testing these is to have the subject pick up the product, hold it within their energy field (such as against the chest) and say a phrase such as "this stuff/food/product (etc.)", followed by the muscle testing. Another method, possibly a little less reliable, is to have the person simply think of the substance, perhaps saying its name. It is not necessary to know the precise name of a product or sub-stance—the person could say "the shower gel I used this morning", for example. If trying to locate the culprit that might have caused an energy toxic reaction, and the hypothesis is that some component of a particular meal had caused the problem, the person can simply say "the meal I had last night"—if the muscle becomes weak, then the precise component can be narrowed down by testing each one in turn. Similarly, if testing whether a particular food or meal would be good to eat, the person can simply think of it or look at it and say "that food" and then test.

Since substances may cause reversals, which can result in the initial muscle test falsely registering the substance as benign, it is important to check for these. This is done by a second stage of testing in which a word referring to the substance is followed by "I want to be well"— as in "this substance ... I want to be well". If the substance causes a reversal, the muscle will test weak to this pairing.

The use of muscle testing in relation to substances can be very impor-tant. Experienced practitioners come to realise that is quite common for foods, products, and environmental substances to cause reactions that appear psychological in content but are essentially caused directly by energy toxins. When these energy toxins are at work, especially if they have caused a general energy reversal, the person will not easily recover. Once the energy toxins are removed or neutralised (with a method such as Dr Callahan's '7 second' treatment), the work with the genuinely psychological components usually then proceeds easily.

Testing for energy toxins, food sensitivities, and nutritional defi-ciencies etc. should be undertaken with caution, recognising that muscle testing is open to error (Kenney et al. 1988; Ludtke et al. 2003; Teuber & Porch-Curren, 2003; Tschernitschek, 2005), although one blind study (Shmitt et al. 1998) found a 90% correlation between food allergies identified with kinesiology and the patients' immunological 'food allergy blood profile', and Yurkovsky (2003) reports a variety of compelling evidence in support of different forms of bio-energetic testing. In general muscle testing suggests hypotheses but does not present facts—and is not equivalent to an objective medical measurement. The point of view expressed in one review article (Pothmann et al. 2003) seems reasonable:

> "In general, AK cannot be recommended for diagnosing nutritional intolerance. However, due to its high sensitivity, it could be a valuable tool to give some preliminary results." [p. 115]

However, regarding the widespread use of muscle testing in the fields of alternative and complementary medicine, it should be noted that many kinesiologists appear not to know about psychoenergetic reversal. This in itself would lead to a high proportion of misleading results.

Testing for a homeopathic remedy

If muscle testing is used to identify a helpful homeopathic remedy, the test result is the opposite of when it is used to identify a helpful nutrient or allopathic medicine. With ordinary allopathic medicines, the muscle will test strong if the substance is helpful (and providing it does not cause a reversal). However, a homeopathic remedy will cause the muscle to test weak. This is because the remedy is based on a substance or its energetic frequency that could, in an allopathic form, cause similar symptoms to those for which the person is seeking relief. A secondary statement must then be muscle tested: "this remedy would be significantly helpful for me". I learned this point originally from the 'Truth Techniques' training material available from www.quantumtechniques.com.

Seeking advice on a course of action

It is possible to use muscle testing as a means of seeking information as to whether a course of action is likely to have a good outcome or not. However, there are certain limits on this. Questions about future events will not result in clear, coherent, or reliable answers; this is presumably because the future is inherently uncertain. On the other hand, it does appear to be possible to pose questions in the form of statements about likely outcomes of a particular action that one might take now: e.g. "this product/action/therapeutic method is likely to be helpful to me". Statements or questions deriving from destructive motives, or ones which lack integrity, do not result in reliable or clear muscle responses. Also, statements or questions framed as "Should I do … X" similarly do not yield coherent answers, presumably because the energy system does not recognise the quasi-moral imperative of 'should' or 'ought'. It would, however, respond to a statement such as "it would be for my highest good to do … X". Statements and questions that 'do not compute' will often result in weak-weak responses, thus answering no to both positive and negative forms of the statement.

Obviously, one should not base important decisions on the results of muscle testing alone. All systems, whether mechanical, electronic, digital, physiological, neurological, linguistic, or energetic, are open to error. Several sources of data should always be considered.

The use of therapy localisation to ascertain meridians to be treated

This use of muscle testing is crucial in finding the correct meridian points to tap, in the correct sequence, when using TFT. It is an application of therapy localisation. The client thinks of the problem (the arm muscle normally goes weak in response to this challenge), then places his or her fingers on various meridian 'alarm points' in order to find the one that makes the arm strong. This indicates the meridian that requires stimulating or treating at that point in the sequence. Note that this is the opposite of the process in therapy localisation to areas of the body where there is a problem; in that situation the muscle begins strong but becomes weak when a problem area of the body is touched.

After the meridian identified through muscle testing has been tapped or otherwise stimulated at the treatment point (which are mostly different from the alarm points), the procedure is followed again to find the next alarm point that makes the arm strong. The previous alarm point will no longer make the arm strong.

This procedure is continued, treating each meridian as it comes up in the sequence, until the person's arm remains strong when he or she thinks of the problem *and* the subjective distress is eliminated.

A further neurological challenge could, in principle, be used at this point, such as the test for oracular lock. The client is asked to rotate the eyes, first in one direction then in the other, whilst thinking of the problem. During this movement of the eyes the muscle may test weak. This kind of challenge formed part of the basis of Dr Callahan's '9 gamut' treatment, involving tapping the thyroid/triple heater treatment point on the back of the hand whilst making a variety of eye movements, followed by humming, counting and humming.

This method of using muscle testing to diagnose the sequence of perturbations in the energy field linked to the target problem cannot be properly grasped from a book and is best learned through the TFT Callahan techniques Step A material, followed by a Step B workshop with Dr Callahan [www.tftrx.com].

The same kind of procedure can be used to locate a sequence of chakra points to treat—although it seems not often to be used in this way.

Self testing

Self testing is easy, providing that the person has established a muscle test that works well for him or her. Learning this takes time and practice. When a person has learned reliably to self-test, he or she is able to check for information such as: their deeper non-conscious knowledge about a situation or a potential choice or action; their own meridian points that may require treatment; foods which are good for them and those which are not; grooming products which are energetically benign versus those which cause problems for that individual, and the answers to all manner of questions regarding situations in the present or past (but not the future). However, self-testing is more prone to error than testing another person, since personal desires and other biases may interfere. Thus, as with all muscle testing but particularly so with self-testing, the results should be taken only as hypotheses rather than objective truth.

Examples of self-testing methods include the following physical movements that require a small but definite amount of effort:

- Raising a finger (such as the index finger): how far does it easily rise?
- Pressing the middle finger on the index finger; how easily does it move?.
- Turning the outstretched hand backwards: how far does it easily turn without effort.
- Flipping the outstretched hand upwards: how far does it easily move up?
- Flipping the thumb upwards or downwards: how far does it move without effort?
- Turning the head to one side: how far does it turn before a sense of resistance is felt?
- Bending down as if to touch the toes: how far can one comfortable reach without strain?
- Pushing on tension apparatus at the gym: how strong is the muscle?
- Leaning sideways, shoulder against a wall, placing one foot on top of the other: how easy is it to push away from the wall with the arm that is next to the wall?
- Rubbing finger against thumb: does the movement feel different (e.g. sticky or smooth) according to whether the statement is true or false.
- The 'O' ring test: make a circle of index finger and thumb; with the fingers of the other hand, try to prise the 'O' apart: how easy is it?

In all these methods the aim is to be able to detect some slight difference between the effort required, or the degree of movement easily achieved, according to whether the statement is true or false. To practice and learn these methods, many trials with statements known to be true or false need to be made.

When using self-testing, it is important to check that one is not reversed and that the results are accurate, by testing statements known to be true (e.g. "Today is …", or "2 + 2 = 4" etc.) and the general reversal statement "I want to be well/sick". Stephen and Beth Daniel, of Quantum Techniques, also recommend checking with statements including "I am 100% free of blocks to accurate testing" and "I am 100% free of spiritual interference with testing".

Extensive information and tuition on self-testing can be obtained from www.quantumtechniques.com.

Surrogate testing

Surrogate testing can be used in cases where direct muscle testing is not possible: e.g. the client is physically injured, or who is physically very weak, or the client is a young child, or the client is not physically present—or, for whatever reason, the client is difficult to test.

The phenomenon of surrogate testing was observed inadvertently by Goodheart quite early in his explorations of AK. He had been testing a particular muscle which registered as strong, but was interrupted by a phone call. When he returned, the woman was holding her baby and now the muscle tested weak. Puzzled by this, he asked her to put the baby down, whereupon the muscle tested again strong. He then asked her to reach out and touch the baby, and now the muscle tested weak again. Initially reacting with astonishment, Goodheart found this to be a replicable and common phenomenon. It seems that one person's energy system can transfer energetic information to another.

The simplest form of surrogate testing is for the surrogate to touch the person whose system is to be tested, whilst the examiner presses on the surrogate's muscle. In this method, therapy localisation to select meridian points can also be used.

Another method is for the examiner to ask questions silently and then test the subject's muscle. This rests upon the ability of one person's energy system to transmit information to another's—an initially startling phenomenon that rapidly becomes commonplace with experience in these methods. It has the advantage that the subject's own conscious beliefs, expectations, or role responsiveness cannot interfere since he or she does not know what the questions are. This method can also be used, very efficiently to elucidate the TFT tapping sequence for the client's difficulty. One way of doing this is for the examiner to therapy localise on his or her own body whilst pressing on the client's arm, looking for the meridian that makes the arm strong. However, it seems to work very effectively and easily if the examiner just *thinks* of the meridian test points rather than actually touching them.

Another form of surrogate testing is for the examiner to ask the question (aloud or silently) and then to test his or her own muscle response. This requires the tester to have mastered a reliable self-test—something that takes a little time and requires cross checking with conventional muscle testing. The same method can be used to discern the meridian tapping points required for a TFT sequence. I use this method frequently, but I do like to cross check and validate quite often by testing the client directly. If the tester is skilled in this method, it becomes possible to work by telephone.

The phenomenon of surrogate testing indicates the energy connections between people—similar to the 'action at a distance' described within quantum physics. It appears that one person's energy system can read another's, even when physically distant.

Ideomotor signalling

These methods have been adapted from hypnotherapy. The subject is asked to raise a finger, for example, as a signal of 'yes'. In fact, the finger raising method seems to combine ideomotor signalling with a true muscle strength test.

A natural indeomotor signal is the slight nod or shake of the head—and many practitioners, including Tapas Fleming, use this.

Dowsing and the use of a pendulum is another common form of ideomotor signalling.

Like other forms of muscle test, ideomotor signalling is prone to error. Hyman (2003) and Spitz (1997) provide accounts which emphasise the need for considerable caution concerning the way that nonconscious movements may respond to expectation, wishful thinking, or fixed ideas.

Auditory, visual, tactile and other submodalities as signalling systems

It is possible to set up a personal internal system such that an internal response gives an indication of the perception of a situation by the deeper unconscious energy mind. For example, a visual 'traffic light' system may be established, such that the person sees green for 'yes' and red for 'no'. Another commonly used modality is the 'smooth' or 'sticky' response as two fingers are rubbed together. The consideration of other modalities can be important, since not everyone is kinaesthetically sensitive. Some people simply cannot grasp muscle testing, for self or others, but can be extremely sensitive and skilled in using sensory modalities that are natural for them—and some may have an extremely accurate sense of just 'knowing' that is not tied to any particular sensory modality.

Inconclusive or misleading muscle responses—neurological disorganisation, psychological reversal, and dehydration

Muscle tests may be inconclusive, may give strong-strong or weak-weak results, or may give reversed answers.

The palm over head test may be used: the palm of one hand is placed down over the top of the head—the muscle should test strong; the back of the hand is placed on the top of the head—the muscle should test weak.

If there is no clear difference between palm up and palm down, neurological disorganisation and non-polarisation may be indicated. This may require one of the standard corrections, such as collarbone breathing, Cooks Hookups, Cross Crawl, or the basic 'unswitching procedure' [press on naval with first three fingers, whilst tapping or rubbing the K-27 collar bone points]. After a correction, the palm test can be repeated to check for the change.

If the results are precisely the reverse of normal, then massive psychological reversal is indicated. The term 'massive' is used because it indicates a pervasive reversal of the normal flow of life energy and will probably be associated with a profoundly negative or sabotaging stance. The negative stance may not be conscious, but may be revealed also by a strong muscle response to "I want to be miserable", or "I want to be ill", or "I want my problem to get worse".

Unclear muscle responses may also be due to dehydration. The client can be asked to drink some water.

Another way of working with strong-strong responses is for the tester to pinch together the client's deltoid muscle spindle cells. This weakens the muscle manually, and the client is then told "this is a no response". Then the spindle cells are pulled apart, which strengthens the muscle. The client is told "this is a yes response". Often this works well.

The client wishes to conceal his or her truth

Another factor preventing accurate responses may be the client's wish to conceal his or her true feelings and beliefs. This can sometimes be revealed by muscle testing the statement "I want to conceal my true feelings".

The psychoenergetic system is not willing to be tested

Whilst operating in some ways as a bio-computer, the psychoen-ergetic system may be regarded as having its own inherent intel-ligence, and at times may have reasons for being 'uncooperative'. Sometimes, when testing results appear confusing and unreliable, I have tested the statement "my system is willing to provide accurate muscle testing data", and have found the response to be negative. It could be that when this is the case on occasion, when the same client has provided reasonably coherent responses at other times, the implicit message is that at this moment the system requires to be left alone rather than undergo further interference.

Areas of the mind may be forbidden to access

Sometimes the client may have no general wish to conceal his or her inner secrets, but nevertheless some areas of the system are labelled forbidden access. This can lead to ambiguous or confusing muscle responses. Paradoxically, muscle testing may reveal this situation if the question is posed correctly—e.g. "there are areas of my system relating to 'X' that are forbidden to access".

The tester may be reversed or neurologically disorganised

Accurate responses may also be prevented by interference from the tester's energy system. The tester may be in a state of psychological reversal—either in relation to a specific enquiry, or a general state of 'massive reversal'.

Blow-out during testing and therapy

Sometimes it can happen that the client will have begun the session by providing clear muscle responses but at some point the muscle seems weak and no longer provides information. This may indi-cate a sudden general energy weakness, either as a result of the cli-ent's general state of energetic health, or sometimes because a past experience of overwhelming trauma or energy wipe-out has been accessed. I have noticed this happening sometimes when working with very early or perinatal trauma and have the impression that the client's system may be re-presenting a state of near death. Perhaps it also occurs on re-encountering a trauma during which the client 'abandoned' his or her body in a state of massive dissociation. For example, in the case of one man, we encountered a state in which he had adopted a fundamental pretence of not existing and therefore of having no body; in this state, his energy system could provide no information.

To correct this it can be helpful for the client to drink some plain water and also to do the Diamond Thymus Thump: lightly thump the upper area of the chest a few times, whilst smiling, thinking of someone who is liked, and saying "Ha, Ha, Ha" on breathing out.

How I use muscle testing

Each practitioner will find their own way of making use of muscle testing data—and many may choose not to use muscle testing at all. My own way is quite varied. With some clients I use muscle testing extensively, sitting near enough that I can comfortably press on their outstretched arm. This is part of the therapeutic frame from the beginning and is what the client has consented to and is comfortable with. However, on the whole, this is the way I work with clients whom I see for short pieces of work of just a few sessions, or with people whom I see over a longer period but on a relatively infrequent basis (e.g. once a month). The relationship with me is not the focus of the work and transference is not prominent; the work is essentially within the client's own psychoenergetic system. In the case of clients with whom I am engaged in more conventional talk-based psychotherapy on a regular basis, with occasional inclusions of an energy intervention, I usually do not use direct muscle testing and sit in my chair some distance away from the client. I may use proxy muscle testing, drawing upon my own subtle finger movement to help assess meridian sequences etc. Of course, any use of energy psychology methods is on the basis of clear consent and request by the client. I still undertake psychoanalytically based therapy that does not incorporate energy methods, when that is what the client requires.

Assuming that I am engaged in the kind of work where muscle testing is central, I apply it to many different aspects, using it as a guide throughout. Thus, I might test for the following: whether the client is generally/massively reversed; whether there is a specific reversal linked to the target problem; whether there are earlier traumas behind the presenting issue (these do not need to be accessed consciously); whether there is inherited trauma; whether there are relevant programmes in the system, which are generating the problematic pattern; the presence of parts of the personality, pursuing different agendas; the relevant meridian points to be tapped and in what sequence; whether the perturbations are cleared, and whether they are completely cleared, and cleared from all parts and layers; whether additional work needs to be done. These are just some of the enquiries I might make.

Here are three examples from my practice today.

The first was a man whom I have been seeing for a while to help with anxiety and depression resulting from very painful and traumatic circumstances in his life, also addressing adverse childhood experiences that were resonating with more recent events. He began by speaking of the very negative mood he was in, feeling angry and depressed, and generally looking on the black side of everything. I muscle tested him and, not surprisingly, he was massively reversed—testing strong to "I want to be sick" and "I want to be miserable", and weak to "I want to be well" and "I want to be happy". Therefore I took him through the usual process of tapping the side of the hand, and tested again. To my surprise he was still reversed. I asked him to rub the neurolymphatic 'sore spot' on the upper left chest, and tested again. He was still reversed. I asked him to say aloud "I accept myself completely even though my energy system is reversed", whilst tapping the side of the hand. The extent of reversal was then lessened—his arm muscle was somewhat stronger than before in response to the positive statements. Clearly something was causing this persisting and recurring reversal—it had been a problem before but not so intractably as today. I asked him what beer he had been drinking (I knew he tended to drink frequently). He told me that recently he had been drinking brand X, saying how much he liked it. I muscle tested him after he spoke the name of the beer. His arm went very weak—and also weak to "this beer [brand X] … I want to be well". I asked if he could think of another beer that he might drink instead, and he mentioned another brand. We muscle tested this, and found that it registered as less toxic for him and did not bring about a reversal. Then I took him through the Callahan '7 second' technique to neutralise the toxic effects of the first beer, using muscle testing to ascertain whether he needed to press on the forehead on the inspiration or expiration of breath (it was the inspiration). This was successful—and the reversal corrected fully. We were then able to continue the session, addressing his current anxieties. I used muscle testing to find the sequences he needed to tap, and he ended the session feeling much more positive. Thus, in this particular session, muscle testing was used in the following ways: to detect persisting psychoenergetic reversal; then to test a hypothesis about an energy toxin that might be causing the reversal; then to generate a hypothesis that an alternative beer might not have this same effect; then it was used to guide the modality of the '7 second technique'; then to test whether this had been successful; then to generate hypotheses that tapping a particular sequence of meridian points would relieve his anxiety and depression. By the end of the session, the muscle testing indicated greatly reduced perturbations in his system, an observation that was congruent with his much-improved mood.

The second example was a woman who comes to see me on an occasional basis for help with certain patterns of emotional distress and unhappiness in her relationships. Today she told me that she was feeling depressed and agitated, and smoking obsessively, having become re-involved with an old boyfriend with whom she tended to have a painful and addictive relationship. She had been shocked at how easily she had succumbed again to his wooing of her, despite her repeated negative experiences of him in the past. He had withdrawn from her, as was his wont, and she was feeling terrible. We muscle tested and she was not reversed. She wanted to feel well and happy. Muscle testing was then used to take her through a diagnosed sequence of meridian tapping points. All this took about 5 minutes. She then reported feeling fine and could detect no subjective distress. Her arm muscle registered strong in response to the phrase "the way I feel at the moment". Wondering what else we should address, I muscle checked for 'inherited trauma' and 'programmes' and both of these registered negative. I tested the statement "there is more we need to do today"—and this too was negative. This was puzzling—it seemed too good to be true that all the necessary work had been done in five minutes. I asked her again how she was feeling. Now she reported an empty feeling in her stomach and began to speak again of her fears of being addicted to this man. We muscle tested the statement "I am addicted to 'Joe' " —this was positive. "I want to be free of this addiction" tested positive—but "All *parts* of me want to be free of this addiction to 'Joe'" tested negative. After tapping the side of the hand, this 'parts' statement registered positive, as did 'I have 100% inner willingness to be free of this addiction to Joe' ". We then tapped a sequence of meridian points, guided by muscle testing. Following this she muscle tested as no longer having the addiction to 'Joe'. However, she then spoke of her relapsed addiction to cigarettes. She muscle tested as strong to being addicted to ciga-rettes—and weak to wanting to be free of the addiction. As we spoke of this, she reported a sudden upsurge of further thoughts about 'Joe' and fears that she was still addicted to him. It occurred to me then to test the following: "I want to be free of 'Joe' " —tested strong; "ciga-rettes—I want to be free of 'Joe' " —tested weak. Thus this appeared to indicate that cigarettes, an energy toxin, were throwing her system into reverse in relation to 'Joe'. Moreover, she told me that cigarettes were very much associated in her mind with 'Joe'. The two were rein-forcing each other—cigarettes causing reversal, driving the addictive craving for 'Joe' (and for cigarettes), and the association with 'Joe' continually calling up the craving for cigarettes. We began trying to clear the reversal and addiction linked to cigarettes and to 'Joe'. This seemed not to be working—again indicated by muscle testing. A further hypothesis then occurred to me that might have a bearing on a factor underlying and fuelling the reversals and addictions— this was too complex to describe here, save to say that it was to do with a particular aspect of her relationship with 'Joe' and how she might have been affected by features within his energy system. This hypothesis was confirmed by muscle testing, which was also used to indicate when the underlying problem was cleared. The outcome was that after an hour of work, this woman felt calm and positive, experiencing no trace of addictive cravings for either 'Joe' or ciga-rettes—and was enormously relieved. Here, muscle testing had been used in the following ways: to test for general reversal (she was not); to find the initial meridian tapping sequence, which dealt with the first layer of her distress; then to check for further issues to address (there appeared to be none at that point, illustrating the shifting and sometimes deceptive nature of muscle responses); then to explore the emerging indications of addictive cravings for both 'Joe' and cigarettes; muscle testing then indicated that we were confused and making little progress with the addictions, reversals, and cravings; it was then used as an initial test of a further hypothesis about a possible underlying factor, and then to guide the work in addressing this underlying factor. The successful outcome provides some, at least partial, validation of the muscle testing procedure and data.

In the third example, a client began by speaking of her headache. Since this was obviously preoccupying her in a distracting way that would interfere with the therapeutic work, we muscle tested for a diagnosed sequence of meridian tapping to clear it away. This brief intervention took only a couple of minutes and was successful. We could then address other issues that were troubling her. She spoke of chronic difficulties in sleeping, which she thought related to having caught a burglar in her house a year or two ago. It seemed likely that part of her felt it was not safe to go to sleep since she lived alone and should stay awake to keep vigil against the danger of a burglar—this hypothesis was confirmed by muscle testing. We then targeted directly the experience of catching the burglar, using muscle testing to diagnose the sequence. After tapping several points, her arm remained strong when she thought of this event. We then muscle tested "I will be able to sleep easily", which registered negative. On muscle testing for the diagnosed sequence relating to this thought that she would not be able to sleep easily, the first point was the little finger heart meridian. Since this point is often linked with anger, I asked if she might be feeling angry. She affirmed that she was—and went on to speak of her current anger with her partner, and it was clear that this had been partly what had been keeping her awake. She indicated that she did want to feel calmer because she was then able to think more clearly about the situation. We then continued muscle testing to diagnose the sequence until she felt calm in relation to her partner and her arm remained strong when she thought about this. After further work addressing some related issues, muscle testing was again used to ask whether there was more we needed to do at that point—the answer was no. Thus in this case, muscle testing was used in the following ways: to diagnose a tapping sequence to clear the client's headache; to check for underlying anxieties and reversals in relation to her difficulties in sleeping; to diagnose a tapping sequence in relation to the burglar trauma; then, as the thought field shifted back to going to sleep, muscle testing indicated the little finger heart meridian as the first point, prompting a fruitful enquiry about possible anger; muscle testing was then used to diagnose a sequence for her anger with her partner; finally, muscle testing was used to check whether further work needed to be done in that particular session.

Personality features revealed through muscle testing

It has occurred to me that a bi-product of muscle testing is its ability to reveal not only the target information indicated by the statement or question, but also aspects of the client's personality.

For example, some people are difficult to test because they will attempt to override the natural fluctuations in their muscle strength. Thus, instead of allowing the muscle to give way as it weakens they will try to compensate by straining harder to maintain the muscle strength. Such people tend to be over-achievers or perfectionists in other areas of their lives and to suffer the consequences of overriding their own bodily and energetic signals. It can be helpful to explain this and to suggest to the client that when he or she feels their arm weakening it is OK to let it go. A similar issue arises with some people who seem to get into a competition with both their own body and the tester, as if determined not to allow the muscle to become weak in response to particular questions, statements, or substances.

Recently I was working with a woman and having difficulty in obtaining clear muscle test results. When I discussed this with her, she explained that she had been assuming that she should try her hardest to maintain the maximum muscle strength she could manage—and that this reflected her desire to please me (and others). She then disclosed that with some statements she experienced a pain in her arm, these being those which would have led the muscle to go weak if she had not struggled to maintain its strength by compensating with extra effort. Once I had explained more clearly that we were looking to find a way for her system to give us information through the differences in muscle strength, and had allowed her to press on my arm to gain a sense of difference in the feel of 'strong' and 'weak', she was able to provide very clearly differentiated responses. I find it can be helpful sometimes to say to the person that if she or he feels their arm beginning to weaken, it is OK to let it go.

It is quite common for a client to suggest that the therapist must have been pressing harder when the arm went weak. In fact, it is the client who is pressing harder in the effort to compensate for the weakening muscle. The reaction is somewhat similar to the 'apex effect', when clients may confabulate explanations of the effect of TFT. A variation in muscle strength in response to a word, a statement, or a visual image, is so startling and unexpected for many people that they reach for the only explanation they can think of—i.e. that the therapist must have been pushing harder.

Other people, of a more secretive and suspicious nature, can be uncomfortable with the idea of their secrets being revealed through muscle testing. They too may attempt to compensate for muscle weakening. In such cases, it can be helpful to treat this as a reversal and have them tap the side of the hand whilst saying "Even though I do not want my secrets to be revealed through muscle testing, I completely accept myself". Often this will allow clearer results to emerge.

Those with a particular need for control may be disturbed by the phenomenon of muscle weakening in response to questions, statements, or substances. They can feel that their body is somehow betraying them with its involuntary responses. The impotence of the conscious mind in knowing or influencing the muscle response can also challenge some people, especially those who are particularly identified with their conscious mind and are not used to accessing deeper sources of knowledge from unconscious areas.

People with an obsessive-compulsive personality style are often preoccupied with whether or not they are doing the muscle testing correctly, and become bothered about whether, and in what way, they might be influencing the response of their own muscle.

Further implications of muscle testing: the work of David Hawkins M.D., Ph.D.

Dr David Hawkins is a psychiatrist and Director of the Institute for Advanced Theoretical and Spiritual Research. In recent years he has written an intriguing series of books exploring the applications and implications of the muscle test as a tool for discerning truth and falsehood. Hawkins was struck by the point that Diamond's work in the 1970s showed that when people listened to tapes of known deceits the muscle tested weak, and when they listened to recordings of statements known to be true, the muscle strengthened even though the subjects were not conscious of whether the statements were true or false.

Hawkins found remarkable consistency of muscle response across subjects. Human beings appear to have the capacity to 'know' whether something is good or bad, true or false, regardless of their conscious view or knowledge.

> "When I was on the lecture circuit, in audiences of 1000 people, 500 envelopes containing artificial sweetener would be passed out to the audience, along with 500 envelopes containing organic vitamin C. The audience would then be divided up and would alternate testing each other. When the envelopes were opened, the audience reaction was always one of amazement and delight when they saw that everybody had gone weak in response to the artificial sweetener and strong in response to the vitamin C. The nutritional habits of countless families across the country were changed due to this simple demonstration." [Hawkins, 1995, p. 59.]

He also found that a mere image produced the same response as if the substance were held. If an apple grown with pesticides were held up, all who were tested would go weak, whilst they would test strong to the sight of an organically grown apple.

Hawkins developed a means of calibrating, on a scale of 1-1000, the relative truth of intellectual positions, ideologies, spiritual beliefs and texts, etc. forming the basis of a map of consciousness. A statement such as "this ... (book, belief system, ideology, teacher, scientist etc.) calibrates at more than 200 (yes/no), at more than 250, at more than 300" —and so on, is checked until the muscle tested weak. By refining the question, the precise calibration of the relative truth of a constellation of ideas could be determined. Hawkins and his research team used groups of testers to find the consensus ratings of many different ideologies, philosophical, spiritual and scientific positions. Thus the Constitution of the United States calibrates at 700, whilst the 'americanism' promoted by white supremacist groups calibrates at only 150. As a nation, the U.S.A. calibrates at 421, the highest of any on the planet currently—reflecting the dominance of science, technology, and rational thought in that culture. The same scale can be used to calibrate levels of consciousness and the energy levels of different emotions. Thus shame calibrates at only 20—a level "perilously proximate to death, which may be chosen out of Shame as conscious suicide or more subtly elected by failure to take steps to prolong life" [Hawkins, 1995, p. 76]. Love calibrates at 500, and the level of Enlightenment, or divine grace, calibrates up to 1000, "the highest level attained by anybody who has lived in recorded history." [Hawkins, 1995, p. 94]. Einstein and Freud calibrate at 499, the level of high intellect and rationality. At 500, the level of consciousness makes a significant leap: "the motivation of Love begins to colour all activities, and creativity comes into full expression, accompanied by commitment, dedication, and expressions of charisma." [Hawkins, 1995, p. 99]. The levels of truth in original spiritual positions can be compared with their subsequent interpretations and practices; thus Mohammed calibrates at 740, but militant Islamic fundamentalism calibrates at 130; Buddha's teachings calibrate at 1000, but Zen Buddhism only at 890. When people's levels of conscious rise, this shift has a powerful effect on others. Framed within chaos theory, higher levels of consciousness can be said to function as strong attractors, tending to draw others into their field.

Interestingly, Hawkins found that in his study, both the person testing and the one being tested had to calibrate at 200 or above for accurate results. Moreover, the integrity of their motivation and questioning is crucial; these too must calibrate at 200 or above. Because of this, the technique thus appears to have a built in safeguard against misuse. Since the motive and intention of the investigator play a part in the reliability of the results obtained, the method can only be used for that which is beneficial to mankind. It seems likely that the need for both tester and testee to calibrate at 200 or above is also related to the phenomenon of reversal—and that states below 200 reflect attractor fields of reversed energy.

Are Hawkins claims valid?

For reasons that may be obvious from this brief account, Hawkins' trilogy, *if his basic stance is valid*, are potentially amongst the most important books ever written, outlining how human beings can access the ability to distinguish truth from deception, and to discern the relative truths of comparative positions on more or less anything of any importance. Hawkins' trilogy have themselves been calibrated. *Power versus Force* (1995) apparently calibrates at 850; *The Eye of the I* (2001) calibrates at 980; and *I—Reality and Subjectivity* (2003) calibrates at 999.8.

> "If a true statement is presented to human consciousness or silently held in mind, the muscles of the body go strong automatically with the recognition of truth. In contrast they go weak in response to falsehood, which has no actual existence. Consciousness is therefore much like a light bulb that goes on with electricity (truth) but fails to light if there is no electricity (falsehood)." [Hawkins, 2003, pp. xxix–xxx].

However, I began to experience doubts about Hawkins' system on reading his more recent Truth versus Falsehood (2005). Here he outlines in much more detail his calibration of all manner of recent and contemporary events, personalities, political and spiritual positions, American companies, particular magazines, newspapers, and television stations, nations and cultures, scientific theories (some of which are simply declared 'false')—and indeed more or less every aspect of life in which a range of views or decisions are possible. Hawkins' vision seems to be one in which all questioning, assessments and decisions can be carried out by a muscle test. Whilst I might be prepared to accept, albeit with some cognitive and emotional tension, the reported very high calibration of the current President of the United States, the information that global warming has nothing to do with the greenhouse effect seemed surprising. Should we base such vital perspectives on muscle test data? Hawkins appears to think so. He does not mention the unreliability of muscle testing, its inherently subjective features, and the vagaries of reversal. Nor does he provide details of his research data and procedure, other than its results. We do not know how many people were used as subjects for each calibration, nor the extent of inter-rater and inter-test reliability. Although Hawkins' ideas are certainly interesting, excessive certainty, particularly in relation to the big issues of science, spirituality, politics, and national foreign policy, can lead to illusion, or even delusion. In many instances, his muscle test data are not cross-checked against any other source of information—and thus his conclusions may demonstrate the error shown by the 'car kinesiologists' in my hypothetical example above. There is no way of knowing whether the muscle test was simply reflecting the political or cultural biases of the person being tested. Even if the collective energy field (collective unconscious) does, in principle, contain the information we seek, and even if it is, in principle, accessible, is it safe to assume that the field does not contain its own reversals, disorganisations, or deceptions, just like the individual human psychoenergetic field? I am not sure that muscle testing is *meant* to be used in the way Hawkins' describes; I feel it could be a *misuse*—and if I muscle test the statement "all Hawkins' claims are correct", the response is no![4]

Notes

1. The author is not a member of the International College of Applied Kinesiology and has not been trained in Applied Kinesiology. Therefore the views expressed here, reflective of the field of energy psychology, may be different from those held by practitioners of Applied Kinesiology. They are not endorsed by Dr John Diamond, or any other member of ICAK. Muscle testing cannot be properly learned from a book alone.

2. Some certified practitioners of Applied Kinesiology may experience disquiet over the widespread using of muscle testing in all manner of other 'kinesiologies'.

3. Judith Swack recommends using the person to 'send' the statement down into the body—into the gut. This seems to provide an additional degree of reliability.

4. I have just muscle tested 'myself on Hawkins's scale'—I am at 925; 'David Hawkins on Hawkins' scale' calibrates at 917; 'David Hawkins' books on Hawkins' scale' calibrates at 640. I conclude that his scale is not valid. His method of calibrating numerically the relative truth or level of consciousness of any cultural object is quite different from the capacity of a child's energy system to register a photograph of Hitler hidden in an envelope as weakening, or for a person's system to register an organic apple as strengthening. Such capacities are commonplace observations in the energy psychology field—but calibrating political speeches, scientific theories, US companies, and news reporting, on a numerical scale is a different matter.

CHAPTER NINE

'Parts' and programmes—and other elements of the structure and functioning of the psycho-energetic system

uscle testing indicates that the human psychosomatic energy system is often organised in 'parts'. Very commonly a person will muscle test strong to "I want to be over this problem" and weak to "all *parts* of me want to be over this problem". This is, in fact, so common that I now suspect that in more or less all cases where there has been extensive childhood interpersonal trauma, the psychosomatic-energy system has evolved protectively into semi-dissociated 'parts'. This does not mean that all such people have a dissociative identity disorder (DID), although the same phenomena are even more marked in that condition. The fragmentation into parts seems to be a typical reaction to severe interpersonal trauma, where no escape or soothing from trusted caregivers is available. It is somewhat analogous to the way that an injured sea vessel may be protected from sinking by sequestering and sealing off an area which has been holed. The 'part' experiencing the trauma will be sacrificed in order to enable the rest of the system to continue its life and development. This means then that the part containing the trauma does not participate in the main development of the rest of the system. That child part may then continue to believe the trauma continues. It is trapped in the trauma and frozen in time. The idea of being over the trauma may be perceived by that part as equivalent to complete abandonment or obliteration of that part. Another perception may be that being free of the trauma may mean being without appropriate anxiety and awareness of interpersonal danger.

The different parts of the mind or personality are able to pursue different agendas—sometimes in conflict. This is most apparent in the case of those with dissociative identity disorder, or multiple personality disorder. For example, one part of the dissociative personality system may seek therapy whilst another part considers this is a very bad idea and will seek to sabotage the endeavour. However, less obvious operations of parts can also be found in people who are not significantly dissociative. Indeed, it may be that the human system is naturally organised into parts, although in more normal circumstances these are *associating*, rather than the *dissociated* parts that result from trauma. The significance of parts has been emphasised by others in the energy psychology field, including Stephen Daniel (www.quantumtechniques.com) and Art Martin (Martin, 1997; Martin & Landrell, 2005).

Psychoanalysis has always dealt with parts of the psyche. Thus, Freud's (1923b) original structural model consisted of the instinctual source (the id), an internalised image of the prohibitive father suffused with the child's own aggression (the superego), and the quasi-managerial ego attempting to mediate between, and reconcile the conflicting demands of, these two and the outside world. Later analysts, such as Klein (1946) and Fairbairn (1952), postulated a variety of internalised and phantasy-based figures in the mind. Some analysts will routinely speak to their patients in terms of parts, or will use a form of words along the lines of "there is the 'you' that feels ... X, and there is the 'you' that feels ... Y" etc, when speaking of conflicts within the personality. Similarly, it is common (particularly amongst those of a Kleinian persuasion) to speak of 'split off' and perhaps 'projected' parts of the mind. The idea of a multiplicity of parts or characters populating the internal psychic theatre is fairly fundamental to the thinking of many analysts In addition, we have the division between 'true' and 'false' selves postulated by Winnicott, with similar ideas proposed by Kohut [see discussion in Mollon,

2001]. The muscle testing data in response to questions/statements about parts thus validates these psychoanalytic perspectives.

Illustration of a 'part'

A simple and vivid illustration of parts was shown by a woman who presented with severe vaginismus. Despite a very loving relationship with her husband she had never been able to tolerate intercourse. She reported partial and fragmented memories of childhood abuse trauma—although its precise nature and the identity of the perpetrators were never clarified, nor were these details necessary for her healing. Muscle testing indicated that a part of her was not willing for her to have intercourse with her husband. She entered the TAT pose and was asked to make contact with that part of her and to have a dialogue. She reported that part to be feeling very frightened and angry and determined not to be hurt again. As she continued with the internal dialogue, she explained to that part that she loved her husband, who was a good man, and that to have sex with him was her choice. In the subsequent session she reported that she and her husband had made good progress towards intercourse, being guided in internal TAT conversation with this part regarding what was tolerable. She said the child part was very appreciative of being listened to and taken notice of. I suggested she return to the TAT pose and have further internal dialogue in the session. The part, whom she now visualised as a little girl dressed in blue, said that sex could be permitted provided it did not hurt. I suggested she explain to the part that, when an adult woman chooses to have sex with a man whom she loves, it does not hurt. She reported that the little girl part responded by asking why, if that was the case, it had hurt her before. I suggested the client explain that a little girl's vagina is not meant to be penetrated and that is why it hurt, but a grownup's vagina is bigger—and suggested the little girl have a look at the adult's body. She reported that the little girl was amazed, not having realised that she had an adult's body. After a few more brief moments of TAT aimed at healing all the little girl part's wounds and pain, the client reported that the girl was saying goodbye and that she wanted to blend in with the rest of her. She felt the child inside her in a very happy and joyful state. This was a deeply moving yet non-dramatic process of contacting a traumatised child part, frozen in time.

The human biocomputer—the parts that run the programmes

The mind may best be thought of as combining information-process-ing properties of a bio-computer with an inner family (or complex society) of parts or sub-personalities that operate its systems and programmes. I do not find any clear form of language or metaphor that seems entirely adequate here, but the data of muscle testing and energy processes persuades me of the validity of this notion of a combination of computer-like functions and inner parts that write and operate the programmes. Kinesiology muscle testing reveals a system that processes information very precisely and literally, often providing different responses to subtle shifts in the form of words and nuances of meaning. Moreover, the information is revealed quasi-digitally: the muscle is either 'on' [locked] or 'off' [spongy]. It has indeed been suggested that the inspiration for the modern digital computer is derived from a 'download' of the operating system of the human brain and mind. John Lilly (1974) was perhaps the first to articulate this metaphor of the brain/mind as a bio-computer. The brain can thus be considered analogous to the hardware of a computer and the mind's fields of information, beliefs, language, cultural signifiers and memes, and so on, correspond to the software, the programmes that 'run' the brain. This software overlaps with the wider network of signifiers and memes that are found in the social world within which each brain is nurtured and programmed.

Let us consider how this system might function—and here my account is strongly influenced by Martin (1997; Martin & Landrell, 2005). Much processing of information clearly is unconscious—and far faster that the conscious mind is capable of. Maladaptive process-ing of information and dysfunctional responses (psychopathology) are the result of largely unconscious activity. Sensory data arrives in the system, is processed in accord with the internal working models (Bowlby, 1980), is evaluated for matching with information stored in data banks, and a response is generated that may have mostly bypassed conscious thought. For much of the time, such automatic processing is adaptive, since conscious attention to every detail of sensory information would be far too slow and cumbersome to enable rapid and potentially life-preserving responses. As we learn and practise our skills, the knowledge that originally was explicit (explicit memory) fades into the realm of the implicit. Thus a learner driver has to think about each movement he or she makes of the controls, but some time later most of these actions are carried out competently but without conscious thought.

In the case of a person who is functioning optimally, thoughtfully and responsibly, and who is prepared to engage with reality and to learn from experience, emotionally significant information is processed partly consciously. With conscious awareness there is choice as to how to respond emotionally and behaviourally. The situation is perceived without resort to psychodynamically defensive strategies that distort or eclipse conscious perception. This openness to experience may involve suffering emotional pain. Experience is thought about, processed, and digested, forming the nutrients for emotional and personality growth—a process described by Bion (1962) in terms of 'learning from experience'.

By contrast, in the case of a person whose level of internal conflict and potential anxiety is such that he or she cannot tolerate a clear perception of reality and the possible pain involved, he or she will avoid conscious processing of emotionally significant information. There will be a failure to take responsibility for the emotional and behavioural response. The incoming information will be diverted to automatic processing, employing a variety of well-known defensive strategies (e.g. repression, displacement, projection and projective identification, denial, manic defences, intellectualisation etc.), and also in accord with core beliefs and internal working models of relationships. In addition to these commonly recognised strategies, there may also be areas of psychosis, childhood 'magic', or other secret internal domains that have been developed during the early years as a form of retreat and respite from unbearable or terrifying emotional experiences. These hidden alternatives to 'reality' often exist latently, unobtrusively, being resorted to only when severe threat or stress is experienced. The entire internal landscape of automatic processing may be populated with a multiplicity of parts—some of which are based on identifications, some express particular emotions or points of view, some are rooted in particular traumas, whilst others have specific organisational roles and functions in maintaining the integrity of the internal defensive system. They may be formed as a combination of self and other, through projection of part of the self into an image of the other—the process of projective identification sometimes described as the basis of 'internal objects' (Grotstein,

1982). Some parts are punitive—partly corresponding to Freud's (1923b) 'superego'—and some may be sabotaging, corresponding to Fairbairn's (1952) concept of the 'internal saboteur', or the 'shadow self' that expresses repudiated anger and aggression.

Through muscle testing I have also found the presence of 'reverse parts', or parts that work with reverse energy. These are death or illness-seeking, and express destructive or perverse aims. These dissociated parts are often deeply traumatised and frightened, as well as feeling beyond the pale of the internal family. They may not believe they can be healed or accepted.

Once the incoming sensory-emotional information has been handed over to automatic processing, then the person is at the mercy of his or her unconscious parts and strategies of defence. Dysfunctional behaviour and emotional reactions will ensue, all of which are organised on the basis of earlier (usually childhood) experiences, fantasies, and perceptions. When automatic processing holds sway, there is no possibility of updating the information in the light of the present situation. The present is reacted to as if it were a direct continuation of the past.

Art Martin (Martin & Landrell, 2005) has hypothesised three basic ways in which human beings may respond to conflict with others: compliance, control, and indifference. The compliance option involves giving up self out of a fear of disapproval—and probably corresponds to Winnicott's (1960) 'false self'. In the stance of control, there is an attempt to change others by expressing disapproval or by instilling fear or guilt. The stance of indifference involves withdrawal or passive resistance, or appearing as if nothing matters. This latter strategy may be linked also to denial—and then to 'denial of denial'. When 'denial of denial' strategies are in operation, the entire awareness of there being a problem is blocked.

In Martin's view, the human system operates with both programmes (the operating software) and parts, or subpersonalities that operate the programmes and carry out the behaviours generated by the programmes. He writes:

> "As we delved into this vast unknown area of the mind, we found that the makeup of the mind was as orderly and smooth running as a computer running an operating system and programs that could be reprogrammed ... Programs cause emotional behaviour, but they must have subpersonalities to act out the emotional behaviour." [Martin & Landrell, 2005, p. 196].

My own experience with kinesiology muscle testing tends to con-firm Martin's findings. Muscle testing will indicate the presence of parts—and also the presence of programmes. These are distinct. Thus the two statements "All parts of me permit me to be free of this problem" and "All programmes within me permit me to be free of this problem" may elicit different muscle responses. 'Parts' may be willing, but 'programmes' may not permit resolution of a problem.

Often the statement "The programmes that lead to my anxiety/unhappiness/self-sabotage are permitted to be deleted or modified" will elicit a muscle response of 'no'. However, if this is treated as a simple reversal, with tapping the side of the hand, particularly if accompanied by a request that the programmes become accessible, it will be cleared. A subsequent muscle test will usually then indicate that the programmes can now be deleted or modified. A further state-ment along the lines of "The software engineer within my system is willing to delete or modify the programmes in order that I no longer experience this problem" will usually elicit an affirmative muscle response. I have found that continued tapping on the side of the hand for half a minute or so whilst stating a request for the software engineer to do this will lead to the desired result. Following this, muscle testing will usually indicate that the harmful programmes are no longer present. It is possible also to ask whether they have been deleted *or* modified, and often the answer is that they have been modified and not deleted. Often the subsequent reports at the client's next session may then reveal positive changes in emotional responses, mood and behaviour. At the time of writing, I am still in awe of the ease with which it is possible to bring about deep changes at this level of the system's 'software'.

If muscle testing indicates that the programmes have been deleted, it is worth asking if they still remain in the system in deleted form (like deleted files on a hard drive) and if they can be re-installed. Often it seems this is the case—and so a further brief step is to ask for them to be permanently deleted so that they cannot be re-installed, and then to muscle test that this has been done.

Enquiries about programmes may be particularly useful in rela-tion to complex patterns of dysfunctional or self-sabotaging behav-iour. This line of exploration may be less relevant in relation to more simple targets, such as anxiety and distress about particular issues or events. These can be targeted and cleared with the simple strategies of classic TFT.

Programmes are much more fundamental and powerful determinants of behaviour than simple traumas and anxieties. Anxieties and phobias may express symptoms (of psychodynamic conflict), or have roots in trauma, or may be inherited through the energy field, or may be induced by energy toxins. By contrast, the deeper programmes are the hidden executive controllers of behaviour and emotional reactions. They comprise the 'software' instructions behind recurrent patterns of dysfunctional or self-sabotaging behaviour. These programmes are intended to avoid danger, whilst also maintaining the fulfilment of basic needs—and thus, in part, are the compromise outcomes of psychodynamic conflict, but are also rather complex sets of instructions governing behaviour in a variety of situations. When a person describes a self-defeating pattern of behaviour, expressing puzzlement at their own motivation, or helplessness in their attempts to change it, then he or she is speaking of a programme. Programmes may have been 'written' in response to traumas, particularly in childhood, but they are themselves distinct from the traumas. A trauma may be cleared but the programme may remain. Symptoms, such as anxiety, panic, inhibitions, self-defeating patterns, and so on, may be expressions of underlying programmes. When this is the case, the overall pattern continues, even though each symptom may be alleviated with an energy psychology method. This persistence of the pattern must be distinguished from the phenomenon of the re-emergence of a previously eliminated symptom as a result of re-exposure to an individual energy toxin—a process that Dr Callahan and other TFT practitioners have emphasised and demonstrated again and again. With the operation of programmes, one has the impression of a more complex intelligence behind a range of dysfunctional behaviours. Another way of putting this is to say that the problematic pattern pervades the personality—or that the difficulties are the expression of a 'personality disorder'.

One analogy might be that clearing presenting symptoms, which can certainly be done easily enough using TFT or other energy methods, is like deleting document files from a computer. The programme that produces the files (the symptoms) still remains. Such a programme may enable a wide variety of documents (symptoms) to be created. The 'software' programmes in the biocomputer are not themselves in consciousness, just as the actual programmes within a computer are not visible on its 'desktop'.

For example, if a person has an 'avoidant personality disorder', he or she will avoid many different situations that evoke anxiety, reflecting a core belief that the world is dangerous and that it is best to stay at home and not risk venturing into unfamiliar places or activities. The pattern will pervade many different contexts. Despite the unhappiness and frustration that this causes, the person will be quite unable to alter this pattern without help. If energy methods are applied to each situation of anxiety, there may be some gradual progress, but the impression will remain of a persisting underlying pattern. This is the programme. Even if the underlying core belief is addressed, progress may be slow and the avoidant personality disorder persists. Some of the childhood traumas and other situations that have given rise to the belief that the wider world is dangerous and should be avoided may be addressed and cleared. Whilst this can help, the underlying programme may remain. If the programme itself is cleared—by locating it with muscle testing, clearing reversals linked to it, and asking the internal 'software engineer' to delete/modify/rewrite the programme—then people often do become much more free in a variety of ways. This is not in any way to question the extraordinary potency of TFT and other energy methods, but is simply a matter of where and at what level in the system the method is best applied.

The elements of the psycho-energetic system

The elements of the mind that we commonly work with in using energy psychology methods include the following:

- Symptoms and other presenting problems.
- Energy fields, including meridian pathways, chakra centres, and the biofield surrounding the body. In relation to the energy field, the phenomena of 'neurological disorganisation' and 'reversal' apply.
- Personal and family/group/tribe energy fields.
- The *information*—or 'perturbations'—in the energy fields.
- Traumas (experiences which overwhelm the coping capacities of the system)—and patterns of trauma (a series of thematically related traumas).

- Simple psychodynamic conflicts — for example, if the expression of anger towards a particular person is perceived unconsciously as dangerous, it may be channelled towards a 'safer' target, or directed towards the self to generate a mood of depression.
- More complex psychodynamic conflicts, involving layers of emotions, whereby a more overt and superficial emotion is clung to in order to ward off a more feared and hidden emotion. For example, a man was resistant to relinquishing his anger about a particular situation because hidden behind this was a more feared and toxic feeling of shame. When his shame was addressed, it emerged that he was resisting releasing this fully in order to avoid facing a deeper feeling of terror. This psychodynamic layering of emotions is unveiled as energy therapy methods progressively unravel the elements of the conflict.
- Parts of the self. These include: [1] internal 'objects' based on a combination of identification with, and projection of aspects of self into, an image of a parent or other significant person; [2] parts that have arisen in response to childhood traumas and carry out important protective functions; [3] child parts, that retain the beliefs, anxiety and distress, and patterns of thought of a young child (perhaps linked to particular traumatic episodes); [4] 'reversed parts', that work with reversed energy.
- Layers of the self.
- Areas of fragmentation and primal wounds. These may be 'walled off', 'denied access' or guarded by designated parts.
- Energy parasites.
- Inherited traumas and pain, not derived from the person's own experience but transmitted down the generational energy fields and thus lodged in the individual's system.
- 'Denied' shame, pain, anxiety, or inherited trauma and pain.
- Core beliefs about the self in the world. These are usually based on recurrent childhood experiences. Core beliefs have something in common with Bowlby's (1980) idea of 'internal working models'.
- Individual energy toxins.
- Energy toxic people (functioning as individual energy toxins).
- Programmes, involving complex instructions for behaviour and emotion in a range of situations. The situations within the remit

of a particular programme may all be thematically linked—for example, behaviour in attachment relationships.

* Deleted files (anxiety and emotional distress) and programmes that remain on the system's 'hard drive' and can potentially be re-installed unless permanently deleted.

All these elements can be identified with muscle testing and can be cleared or modified using energy psychology methods. They are all concepts that appear meaningful to the clients' energy systems that I have muscle tested—i.e. the client's system will give clear muscle responses to statements incorporating these concepts and the muscle responses will change as a result of energy tapping work focused on these same concepts—and, crucially, the client reports subsequent changes and benefits in his or her behaviour and experience. Of course there is potentially any number of further elements that others may discover. At the time of writing, the above categories are the ones that I have found important and which form a routine part of my clinical work when using energy methods.

Conscious and non-conscious elements of the psycho-energetic system

Some elements are within, or potentially within, consciousness—such as memories of trauma, anxiety, and other symptoms. Core beliefs may become accessible to awareness through introspection or 'Socratic questioning'. Others, even though of a potentially experiential nature, are likely to be obscure to consciousness—such as inherited trauma and pain. Similarly, 'parts' may not be in consciousness. Many elements and qualities of the system *inherently* do not feature in consciousness—such as 'software programmes'. The contents and qualities of the energy system itself are usually not directly accessible to consciousness or the organs of sensation, although those with some energy sensitivity may discern subtle qualities. Other elements are potentially conscious but are labelled 'denied access'—this idea of 'denied' functioning as a kind of password that allows their presence to be revealed through muscle testing.

It is fortunate indeed that we do not have to rely on consciousness for access to the elements that we need to address in energy psychological work. We can use consciousness simply as a vehicle to channel intention and requests to the deeper psycho-somatic-energy system with its biocomputer qualities. It is not necessary for consciousness to understand all the details of the changes that are taking place in a person's system. The practitioner may be busily working with the client's energy system, using consciousness combined with muscle testing as a channel of access to this, but without the person's conscious understanding of the content of what is going on. In such situations a fuller explanation and discussion may take place after the work has been done. There are indeed times when conscious discourse with the client's mind would greatly slow the process down.

Inherited pain, trauma, attitudes, and behavioural patterns

One of the many advantages of muscle testing it that it can reveal hidden areas and qualities of the system that would never be grasped through talk and consciousness alone. Some of these are not, strictly speaking, part of the individual's self. One example is the area of inherited pain, trauma, attitudes and desires. These qualities may profoundly influence a person's experience and behaviour but they do not stem from the individual's own lifetime or experience. They are transmitted down the generational lines through the energy fields. We are conceived and nurtured in the information-rich energy field of our mother, inseminated with a sperm carrying a hologram of the energy field of the father. This transmission down the generational energy fields is one aspect of Jung's collective unconscious. It may also be linked to the homeopathic idea of the inherited 'miasms'. Parts of the self may be attached to inherited trauma or pain and may be organised around it; thus the threat of clearing it may initially evoke resistances or reversals due to these parts' fears of feeling lost, disoriented, or abandoned. Once the resistances or reversals are removed, the inherited trauma, pain, or patterns of desire and attitude, will clear quite easily with simple tapping sequences. However, it is important to check whether they have been permanently deleted, or still exist in the system as 'deleted files' that could potentially be re-installed. If the latter is the case, it is necessary to check for resistances to permanent deletion, and once these are cleared a brief tapping sequence will 'delete the deleted files'.

Transmission through the energy fields has been illustrated in studies reported by biologist Rupert Sheldrake in connection with his concept of morphic fields. These morphic or 'morphogenetic' fields are "self-organising regions of influence, analogous to magnetic fields and other recognised fields of nature" (Sheldrake, 1999, p. 258)—and Sheldrake proposes, on the basis of a variety of observable phenomena, that these fields contain information, have memory, and are capable of learning. When one group of organisms learn a new behaviour, others within the same species may rapidly develop the same behaviour, even though they are remote in space and time—as documented, for example, in the relatively sudden development all over the UK of the behaviour of blue tits in pecking the tops off milk bottles on door steps in order to consume the cream. In one experiment, newly hatched batches of chicks were shown a small yellow light and after they had spontaneously pecked on it were injected with a substance that would make them feel ill. The chicks rapidly developed a conditioned aversive response and avoided the yellow light. Subsequent generations of chicks showed aversion to the yellow light when first exposed to it, even though they had not received the injection, nor observed others receiving it. This simple experiment illustrates the principle of 'inherited trauma' influencing organisms, even though the trauma has not occurred within the individual's own lifetime; it is a model of an inherited phobia. There is also an obvious similarity between the idea of inherited morphic fields and Jung's concept of the 'collective unconscious', the universally accessible storehouse of images, archetypes, fears and other thought forms.

Family/group/tribal fields

The existence of family fields occurred to me one day when, in puzzling over a persisting problem, I muscle tested the statement "there is a prohibition on ...X... in my family field", and this tested positive, even though the prohibition had been removed from the personal field. As a result, I began to test for family/group/tribal fields in cases of persisting problems and have found that these often test positive. They can be cleared quite easily in the same way as prohibitions and programmes in the personal field. Perhaps they are somewhat similar to inherited trauma, pain, behaviours and attitudes. Such prohibitions in the family field appear to function as invisible prisons, rules encoded in a field of influence that is not within consciousness.

Reversed parts

Reversed parts—or parts that work with reversed energy—can be like concentrated expressions of the 'death instinct' (in Reichian terms, 'Deadly Orgone'). These may result from periods of trauma, profound feelings of despair, or experiences of believing the self to be utterly unwanted or condemned to death. They may be pervaded with absolute feelings of guilt and badness. Their origins may be very early in life. These hidden parts may be expressed in illness, perversion, or self-destructive acts. They will tend to generate reversals generally in the energy system—and may also give rise to confusion when attempting to muscle test.

The domain of reversed parts can provide a point in which parasitic energies can gain hook-hold and remain hidden. Parasitic energies appear to be malignant 'life-forms' within the energy fields—the interacting energy fields of individuals, families, groups, lovers, societies etc., all within the background energy ocean (Modi, 1997; Stibal, 2006). They feed on the negative energies of reversed parts—and thus have an investment in maintaining parts in this distorted condition. Whilst it is possible to speculate on their origins, it is not necessary to do so in order to detect and remove them. There is no need for any particular emphasis or fuss to be made about energy parasites since they are simply another of the various elements that can be detected and cleared with energy psychological methods. Muscle testing a statement such as "there are energy parasites in, or attached to, my system" or "there are parts within me that are not truly part of me" will, as far as I can judge, reveal their presence if they are there. It is important to distinguish dissociated parts of the self from parasitic energies that are simply masquerading as parts of the self, rather in the way that viruses and other physical entities seek parasitic asylum within the body. Removal of energy parasites is simply a matter of tapping a suitable sequence whilst the person voices the intention that they depart or be removed by the 'energy body's immune system'—the latter being a metaphor that nevertheless appears to find an appropriate resonance in the energy system.

Breaches in the energy field

Other areas and qualities of the system that are accessible *through* consciousness in conjunction with muscle testing, but are not usually *in* consciousness, include breaches and wounds to the energy field. Such wounds may arise through trauma, or are left in the wake of parasitic or otherwise damaging relationships, especially ones in which there has been an exchange of parts of the self (through projective identification etc.). Clues to these may be found in states of exaggerated energetic sensitivity, feelings of being easily invaded and weakened by others, or a general lack of psychosomatic resilience. Some people are naturally very sensitive and affected by others—phenomena described well by 'energy psychiatrist', Judith Orloff (Orloff, 2006). Such states do not necessarily indicate breaches of the energy field, although simple energy methods combined with intention can be helpful in strengthening the field.

Information and energy

Are we dealing with energy, energy flows and blockages, or information? Dr Callahan emphasises he is addressing information—the perturbations in the energetic 'thought field'—and by clearing this away, in a manner perhaps akin to smoothing the ripples in a pond, the disturbance in mind and body is eliminated. Ripples in a pond are indeed a form of information, providing indications of the nature and impact of whatever has caused them (e.g. the size and weight of an object that landed on the pond surface). They are also a wave-like flow of energy. Flows of energy can be blocked, causing diversions or backward flows, all of which themselves contain information. We might recall Freud's (1905d) concept of libido, the energy that lies on the border between psyche and soma, which, when blocked, for either psychological or physical reasons, flows backwards along the earlier paths of development and bodily zones of pleasure. This blocked flow, and resulting regression-reversal, gives rise to a psychological or physical disturbance—but such disturbance, a neurosis, for example, is dense with information regarding its origins, which the psychoanalyst can, in principle, decode. Through such considerations, it becomes possible to see that we are dealing with *information* encoded in the energy field, *flows* of energy, and *blockages* or *disruptions* in the energy flow. It may be important to be aware of these subtle distinctions.

CHAPTER TEN

Energy toxins

A friend called to see me in a state of great anxiety. She had a sophisticated understanding of methods of energy psychology and had been frantically applying these. Her assumption was that she had got into a state of panic about the prospect of her daughter leaving home imminently—and feared there must be profound and complex layers of psychological conflict and trauma behind her distress. This was not an unreasonable hypothesis. I listened to her and the thought came to me that she needed to do the collar bone breathing technique. Slightly surprised by this intuition, but willing to go along with it, I shared the thought and we both did the exercise. Two minutes later she reported feeling completely relaxed. Her anxiety had entirely disappeared. Wondering what had caused the state of neurological and energetic disorganisation that had been corrected by the collar bone breathing, I asked if she had been using any new perfume or other products in the home. She said she had been using some new foot cream—rather fancy, expensive and aromatic cream. We muscle tested her as she thought of this cream—her arm collapsed with no strength at all. She realised that her state of anxiety coincided precisely with the period that she had been using the cream. Moreover, it struck her that she had been feeling particularly anxious at home, where the cream was kept. This was a vivid example for both of us of the significance of energy toxins in some cases. What had appeared to be a psychological disturbance, rooted perhaps in deep anxieties and childhood insecurities, turned out to be caused directly by an energy toxin that had been causing havoc with her system.

Excess alcohol

People who are troubled are sometimes inclined to drink excessive amounts of alcohol. I find that clients who do so tend to have energy systems that are in a state of general reversal. This condition of energy toxicity is associated with a negative and self-destructive outlook, as well as an absence of response to TFT treatments. It is also linked with increased desires to drink more alcohol. Clearing this reversal often involves a combination of tapping the side of the hand, rubbing the left neurolymphatic 'sore spot', and perhaps also the Callahan '7 second' technique. Tapping the side of the hand can be accompanied by a statement such as "Even though I have poisoned myself with alcohol and my energy system is in reverse, I completely accept myself". Once the general reversal has been corrected, the person feels more positive in mood and outlook, the self-destructive inclinations fade, and the urge to drink alcohol disappears. Sometimes the transformation in mood, within the space of just a few minutes, can be startling. Alcoholic drinks can be powerfully energy toxic for some people (but not everyone), generating self-destructive addictive cravings, sucking them ever deeper into a mire of hopelessness and despair—often expressed in characteristically repetitive speech (even when not overtly intoxicated). Fortunately, the right combination of TFT techniques can rapidly set the person free of these profoundly damaging traits.

Toxins and psychological problems—Dr Callahan's discoveries

The influence of toxins in creating psychological problems has been known for some time—for example, in the pioneering work of Doris Rapp (1991) in relation to hyperactive and disturbed children, and the report for the American Psychological Association by Travis et al. (1989) on environmental toxins. However, it has been the use of kinesiology in relation to psychological conditions, especially through Dr Callahan's Thought Field Therapy, that has brought this issue more fully into focus.

The full extent of the role of toxins in triggering seemingly psychological problems was only discovered as a result of the strikingly effective nature of TFT. Dr Callahan found that some clients would not benefit from a TFT treatment until a toxin was removed. The effect of removing the toxin from the person's diet or their immediate environment would be clear—resulting in either a subsidence of symptoms or a capacity to respond easily to TFT. A further very important observation of the effect of toxins was that they could cause a previously successfully treated problem to be reinstated. This reinstatement is one version of a wider phenomenon known in biology as 'atavism', meaning a return to an earlier form. Biological atavisms—such as a baby born with characteristics of an earlier ancestral form (a tail, for example)—are known to be caused sometimes by toxins, such as radiation. Through his work with TFT, Dr Callahan discovered that toxins can trigger the return of a previous problem which had either been successfully treated or had been overcome in the normal course of maturation—thus he thinks of this phenomenon as a biological atavism occurring within a single generation (Callahan, 2003). It is important to note that the problem of toxin effects is not unique to TFT—toxins have their effects anyway, but it is only because TFT is an unusually effective and precise treatment that it was possible to observe how toxins affect the energy system and then the physical and mental systems. Dr Callahan is keen to emphasise the important point that it is only in the case of effective therapies, such as TFT and EMDR, which often succeed in completely eliminating symptoms and therefore bringing about a cure, that it is possible to observe the undoing of a cure and attempt to track the cause of this undoing, It is not the case that the cures produced by TFT are uniquely susceptible to relapse and to the effects of toxins, nor that failures in TFT are 'blamed' on toxins as a post hoc excuse; rather it is that methods which do not produce cures do not create the circumstances in which the undoing of a cure by a toxin can be observed. By identifying toxins, and either neutralising them, or eliminating them, it is possible to make TFT and related methods even more effective for more people.

Dr Callahan prefers to speak of 'individual energy toxins', because they are often very specific to the individual. A food or product that acts as a toxin to one person may be fine for someone else. Sometimes foods or products that are highly nutritious and health-promoting for most people can be an energy toxin for a particular individual. A brand of perfume may be harmless to one person but may wreak havoc in the energy system of another person. However, although Dr Callahan calls these *energy* toxins, he emphasises that they are genuinely toxic—they cause harm to the person's body.

Toxins can create any kind of symptom

It is now generally recognised amongst energy psychologists who are familiar with this field that energy toxins can create almost any kind of psychological or physical symptom. Anxiety, panic, mood disturbance, agitation and irritability, are just some of the symptoms that commonly can be triggered by toxins. This is not to say that in every case these are toxin-based reactions, but in some cases they are and they do not then respond well to a purely psychological focus. Also, it has been observed that problems that appear particularly complex and entrenched often have a toxin component. People with obscure syndromes that combine multiple psychological and somatic symptoms—such as chronic fatigue, fibromyalgia, autoimmune diseases, and states of psychosomatic exhaustion—usually seem to have roots partly in the effects of energy toxins. Obesity often has an energy toxin component, partly because toxins can trigger excess appetite and cravings, and also because the body may use fat tissue as a means of storing toxins to protect the rest of the system—similar to the problem in the wider environment of storage and disposal of toxic waste. For similar reasons, toxins may cause the body to retain more water than otherwise.

The effect of individual energy toxins in blocking treatments, or in causing previously treated problems to return, is in addition to the well-known allergic and sensitivity responses to particular substances. The latter are increasingly recognised today.

Toxins and toxic experiences (traumas) all can cause psychological and physical symptoms. There is one important difference. Individual energy toxins cannot be treated so easily or completely using TFT or other energy-based methods. They may be temporarily neutralised, using the Callahan '7 second' technique, but permanent elimination of the reaction is more problematic. Often toxins have to be avoided, at least for some time.

Toxins and trauma

Sometimes it is suggested that toxins have their effect because they have become associated with traumas—perhaps being in the person's environment or body at the time a trauma happened. Thus the body would develop conditioned responses to the substance. An observation that might seem to favour this idea is that people who have experienced a great deal of abuse trauma in childhood often seem to develop multiple food and environmental sensitivities. Some years ago I worked with a very unfortunate patient who presented with a background of very extensive and sadistic abuse within a network in Belgium; she suffered with such extreme sensitivities that her diet and the products she could use in her home were severely restricted, to a degree which seemed to me at the time to be quite astonishing and yet absolutely genuine. It was as if her system were registering the world in general as toxic and threatening. In such cases of allergic and sensitivity responses, it is as if the body is reacting with a sort of physiological phobia to substances that are not actually harmful. Tapas Fleming (www.tatlife.com), Sandi Radomski (www.allergy-antidotes.com) and Stephen Daniel (www.quantumtechniques.com) have all emphasised the possible links between sensitivities/allergies and traumas. The role of ancestral traumas, patterned into the inherited energy fields, tends to be part of this line of enquiry.

Toxins are toxic

However, Dr Callahan makes two points about this kind of hypothesis linking toxins and trauma. First, if toxic effects were essentially trauma-based, it should be easier to clear them, since TFT can treat trauma reactions very simply. Second, he suggests that the substances that trigger allergies and sensitivities, and which interfere with treatments, are *actually* toxic—the effect is not an illusion or a mistake on the body's part. He quotes the arguments of Margie Profet (1991) that food sensitivities and allergies are due to toxins in plants, even though some people's bodies may be able to cope with these. One natural defence that plants may develop against being eaten by predators is to manufacture toxins. It has also been suggested that current strains of grains, such as wheat, cultivated and adapted for their relative resilience against pests, have this quality because of the toxins they naturally produce. Dr Callahan suggests that the overall state of a person's system, including their current level of stress, may play a part in determining their response to toxins. When healthy and relatively free of stress, the body may be able to cope with a level of toxins that would provoke a reaction when their health is compromised or they are under stress. Another factor is the so-called 'barrel effect'. If we imagine that the body places toxins in a protective barrel, then provided the barrel is not full the body suffers no reaction, but if the barrel is full and over-flowing, because of the *amount* of toxins that have been consumed, then the system is poisoned by each additional exposure to the par-ticular substance. This analogy may be developed further, with the idea that stress may reduce the size of the barrel, so that less toxin be tolerated at such times.

Toxins, atavism, regression, and reversal

Dr Callahan compares the actually toxic nature of energy toxins to the way in which phobias usually relate to objects or circumstances that were actually dangerous at some point in our evolutionary past. Thus, phobias have an atavistic nature—a reactivation of a terror that in certain circumstances, or at certain times in the personal or evo-lutionary past, may be appropriate even though there is no realistic danger in the present. It is perhaps possible also to link this with the psychoanalytic and neurological concept of regression—the rever-sion to an earlier mode of functioning. This can come about through brain trauma or psychological trauma. To these we can now add toxins as another trigger for regression.

In addition to causing regression, toxins cause psychologi-cal reversal. This is perhaps a major way in which they have their damaging effect. It is also a good indicator of the likely influence of a toxin if a person presents in a state of general reversal—indicated by muscle strong to false statements and to "I want to be sick/miser-able", and weak to true statements and "I want to be well/happy". Recurrent reversal, where almost as soon as it has been cleared it comes back again, is another sign of toxins. Another clue is if the side of hand treatment for reversal does not work well and the rubbing the 'sore spot' neurolymphatic area is required.

Interplay of toxin sensitivities and emotions

Sometimes a clear interplay of food sensitivities and emotions can be revealed as energy work proceeds. In a workshop I once worked with a man who knew he was sensitive to cow's milk. First we used the Etox laser, with the method taught by Sandi Radomski [www. allergyantidotes.com], whilst he held a vial of water imprinted with the energetic frequency of cow's milk. He began to report a series of rapid impressions of the kinds of allergy reactions he recalled as common in his childhood after he ate or drank dairy products. These soon settled and he reported a strong feeling of happiness. He also mentioned that he had been weaned from the breast and put on cow's milk at nine months. However, when we then tested for the sensitivity, his arm still showed partial weakness, although not as much as initially. We moved on to working through a diagnosed sequence of TFT in relation to the cow dairy products. As he proceeded through this tapping sequence, he reported feelings of sadness, then anger. I commented that he was perhaps angry and upset about the loss of the breast, represented by his previous sense of happiness. This made much sense to him, as we continued finding and tapping the sequence. Soon there were no perturbations left as he thought of cow's milk, or held the imprinted vial. This was a vivid and rapid cycling through early experiences of happiness at the breast, followed by distress at the substitution of cow's milk, and his system's rejection of this, expressed in both physiological and emotional responses. Both these components were cleared using a combination of energy methods.

Toxins and addiction

Toxins often form the basis of an addiction. It is now commonly recognised that people may crave substances that they are sensitive to. These may cause specific reversals in relation to the particular substance. In such instances the person will muscle test strong to "name of substance"—but weak to "name of substance—I want to be well"—revealing the reversal that is tricking the system into registering the substance as desirable (muscle test strong). This is almost always the case with smokers of cigarettes and is readily demonstrated. Dr Callahan notes that people who smoke cigarettes are much more inclined to experience the return of a previously treated problem, because of the multiple toxins in cigarettes. Interestingly, it has sometimes been observed that pure tobacco is much less toxic and addictive, but modern cigarettes have many additives which may contribute substantially to the addictive potential.

In the case of cravings for alcoholic drinks, Stephen and Beth Daniel of Quantum Techniques note that people may experience particular alcoholic drinks as toxic, and therefore addictive, whereas other drinks may not have this effect. Thus, they hypothesise that it is not the alcohol per se that functions as the energy toxin, but the particular grain from which the drink is fermented.

The Daniels also note that once an addictive craving has been overcome with energy methods, it can sometimes be reactivated by exposure to some other quite different toxin. Once this other toxin is identified and neutralised, the craving subsides.

The many kinds of toxins

Energy toxins are many and varied—and are specific to the individual. They include the following:

Foods (including food supplements)
Perfumes
Toiletries
Detergents (particularly detergent perfumes)
Moulds
Environmental chemicals: petrochemicals, pesticides, heavy metals etc.
School/office products: e.g. paper, ink, chalk.
Vaccines
Insect bites
Bacteria, viruses, parasites, and other infectants.
Coloured light (e.g. through pink tinted spectacles).
Medications
Animals (hair, faeces etc).
Dust
Pollen.
Accessories, such as jewelry.
Electromagnetic frequencies

People—particular people's energy.

Places—geopathic energy.

Areas of dense attractor fields of reversed energy (e.g. generated by highly destructive acts, or by gatherings of people in a state of high emotions and committed to a destructive ideology).

Endogenous toxins—the body's own hormones, neurotransmitters, and other biochemical substances.

The body's own blocked energy.

The person's own emotions.

Sometimes the various toxins are classified into ingestants (e.g. foods), inhalants (e.g. perfumes), contactants (e.g. jewellery) and injectants (vaccines, bites). Dr Stephen Daniel, of Quantum Techniques, indicates that these different categories may interact. For example, if a person eats an ingestant toxin, this may make them more sensitive to inhalant toxins (e.g. pollen) that they might otherwise be able to tolerate.

Food sensitivities commonly involve the following:

Milk
Eggs
Chicken
Fish
Wheat
Corn/maize
Soy
Refined sugar
Caffeine
Peanuts
Pepper
Food colouring
Food additives
Monosodium glutamate
Artificial sweeteners

Testing for toxins

The Callahan method of testing for toxins is essentially as follows. After checking that the person's system is appropriately polarised and is not generally reversed, the substance is held to the throat or solar plexus, or the name of the substance is spoken or thought of, and the muscle is then tested. If it is weak, this indicates the substance is toxic. Then the following statement is muscle tested "name of substance ... I want to be well". If this tests weak, the substance causes a reversal. Finally, if the previous two have tested strong, a further test is to the statement "name of substance ... I want to be sick". If the last statement tests strong, it means that the substance is toxic for both the person being tested and the one doing the testing; whilst not an intuitively obvious conclusion, this has been found to be the case. To use this method, the full details should be obtained from the Callahan techniques 'toxin pack' [Callahan & Callahan, 2003; www.tftrx.com]

An objective indicator of the effect of energy toxins is a measure of heart rate variability. Dr Callahan is keen on this measure because it is objective and not open to influence by expectation or suggestion. HRV is not easily influenced—but it does respond to toxins, often showing dramatic drops from optimum levels, and also can be restored by TFT. This objective measure can be useful in assessing whether a purported energy treatment for energy toxins has actually been successful. Guidelines on purchasing appropriate HRV measuring equipment can be obtained from www.tftrx.com.

Neutralising toxins

Having identified the toxins, these can be temporarily neutralised using Dr Callahan's '7 second treatment' (now elaborated so that it takes a little longer than 7 seconds!). The method is best learned from a Callahan Techniques workshop, but basically it involves having the client hold one hand over the forehead and another behind the head, whilst lightly pressing during breathing in or breathing out. It is necessary to test whether the pressure should be on the inhale or exhale, and there are various other complexities to address. This method will usually (but not always) neutralise the toxic effect long enough for further TFT to be carried out. A muscle test before and then after the 7 second treatment will show the difference.

Full details of how to identify and neutralise individual energy toxins can be found in the training material available from Callahan Techniques Ltd. www.tftrx.com.

Endogenous toxins

Dr Callahan has tended to emphasise the role of exogenous toxins. However, others, such as Sandi Radomski, have drawn attention to the possibility that people can react to their own bodily organs, blood, hormones, neurotransmitters, and so on—as well as to bacteria, viruses and their toxic products. It is possible to muscle test all of these, to find which are registering as toxic. One might begin by muscle testing globally—for example "my hormones", "my hormones I want to be well". If testing weak on either of these, a more detailed list of specific hormones can be checked. Adrenaline typically may register as toxic and may also cause reversal. As a result, the person's system may develop an addiction to adrenaline—and will therefore non-consciously seek stress and anxiety. Similarly a list of neurotransmitters [see list at the end of the chapter] can be worked through. Such testing can be done either by having the client hold vials containing samples of substances, or by simply saying the name. It does not seem to matter whether the person consciously knows what the substances are—again illustrating how the kinesiology test taps into a wider field of knowledge than that contained within the subject's own mind.

Recently I worked through a list of neurotransmitters with a client who had become severely disabled by pervasive chronic anxiety and panic. Her system muscle tested as finding several of these toxic, and some caused reversal. She reported that following this she felt unusually calm, finding this initially somewhat strange since it seemed unfamiliar, but a couple of days later realising that for the first time in years she had begun to feel normal.

Endogenous toxins and ADHD—Quantum Techniques

Stephen and Beth Daniel, the husband and wife team who developed Quantum Techniques, with backgrounds in clinical and educational psychology, have produced an excellent resource on energy treatment of ADD and ADHD (available from www.quantumtechniques. com). Amongst the many aspects they discuss, they draw attention to the effect of ingested toxins on neurotransmitters. There are actually more neurotransmitters in the gut than in the brain. When a person ingests an energy toxin through the mouth, this can shift the system into reverse in relation to the neurotransmitters, contributing to symptoms of brain fog and difficulties in attention and concentration. The Daniels report a specific energy test for neurotransmitter reversal, based on the brain-body integration approach known as Neurolink, developed by Dr Allan Phillips (www.neurolinkglobal. com). To do this test the person blinks rapidly a few times and then muscle tests the standard reversal statement "I want to be well"; if this tests weak, there may be reversal associated with neurotransmitters. The Daniels supply a specific meridian sequence code for treating this. Alternatively, a diagnosed treatment sequence could be used.

The Daniels find that amygdale imbalance is often a feature of ADHD, generating fear and a tendency to be continuously scanning as if for danger. This would link with the process described by biologist Bruce Lipton (2005) whereby blood is withdrawn from the frontal areas of the brain, involved in thinking and planning, and directed towards the hind brain and limbic areas involved in fight-flight responses. They describe a test for amygdala imbalance, again derived from Neurolink. To do this test, the person holds the fingers around the ear and muscle tests the statement "I want to be well" (first one ear and then the other). If the muscle tests weak, the amygdala is imbalanced. The treatment for this is to tap around the top of the ear a few times.

Another specific test they describe, also based on Neurolink, is for cortical integration. For this, the person taps a few times on both sides of the body simultaneously, and muscle tests the statement "I want to be well"; if this tests weak, problems of cortical integration are indicated. Quantum Techniques can provide a treatment sequence for this by phone. However, I have the impression that collarbone breathing also works well in correcting this problem.

A further endogenous imbalance the Daniels test for is to do with the digestive valves. To perform this test, the person clenches his or her teeth and then muscle tests the statement "I want to be well"; if the muscle tests weak, then imbalance in digestive valves is a problem. Specific treatment for this can be provided by telephone consultation from Quantum Techniques. Alternatively, I have found that a diagnosed meridian sequence can help this, although clearing the associated reversal can be important; it may be necessary to use the diagnostic treatment procedure in relation first to 'digestive valves' and then to 'digestive valves balance'. If attempting correction of this at an energetic level, the clenching the teeth test can then be repeated to check for a change. Digestive problems can become a self-reinforcing spiral—triggered by toxins, but in turn generating further toxins. Incomplete digestion can lead to fermentation in the gut, which can in turn feed fungal infections such as candida, which can be a factor in leaky gut syndrome, allowing toxic products to enter the blood stream.

Candidiasis—a common source of endogenous toxins

Overgrowth of candida in the gut may be a common source of endogenous toxins that create psychological symptoms. Krebs (1998) gives a clear account of this. Candida albicans is a naturally occurring yeast that inhabits the human intestinal system. Its normal growth pattern, of budding asexually, is slower than that of bacteria, and therefore, in the competition for surface area in the gut, the bacteria tend to limit the amount of candida. A common factor disturbing the balance between candida and bacteria is the use of antibiotics, which kill bacteria but not candida. Given the chance, the candida shifts into a mycelia overgrowth form, generating horizontal growth tubes that can penetrate the intestinal tissue, thereby entering blood capillaries and allowing the yeast itself as well as biproducts of digestion to enter the blood stream. When partly digested proteins then enter the blood stream, the immune system registers them as antigens and generates antibodies. This forms a basis for sensitivity reactions to foods. Sugary food and refined carbohydrates, often craved by people with candidiasis, feed the yeast. Two toxic products of the yeast overgrowth are acetaldehyde and alcohol. These can cross the blood brain barrier, causing loss of brain integration, with accompanying 'brain fog', depression and mood swings, and other disturbances. The immune system can become depressed by these various reactions, leading to infections and further physiological stress. It has also been noted that candida is associated with diminished serotonin levels. Most serotonin is produced and located within the gut and it is associated with peristaltic movement of material; it is plausible that lowered production of serotonin, and thus slower movement of the gut, might facilitate candida—and thus a capacity to bring this about might have been selected by evolution of this fungal parasite.

Appropriate treatments for candidiasis can include diagnosed TFT in relation to the candida, combined with restriction of foods that encourage yeast growth (such as sugar, alcohol, brewers' yeast, mushrooms, wheat and maize, dairy, dried fruits, and certain soya products). Probiotics may also be used. The practitioner should seek specialised guidance regarding treatment of candida. A blood test for candida antibodies is available. Aggressive treatment of severe candidiasis can be dangerous because of the potential release of large amounts of toxins.

Toxic emotions

Something I found rather startling when first encountered was the way in which people may register certain of their own emotions as toxic—a phenomenon highlighted by Sandi Radomski. Thus, it is possible to work through a list of emotions, muscle testing each one in the normal way: e.g. "anxiety/anger/sadness/frustration/ jealousy/shame etc." and then also pairing the emotion with "I want to be well". Although an emotion may be inherently painful, it will not necessarily register as toxic, but some may do so and may also create reversals. The precise naming of the emotion may be important. If an emotion is experienced as toxic, then it will have a 'double whammy' effect within the system, generating further reactions in response. This may be part of the process whereby people become anxious about being anxious, or depressed about feeling depressed. One emotion may trigger further emotions in response, or more of the same emotion, thus spiralling the system into affect overwhelm. If an emotion creates a reversal, the system may be addicted to that emotion. Such processes are energy-somatic, not psychodynamic, and are not accessible to consciousness, although the emotions may be experienced in consciousness. Once this idea is grasped it is not difficult to think of people who seem compulsively (albeit unconsciously) to generate particular emotions, sometimes by manoeuvring interpersonal situations so as to evoke or justify these.

A woman who developed an addiction to casinos illustrates the effect of toxic emotions. She would experience great excitement, as well as anxiety, whilst in the casino and would lose large amounts of money in an altered state of consciousness. Subsequently she often could not remember very clearly what had gone on. The emotional states of 'anxiety' and 'excitement' tested toxic for her and induced reversal (whilst other emotions did not register in this way). It became clear that the combination of anxiety and excitement created a toxic effect in her system, inducing reversal, with its accompanying self-destructiveness, addictive craving, and stupidity. When I commented to her that toxins that generate reversals, in effect, make people stupid, she replied with amusement that her boyfriend had complained that in the casino a peculiar look of stupidity would appear on her face.

Toxic 'libido'

I have also found that people may sometimes register the word 'libido' as toxic, or as causing a reversal. This is interesting since it reminds us of Freud's original explorations of blocked libido as toxic, in his concept of the *actual neuroses*, in which anxiety states and neurasthenia were a direct effect of these:

> "… the symptoms of these patients are not mentally determined or removable by analysis, but … they must be regarded as direct toxic consequences of disturbed sexual chemical processes." [Freud, 1925d, p. 26]

He also continued to consider there may be an 'actual neurotic core' to other anxiety states that reflect psychodynamic conflict. It can be worth muscle testing the word libido in cases of sexual disturbance or inhibition.

Blocked energy

The phrases "blocked energy" and "blocked energy—I want to be well" will cause people to muscle test weak (unless they are generally reversed)—thus indicating that blocked flow of meridian energy is itself registered as toxic and as causing reversal. This is a highly significant observation. It means that when trauma, toxins, or psychodynamic conflict block the normal flow of subtle energy, the stagnant build-up is registered as toxic. Energetic reversal would then appear to be a direct expression of a block in the flow of subtle energy which has caused a reversal of the direction of flow.

States of severe anxiety and stress exhaustion

States of generalised anxiety and stress exhaustion can become very entrenched and difficult to treat by any method, including simple forms of TFT. In such conditions the person exhibits continual or frequent overwhelming levels of anxiety, often of an agoraphobic nature, panic when faced with any disruption of a familiar routine, childlike clinging, with intense reactions to separation. This constellation may contrast markedly with the person's previous personality and behaviour—and may therefore be very humiliating. It may arise in the wake of periods of prolonged and overwhelming stress, or may follow severely traumatic events or a series of traumatic events. In such cases muscle testing may indicate that the person registers many internal stress hormones and neurotransmitters as toxic and as generating reversal. Adrenaline is often strongly implicated. The impression is that the prolonged onslaught of stress hormones and related physiological reactions has sensitised the system to these, such that much of the person's own internal biochemistry is registered as toxic and generates further stress reactions. Thus the condition, probably associated with a severe disturbance of the hypothalamic-pituitary-adrenal axis, becomes self-perpetuating and may tend to worsen over time. This can be very debilitating indeed.

Another aspect of this condition can be understood in terms of Dr Callahan's concept of biological atavism within the same generation. The intense anxieties experienced by the adult in this state of being overwhelmed with generalised stress are characteristic of frightened young children, who may panic on being separated from the mother, for example. The adult may be perfectly aware that these anxieties are not rational, but nevertheless their intensity persists. It is the reinstatement of an early state of infantile anxiety that had previously been subsumed in the course of normal development—a 'regression', to put this in Freudian terms. This regression or atavism appears to be triggered by a combination of trauma and an excess of internal stress physiology that becomes registered as toxic. In addition, exogenous toxins may play an important role—and people in this condition do often register many substances and foods as toxic. By working gradually through the many different realms of traumas and toxins, using TFT and related methods, and with attention to the person's overall health requirements, it can be possible to resolve these conditions.

Toxic perceptions

Recently two clients presented material that drew my attention to the way in which certain perceptions may be experienced as toxic because they cannot be metabolised by the mind. These result in either physical reactions or pathological behaviours, but the link to the toxic perception is not conscious.

In one case, a woman received a text message from a male friend that appeared ambiguous, offering a potential meaning of expressing some kind of paedophilic interest. Such a possibility was not congruent with what she knew of this man, but it did resonate with certain of her childhood experiences. The message disturbed her, but she had not been able to process it. Subsequently she found herself drinking heavily over a weekend, something she had done often in the past but not recently prior to this. Until we explored the sequence of events she had not been aware of the link between her drinking and the disturbing message.

In the second case, a man had grown up in family circumstances that had contained a secret relating to his own paternity. He had felt certain tensions in relation to his 'father' and had experienced subtle feelings of being somehow on the outside by comparison with his siblings. These obscure childhood states of unease had been stirred up again following a family gathering. The following week he developed a migraine. He reported that this suddenly began at a particular moment on leaving his work when he stood briefly outside the building and saw through the door a group of his colleagues standing together. As we explored this, it began to seem plausible that this perception of the group together, whilst he was on the outside, had joined up with memories of the childhood situation, functioning then as a toxic perception that he could not metabolise.

Toxic perceptions are closely analogous to physical energy toxins. In the case of the latter, the body does not know how to metabolise or otherwise deal with the substance, whilst in the case of toxic perceptions the *mind* does not know how to process them. It appears that mental or perceptual toxins can affect the body and behaviour, just as physical toxins can affect the mind.

The concept of toxic perceptions appears to have some similarity to the 'conflict-shock' postulated by Dr Ryke Geerd Hamer as the hidden factor commonly triggering cancer—in his challenging but controversial approach called New Medicine [www.newmedicine. ca]. According to Hamer's observations, the crucial conflict-shock life event has qualities of being dramatic, difficult or impossible to resolve, and isolating. The person's coping capacities are overwhelmed, the conflict cannot be resolved, and he or she has no-one to talk to about it. Moreover, the shock registers simultaneously on three levels, of the psyche, the brain, and the organ where the cancer forms. Evaluation of Dr Hamer's ideas are beyond the scope of this discussion.

Treatment of energy toxin sensitivities

Treatment of sensitivities to energy toxins is essentially similar to methods used for treating trauma, anxiety and other 'toxic' experiences. An early proponent of such work, who has inspired or influenced many in the field, is Dr Devi Nambudripad, a chiropractor and acupuncturist who originally suffered with many food sensitivities, with multiple resulting symptoms, such as bronchitis, aches and pains, arthritis, brain fog, dizziness, and digestive problems. She discovered one day by accident, in 1983, that treating herself with acupuncture whilst carrots were in her energy field resulted in her body being able to cope easily with carrots whereas previously they had provoked reactions. She subsequently developed a method called Nambudripad Allergy Elimination Technique (NAET), based on acupressure to specific meridians. The NAET Foundation is associated with ongoing research on the outcome of this method, including brain scan data before and after treatment.

Tapas Fleming, a California Acupuncturist, influenced by Nambudripad, developed her Tapas Acupressure Technique originally as a method for treating allergies and sensitivities—subsequently realising its applications for many other kinds of problems. She no longer uses acupuncture with needles, finding that TAT is more effective.

Sandi Radomski, who has a background as a naturapath (as well as social work and counselling) has specialised for a number of years in treating sensitivities and allergy-like reactions using a variety of energy psychology methods. She describes (Radomski, 2002) how she became interested in this work after undertaking TFT training with Dr Callahan and finding around the same time that her husband had developed widespread food and environmental sensitivities. A telephone consultation with Dr Callahan helped to identify the toxins and avoiding these resolved the symptoms. However, her husband's symptoms were so widespread that they embarked on a search for ways of actually treating the toxin sensitivities, initially working with Nambudripad allergy elimination. She finds that, in addition to the Nambudripad method, many other approaches, including TFT, EFT, TAT, and Seemorg Matrix,[1] are often effective with these problems.

Radomski has developed a simple method she calls Spinal Release, based on stimulating the 'associated points' for the meridians, which lie along the bladder meridian that runs down either side of the spine. By tapping on all 14 of these associated points whilst the person holds or thinks of the substance the meridians become balanced, or cleared of perturbations, in relation to that particular substance. She also combines this with a cycle of breathing, with pauses after breathing out and in, somewhat similar to Callahan's collar bone breathing technique, and also incorporates circular eye movements. The method of tapping on all the associated points is somewhat similar to EFT, in that all the meridians are covered. However, she also describes a more specific approach, somewhat similar to the TFT method of diagnosing specific points and sequences. In this version of Spinal Release the practitioner uses one hand to touch the specific associated points whilst muscle testing the client; when a point is found that muscle tests weak, that point is pressed until it muscle tests strong; then other points are tested until they all register strong. Full details of the Spinal Release method, along with other simple procedures for meridian tapping (including 'body talk', the Holloway technique, and the karate chop 33 method), are provided in Sandi Radomski's trainings and in her manual (www.allergyanti-dotes.com).

Another method favoured by Radomski, and originally developed by her husband Bob Radomski, is the use of a 'laser ear spray'. The ear, like the foot, contains a hologram of the entire body, and all the meridians are represented there. A special laser, with a frequency of healthy cells (630-670 nm) is directed at the ear whilst the client holds or thinks of the substance. This can also be used on the hands or the feet.

Muscle testing is used at all stages in Radomski's work. First to identify the toxins, then to test for reversals and for willingness to undergo treatment and to get well. Tests for whether it is safe to treat an issue are recommended. Muscle tests to statements of 100% willingness may be used, and are also recommended by Stephen and Beth Daniel of Quantum Techniques: e.g. "I am 100% willing to be free of this problem". Bob Radomski uses a simple version based on permission: [1] "you give me permission to treat you"; [2] "you give yourself permission to get well"; [3] "you give yourself permission to accept this treatment". Muscle testing is also used to check whether the treatment is complete, whether the treatment needs to be completed, and whether and for how long the person needs to avoid the substance.

A further dimension of Radomski's approach is to test for emotional factors linked to a substance sensitivity by holding the 'emotional points' across the forehead (located above each pupil); if the substance now registers strong in a muscle test, emotional factors are indicated. Radomski would then work through a range of emotions, muscle testing each to find the most relevant, and would also test for the age and situation connected with the substance sensitivity. These are then treated using any of her usual energy clearing techniques.

Radomski notes that often patients can become very tired through using these methods and negative reactions can occur. Commonly the negative reactions are basically fatigue, perhaps accompanied by dizziness and feeling overwhelmed. At such times, Radomski recommends the patient hold their 'resuscitation points' for a few minutes. These are under the nose, the governing vessel, where two fingers are placed, and the back of the head where the other hand is placed.

Tapas Fleming recommends the use of TAT for sensitivities, provided that muscle testing indicates that the person's system permits this. As always with TAT, the method is gracefully simple: the TAT pose is assumed and the person thinks of his or her difficulty with the substance; next, the person thinks of the idea of being perfectly comfortable with the substance; then the usual further steps of TAT are followed, allowing the thought that all origins of the problem are healing, all the places in the body and mind relating to the problem are healing, and so on.

Krebs (1998) describes the use of kinesiology to clear certain allergies and sensitivities. He gives the example of a brief treatment of boy who was very allergic to cat hair, and who would develop skin pustules if in contact with the allergen. Krebs had been visiting the family.

"Because I was there, I offered to balance the boy for his allergy to cats. He was disbelieving. I asked him to lie down on the table, got some cat hair and placed it on his navel. The muscle immediately indicated severe stress. After going through a series of balancing techniques, the last of which was age recession, I found that the cause was an event that occurred at the age of two-and-a-half. Even though there was no conscious memory of this event, kinesiology identified an issue of anger with his father. There was also a cat involved and that was all we needed to know.

I then did Frontal Occipital Holding to defuse the emotional stress on this issue. As soon as I had finished, he no longer demonstrated any reaction to cat hair being placed on his navel. The boy got up and reported he was feeling very strange … He picked on of the cats up and smelled it. No response: no streaming eyes, no blocked nose. He put the cat on his shoulder and the cat began rubbing on his neck. Again, no physiological response. The cat slipped, digging a claw into his shoulder and again there was no response. His old reaction to cats had been eliminated." [Krebs, 1998, p. 292]

Subsequently the boy asked his father what might have happened in relation to cats at age two-and-a-half. His father replied that at that age the boy used to go to a babysitter's house but the cat bit and scratched him and that the boy would make such a scene that the father stopped taking him there. Krebs considers that sometimes it is possible to clear allergy and sensitivity responses and sometimes it is not.

Quantum Techniques provide much information on clearing toxin sensitivities (www.quantumtechniques.com). Stephen and Beth Daniel recommend muscle testing for a variety of issues that might be associated with the sensitivity, including trauma, ancestral trauma, and bacteria and viruses. In order to check whether all the relevant aspects and roots of the sensitivity have been accessed, they recommend muscle testing the statement "We have 100% of the field (or information) required to treat this issue"; if this tests weak, then more enquiry is needed. Their own impression is that most food sensitivities are ultimately trauma based (perhaps through the ancestral energy fields)—and that as the traumas are cleared, and as the body is healed, the sensitivities lessen. An important distinction the Daniels make is between food sensitivities to energy toxins, where a minute particle might trigger a reaction, and digestive intolerances, where the amount is crucial.

All those who work to treat severe allergies or sensitivities with energy psychology methods emphasise the need for caution and medical supervision. *Serious allergy reactions are obviously dangerous. Anaphylactic shock is a life-threatening medical crisis.* These cannot be safely tested in the same way that one might test the treatment of a phobia by exposure to the previously disturbing stimulus.

A question sometimes raised is that, if energy toxins are actually toxic, as Dr Callahan indicates, might it be harmful to use energy methods to eliminate reactions, especially if this means the person may then ingest more of the toxin? In response, I am reminded of Dr Callahan's observation that when his patient, Mary, was suddenly liberated from her phobia of water, she ran to his swimming pool, but did not jump in. Mary knew that she could not swim and so her normal life-preserving instincts were intact. I am inclined to think that, especially if the work is guided by muscle testing (including checks for reversals), the body will not generate false harmony with a substance that is actually causing damage—but, of course, I could be wrong.

My own approach to toxins and sensitivities

Whilst I mention the work of Radomski and others in relation to healing sensitivities and allergy-like reactions, my own experience in this area is limited. I do not offer directly to clear allergies and sensitivities per se—such work would be beyond my present scope of practice—and so I cannot verify from my own experience to what extent it is possible to clear allergy-like and sensitivity reactions. However, in the course of working with psychological presentations, it often becomes apparent that energy toxins may play a part. Pursuing a purely psychological perspective when the underlying issue may have a more physical and energetic basis would be unproductive. Moreover, there are very often clients who present with a combination of psychological and physical problems that, on investigation, almost always are rooted in a mixture of trauma and toxins. Identifying possible toxins, so that the person can experiment with avoiding them, can be crucial. Unless this is done, the person may be unable to respond to energy psychology methods. This is basic to TFT.

The identification of energy toxins through muscle testing should not be regarded as entirely objective or foolproof. Many factors can influence the outcome of muscle testing. However, it can provide useful hypotheses. These hypotheses are tested by observing the results when [a] the food or substance is neutralised with an energy method such as Callahan's '7 second treatment', or [b] the substance is avoided for a period of time. Muscle testing is not in itself the confirmation of the hypothesis. The only relevant test is whether the work guided by muscle testing is helpful to the client.

The Callahan 7 second toxin treatment is invaluable as a rapid means of neutralising toxins.[2] Its effect is easily demonstrated by before and after muscle testing. Moreover, it can function as a powerful confirmation that a toxin is blocking treatment if the TFT is found to work rapidly after the 7 second technique whereas prior to this it was severely blocked.

I also find that rubbing the neurolymphatic 'sore spot' whilst saying the name of the toxin, or simply thinking of it, can be very effective. Certainly it will usually clear the reversal linked to the toxin. To some extent, it is possible to apply ordinary TFT tapping, using a diagnosed sequence, and achieve some reduction in the potency of a toxin. Work with addictions inherently addresses toxins, and the associated reversals and cravings.

What I have found very important sometimes is the work with endogenous toxins, where a person's system has become sensitised to their own body's physiology, hormones, and neurotransmitters. In the case of people suffering intense and pervasive anxiety, I have often found that adrenaline toxicity and associated reversals, some-times with adrenaline addiction, can be central to the syndrome. It is quite easy to test for this in the normal way: muscle test "Adrena-line"; then "Adrenaline—I want to be well". If either of these test weak, then adrenaline is registering as an energy toxin. Similarly it is possible to work through a list of hormones and neurotransmitters, finding which ones muscle test weak, or cause reversals.

Endogenous energy toxins, when these are the body's natural substances, seem relatively easy to treat. I have found the following method, with variations, seems to work well. First I ask the person to tap the side of the hand, small intestine reversal point, and say, for example, "Even though my system is registering adrenaline as toxic—even though my system is addicted to adrenaline—even though my system and adrenaline are not in harmony—I com-pletely accept myself". This initial step has two functions, first that of correcting reversals in relation to the substance, and second the task of tuning the person's system to the target problem. Then I obtain a diagnosed tapping sequence for the target substance—e.g. by asking the person to say 'adrenaline' whilst muscle testing for the sequence of meridians that make the arm strong. If the name of the substance is muscle tested again, it will usually then register as strong and no longer as toxic.

Similarly, it is possible to muscle test a list of emotions to find ones which the person's system registers as toxic. Then the client can be asked to tap the side of the hand whilst saying "Even though my system registers anger (for example) as toxic—even though my system and anger are not in harmony—I completely accept myself". Then a diagnosed tapping sequence is carried out and the emotion is muscle tested again. Usually these are very easy to treat. Subsequently the person may experience the emotion as painful, but since it does not register as toxic, the additional spiralling reactions and reversal do not occur. It can be important to be precise about the emotion. For example, 'anxiety', 'terror', and 'panic' may all register differently. Neutralising the toxic effect of one may not neutralise other, similar but differently nuanced, emotions.

Trauma, toxins, reversal, and psychodynamic conflict

The three paradigms of trauma, toxins, and psychodynamic conflict are intertwined. Toxic experience (trauma) and chemical trauma (toxin) disrupt the body's energy flow. Psychodynamic conflict, stimulated by anxiety about the expression of a particular emotion or impulse, also blocks energy flow, causing it to register as toxic—as in Freud's original insights into the toxic nature of blocked libido, later elaborated by Wilhelm Reich (1948/1960). The blocked energy not only registers as toxic, but is associated with reversal. Regression along developmental and energetic pathways ensues, with cathexis of atavistic positions, such as infantile anxieties, phobias, and sexual desires, these generating further anxiety and shame. The psycho-energetic reversal gives rise also to destructive and self-destructive, anti-life trends—i.e. the preponderance of aggression and death instinct that classic psychoanalytic theoreticians noted in states of regression (e.g. Jacobson, 1964) and which energy psychologists recognise as characterising states of massive reversal. Cathexis of

developmentally atavistic positions, and the emergence of destructive (reversed) emotions and impulses, generate increased need for
psychodynamic defence, exacerbating the block on energy flow. In
such circumstances, the system is being poisoned by its own blocked
energy, registering as toxic, and generating stress responses. Wilhelm
Reich called this toxic blocked energy 'deadly orgone' (1952/1960).

This perspective brings the findings of energy psychology into
harmony with Freud's original (pre-1926) formulation of the genesis
of neurosis, as elaborated (controversially) by Reich (1948/1960):
anxiety or trauma creates a block in the flow of energy (libido); this
blocked energy is registered as toxic and generates further anxiety
(Freud;s 'actual neuroses' as a transformation of dammed-up libido);
the blocked flow also results in energetic reversal (Freud's regression);
the toxic nature of the blocked energy, combined with the reversal,
leads to developmental regression, with the cathexis of previously
abandoned psychoenergetic positions (the re-activation of infantile
sexual stages, including incestuous desires and primitive phantasies); the re-activation of infantile desires and phantasies, which are
unacceptable to the adult's conscious mind, results either in perverse
sexuality or is subject to repression, resulting in a neurosis. To this
classical perspective we can now add the role of energy toxins as
triggering blocks in the normal flow of subtle energy (libido), which
then create conditions in which the body's own energy is registered
as toxic.

Cautions regarding muscle testing for toxins

The startling phenomena of muscle testing, combined with observation of the important effects of energy toxins, and the benefits experienced when these are avoided or neutralised, can potentially lead to
excessive enthusiasm and confidence in the reliability of the method.
I find that muscle testing is most helpful if used with caution and
due regard for its inherent vagaries. It is rather like an extremely
useful measuring instrument, that provides invaluable data, and yet
possesses an inherent variability due to a wide range of factors that
influence the processes within both client and tester and the relationship between them. Whilst some studies have demonstrated a basic
validity and reliability of muscle testing (e.g. Cuthbert, S. C. & Goodheart, G. J., 2007; Jacobs, 1981; Monti et al. 1999), others have cast

doubt on these and emphasise the need for caution (e.g. Kenney et al. 1988; Klinkoski et al. 1990; Ludtke et al. 2001; Peterson et al. 1994; Teuber & Porch-Curren, 2003). Further research is needed. Whilst muscle testing generates hypotheses for further enquiry with the client, these obviously should not be presented as objective 'facts'. Excessive restrictions on diet and the use of other products are merited only if the results are clear in terms of benefit for the client.

The beliefs and prejudices of the examiner can influence the results of muscle testing. Frost (2002) reports the example of Dr John Diamond, who believed that everyone (unless reversed) would test weak with white sugar in their mouth. However, when other researchers tested this hypothesis their findings were different—and in cases of low blood sugar, white sugar in the mouth was sometimes strengthening. Similarly, Asha Clinton, developer of Seemorg Matrix, who uses muscle testing extensively in her approach, cautions in her workshops that it is quite possible, through force of will, to influence the outcome of the test. Muscle testing is an art rather than objective science—a mode of communication between client and therapist. Like all forms of human communication, it is prone to error, misunderstanding, conscious or unconscious deception, as well as having the potential to convey truth.

A further caution relates to the danger of engaging in a search to identify toxins whenever a client's problem fails to resolve rapidly or recurs after an apparently successful treatment with TFT or a derivative method. Sometimes the more relevant factor may be that other or deeper *psychological* aspects of the problem have yet to be addressed. To give a simple example, a phobic client may easily reach a zero level of subjective distress when thinking of the phobic object or situation whilst sitting in the therapist's office, but may experience a surge of anxiety when faced more directly with the stimulus for the fear. Such a phenomenon may have nothing to do with toxins but simply the fact that in vivo TFT is required. Clients who are phobic are often highly avoidant and manage to dissociate or otherwise block their cognitive-emotional processes such that the full extent of the relevant thought fields are not activated in the consulting room despite the therapist's best efforts. Other factors might include related traumas that had not been addressed, hidden blocking beliefs, or latent reversals that had not been identified. On the other hand, energy toxins *can* sometimes re-evoke previously treated anxieties.

As always, a stance of cautious enquiry is usually the most appropriate.

List of neurotransmitters

Although it is possible to obtain vials containing samples of these [e.g. from www.allergyantidotes.com] for the client to hold in their energy field whilst being muscle tested, it seems to work well often to have the client simply say the name of the substance. It does not seem to matter whether either the client or the therapist have much detailed idea of the nature of the substance and its functions.

Acetylcholine
Cholinesterase
Dopamine
Epinephrine
Gaba
Gluntamic acid
Histamine
Histidine

Malvin
Melanin
Melatonin
Norepinephrine
Phenylalamine
Serotonin
Taurine

List of hormones

There are many hormones in the human body. They include the following, any of which can be muscle tested.

Adrenalin
ACTH
Adrenocorticotropic Hormone
Aldosterone
Bradykinin
Calcitonin
Cholecystokinin
Cholesterol
Chorionic Gonadotropin
Corticosterone
Cortison
DHEA

Estrogen
Estradiol
Estriol
Estrone
Etiocholanolone
FSH
Glucagon
Gonadotropin
Growth Hormone
Hydrocortisone
Insulin
Lactogenic Hormone

Epinephrine
Epogen
Melatonin
Neurostensin
Olytosin
Parathyroid Hormone
Progesterone
Prolactin
T3—Tryodothyronine
T4—Thyroxine
TSH
Testosterone
Thyrotropic Hormone
Thyrotropin Releasing Hormone
Vasoactive Intestinal Hormone
Vasopressin

Lepsin
Luteinizing Hormone

Notes

1. Asha Clinton has developed a variety of sophisticated ways of incorporating allergy and sensitivity clearing into her Seemorg Matrix protocols. www.seemorgmatrix.org
2. Although the Callahan Techniques '7 second technique is not designed for use in medical emergencies, I know from personal experience with a family member in an allergic crisis that it can, on occasion, and in the absence of other medical assistance, be lifesaving.

CHAPTER ELEVEN

Working with the chakras

"Of course you must take a case history. Of course you must perform a clinical examination, and of course you must take notes, but, and this is a very important *but*, at some point you must stop all this busy 'doing'. You must be still. You must, in effect, just 'be', and in that state of 'being' you must listen to what the patient's body, mind, and spirit are trying to whisper to you in a language you will only understand if you allow yourself to tune in." [Charman, 2006, p. xv]

Whilst Thought Field Therapy and many of its derivatives address primarily the meridian system, it is also possible to work with the energy centres of the chakra system. Dr Callahan does indeed teach, in his Step B trainings, the adjunctive use of the chakra system as an occasional additional step after working with the meridian system. Others, particularly in the Seemorg Matrix approach, developed by Asha Clinton, work *primarily* with the chakras—whilst yet others, such as Dorothea Hover-Kramer (2002) work with meridians, chakras, and the biofield in a broad integrated energy psychotherapy.

I find that work with both the meridians and the chakras blends together very well. In common with some other practitioners, I have the impression that the chakras tend to be the natural focus for more deep-seated dysfunctional patterns of belief and emotional reactions, whilst the meridian system tends to express responses to more specific traumatic events or phobic anxieties. This is not an absolute distinction by any means and is more a matter of subtle degree.

The meridian and chakra systems together may be thought of as analogous to a 'skeleton' at the energy level—a main structure that acts as a vehicle for the biofield that surrounds the body. Within this analogy the chakras are like the backbone, the most crucial structures. The chakras are indeed arranged along the spine. Clairvoyants see them as spinning vortices of coloured energy. Tansley (1975) describes a 'subtle spine', of etheric matter, on which the fiery wheels of the chakras are arranged. This subtle spine consists of three streams of energy, two spirals moving around a central column—reflected also in the double helix of DNA.

Another analogy that makes some sense to me in comparing the meridians and the chakras is in terms of what happens when a file or programme is deleted from a computer. When a perturbation is 'deleted' from the meridian system, it usually remains gone. However, there can be circumstances that can trigger its re-installation. This may be viewed as similar to the way in which a deleted computer file remains in latent form on the hard drive, and can, given appropriate software, be reinstalled as an active file. Working with the chakras seems more equivalent to clearing a programme permanently from the hard drive.

The location and qualities of the chakras

Knowledge of chakras is a part of ancient traditions, found in Hindu, Buddhist, and other esoteric realms, and discerned intuitively by practices such as yoga. Crawford (1990) describes chakras as follows:

> "A chakra or force centre, is a junction on the surface of the etheric double where many strands of energy meet and pass one another— like major railway junctions. They receive and transmit energy and appear as dull, scarcely moving discs in the undeveloped person, but as rapidly whirling suns in the developed person. These centres are not physical things. They are whirlpools of force that swirl etheric, astral and mental matter into activity. The action being rotary, the result, as seen clairvoyantly, is a circular effect, like a fiery wheel." [p. 43]

Different writers present slightly different perspectives, but the general picture is fairly consistent across diverse accounts. Most commentators refer to seven major chakras running down the centre of the body, from the crown of the head to the base of the spine. A variety of minor chakras have also been noted; for example, Asha Clinton makes use of the left and right minor heart chakras, and the left and right root chakras.

Although not themselves physical or anatomical, the chakras do have neurophysiological correlates, such as high concentrations of neuropeptides. Thus, neurobiologist Candace Pert (1999) has described them as like 'minibrains' since they are centres where electrochemical information is received and processed.

According to the insights of David Tansley (1972), the primary subtle energy enters the centre of each chakra, where these are located in the etheric body. It seems likely that the energy Tansley refers to is that of Chi, prana, tachyon, or orgone — different terms that all designate an energy that is ubiquitous and essential to all living beings. The chakras then differentiate (or refract) the primary energy into secondary energies that flow along the 'nadis' — a term which may refer to something similar to the energy meridians of traditional Chinese Medicine. After the energy has passed through the nadis, the nervous system then responds, in turn stimulating endocrine glands associated with the particular chakras. The condition and level of activation of each chakra has a great bearing on the overall functioning of the body and mind. Tansley (1972) describes how a chakra can be in one of five states of arousal: [1] in one state, the chakra is clairvoyantly perceived as "a saucer-like depression, closed and inert, or rotating very slowly" (p. 25); [2] a state of beginning arousal is seen as a circle with a glowing point of energy in the centre, with a more rapid rotation; [3] further arousal gives the impression of a divided circle, the central vortex of energy glowing more brilliantly; [4] a still greater intensity of arousal is indicated by the circle appearing divided into four, this internal cross itself rotating "creating an effect of great beauty" (p. 26); the highest level of activity has the appearance of a fiery wheel "blazing and radiant throughout" (p. 26), more like a sphere than a wheel.

The main chakras are commonly described as follows:

- The first chakra, known as the root or base, is situated at the base of the spine, between the anus and the genitals. It is concerned with survival, 'rootedness' or 'groundedness', and the sense of security. Asha Clinton regards the root as having associations with feminine and mother aspects. Nelson (1994) comments: "The first chakra guides the development of a fetus and infant before it forms a bounded self ... For people centred at this chakra, relationships with others are dependent and clinging, based on need." [p. 163]. Cross (2006) links the root chakra to the negative emotions of insecurity, doubt, and many phobias. It is usually perceived as red.

- The second chakra, known as the sacral, is located a little higher, between the umbilicus and the pelvis. It is concerned with sexuality and the reproductive system. Pleasure in relationships and sexual activity is linked to the sacral chakra, but in its negative aspects, jealousy, envy, and lust are also found here (Cross, 2006). Nelson (1994) comments: "The second chakra operates throughout early childhood as self-boundaries gradually wall off a separate identity within the Ground, but are still far more permeable than those of most adults ... The primary modes of the second chakra are unbridled desire and free-form sexuality" [p, 163]. It is usually perceived as orange.

- An additional chakra not usually listed, but used by Asha Clinton, is that of the navel (situated just below the navel). This is thought of as the body's energy centre.

- The third chakra, known as the solar plexus, is situated under the sternum. It is commonly associated with issues of power and control. Nelson (1994) comments: "The consciousness of the third chakra infuses a young adult throughout his quest for a career and suitable mate as he establishes himself as an effective and competent force in the world ... People centred at this chakra are uncomfortable in the company of anyone operating at higher levels. Relationships are competitive and manipulative." [p, 163] Cross (2006) links the solar plexus chakra to depression and anxiety. It is usually perceived as yellow.

• The fourth, or heart, chakra is located in the mid chest. It is associated with love, compassion and the intelligence of the heart. Nelson (1994) comments: "The fourth chakra rises above attachments to the material and social worlds and toward an impassioned union with humanity, indeed with all sentient life. In its capacity to lift the self above the ego and initiate a gradual reopening to the Ground, it is the first spiritual level." [p. 163]. Tansley (1972) links it to the thymus gland, involved in the immune system and fight-flight reactions. He cautions against allowing excess energy to flow through the heart chakra. At his time of writing, in 1972, he commented: "At present the full functioning of this centre is unsafe due to man's point of inner development, which is reflected in the general imbalance of the average endocrine system. Energy flooding uncontrolled through this chakra would have devastating effects upon the personality of the person concerned." [p. 41]. Cross (2006) links the heart chakra to states of tearfulness, anxiety, depression, and detachment. It is usually perceived as green, perhaps mixed with pink.

• The fifth chakra is situated over the throat. It is thought to be associated with self-expression, particularly of the authentic self and of higher truths. Nelson (1994) comments: "The fifth chakra further reopens the self-boundary to the Ground, allowing an influx of higher consciousness that seeks creative expression through an expanded self. This is the level of majestic wisdom, access to universal symbols, surrender to divine power, and partial detachment from specific worldly outcomes." [pp. 163–164] Tansley (1972) links it to the thyroid gland. Emotional shock will affect this chakra, which governs the lungs and alimentary canal. Cross (2006) links the throat chakra with states of shyness, introversion, and paranoia. It is usually perceived as blue.

• The sixth, or brow, chakra is situated between the eyebrows, just above the eyes. It is associated with awareness, intuition, and spiritual vision. Nelson (1994) comments: "This is the level of benign sorcery, visionary power, and prophecy. It is character-ised by expanded vision and direct access to universal knowl-edge. Its primary mode is *insight*." [p. 164]. Tansley (1972) links it to the pituitary gland. Cross (2006) links the brow chakra with states of anger. It is usually perceived as a deep blue or indigo.

- The crown chakra is situated at the top of the head and is generally regarded as the link to higher spiritual energies and knowledge. Nelson (1994) comments: "The seventh chakra marks a return of self to Source, a voluntary dissolution of self-boundaries, a merger of a fully developed soul with its divine essence." [p. 164]. Tansley (1972) links it to the pineal gland, and adds some interesting points: "The crown chakra contains within it a replica of each chakra … Average and advanced man works through all his chakras, but the highly advanced initiate increasingly works through the counterparts in the crown chakra, all his life force being tuned in to the ultimate reality of the macrocosm … One may liken the crown chakra to a master control panel which processes information flowing in from the external environmental fields, and outward from the inner spiritual realms." [pp. 44–45] Asha Clinton regards the crown as having associations with masculine and father aspects. Cross (2006) links the crown chakra with states of melancholy and certain phobias. It is usually perceived as violet, gold, or brilliant white.

- Some commentators, including Dr Callahan, also refer to a higher, or halo, chakra located perhaps a couple of feet above the head.

Correspondences and links with other psycho-somatic-energy systems

Cross (2006) draws attention to many correspondences between individual chakras and particular glands, meridians, organs, muscles, emotions, spiritual connotations, and aspects of the central nervous system. In addition, he reports an inherent coupling relationship between certain chakras: thus, the crown and brow are linked to the base; the throat is linked to the sacral; and the heart is linked to the solar plexus.

The link between particular chakras and particular meridians can be useful to consider if a chakra appears unusually 'stuck' in some way. Cross (2006) describes how the meridian relationships can be used as a 'backup' energy system when working with the chakras. He lists the correspondences as follows:

the crown chakra—triple warmer or thyroid meridian;
the brow chakra—gallbladder meridian;
the throat chakra—large intestine and lung meridians;
the heart chakra—heart and small intestine meridians;
the solar plexus chakra—liver and stomach meridians;
the sacral chakra—spleen and pericardium meridians;
the root chakra—bladder and kidney meridians.

A meditative attunement to the chakras provides a window into infinitely deep realms of human existence, bridging physical, developmental, psychodynamic, and spiritual aspects. Nelson (1994) outlines how the opening of the seven major chakras correlates with the individual's personal and spiritual progression: "… the system of the seven *chakras* is a five-thousand-year-old way to integrate body, mind, and spirit. It elegantly maps the progress of personal consciousness from its first quickening within a living embryo to the highest stages of self-realisation and ultimate reunion with the divine Source." [p. 161]

How to work with the chakras

Just as it is possible to muscle test, diagnostically, for the correct TFT meridian sequence expressing the perturbations in a particular thought field, in a similar way we can discern sequences of chakras that may be relevant to the target problem. For example, the chakra sequence for a man I have just worked with in relation to his general state of stress was: sacral, solar plexus, sacral, brow, heart. Sometimes it may also be relevant to hold two chakras at once. All the usual principles of checking for reversals, including mini-reversals, and neurological disorganisation, apply in work with chakras just as when addressing the meridian system. Rather than tapping on energy points, as commonly done with the meridians, it seems more natural simply to touch or hold the chakras for a minute or so at a time. The therapist can use his or her own proxy muscle test to guide how long the client should hold each chakra.

To muscle test for sequence of chakras, the basic principles are the same as with testing for meridian sequence. When the client thinks of the target problem, the muscle will normally test weak. The various chakras can then be touched by the client's other hand in order to find one that will make the muscle test strong. That chakra can then be held for a few moments, perhaps for the duration of a one complete breath or longer, or can be gently rubbed for a few seconds. Then the next chakra is found that will make the muscle test strong when the person states or thinks of the target problem. This chakra is then stimulated by holding or rubbing. Then the next chakra is found—and so on, until the muscle remains strong when the person states or thinks of the target problem.

The meridians and chakras may be woven together in the same sequence. Thus, instead of thinking in terms of just the 14 main meridians, the clinician can bear in mind the additional 7 main chakras, and perhaps also various minor chakras. Of course it would take a long time to work randomly through 21 possible energy locations in order to find each specific point in a sequence. However, the experienced practitioner will be guided a great deal by intuition, which is then checked by muscle testing. In addition, the therapist may shorten the choice by muscle testing as to whether the meridians or the chakras are needed at any particular point. Often it seems that working through the meridians for a particular problem is a natural first step before proceeding to the chakras—and sometimes it may be appropriate to shift back from the chakras to the meridians. It can sometimes be the case that most of the perturbations have been cleared from the chakras but some remaining distress is still located in the meridians.

Working with the chakras often has a slower and more meditative quality compared to work with the meridians. Some clients like to speak of the various thoughts and emotions that emerge at each chakra. When addressing target problem, the chakras seem to function like energy prisms, refracting the perturbations into their underlying emotional colours and aspects.

As the particular chakras come up in turn, it is possible to tune in to the associated psychological quality and injury at each point. Thus, the heart tends to relate to emotional injury, the solar plexus to injuries to personal power, the sacral to injuries to sexuality and creativity-generativity, the root to fundamental security, the throat to capacities for personal expression, the brow to injuries or inhibitions in perception, and the crown to injuries to spirituality. If one of these predominates, or comes up several times in a sequence, this may help client and therapist to tune in to a core component of the disturbance. For example, I have noticed that if the brow chakra is significant in a sequence it may relate to difficulties a person has had in tolerating their own perceptions of the mother of infancy (or father), or of a current partner. This may express a personal 'blinding' owing to the true perception being intolerable.

Example of working through emotional 'blindness'

In the case of a man struggling to come to terms with his recognition of the exploitative and abusive behaviour of his ex-partner, the following chakra points came up in sequence: heart (reflecting his deep injury in 'matters of the heart' in relation to the ending of the relationship); solar plexus (expressing his sense of loss of personal power and his feelings of helplessness); brow (relating to his disavowal of perceptions of his ex-partner's treachery); throat (indicating his difficulties in personal expression); heart (as he returns to his emotional injury); chin (relating to the shame evoked by his partner's rejection of him); crown (expressing his need for new sources of inspiration and energy, and for reassessing his life goals); heart; solar plexus; brow; throat; solar plexus, brow. At this point he spoke of his thought that if he accepts his recognition of his ex-partner's characteristics, he is then faced with further worries about his children being in her care. He then spoke of his realisation that early events in their relationship had led him to know that something was seriously wrong, but he had overruled this perception at the time; this had caused him to lose faith in all his judgements. He talked of his realisation of how angry he felt towards her. The heart chakra then came up again as the next one in the sequence—expressing his further working through of this heart-felt emotional injury. This was followed by: brow; heart; crown; throat; crown; heart; crown—expressing his working through of injuries to his heart and perception, and his seeking of new inspiration and spiritual nurturance. He talked then of his realisation that he had misperceived the neediness she had displayed at one time for love—and he saw how she had now discarded him. The brow chakra came up again—indicating how he was continuing to repair the distortions in his perception.

Working through the chakras in relation to a weight problem

A woman presented with a difficulty in losing weight. Muscle testing indicated a 'desire' to be fat and not to be attractive to men—a position that was entirely at odds with her conscious view. After muscle testing various possibilities as to why this might be so, we arrived at the hypothesis (validated by muscle test) that she believed she must not be slimmer or more attractive than her mother, who had herself been overweight. She spoke of paradoxical messages and attitudes expressed by her mother—overfeeding her and insisting that she eat everything on her plate, on the one hand, whilst also putting her on a diet at a young age. We worked with the chakras using the phrases "the patterns of eating given to me by my mother" and "trying to be what my mother wanted". The following sequence emerged: sacral; heart; brow; heart; throat. At this point she suddenly remarked "my mother lost a little boy before me"—then indicated astonishment at the implications of this new revelation that she had been a replacement child. The following chakras then came up: solar plexus; sacral; heart; brow. We also concluded with meridian tapping on: eb c a e c. Muscle testing then revealed a strong positive desire to lose weight and to be attractive to men—a striking contrast to the earlier response.

Working through the meridians to facilitate clearing the chakras:

E.g. 1. Sexual guilt and anxiety in the sacral chakra
One woman was troubled by obsessional anxieties and rituals, particularly focussed around a fear that she had sexually transmitted infection on her hands and might contaminate others. Her obsessions had begun in adolescence when she felt she must wash her hands continuously because they were 'dirty' from masturbation. She also felt anxious and guilty about a period of promiscuity some years back. As we worked through the chakras in relation to her obsessional anxieties, we found that the sacral chakra played a central role, but it did not clear even after several minutes of her holding this point. I asked her to tap on her index finger for a minute or two, whilst thinking of all her feelings of guilt about sex, followed by further tapping under the eye, under arm, and collar bone. We then returned to the sacral chakra, which now cleared. This seemed to illustrate the way in which great feelings of guilt and anxiety about

sex were located in the sacral chakra—but we had to divert to tapping on relevant aspects of the meridian system, to do with guilt and
anxiety, before the sacral chakra itself cleared.

E.g. 2. Guilt and anxiety blocking the heart chakra
A woman was troubled by severe and deep-rooted self-hatred, a
primal sense of guilt about her very existence. This had led to many
serious mental health problems, including suicidal states of mind. It
seemed likely that the origin of this self-hatred lay in her mother's
postnatal depression, wherein she failed to experience a sense
of being lovingly welcomed into the world. As we addressed this
through the chakra system, the heart (loving connection) and brow
(perception) chakras seemed particularly important. However, at a
certain point the process seemed to stick, although there had been
no reversals detected initially. A further check for reversals revealed
one in relation to deservedness, and also to a lesser extent in relation
to safety. These did not easily clear. We shifted to tapping the index
finger, large intestine meridian, since this is often associated with
guilt, and then moved to under the eye. Following this, we returned
to the chakras, which now cleared.

Work with meridians can combine seamlessly with attention to
the chakras. Usually one might work through the meridians first—
but then, especially if the target issue is not clearing easily, or if the
target is a very deep-seated pattern, then its location and encoding
within the chakras can be addressed. The process of clearing perturbations and dysfunctional patterns from the chakras has a deeper
and more introspective quality than that experienced when working
with meridians. The slower process of spending a minute or more
at each chakra facilitates the emergence of new thoughts, memories
and insights in relation to the target problem.

Installing and eliminating qualities through chakras

Some writers suggest 'spinning' the chakras by moving the hand
in a circular motion at each point. To eliminate a perturbation, or
dysfunctional belief, from a chakra, the movement would be anticlockwise (picturing the body as a clock facing outwards); to install
a new belief or desired quality, the movement would be clockwise.
However, there seems to be some lack of clarity over this question of

the direction of movement, since some practitioners appear to state the opposite; moreover, there can be much confusion resulting from a reference to 'clockwise' or 'anticlockwise' without specifying carefully the orientation of the 'clock'. Personally, in my present practice I do not make use of the 'spinning' method.

Asha Clinton recommends the upward movement through all the chakras from the root to the crown for installing positive qualities. This is often useful after the relevant traumas and other adverse experiences have been cleared. Sometimes there has been a dearth of positive experiences and benign figures in the person's life, thus creating a deficit of positive internal resources. Just as in using EMDR, it can be important to endeavour to 'install' resources by adding these in through affirmation, imagination, or emphasis upon such positive experiences as there have been in the person's life. This is also somewhat akin to John Diamond's use of affirmations related to particular meridians [e.g. "I am full of hope" whilst tapping the thyroid meridian point, or "I am secure" whilst tapping the spleen meridian]. It can, however, be important to check for reversals against the positive installations. For example, after clearing various experiences and patterns of rejection from her chakra system, I worked with a woman to install feelings of love and security. After we had worked through the chakras with this idea, she was tearful, saying she wished she could feel these things but did not. I checked for reversals ["I am 100% willing to feel loved and secure"], which tested weak. After correcting this, we tried again. This time her response was quite different. She reported that she had found herself thinking of various experiences during her life in which she had felt loved and cared for.

Seemorg Matrix

The method of working with the chakras called Seemorg Matrix, as developed by Jungian psychotherapist Asha Clinton, is undoubtedly one of the most deep and comprehensive of the energy psychology approaches. In a manner consistent with her analytic background, Clinton addresses the childhood roots of the presenting problem, as well as the matrices of dysfunctional cognitions that have arisen from traumas and other adverse experiences. This attention to deep patterns of core cognitions makes Seemorg Matrix particularly suitable for work with people with personality disorders.

Competent use of Seemorg Matrix requires training with Asha Clinton or one of her appointed teachers. The brief outline here is intended only as a schematic introduction.

Clinton makes an important link between what she calls the initiating trauma (the recent event that has precipitated the need for help), and the originating trauma (the childhood event(s) that predisposed the person to repeat thematically similar events as an adult and to be particularly vulnerable to these events). Both of these are treated by removing the relevant perturbations from the chakras. In addition, the *patterns* of thought, emotion and behaviour that have resulted from the childhood traumas are treated. Thus one of the basic Seemorg approaches is to treat the following components by clearing the perturbations in the chakras: [1] the originating trauma(s) and aspects; [2] the more recent initiating trauma(s) and aspects; [3] the connection between the originating and initiating traumas, using a phrasing formula such as "because X happened in my childhood, I now do Y"; [4] the traumatic patterns, using phrasing such as "all the times and ways in which X happened"; [5] the core beliefs that have resulted from the traumas.

An important technical feature of Clinton's approach is that the client is invited to select one chakra that is particularly relevant to the target problem. This may be done through simple intuitive choice, or through muscle testing. The client then keeps one hand on this chakra throughout the subsequent sequence, whilst the other hand moves progressively down the chakras beginning at the crown. In this way a bioelectrical circuit is created between two chakras at each point in the sequence—and this may play a significant role in the effectiveness of the Seemorg method. Clinton also makes use of some minor chakras, giving rise to a total of 12, and routinely includes in addition the central meridian point at the chin.

In common with many contemporary psychologists and psychotherapists at the forefront of the new effective methods, Clinton sees trauma at the root of most emotional and psychological problems. She defines trauma as follows:

"A trauma is any occurrence which, when we think of it or it is triggered by some present event, evokes difficult emotions and/or physical symptoms, gives rise to negative beliefs, desires, fantasies, compulsions, obsessions, addictions or dissociation, blocks the development of positive qualities and spiritual connection, and fractures human wholeness." [*Seemorg Matrix The Basic Manual*, 2005, p. 11].

and she adds that, given this perspective, psychotherapists primarily treat the consequences of traumas, which are:

"the intense and negative emotions, the physical sensations, symptoms, and involuntary movements, along with the resulting negative beliefs, desires, compulsions, fantasies, obsessions, and addictions that either remain dissociated or are experienced, even expressed, in the present." [p. 12]

Thus, it is possible to see that Seemorg Matrix, and similar methods, may be able to resolve most psychological disorders, and may also help in the case of psychoses and physical diseases that may, in part, have an emotional or traumatic basis.

For Clinton, traumas involve a "fracturing of human wholeness" [2005, p. 13] such that the person is no longer fully present to him or her self. She also explains that traumas and all their associated emotions, sensations, beliefs, fantasies, addictions, and so forth, become a 'template for future experience', a working unit like Jung's idea of the 'complex'. Subsequent traumas interact with this complex or template so as to mutually confirm each other and entrench the belief that this is how things are. Thus the trauma complex becomes reality for that person—"a grid through which negative experience is selectively taken in" [p. 13]. Trauma cuts the person off from their own personal centre and also from spiritual light, resulting in 'a life lived in darkness'.

The Seemorg approach allows for many different varieties of reversal to be muscle tested, based in the extensive matrices of dysfunctional cognitions. Commonly these relate to concerns for safety, deservedness, secondary gain, identity, fears of deprivation, fears of being criticised or humiliated, belief that resolution of the problem is not possible, and other fears regarding the consequences of becoming free of the problem. Reversals are repaired by rubbing the neurolymphatic 'sore spots' on the side of the chest, and repeating the kind of phrasing suggested by Gary Craig, along the lines of "Even though I feel ... I deeply and completely love and accept myself and forgive myself ...". As with other approaches, the Seemorg method begins with routine checks of neurological disorganisation (using the palm over the head check) and dehydration (tugging on a strand of hair or pinch of skin to check that the muscle does not go weak).

An innovative tactic for reducing the problem of reversals is the use of what is termed the 'Seemorg Covenant'. This involves first muscle testing, and treating, two particular Core Belief Matrices. One of these relates to willingness to recover and the potential secondary gains from remaining ill or suffering. The second concerns the willingness of the *unconscious mind* to heal the wounds in various levels of the person's system. After all these potential reversals have been treated, the client is invited to repeat a brief statement, somewhat similar to that used by Larry Nims in his BeSetFreeFast, expressing the intention that every trauma or traumatic pattern that is addressed will be fully and permanently treated.

Asha Clinton has compiled many matrices of core beliefs, concerning self, the world, and relationships with others, many of which develop from trauma or other adverse early circumstances. Each negative belief is paired with a realistic positive belief. Muscle testing can be used to find which negative beliefs register as present for the person. These are then cleared by repeating the negative belief as the client places a hand on each chakra, moving down from the crown. In this procedure with the negative beliefs there is no need to use a stationary hand. With very disturbed clients, who have experienced substantial and repeated trauma and other adverse events, several rounds of chakras may be required before muscle testing indicates that the negative belief has been cleared. Once the negative cognition is no longer experienced as true, the associated positive belief can be installed. For example, if the negative belief is "I deserve bad treatment", the positive belief to be installed could be "I deserve to be well treated". To install the positive belief, the client selects the most relevant chakra for a stationary hand, and then moves up the main chakras, repeating the new belief at each point. In her emphasis upon the importance of working with the core beliefs that have developed from traumas, Clinton is in line not only with contemporary cognitive therapy (particularly Young's schema focussed therapy), but also Francine Shapiro's Eye Movement Desensitisation and Reprocessing [EMDR], and other highly effective modern therapies.

Seemorg can also be used to install positive qualities—for example, empathy, compassion, intuition, patience, fortitude, elegance, courage—or any other desired personal quality. This is done in a similar way to installing positive beliefs, by repeating the name of the quality whilst moving the hand upwards to each chakra, beginning at the root. Repetitions of the name of the desired quality can then be made on a daily basis for some months.

Like others in the energy psychology field, Clinton has developed ways of resolving food/substance sensitivities and allergy-like reactions. As always, great care should be taken when working with true allergies, which can generate life-threatening anaphylactic shock. However, she tends to recommend treating these sensitivities as an adjunct to work with other traumas. In this process, the client may hold a sample of the substance, or a vial of water carrying the energetic imprint of the substance (based on the principles of EAV, which stands for Electro Acupuncture according to Voll), or may place on his or her body a piece of paper with the word of the substance written on it. At the same time the Seemorg procedure for clearing traumas is followed, even though the target trauma may not appear directly related to the substance sensitivities. My impression is that Asha Clinton recognises the importance of food and substance sensitivities, and the havoc they can wreak on a person's energy system, but she aims to clear them as rapidly and efficiently as possible so as to allow the main focus to be upon healing the traumas to mind, body, and soul, that have fractured the person's wholeness and capacity to be fully present to self, others, and to the spiritual source or centre.

The Seemorg focus on negative core beliefs can provide a useful starting point for deeper exploration of the client's personality and formative experiences. For example, one man was muscle tested for a statement in the Seemorg 'boundaries' matrix: "Others can do anything they want to do sexually with me when they want to". This tested strong, indicating this idea was believed to be true within his mind-body-energy system. He had no idea how such a belief or attitude might have arisen. Further enquiry raised the hypothesis of preverbal sexual abuse by an older boy who was known to have been hostile and disturbed—and this was then processed using the Seemorg trauma protocol. This then led to thoughts of feeling inferior to his sister who was regarded as the clever one, and who also had made no secret of her early hostility towards her younger brother. The man reported a general feeling that he was intellectually inferior and defective. As this was explored further, he realised this was based on a more fundamental view of himself as essentially defective in some way. His associations then flowed to his knowledge that his mother had preferred girls and had been disappointed when he had been born. He recognised also that his mother had almost certainly become withdrawn from him during his second year of life because of the suicide of her own mother at that time. As he proceeded through the Seemorg process in relation to this trauma, he experienced vivid and intense sensations at certain chakras—a sense of utter collapse as he held the central heart chakra, and a sensation of bleeding and flowing out of himself at the navel chakra. After finishing the trauma protocol he felt a great sense of peace and muscle testing indicated that the distress relating to his mother's early withdrawal had been cleared. Thus, by beginning with a belief within the boundaries matrix, the work had plunged into a variety of deeper traumas: the possible early sexual abuse from a hostile older boy; the hostility from his sister; his feeling of intellectual inferiority; his general sense of being defective; his sense of being a disappointment to his mother; the trauma of his mother's withdrawal from him in his second year. This illustrates the rapid and deep flow of psychodynamic material that can take place during Seemorg work, especially if both therapist and client are receptive to this.

There are now many Seemorg protocols and specific workshop trainings, focussed on different target problems, including personality disorders, wounds to the body, and physical illness. The basic Seemorg method is so elegant and simple that the limits of its application are unknown. As is the case with some other energy approaches, Seemorg reflects the personality and personal qualities of its developer, Asha Clinton. Not only does she bring to her clinical work an academic background in cultural anthropology, as well as training and many years of experience in Jungian psychotherapy, but also a deep grounding in meditative spiritual practice. The latter may have contributed significantly to the impression of remarkable coherence, clarity, and order in Asha Clinton's writing and teaching.

Attunement, attention, and presence—on 'seeing' chakras

Attunement to the chakras can enhance the practitioner's intuitive knowing of the client, facilitating more accurate and subtle interventions. With practice, it is possible to 'see' the chakras and their condition. This is not a physical seeing whereby light falls on the retina of the eye, but more like a sensing in a visual modality. The seeing is *in the mind's eye* rather than in the physical eye. It may be easier for some people than others—and there may be variation in the sensory modalities with which different people access the information. The way it works for me is as follows. I sit in a relaxed and receptive state (as I aim to be most of the time when I am working therapeutically) and I inwardly ask to see the client's chakras. Usually I can then 'see' the chakras, in particular colours and states of excitation, imposed upon or within the client's body. The ones that stand out or appear unusually subdued, 'greyed out', or dead may be those that require particular attention.

For example, this morning I noticed that a client's heart chakra appeared particularly fiery and red. This began to make some sense as he went on to speak of his dawning awareness of intense, but mostly hidden, anger relating to abusive experiences in his childhood. He spoke of how his anger had fuelled his dedication to helping those who are vulnerable and suffering. Thus his anger, combined with compassion for suffering humanity, was naturally expressed in the impression of a flaming red heart chakra. However, he feared that if he lost his anger he might lose his motivation. I noticed that the other chakra that particularly stood out was the brow, a vivid deep blue. Therefore I invited him to hold his heart and brow chakras whilst he reflected on what he had been saying—his feelings of being over-whelmed with anger but fearing that loss of his anger would mean loss of his motivation. After a couple of minutes he reported feeling very calm, saying he felt a kind of freedom and also an inner peace and silence.

Another patient presented with long-standing fibromyalgia, suffering pains all over her body in her joints and muscles. As she talked about this I 'saw' her heart chakra as if it had been blasted away. Initially I had no idea why it had this appearance—but later she talked of her four very traumatic marriages and her preference for living alone now. It began to seem quite likely that her emotional traumas, the injuries to her heart chakra, had contributed to the expression and experience of somatic pain.

In another example from today, I 'observed' that a woman's heart chakra had an appearance like a tired and drooping water plant. The context of her discourse evoked the phrase 'heart weary', as an expression of her state of emotional exhaustion in relation to men. I did not immediately comment on this but continued listening and observing. The image of the drooping plant gradually elaborated into a scene of a stagnant pond in her heart chakra area. A little later in the session, she had become more lively and I 'saw' some flowers on stalks growing out of the dank watery scene. Then, to my astonishment, she spoke of a slip of the tongue she had made at work in referring to a situation as 'stagnant' when her conscious meaning had been 'static'. This had led her to reflect on a sense of herself, or aspects of her life, as somehow being *like a stagnant pond*. I did not tell her of my own prior image of the pond, but continued to listen. Her narrative prompted me then to comment that she seemed to be speaking of a lack of a replenishing and refreshing flow in and out, as with a stagnant pond, and her feeling that although there was a man in her life who had impregnated her physically, she was lacking a sense of emotional intercourse that could make her feel psychologically fertile and creative. She found this a particularly apt perspective—and went on to speak of feeling weary of it all, again linking to the 'heart weary' phrase that had occurred to me earlier. Although I might have discerned a somewhat similar meaning in her discourse without attention to her chakras, I feel my receptiveness to chakra imagery gave rise to a clearer resonance through the shared metaphor of the stagnant pond (even though I had not explicitly revealed this sharing).

Thus it appears that the chakras have a communicative-transmittive function, providing the energetic component of the unconscious communication described by Freud [1912c]:

> "[the analyst] must turn his own unconscious like a receptive organ towards the transmitting unconscious of the patient. He must adjust himself to the patient as a telephone receiver is adjusted to the transmitting microphone." [p. 116]

When two (or more) people are closely attuned, it seems their chakras are engaged in continual communication. However, just as Freud cautioned that the analyst needs to be free of resistances that would distort perception of the patient's communications, similarly, the chakra-oriented psychotherapist must aim to be as open as possible to communications from his or her own energy system.

Certain chakra patterns become apparent in relation to different personalities and mood states. Very depressed people often appear to have chakras that are dark or switched off. One deeply suicidal young woman was asked to observe her own chakra system in her mind's eye (as part of our efforts to address the energetic aspects of her condition); she reported them all to be black, except for the root that was fiery. This had an ominous 'flames of hell' quality, as if sucking all her life force downwards into the earth. Shortly afterwards, she died—not of active suicide but by succumbing to some kind of flu-like condition. Those who have experienced sexual trauma may give the appearance of a blacked out (or burnt out) sacral chakra. People with a particularly spiritual orientation will often appear to have a very lively and vivid crown chakra, with all the others alight and somehow streaming upwards. More earth-bound people may appear to have chakras streaming downwards.

People vary in their preferred or dominant sensory modality. Psychoanalysts and psychotherapists often have a strong orientation to the auditory modality. Physical and body therapists may be more kinaesthetically dominant. It can be helpful to try to develop additional modalities of sensing. John Cross (2006), a physiotherapist who also uses a variety of energy healing modalities, gives an interesting description of his use of what he calls 'listening posts', which are areas of the body that enable the practitioner to tune in to energy imbalances in the client's system. He describes how the 'vault hold' may be used, particularly in craniosacral therapy, whereby the therapist's hands are placed under the occipital area at the back of the head. He writes:

> "The contact must be light and 'airy', with no pressure whatsoever ... After approximately one to two minutes a 'cranial rhythm' should be felt... There are many schools of thought as to exactly what is being felt—some authorities insist that it is the physical movement of the CSF, whereas others would say that it is the flow of chi or vital force ... This energetic sensation can be likened to the movement of the tide on a beach—it is in constant flow. It is important that you feel this rhythm for a few minutes before you begin with the analysis. Your brain should be 'in neutral' as much as possible during this phase ... After a short while, a definite shift of emphasis will be perceived ... this is when yours and the patient's vital forces are resonating in the alpha-theta frequency ... Once this has been reached, the task of 'body dowsing' and 'tuning in' can be commenced—and *not before*.

The next phase of analysis using the vault hold involves the use of thought and intention. These are both powerful tools and can be quite manipulative, so it is best to use them wisely and with deference to the task in hand. Now you ask questions about the patient's chakra energy system. On no account should you speak aloud or obviously change your hand position to suggest to the patient that something is occurring … When the answer to the question is yes … the rhythm will appear to stop or stall. It will recommence after a few seconds …" [pp. 251–252]

Although this is an account by a physical therapist who uses hands-on touch, I believe it contains insights valuable to psychotherapists who do not touch their clients. Cross describes waiting patiently as a resonance and attunement is developed between therapist and patient, and then, when in that meditative and receptive state, silently asking questions and 'listening' for the response that he perceives through his hands. The psychotherapist too can 'listen' in a variety of modalities (without touching the client). One can observe subtle changes in the client's breathing, posture, skin colour, muscular tone etc., and may also sense shifts in one's own body sensations, as well as information appearing in one's 'mind's eye'. By sensing in these multiple modalities it becomes possible to 'see' where the problem lies and be guided more deeply and clearly by intuitive knowing.

There are many ways of working with the chakras. Each practitioner can find their own variants. For example, I have recently found that having one hand holding the two bladder 1 points at the corner of each eye and the nose, with the middle finger on the forehead brow chakra (part of the TAT pose developed by Tapas Fleming), whilst the other hand rests on the chakra most relevant to the target problem or issue, can be helpful in generating relevant new insights and perspectives. A woman was very worried that her daughter might be repeating some of her own tendencies to be over-conscientious and depressive, and was wondering what she might best do to help. After a few moments with one hand in the partial TAT pose and the other on her heart chakra, she smiled peacefully and remarked that she realised her daughter had to find her own way.

The chakras may be considered not only centres of energy but also of *intelligence*. By placing attention on a particular chakra and seeking 'advice' regarding an issue or problem, the perspective most relevant to that chakra's role and function may often emerge into consciousness. As with many aspects of energy-based work, what is required may be receptive attention rather than hard work, effort, and active enquiry. Since this quality is greater than conscious mental attention, but rather involves one's whole being, the term 'mindfulness', derived from meditative practice and popularised in contemporary cognitive therapy, may be better substituted by Asha Clinton's concept of 'presence'.

Esoteric aspects of the chakras

The study of the chakras leads into many esoteric realms that one might study for a long time. Tansley (1984) provides some windows into these, linking to the writings of Alice Bailey (e.g. Bailey, 1995). He indicates how each chakra is linked to one of the so-called '7 rays', these being different energetic qualities that provide the components or building blocks of the personality. Each person has their own particular constellation of these 7 rays, accounting, in part, for the rich variation in human temperaments. It is possible to develop intriguing personality profiles based on the configurations of the 7 rays, which help to reveal some of the inherent tensions there can be within the makeup of a person's temperament (Hodson, 1953; Lansdowne, 1989; 1993).

CHAPTER TWELVE

Some thoughts on Tapas Acupressure Technique [TAT]

"That was amazing—I saw a door opening in my head— loads of stuff was pouring out—like angels flying! That was the most powerful thing I've ever done!"

[A comment by a woman having just done a couple of minutes of a few brief steps of TAT on her bitterness about her dead father who had abandoned her at age 4; previously she had used other energy psychology methods extensively, without such dramatic effects.]

I t is in a mood of reverence that I begin writing about TAT—the inspired method developed by California acupuncturist Tapas Fleming. This is an awesome and profound approach to emotional healing—startling in its seeming simplicity yet full of mystery at its core. The client holds two hands around the head in a particular pose, whilst focusing on a sequence of thoughts and perspectives in relation to the trauma, anxiety, physical illness, or other form of distress. It is then as if the person's own hands become transformed into those of a healer, as the mental, physical, and energetic residues of pain are gently cleared.

273

The human mind and body appear to run on a combination of thought and energy. Our thoughts direct the form and direction of the energy—although mostly we may be unaware of this. Tapas Fleming has identified a sequence of core thoughts about the target problem that a person is invited to focus upon whilst holding a pose in which the fingers of one hand hold the first bladder meridian points in the corner of each eye, as well as the third eye chakra, and the other hand holds the occipital area at the back of the skull. The sequence of thoughts—the steps of TAT—involve (schematically): [1] an acceptance of the problem; [2] an alternative or opposite idea (e.g. that the problem is healed or that the original statement is not true); [3] a thought to do with healing of the *origins* of the problem; [4] a thought of healing of all the *places* the problem has been stored in the mind, body and life; [5] acknowledgement and healing of any part of the self may have benefited from the problem; [6] a thought to do with forgiveness of self and others; [7] a thought of seeking forgiveness from those who may have suffered through the person having the problem; [8] a thought of healing any remaining aspects. After each step the person is asked what he or she experienced while doing it. Full details of TAT can be obtained through the material available from the Tapas Fleming's website (www.tatlife. com) and the method should be learned through workshops run by official teachers of TAT. I also recommend that potential practitioners take at least one workshop with Tapas Fleming herself, since so much of the essence of TAT is conveyed through her personal presence.

Trapped in error

Through the brief process of TAT, it seems that the person's mind-body-energy system *realises* that it had been trapped in an error—in thinking that a trauma or injury was still happening—and had become attached to, and *identified with,* the trauma. In that moment of realisation, the system is set free from the past to experience its joy and well-being in the present. What had been a frozen instance of pain, stretched through time to darken the present, is illuminated and melted in the light and warmth that flood in through the simple TAT pose. All the underpinnings, ramifications, and associated complications are similarly washed away in the gentle flow of energy released in TAT. The person realises "I am not that bad thing that happened—and I do not have to remain attached to it".

Thus TAT appears to open a window to healing—a portal to grace—with almost limitless applications. It is indeed simple, but there are many subtleties in using it effectively. A key aspect of Tapas Fleming's approach is the yoga-inspired idea of the contemplation of opposites. By considering first the thought that "this trauma happened", followed then by the thought that "it's over and I am Ok", the person tends to become free of identification with the trauma-based point of view. A space opens up between the contrasting ideas—and in this space there is a centre of peace. At a deep level, not necessarily consciously articulated, the person becomes aware that he or she is more than the body and more than the ego—the ego being really just a precipitate of identifications with words, images, and roles offered by the socio-cultural world (including the family).

Tapas Fleming explains that the focus on the opposites is not done in order to impose a positive belief over the negative one. It is not a form of simplistic positive thinking. First the problem is acknowledged and accepted. This is important because up to this point the person is likely to be in a state of resisting the belief or thought at the same time as wishing it were not true. Then, by contemplating the opposites, we have access to the wide spectrum of possible responses and thoughts in relation to our situation. We do not have to become identified and stuck with any one point of view. An important part of this is to become detached from our emotions—not in order to deny our emotions but to be able to accept and observe them.

Information, energy and light

Like Dr Callahan, Tapas Fleming emphasises that our body-mind-energy systems run on information, and this information organises our thoughts, emotions, physiology, and behaviour. Unhelpful information may become encoded in our system as a result of trauma or faulty teaching and programming by our caregivers, teachers, and other significant people. When this faulty information is accessed, whilst the person is in the TAT pose, it is rapidly exposed to re-evaluation in the light of healing, and will then, often more or less instantly, clear from the system. As a result, the person's thoughts, emotions, physiology and behaviour immediately change in a positive direction. Tapas quotes the work of cell biologist Bruce Lipton, who surveys a vast amount of evidence that our beliefs and perceptions profoundly influence our physiology and genetic response at fundamental levels. TAT demonstrates this rapid effect on both emotions and the body through shifts in our thoughts.

Tapas is fond of pointing out how a person appears to glow with light after a session of TAT. She links this with the emerging research indicating that cells communicate through tiny amounts of light—biophotons. When in the grip of depression or fear, a person appears subtly dark—but after TAT this darkness has been replaced by light.

Traumas imprinted in the mind and body are like whirlpools, described in Indian yogic traditions as vrittis. These act as vortices sucking our attention into their forcefield of negative emotions of fear and anger. When our mind is full of vrittis, our capacities to think calmly and to relate to others are impaired. TAT acts to still the mind, calming the vrittis, allowing clarity of thought and loving relatedness to others to emerge.

Tapas speaks of a person's problem as being like a hologram, such that whichever aspect is presented it contains the whole issue within it. Even just a tiny filament of the problem connects to the whole that is contained within the whirlpool of the turmoil. For this reason, it does not matter where the work begins with TAT. Whatever the client presents is likely to be a good place to begin.

Because thoughts are so important in their capacity to influence our emotions and physiology, Tapas emphasises attention to their subtle qualities—of mass, energy, space, and time. As she states in her Professionals' Manual [2007], "Thoughts are things. Even though they are invisible and not commonly measured, they do indeed exist" [p. 34]. She points out, for example, that a person may refer to feelings of heaviness (*mass*) as they speak of a problem, or may display strong emotions (*energy*) as they focus on it, or may give the impression of being far away and alone (*space*), or the element of *time* may be present in the client's account. Where a thought constellation has any of these qualities of weight, emotional energy, space, and time, this may be an indication of stagnant or stuck energy which needs to be released and allowed to flow.

Tapas recommends that the TAT practitioner seek to achieve a stillness of mind—partly by using TAT to clear as many as possible of the whirlpools of turmoil. By resting in a state of inner peace, like the surface of a still pool, the impact of the 'pebble of your client's thought' can be observed more clearly. She also emphasises the importance of the practitioner's transcending of ego-involvement in the process of healing. Instead of the practitioner needing to be clever or highly educated in order to facilitate the client's healing, it is more "a sense that we are resting in grace" (p. 31 of TAT Professionals' Manual), witnessing what takes place. It is also advisable for the practitioner not to be too focused on emotions, which can be a compelling realm for many psychotherapists. Tapas Fleming's stance is similar to the 'mindfulness', derived from yogic practice and advocated by contemporary cognitive therapists.

The 'veils of thought'

Sometimes the direct access to the target problem is blocked and the blockage itself has to be addressed. One metaphor that Tapas Fleming uses is of the river of healing which the practitioner and client enter together when doing TAT. At times there will be hidden obstacles that hold the client locked in to the problem and prevent him or her being carried by the river of healing. She describes these obstacles as often consisting of "subtle layers of thought ... invisible, impenetrable veils ... so thin, often made of only one thought" [p. 39 of TAT Professionals' Manual]. Such thoughts consist of beliefs that healing is not possible, the problem is too big, too difficult, too complex, or too confusing, or that there are dangers (to self or others) inherent in recovery. These correspond both to the 'automatic thoughts' identified by cognitive therapists and to the reversals addressed in TFT and other energy psychology approaches. The TAT approach to these is to do the Step One as either the problematic thought itself, or the idea of "the event that put this thought in place". This is then followed, in the normal way of Step Two, by an idea representing the opposite. The blocking belief or automatic thought may then have cleared, but, if not, the further steps of TAT can be followed. After the 'veils of thought' have been adequately addressed, the original target problem will usually easily respond to the healing river of TAT.

I find that in working with seriously troubled people in a mental health setting, TAT is particularly useful in highlighting the layers of problematic thoughts, or 'veils', that hold the whirlpools of cognitive-emotional turmoil in place. The inner observational stance of TAT and the procedure of asking the client what he or she experienced after each step are valuable in facilitating detailed reports of these. Sometimes, much work has to be done over a period of time on the veils of thought before the target can be addressed—and it can be important to be patient about this. For example, a client and I identified her core belief about herself that she was 'loathsome and worthless'. I suggested she begin Step One with an acknowledgement of this basic belief. After staying in the pose with this for a short time, she reported that it was too frightening to face this view of herself. Therefore I suggested she do the pose whilst focused on acknowledging the fear. This time she said the fear itself was too frightening and that she just felt enveloped in fear and wanted to curl into a ball and hide. I then suggested she focus on the idea that the fear was too frightening to face. Following this, she reported feeling slightly calmer. I suggested Step Two as the idea that it was possible to face her fear and other feelings. She tried this but then reported that she could not allow this thought. This was enough work for that session. The TAT had allowed both of us to witness very clearly the layering of the thoughts and fears and self-condemnation. Her core negative belief that she was 'loathsome and worthless' was too frightening to face, but her condemnation of herself for having this belief added to her inner turmoil. As she looked into the whirlpool she felt even more frightened. However, there is something very reassuring to clients in the idea that each layer of their distress and terror can be addressed carefully one at a time; this helps to counter the dread of being sucked irrevocably into the black hole of the mental whirlpool.

Pains in the back—ghosts in the body

Because TAT helps to release a person from their cognitive prison, it is particularly good at facilitating the incorporation of new perspectives. When in the TAT pose, new ideas seem to settle more deeply into a person's psychosomatic system—and, of course, the soma is partly determined by the thoughts in the psyche. Recently I worked with a patient, Pat, who had been hospitalised on a psychiatric ward for some weeks with pains in her back (as well as depression and anxiety) for which no adequate physical cause had been found. Psychiatrists had told her that she suffers from a somatoform disorder, an idea that she was willing to accept in principle, although it had little emotional meaning for her. We have met a number of times, exploring various aspects of the thoughts and emotions that might play a part in her condition. As we moved through some of the steps of TAT Pat began to report an increased sense of relaxation, and then went on to describe, with surprise, a sensation of the pains shifting location and the intensity lessening. This prompted her to appreciate more fully that her pain in her spine might not be due entirely to physical damage in her spine. As she remained in the TAT pose, I put to her the idea that the movement of the sensations showed that they were on the border between her mind and her body. Pat accepted this perspective. I spoke of the sensations as being like ghosts in her body—the energetic residues of previous traumas and emotional pains. Again this idea was meaningful to her—much more deeply so than if it had been put to her without her being in the TAT pose.

The next time I saw Pat, a few days later, I noticed immediately that her movements and pace of walking seemed much faster. She remarked that pains in her back had not been bothering her so much. We moved into further TAT, now focused on her remaining pains and other sensations. When invited to focus on the thought or idea of being free of these, she commented that this seemed very hard to consider since she had had the pains so long she could not imagine being without them. Therefore I asked her to focus on the thought that she could not imagine being free of the pains. Following this step, Pat was then able to entertain an idea of being without pain, which she found a deeply pleasurable reverie. We then moved into the idea of the ghosts of past traumas and emotional pains being lodged in her physical sensations, with the additional idea that these energetic patterns could be calmed and healed and could leave her body like a ghost passing through a wall. This led to a significant drop in the intensity of her pain. Finally I asked her to focus on the idea that all that had led up to these ghosts and pains in her body, from whatever time, place, or circumstance, was healing now. Following this Pat reported a deep feeling of peace and relaxation, declaring that she felt she had let go of all that had been troubling her.

A few days later, Pat spoke of a marked lessening in the pain, which she now experienced as wave-like sensations moving around her body. I put to her that these were the old energy patterns, the 'ghosts', gradually finding their way out of her body. This idea made sense to her. Pat then complained of another, less acute, problem that troubled her—the absence of her emotions. Somehow it seemed that the onset of her physical distress had coincided with the loss of direct experience of her emotions. By now she had become enthusiastic about TAT and needed no encouragement to assume the pose and to put her attention on the thought of her loss of emotions. She reported that in response the wave-like sensations were increasing. I asked her then to focus on the idea that the waves contained her emotions and that these could re-enter her mind. As she came out of the pose she suddenly remarked "I think my mind is full of anger". The next TAT step was to focus on the feelings of anger, and to consider the idea that her body and mind were full of anger. She spoke of people she was angry with. Next she focused on the idea that the anger had left her, the ghosts of old experiences and emotions having found their way out of her body as she forgave those she had felt angry with. She reported feeling peaceful, the pain having gone.

A couple of days following this session, Pat created an angry scene on the ward, complaining vigorously and in colourful language about various aspects of the care that was not to her liking. She told me about this with evident pleasure, and added that her spine felt much better. Now she realised with absolute clarity that in some way her spine had been containing her warded off rage. Moreover, she was indeed feeling at least some of her emotions again.

Dragons along the path

There is an essential simplicity about TAT. Within the TAT pose, a person's system will do whatever it is instructed or invited to do, provided the request is stated in clear and simple terms, and provided the inherent objections to doing so are addressed as they emerge. The 7 basic steps of TAT provide a kind of template of where to aim the focus. However, there are often competing beliefs and motives—like dragons to be slain—along the path to these 7 steps of healing.

For example, a man reported a reaction of anxiety after attempting step 3, saying that for some reason the thought of losing all his problems seemed frightening. I suggested he go back into the pose and put his attention on the thought that it was frightening to lose his problems. He did this and reported the anxiety collapsing. I then suggested he focus on the thought that losing his problems would be good and desirable rather than frightening. Following this he was able to proceed through the further steps quite easily.

I find that a crucial strategy in using TAT is to target each resistance that emerges within the basic steps. This is done simply by shining a light on it. Typically what happens is that while attempting to do a step of TAT the person encounters an inner objection, which might take the form of another fear, or a feeling of undeservedness, or some fundamental blocking belief that is in opposition to the proposed change, or it may be more like a counterargument by another part of the self. Sometimes the objection will be processed and resolved within the TAT step—the objection appears momentarily before fading. In other cases, however, the objection forms a more persisting challenge and obstacle—a dragon on the path. The solution then is to shine the light on it directly rather than trying to fight it or force the process past it. When the objection is directly attended to, it almost always fades or transforms in some way. With very substantial 'dragons', a number of TAT steps may need to be addressed to that objection itself, including attention to the idea of 'the trauma that gave rise to this objection'. Following the processing and fading of the objection, the original target can be addressed again.

If there is an attempt to avoid or run from a 'dragon', it will usually come in pursuit, determined to protect or even expand its territory. Thus if a person attempts to focus on an idea of healing, an internal dragon may rear up snarling that this is not possible, that he or she will never be better, and that it is better to remain ill or disabled because that is safer than risking further suffering by getting better and trying again (or any number of other discouraging messages). As a result the person may feel momentarily worse as they attempt to engage with TAT. This reminds me of certain experiences with dogs when I was a young boy. In the town where I lived, there often seemed to be dogs roaming the streets unattended—a sight less commonly seen now. I became very frightened of my journeys to and from school where I might be pursued by terrifying barking dogs. One day, in a sudden mood of rage and rebellion against the intimidation I felt from these creatures, I stopped running away from a particular dog and turned around and ran directly at it. To my delight and amazement the dog turned and ran away.

This became my regular tactic when confronted by these threatening beasts—although, to be honest, I am not sure that I would have the courage to use this same ruse now as an adult! In a similar way, the dragons within the mind become subdued and tamed, or simply dissolve and fade, when directly faced, particularly when done so with the light of TAT.

The pausing and checking in with the client between each step allows important and detailed information to be accessed regarding the client's inner thoughts, fantasies, and emotions. This helps to fine tune the focus of TAT. For example, a woman reported difficulty with the idea of her traumas healing because there seemed so many and they were so deeply rooted. Therefore I suggested she focus on precisely this thought, that there were too many traumas and that they were too deeply rooted. Following this, she reported that it seemed easier and that she had a sensation of light coming in to her. However, when we moved to the idea of all the storage places of the traumas in her mind and body, she said the light seemed to have difficulty penetrating her body. I invited her to focus on this thought, whilst in the TAT pose, and then to shift to the thought that the light could penetrate all areas of her body. She found that this did lead to her experiencing her body and mind as filled with light.

Permission to live—the chief dragon

Sometimes Tapas Fleming has recommended an initial TAT step for certain clients based on the thought "I do not deserve to live—I deserve to die", which is then followed by the next step of "I do deserve to live". Whilst some clients (and practitioners) may be disturbed by such statements, I find this step can be extremely apt and useful with those who are in the grip of serious depression or other very negative states of mind. If a person has a fundamental belief that he or she does not deserve to live—perhaps based on a sense of having been hated by the mother, or perhaps linked to the mother's wish (conscious or unconscious) to abort the baby—then it will be very difficult for them to benefit from TAT or other methods unless this is addressed. Such a belief in not deserving to live may also be viewed as form of massive and major 'psychological reversal', to use Dr Callahan's terminology. By applying TAT to this fundamental 'dragon', the path to healing becomes opened.

Working through the psychodynamic layers of severe depression

The following case illustrates the importance of checking the client's response to each step of TAT and systematically addressing each aspect that emerges. Hannah, a woman in her forties, presented with moderately severe chronic depression. She began this session by speaking of recent struggles against impulses to take all her paracetamol and kill herself, in order to "end all the pain"—going on to list this pain in terms of a series of features of her childhood that had involved neglect, abandonment and abuse. She emphasised her sense of having felt very alone with no-one consistently available to provide support.

After the first step of TAT, focused on the thought "there was no-one there for me", she reported: "I felt God was saying to me that he was there for me—so I wasn't completely on my own". This seemed a positive start! However, she then went on to speak of the fact that her dear grandfather, who died when she was 11 but had always loved her, had made some kind of sexual advance to her after he had suffered several strokes (she had talked about this before). She emphasised her sense of confusion and shock about this: "it was hard to believe that the granddad who was there for me was the same one who frightened me." I suggested she do the next step of TAT focused on the thought that it was a shock when her granddad frightened her. Following this she spoke more of her childhood state of shock and confusion—her complete inability to make any sense of why her grandfather had behaved as he did, how she wanted to run away, and how she did not know whether to tell her grandmother who was in the kitchen at the time. I guided her back into TAT, focused on precisely what she had just said. Following this, she spoke of realising that she had still loved him and they had remained close despite his aberrant behaviour on that one occasion—and that just before he died she had spent a morning with him. However, she then added: "I just wish he hadn't done that—I feel it has spoilt everything".

I asked Hannah to focus on the thought she had just expressed, that what her grandfather had done had spoilt everything, as the next TAT step. She then spoke of her appreciation that her grandfather would never have tried to hurt her, but on the other hand this thought did not alter her feelings—she felt that her head was fighting with her feelings. I suggested she enter the TAT pose whilst focused on the thought of these two parts of her (her head and her feelings) in conflict. Following this she remarked: "Its not just to do with my grandfather—its everything". Sensing that this was a very angry remark, I suggested the next TAT step be focused on the thought that she was full of anger. After this step, she said she knew that other people had commented that she was very angry, and she realised that in view of her experiences she might be expected to be angry, but she could not be aware of her anger. She asked how she could express anger if she was not aware of it. I commented that perhaps her whole state of depression, and her suicidal thoughts, *were* her way of expressing anger—and I further pointed out that her list of problems in her childhood, that she had recounted at the beginning of the session, came across like a set of angry complaints. She looked surprised, but agreed that it did indeed appear that she was very angry. I wondered aloud whether there was within her some kind of taboo on anger. In response she commented that her grandmother, with whom she had spent most of her childhood, had frequently instructed her that "children should be seen and not heard".

Having identified this crucial childhood injunction, I asked Hannah to assume the TAT pose and attend to the thought "children should be seen and not heard". She emerged from this looking very thoughtful and stated her realisation that she was never allowed to express her anger: "Every time I attempted to express anger, my grandmother would interrupt me and tell me off." I suggested the next TAT step as "It is not true that children should be seen and not heard"—and after a few moments, I added the further thought that "it is OK to be angry". Following this, she remarked: "Before you had even said that, I had the thought that it is OK to be angry—I feel such relief—it feels like I've been bottling up so much all my life—there have been so many things ...".

For the next TAT step I suggested she focus on the thought "Everything that caused or led up to my problems with anger and depression happened" (a variant of step one). She reported feeling calm. Then she focused on the TAT step two idea that all these contributing events were healing now. She described an image of there being so much rubbish in her life and she saw herself sweeping this up into bags. For the next TAT step (a variant of step 4), she focused on the thought that the rubbish was being cleared out from all the places in her mind, body and life, and being disposed of. She described seeing herself sweeping out all the nooks and crannies and putting all the rubbish in the bags, which were left outside for the refuse collectors. I suggested a further TAT step focused on the thought that the rubbish was being carried away. She reported seeing the refuse truck driving off whilst she waved goodbye. She remarked: "I felt a huge relief—it was gone—I did not have to take responsibility for it any more—I feel so much lighter". She looked radiant and smiling, thanking me warmly as she left.

This was a successful TAT session, but there were many twists and turns and layers to address along the way. At each moment, the client's own thoughts, images, and emotions were the focus and the signposts of the direction to follow. We moved from the original list of depressive reproaches (against life, God, and reality) to her more specific complaint about the trauma and shock of her grandfather's inappropriate behaviour following his brain illness. By focusing on each disturbing thought in turn, she gradually arrived at a more comfortable stance towards her grandfather, realising that they had remained close despite his having frightened her with his behaviour. Her general anger then came more into view—and her difficulty in being aware of this. She recalled the childhood message that children should be seen and not heard. Focusing on this idea in the TAT pose, led her to a realisation of how pervasively she had been discouraged from expressing anger as a child. A step two idea that it was OK to express anger and not true that children should be seen and not heard led to great feelings of relief. The step three idea of the contributing problems being healed led to the imagery of clearing out the rubbish into sacks for the refuse collectors. This neatly led into the step 4 idea of the rubbish being cleared from all the storage places—and then taken away by the refuse truck whilst she waved goodbye, feeling wonderfully light and free of this burden.

Some of the ideas addressed within the TAT pose were those of the basic mutative steps of healing outlined by Tapas Fleming. Other ideas were the associations, competing thoughts and feelings, and objections that needed to be addressed along the way to the mutative steps. Each of these ideas melted or transformed when attended to within the TAT pose.

Resolving low self-esteem

The following TAT session flowed easily and elegantly. Ellen had benefited from various energy psychology modalities, but complained of continuing low self-esteem and difficulties in asserting herself. We began TAT with step one along the lines of "Everything that has led to my low self-esteem and difficulty in asserting myself happened"—followed by step two as "it is all in the past and not affecting me now—I am free to live in the present". Ellen reported feeling a sense of peace, but marred by the thought that even if she were free of these past events, members of her family might still undermine her. I asked her to enter the TAT pose and attend to the thought that members of her family might undermine her. Following this she said she accepted that they might still put her down and that she has no control over their behaviour. For the next TAT step I suggested the thought that she is responsible only for her own reactions and not for others' behaviour. She reported feeling better—thinking that she can control how she feels but not how others behave—and that she could switch off if members of her family are speaking critically or attempting to undermine her. The standard steps three, four and five proceeded easily without complication. After step six, she said she could see a new chapter opening in her life, but although she could forgive her brother, she was aware that he would still try to dominate her as he had in the past. I asked her to go into TAT and put her attention on the thought that her brother would continue to try to dominate her. She reported the thought that she could just let his behaviour go over her head and she was not going to allow him to hurt her as he had before. Step eight was uneventful. A further step, focused on any other aspects now being healed, led her to declare that she felt much better and very happy.

In this example, most of the standard mutative steps of TAT proceeded easily. At a couple of points, potential internal objections arose, based around fears of the potential for further undermining behaviour from members of her family. By directing TAT on these thoughts, they changed towards a more positive perspective in which she realised she did not need to allow her family's behaviour to affect her in the same way as before.

Shadows on the path to wholeness

The vision of the human situation revealed by TAT is that we are potentially inherently whole and healed, but this knowledge is blocked by false thoughts and beliefs. These form extensive webs and networks of illusion and internal intimidation—ghosts and dragons that colonise the mind, generating propaganda and fear in order to maintain their parasitic organisation. They are like tumours in the psyche—sometimes small and easily removed, and sometimes extensive and deeply embedded. When the light of TAT is shone upon these false beliefs and bogeymen of the psyche, they melt away.

Sometimes the beliefs are linked to denial of a person's underlying true feelings—particularly those that may be associated with shame or guilt, such as deep feelings of resentment, hatred, envy, triumph over others, and so forth. Many such monsters from the psychic depths can seem disturbing when first glimpsed, but when exposed to TAT they rapidly lose their power and energy—and are replaced by love. It is not that we become free of emotions and strivings, but these become more able to find expression in the continual flow of our thoughts and feelings. The natural state for human beings is one of wholeness and love, but this is rarely seen because of the many networks and layers of illusion—what Tapas Fleming calls the 'veils of thought'—covering and distorting this inherent truth. The veils may be extensive—they may be complex—there may be many of them—but gradually TAT clears them all away.

Partly the problems arise through trauma—including that experienced around birth, which is often a time of anxiety, pain, and distress for human beings. Trauma induces a shock reaction, in which the mind-body system freezes. The flow of emotions and energy is blocked. Trauma produces a kind of energetically dead and toxic area in the system. It is rather as if some foreign body had become stuck in the gut, remaining undigested yet generating toxic products. The system might attempt to wall off the toxic area in some way, as a partial solution that enables survival to continue. Something like this goes on in the mind too. The traumatic experience is walled off and avoided. Layers of thoughts are woven around it, designed to prevent access and minimise the danger of encountering a similar trauma again. Where there has been repeated interpersonal trauma in early childhood—where the perpetrator is a caregiver or close

relative—the mind may react also by severing itself into compartments, so that experiences are kept walled off from one another. In
severe cases, Dissociative Identity Disorder develops. All of these are
compromises of integrity and wholeness. Areas of the mind are shut
down and walled off and sometimes compartmentalised. Energy
and emotions cannot then flow. The stagnant energy becomes itself
toxic. Layers of protection are laid down around the traumatic experience. Partly these layers of protection take the form of thoughts
that block access (as addressed by cognitive therapists) and aim to
prevent re-experience of similar trauma, and partly they take the
form of muscular and other bodily tensions (as originally described
by Wilhelm Reich). By shining the light of TAT, first on the layers
of protective thoughts, and then on the traumas themselves, these
complex traumatic networks can be gradually dissolved. The underlying potential wholeness and healing is then revealed.

How I use TAT with complex problems

In my work in a psychiatric setting, with clients whose problems
are often rather deep and extensive, I find there are some subtleties
and complexities in the effective use of TAT—even though the basic
template of TAT, as developed by Tapas Fleming, remains the core.
Here is, schematically, what I do.

I listen, as I would in any psychotherapeutic consultation, being
alert to the crucial anxieties, emotions, beliefs, self-images, traumas,
and so forth, as these emerge in the client's discourse. Eventually a
key issue (e.g. a trauma, a series of traumas, a self-image, or a belief
about the self in the world) comes into view as a potential initial
target for TAT. A succinct formulation of this issue becomes the focus
of step one of TAT. The standard mutative steps of TAT are then
followed. However, at any of these steps, the client may report some
internal objection, or some new direction of thought and emotion.
I follow the client, asking him or her to focus on each emerging
'blocking thought' whilst in TAT. It is not that every thought is to be
targeted specifically—many of the emerging thoughts are part of the
positive transformational flow of TAT. Rather, it is specifically those
thoughts that form a block to the basic mutative steps of TAT.

Sometimes I picture this as like looking into a computer screen
where objects are continually forming and beginning to increase in

size; if left unchecked, each one of these objects (thoughts) would come to dominate and take over the screen. However, by directing the pointer at each one as it forms, it is neutralised or eliminated. This is like the effect of directing attention at each emerging 'blocking thought' whilst in TAT.

In my own experience, TAT can be very free-associative. We follow the client's lead, wherever their flow of thoughts take us. Whilst mindful of the task of getting down to the main mutative steps as developed by Tapas Fleming, we may have to keep directing TAT also at the numerous blocking thoughts (or dragons) and side issues as they arise. With complex problems the work can be complex— albeit always with an underlying simplicity if we have faith to follow the inherent direction of the process.

Time spent specifically in TAT may be interspersed with much other exploration that is conventionally verbal. Premature or hurried TAT, when there has been insufficient time for the most relevant issues to be expressed, is unlikely to be optimally effective—whereas patient and skilled listening, followed eventually by carefully targeted TAT, is frequently awesome in its positive effects.

The scope of TAT

Tapas Fleming originally developed TAT in the context of her work with allergies. She began to realise that many allergies and sensitivities are actually linked with traumas—and that TAT works very well in relation to traumas. Over time, the scope of TAT has steadily broadened, to include all manner of psychological and physical problems. Although there is no claim that TAT cures physical illness, it can certainly support healing by addressing emotional, psychological, and energetic aspects [see the DVD Healing the Emotional Aspects of Cancer with TAT]. Recent published research, using a randomised design with control groups, indicates that TAT can be very helpful in supporting people who have needed to lose excess weight and to maintain this weight loss, and more effective than a cognitive-behavioural method (Mist et al. 2006; Elder et al. 2007). At the same time, Tapas Fleming has always sought to simplify the procedure and render it as elegant and efficient as possible. She has found that it is not necessary for the details of what lies behind a problem to be known consciously; the wording of the opening step one can be something like "the most influential trauma behind this problem happened" or "everything that resulted in this problem happened". Thus the mind-body-energy system is invited to search for the most relevant traumas, beliefs, conflicts and other relevant factors that underpin the target problem. It will graciously do this when given simple and clear instructions. Conflicting parts of the self can also be brought into clearer dialogue and reconciliation through TAT. Recently Tapas Fleming recommends beginning TAT with a statement of intention that the healing will be of benefit to family, ancestors, everyone involved in the problem, and all parts of the self and all points of view held within the self.

By broadening, with clarity, the instructions and intent, the synergy of thought and energy mean that the scope of TAT becomes almost limitless. Such a statement is not intended to imply that TAT is magical or omnipotent—it is a precise procedure with observable and potentially measurable results. However, anything that it is possible for a human being to think can be placed within the light of TAT- and thus more or less any human discomfort or misery can, in principle, be alleviated with TAT.

CHAPTER THIRTEEN

The energy perspective

M any practitioners from conventional psychotherapeutic backgrounds find energy psychological methods intriguing, perhaps exciting, but also problematic. The 'problem' appears to arise from the way in which a method such as Thought Field Therapy, or its derivatives, is not only a novel therapeutic *technique*, but also works with what is for many people a novel *realm of reality*—the energy system. Some mistakenly believe that these methods are based on strange theories about mysterious energy fields. They are not. The energy psychological methods are based on investigations, using simple and replicable procedures, of that area of reality that is known as the energy system. It is not a hypothetical realm but one that is palpable and observable—and when certain simple procedures are followed, a distressed, traumatised, or anxious person will experience relief. Muscle testing, using routine kinesiological methods, readily reveals the energy system, the information it contains, and the profound intelligence manifest in it. It is common for people to be astonished on witnessing such demonstrations for the first time, and yet for energy psychological practitioners this realm is part of our ordinary reality. By contrast, most of the 'official' disciplines of knowledge and science have yet to embrace this.

A failure to embrace modern physics

Bruce Lipton is a cell biologist who strongly supports energy psychology methods and perspectives. He (Lipton, 2005), along with others, points out that most of the sciences above physics, including biology and psychology, have not taken account of the implications of quantum physics and the energy perspective. Instead, biology, pharmacology, and psychology still maintain a quasi-Newtonian 'matter-based' theoretical basis. After listing a long list of applications of quantum physics in the physical sciences, Lipton asks:

> "But what great and marvellous advances in biomedical sciences can we attribute to the quantum revolution? Lets list them in order of their importance:
>
> It is a very short list—there haven't been any." [Lipton, 2005, p. 109]

Lipton summarises the prevailing Newtonian paradigm as follows:

> "... conventional biologists are reductionists who believe that mechanisms of our physical bodies can be understood by taking the cells apart and studying their chemical building blocks. They believe that the biochemical reactions responsible for life are generated through Henry Ford-styled assembly lines: one chemical causes a reaction, followed by another reaction with a different chemical, etc ... This reductionist model suggests that if there is a problem in the system, evident as a disease or dysfunction, the source of the problem can be attributed to a malfunction in one of the steps along the chemical assembly line. By providing the cell with a functional replacement part for the faulty element, by prescribing pharmaceutical drugs for example, the defective single point can theoretically be repaired and health restored. This assumption spurs the pharmaceutical industry's search for magic-bullet drugs and designer genes. However, the quantum perspective reveals that the universe is an integration of interdependent energy fields that are entangled in a meshwork of interactions." [Lipton, 2005, pp. 102–103]

Energy fields influence biology

Lipton goes on to point out that it is now well-established that energy fields of the electromagnetic spectrum profoundly affect or disrupt biological regulation. Such energies include microwaves, radio frequencies, visible light spectrum, acoustic frequencies, extremely low frequencies, and scalar energy. Moreover, a study over 40 years ago showed that energetic signalling mechanisms are a hundred times more efficient than physical signals such as hormones, neurotransmitters, and growth factors. Lipton further points out that the speed of electromagnetic energy signals is 186,000 miles per second, whilst the speed of a diffusible chemical is less than 1 centimetre per second. He comments:

"Energy signals are 100 times more efficient and infinitely faster than physical chemical signalling. What kind of signalling would your trillion-celled community prefer? Do the math!". [2005, p. 112]

Every atom and molecule has its own specific electromagnetic frequency. This comes about because the distribution of 'particles' within the energy vortex of the atom is not even. The uneven distribution of charge imparts a kind of wobble to the atom, which generates the frequency. If a hypothetical voltmeter, of sufficiently small size, were placed alongside an atom, its pointer would fluctuate back and forth at a rate that was that atom's frequency.

James Oschman, another eminent cell biologist, points out that the conventional model of biochemical communication is actually implausible at the physics level of understanding:

"In the conventional picture of biological regulation, structurally matching molecules exchange energy and information by billiard-ball type direct impacts. Signal molecules diffuse, wiggle, and bump about randomly until they chance to approach a receptor site, at which time electrostatic, short-range (two to three times the molecule size) forces draw them together so that 'the key can fit into the lock'. It is not generally appreciated that this kind of random encounter, taking place in a sea of other molecules, gives these molecular meetings a statistically low probability. The simplest biological event or regulatory process should require a very long time to happen." [Oschman, 2000, p. 196]

Instead, Oschman proposes that molecules communicate by electromagnetic signals that do not require direct contact:

"In living systems, long range electromagnetic fields transmit messages between distant molecules, as long as their emission and absorption spectra match. Non-resonating, unwanted random signals are excluded ... Molecular electromagnetic communications can account for the rapid and subtle and integrated functioning of living systems. Millions of molecules can communicate with each other in this way. The upper limit on the signal velocity is the speed of light." [pp. 196–197]

This idea is also strongly supported in the research of others, such as Benveniste [www.digibio.com] and Smith [1987], showing, for example, that playing digital recordings of the electromagnetic signatures of signal molecules can trigger receptors in biological systems to respond just as if in physical contact with the molecules.

As early as 1923, Georges Lakhovsky, a Russian engineer, built an apparatus to measure microvoltages from human cells, plants and microbes, and was able to demonstrate oscillations in the radio and colour frequency spectrum emitted by living organisms. Cells in each organ of the body emitted frequencies specific to its particular organ or tissue, and cancerous cells emitted an abnormal frequency. Harmful factors, such as bacteria, viruses, toxins, or poor nutrition, would weaken and distort the electromagnetic fields prior to the onset of overt illness. Yurkovsky [2003] reports that Lakhovsky "concluded that health is nothing but a state of electro-magnetic equilibrium of body cells, while diseases and death represent just the opposite—a broken energetic balance". Lakhovsky went on to develop a radio-electrical apparatus called a 'Multiple Wave Oscillator' which he used to send healing frequencies as a means of treating cancers. This was used successfully in French hospitals in the 1930s, including in treatment of the Pope. His ideas were later taken up by Bjorn Nordenstrom, a Swedish Professor of Radiology, who used electro-frequencies to bring about recoveries in patients with advanced cancers. Similarly, Robert Becker, a Professor of Orthopedic Surgery, found he could enhance tissue and bone healing in severely ill patients by applying small currents of electricity. He criticised the reliance of conventional medicine on the chemical-pharmacological approach to the neglect of the body's energies and the energy therapies such as homeopathy and acupuncture (Becker & Seldon, 1985). In 1968, Soviet scientists announced their finding that all living entities have an energy body alongside their physical body, observable through an electron microscope; they called this the 'biological plasma body', and like others found that this could be distorted through stressful events or exposure to toxic substances [reported in Yurkovsky, 2003, p. 18]. Another indicator of the fundamental role of energetic frequencies in biological life is the repeated finding that allergic patients showed the same reactions when exposed merely to the electromagnetic frequencies of a substance as they did when in contact with the actual substance [reported in Yurkovsky, 2003, p. 21].

William Tiller, Professor Emeritus of Materials Science at Stanford University, also gives the following striking example of the role of frequency information in relation to biological processes [Tiller, 2003]. It is well-established that colloidal silver will kill bacteria. However, it has been found that focussing the electromagnetic emissions from colloidal silver will also kill bacteria without any direct contact. Even more surprisingly, simply focussing light frequencies that closely match the optical spectrum of silver will also kill the bacteria. Thus it is the specific information pattern inherent in the silver atom that kills the bacteria rather than the physical contact with silver. Tiller proposes that there are two broad levels to physical reality: the coarse particulate part and the fine informational wave part. Homeopathy and other energy methods act on the informational wave aspect. He comments:

> "Allopathic procedures and techniques have taught us a great deal about the coarse particulate patterns of the hierarchy while homeopathy, acupuncture and advanced kinesiology ... are beginning to teach us a great deal about the fine information wave patterns of this information hierarchy." [Tiller, 2003, pp. xvii–xviii]

Homeopathy as a model of frequency signalling

One of the strongest indicators of the energy-informational regulation of life is the fact that homeopathy works even though the remedies may contain no chemical trace of the original substance. Despite prevalent misinformation to the contrary, there is substantial clear evidence of the effectiveness of homeopathy. For example, early British double blind studies during the second world war found that subjects given a combination homeopathic remedy experienced significant improvement in burns from mustard gas compared to those given a placebo [Paterson, 1944; Owen & Ives, 1982]. Similarly, subjects given a homeopathic remedy for hay fever suffered six times fewer symptoms than those given a placebo [Reilly et. al. 1986]. Double blind studies with animals also show significant effects of homeopathy [Ullman, 1991, pp. 62–63]. A 1991 review article in the British Medical Journal analysed 107 controlled trials and concluded that 80% of these were of sufficiently high quality to demonstrate the effectiveness of homeopathic remedies [Kleijnen, 1991]. Similarly, in 1997 The Lancet reviewed 186 trials and concluded that homeopathic remedies were active treatments and not simply placebos [Linde, 1997]. The assumption from the homeopathic perspective is that the remedies work, not because of a chemical effect, but because they provide an energetic signal to the body—an informational feedback—indicating what needs to be corrected. Moreover, it has been found that electronic digital cloning of homeopathic remedies is as effective as those derived from the original substance [Yurkovsky, 2003, pp. 89–91].

Meridians and the 'X-signalling system'

James Oschman [2000] draws attention to the work of scientist-acupuncturist Yoshio Manaka, who has developed the idea of the 'X-signal system' concerned with fundamental aspects of energy and information flow. Manaka bases his theorising on a range of observations to propose that the X-signal system is an evolutionarily early mode of biological communication, present in single celled creatures that do not have a nervous system but nevertheless react to external stimuli to avoid harm and seek nourishment. He hypothesises that this system has important functions in the human body and is separate from the nervous system—and that it is linked to the energy fields addressed by many forms of energy medicine. Oschman comments:

> "The living matrix, the energy fields, the acupuncture meridians, and the various biocircuits that energy therapists interact with during their therapy sessions are all related and are components of Manaka's system." [p. 70]

The meridian system is generally considered to have some kind of link to bodily organs and systems, but at the same time to be somewhat independent of the physical body. Whilst being linked to points of lowered electrical resistance on the skin, ultrasound attenuation, and conduction of light, the meridians do not correspond to any fixed anatomical structures—and may indeed have an inherently shifting location. This system, operating with bioelectromagnetic energy, appears to transmit information very rapidly form one part of the body to another, as well as containing a blueprint for the physical system.

Morphic fields

Biologist Rupert Sheldrake [e.g. 1985; 1988; 1999] has over a number of years been developing the theory of morphic fields: "self-organising regions of influence, analogous to magnetic fields and other recognised fields of nature" [Sheldrake, 1999, p. 258]. His interest began with his puzzlement over how it is that a biological organism grows into the form characteristic of its species, and how each organ within it knows what form it is meant to assume. Since every cell in the body contains the same DNA, an explanation in terms of genetic programming is insufficient. Sheldrake's theory is that organisms are shaped by morphogenetic fields that are like invisible blueprints for the body. Crucially, Sheldrake also proposes that these fields communicate with one another across groups and also that they can acquire new information and thus learn. Species will therefore have collective energy fields, containing information that is relevant to the survival of that species. These ideas, and the evidence that Sheldrake has amassed, are entirely consistent with the emerging perspectives on the energy field basis of life, and with the principles of Dr Callahan's Thought Field Therapy.

Conventional medical use of energy-information

Although the energetic basis of biological life has not yet been generally embraced, modern medicine does make use of energy-scanning technology that analyses the specific frequencies emitted by healthy and diseased parts of the body. A new technique for eliminating kidney stones uses constructive interference, whereby a focused energy waves of the same frequency as the kidney stone are used to disintegrate the stone. Lipton concludes: "… there is enough scientific evidence to suspect that we can tailor a waveform as a therapeutic agent in much the same way as we now modulate chemical structures with drugs" [2005, pp. 118–119]. A further specific example of this is the findings that transcranial magnetic stimulation of the brain, an electrical organ, can have a powerful therapeutic action against depression. Similar use of pulsed magnetic stimulation machines have been found to be effective in treating a range of disorders, including Parkinson's disease and epilepsy. Church describes the principle behind such use as follows:

> "A normal cell has an electrical potential of about 90 millivolts. An inflamed cell has a potential of about 120 millivolts, and a cell in a state of degeneration may drop to 30 millivolts. By entraining the electrical fields of the cells within its range to the magnetic pulses emitted by the PMS machine, cells can be brought back into a healthy range." [Church, 2007, pp. 67–68]

This possibility of entraining the electromagnetic fields of biological systems into a healthy frequency provides obvious partial answers to the question of how it is that healer's hands, that do emit measurable electromagnetic fields [Oschman, 2000], have a therapeutic effect. Increasingly it appears that the body-brain-mind system generates an information-transmitting electrogmagnetic field that contains information and has important regulatory functions. The field provides information that is detectable by an external observer (frequency changes) and it can be influenced by energy therapeutic procedures, which in turn bring about changes within the body-brain-mind system.

Attacks on energy medicine

However, the American medical professions, supported by the pharmaceutical industry and the self-styled 'pseudoscience debunkers' and their websites (Mollon, 2007), have consistently attacked homeopaths, chiropracters, and other energy-based practitioners who do not use drugs. One well-known 'quackwatching' organisation even states on its website that it is interested in prosecuting homeopathic practitioners and those who sell homeopathic remedies, and asks for information from any person who has purchased a remedy that did not work. Yurkovsky [2003] gives a clear account of the history of attacks on homeopathy driven by economic and territorial motives. He comments:

"On occasion, spokesmen for mainstream allopathic medicine make claims that homeopathy has been rejected by the majority of the medical profession because it has failed scientific investigation. Such claims are false; no scientific investigations have been conducted whose results were detrimental to the credibility of homeopathy." [Yurkovsky, 2003, p. 205]

The history of attempts to suppress homeopathy date back to the mid-19th century. Orthodox medicine, that embraced methods such as bloodletting and the use of leeches, denounced homeopathy as 'quackery', 'unscientific', 'devilish' and 'unmanly' [Ullman, 1991]. In 1855 the American Medical Association established a 'consultation clause' in their code of ethics, forbidding any member to have anything to do with a homeopath [Coulter, 1977]. This restriction was fiercely imposed; for example, a New York doctor was expelled for making a purchase from a homeopathic pharmacy. However, the true motivation for this hostility was expressed by a respected orthodox physician at a meeting of the AMA in 1903: "We must admit that we never fought the homeopath on matters of principles; we fought him because he came into the community and got the business." [Kaufman, 1971, p. 158]. Similar campaigns were sustained against other practitioners whose work lay outside the orthodox paradigm. In 1990, the American Medical Association was found guilty by the US Court of Appeals of an 'unlawful conspiracy in restraint of trade' in their efforts to destroy the profession of Chiropractic, a system of knowledge and skill to do with the flow of energetic information along the vertebral column. The years of litigation over this issue illustrate the trade and professional territorial protectionism that often masquerades as scientific rigour. Moreover, the claims by orthodox medicine for scientific integrity and clinical success should be tempered by a recent finding, on the basis of a ten year survey of government statistics, that iatrogenic illness is the leading cause of death in the United States [Null et al. 2003].

Biology and the energy of thought

If biology is regulated by energetic information, how much is the physiology of the body influenced by the energy of thought? Lipton [2005] draws attention to intriguing instances that are normally regarded by conventional medicine as anomalies. For example, in

1952 a Dr Albert Mason treated what he thought was a boy's severe case of warts using hypnosis. The warts, which had covered most of the boy's body, completely healed, leaving healthy skin. Subsequently, Mason was told that the skin problem had not been warts but a rare lethal genetic illness. Thus it appeared that, simply by using thought, a seemingly incurable disease had been healed. Mason was not able to replicate these results with other patients with this disease—and he attributed this to his loss of belief in relation to his original treatment of what he had thought was a case of warts. The role of thought and expectation is also revealed in a study of data from drug clinical trials, which found that 80% of the effect of antidepressant medication could be attributed to placebo effect (Kirsch, 2002). One participant in a clinical trial for a leading antidepressant was astonished to find she had been on a placebo since not only had her chronic depression lifted but also brain scans revealed enhanced activity of the prefrontal cortex (Leuchter et al. 2002). In another study, a knee surgeon divided his patients into three groups: two groups received somewhat different kinds of legitimate surgical intervention, whilst the third group received fake surgery. The placebo group improved just as much as the two groups who received genuine surgery (Moseley et al. 2002).

Lipton compares the power and efficiency of the conscious and 'subconscious' minds:

> "When it comes to sheer neurological processing abilities, the subconscious mind is millions of times more powerful than the conscious mind. If the desires of the conscious mind conflicts with the programs in the subconscious mind, which 'mind' do you think will win out?" [2005, p. 128]

Lipton sees the subconscious mind as a huge database of stored programmes, some of which are hard wired and others are derived from life experiences and messages from parents, teachers and others in childhood. Crucially, he notes that between birth and 6 years of age, the child's brain state is predominantly operating either within delta or theta wave frequencies. Such states are characteristic of those of patients undergoing hypnosis—i.e. states of heightened suggestibility. This enhances the child's capacity to take in the messages, whether helpful or dysfunctional, provided by parents:

"This gives us an important clue as to how children, whose brains are mostly operating at these same frequencies between birth and six years of age, can download the incredible volume of information they need to thrive in their environment. The ability to process this vast quantity of information is an important neurologic adaptation to facilitate this information-intense process of enculturation. Human environments and social mores change so rapidly that it would not be an advantage to transmit cultural behaviors via genetically programmed instincts. Young children carefully observe their environment and download the worldly wisdom offered by parents directly into their subconscious memory. As a result their parents' behaviour and beliefs become their own." [Lipton, 2005, p. 163]

Since the child does not have the capacity to evaluate parental messages for their truth status, negative messages (along with those that are positive) are downloaded as 'facts', forming the software programmes that generate emotions, behaviours, as well as states of health and sickness, in the human biocomputer.

Implications

There are a number of implications of the overall thesis presented by Lipton, Oschman, and others. The body-mind system operates with energy-information. Energy affects biology. The brain's energy is thought. Thought and belief powerfully affect biology. Intention, thought, and energy interact with biology—and this dynamic interaction allows healing (as in the energy psychology therapies) as well as generating dysfunction (through destructive information arising from traumas and negative parental messages).

Placebo as energy-information

The commonplace 'placebo effect' is often regarded as somehow an artefact, false, and inferior to a 'real' effect—as if a person who gets better on the basis of a placebo has deceived himself and is in the grip of illusion. By contrast, the effect of an active drug is considered real and true. When the informational aspect of illness and healing is understood, then it becomes easier to appreciate the placebo effect as being just as real as a drug effect. A person who invests an otherwise inactive pill with the idea of healing is transmitting to his or her own system the energy-informational instruction to get better. The result is just as real and valid as the non-local effects of frequencies on biological processes even when the substance generating the frequency is not in direct contact—as in the case of the silver frequency described by Tiller.

Clearing dysfunctional information; installing new information

When we use energy psychology methods, we are either clearing dysfunctional information or putting new and corrective information into the system, designed to encourage healing. In the original diagnostic Thought Field Therapy procedure, the energetic meridian coding is ascertained through muscle testing. The psychological content of the target problem does not need to be known consciously. By tapping the resulting code back into the system the issue is healed—the perturbations that had previously generated the distress are cleared from the energy-informational field. This remarkable effect is entirely reliable and replicable—a routine procedure that is easily learned by any person with sufficient sensitivity to discern subtle shifts in muscle strength. On the other hand, when we use Emotional Freedom Techniques, or any other of the energy psychology methods that employ a standard format for stimulating meridians or chakras, we use a word, phrase, or a simple thought (combined with tapping or touching) as a means of instructing the system to heal a problem. In the TFT diagnostic procedure, using muscle testing, the client's *energy system* gives us the information that we then feed back through tapping the code into the meridians and chakras. In the EFT type of method, the client's *mind*, through conscious discernment of the issues, presents the information (the target problem) that is then put back into the energy system through the combination of words and tapping. Both methods appear to work well. By contrast, if the therapy consists merely of talking (albeit deriving insights, emotional awareness, cognitive restructuring, and so forth), without engaging the body and the energy networks, most of the person's system is not activated in relation to the problem—and hence not a lot changes.

The energised word

It appears that when a word (or phrase, or simple statement) is combined with tapping on the energy system it acquires great power, far beyond that when using the word on its own. The simple repetition of a word alone is unlikely to result in much emotional shift—but if the repetition, or even just the thought of the word, is combined with tapping on meridian points there will often be a substantial drop in emotional distress or anxiety. Thus it is as if the word combined with tapping transforms it into an energetic frequency that the body-mind system can respond to.

Paradoxically, the 'word combined with tapping' can be either a representation of the problem—thus functioning like a homeopathic frequency—or it can represent new positive information. Usually the recommended procedure would be to clear the negative information (e.g. traumatic experience and associated beliefs) before introducing the new positive idea. A similar phenomenon is found in using Eye Movement Desensitisation and Reprocessing, whereby bilateral stimulation, such as eye movements, can be used both for clearing the negative and also for installing the positive.

The basic idea of introducing positive new information into the mind-body system through affirmations, or autosuggestion, was established decades ago when Emile Coue first recommended a daily repetition of the statement "Every day, in every way, I am getting better and better". Variations on this theme have been a staple of the self-help literature. Intuitively we feel there is something in the idea—and yet the common experience is that they do not seem to work very well, or may even paradoxically provoke negative results. The problem appears to be that a positive statement will evoke a negative thought in response—an internal disagreement, deeply rooted in the person's beliefs, which will function as the real affirmation. Gary Craig calls these automatic internal disagreements the 'tail enders'. They can themselves be targeted and cleared, with the result that affirmations are then more effective. Patricia Carrington combines EFT with affirmations in her 'Choices method' [www.eftupdate.com], formulating the positive in the form of 'I choose', which is less likely to evoke internal resistance than 'I will' or 'I am'. However, what is often noted is that if a person repeats an affirmation whilst tapping on the energy system, after a little while the 'tail enders', or internal objections, begin to subside. The negative information starts to clear away and the positive is installed. This process is enhanced if the negative beliefs and thoughts are voiced whilst tapping, and then at a certain point there is a shift to voicing the possibility of the positive—a way of using EFT that has been particularly developed by Carol Look [www.carollook.com]. What seems to be happening then is that the negative internal messages are played back to the system, thereby being highlighted as target problems to be cleared; the system is then able to embrace the positive message.

The subtle differences between TFT and EFT

It becomes possible then to characterise the difference between TFT and other energy psychological methods such as EFT as follows. TFT (at the muscle testing diagnostic level) takes a reading of the energetic coding of the target problem. This reading is given back as a healing code by tapping on the meridians in a precise sequence. EFT and related methods combine a word with tapping on meridian points, thereby transforming the word into energetic information. The 'word-energy' quantum is used either to signal the target problem that needs healing, or to introduce a healing intention, as in Carrington's 'Choices method'.

The overall energy perspective

A clear picture begins to emerge as we survey the range of emerging evidence regarding the energy-informational basis of life. Biological systems are organised and regulated by energetic fields of information. These provide the *template* for the body (morphogenic fields), *acquire new information* through experience, and *transmit information* far faster than can be achieved through biochemical reactions or through the nervous system. Whilst correlated to the physical body, the energy system, with its meridians, chakras, and biosphere, is partially independent of it. States of health and sickness, as well as the 'thought field' are encoded in the energy system. Specific organs and sites of the body emit particular frequencies according to whether they are in a state of health or sickness. Health can be improved by directing optimal frequencies at the body—either frequencies characteristic of health, which then entrain the system, or homeopathic-style signals of illness that provoke a healing response. One person's energy field can affect another person's—in both good and bad ways. When a healer is working, it seems most likely that his or her energy field is transmitting information that entrains the client's energy field in the direction of health, healing, and peace. This entrainment by the healer's energy is probably able to override, in some cases, the psychological reversals that might otherwise be found in the client's system. When we use energy psychological methods, we access the relevant energy information through a combination of language, thought, and muscle testing — and transmit a healing code back into the client's system.

Information and energy

Dr Callahan often emphasises that Thought Field Therapy addresses the *information* in the energy field and is not simply to do with blockages in the flow of energy. This is an important point. The 'thought field' is the expression in the body's energy field of the information — the 'perturbations' generating the distress — associated with the thought. Similar principles are found in homeopathy, where it is a frequency imprint (i.e. 'information') of the substance that generates the therapeutic effect rather than a direct biochemical interaction with the body.

Because a signal in the energy field has little inertial mass, a shift at an energetic level can be very rapid. This can result in more or less instant changes in emotional state in some cases. However, changes in the physical state of the body, arising from shifts at an energetic level, may be slower since there is greater inertial mass and perhaps a need for organic tissue growth.

An analogy with road traffic lights may be helpful. A red traffic light appears to cause cars to lose power and come to a halt, whilst a green light appears to cause them to gain power and move, sometimes at high speed. Does the green light somehow transmit energy to the car whilst the red light absorbs it? Obviously we known that what actually happens is that the lights are forms of information, generating certain behaviours in drivers, which in turn alter the energy provided to the engine. The amount of energy involved in the shifts within the traffic light itself is relatively minimal. If traffic lights are working well, the flow of traffic is optimal, but if they are out of phase, reversed, or in other ways disorganised, havoc may be caused in traffic flow. However, if a car breaks down (analogous to a breakdown in the hardware of the body or brain), or if it runs out of energy/petrol (analogous to nutrition for the body), then the system cannot respond to the signals and traffic will pile up. If one set of lights are stuck on green there may be excess traffic down one highway at the expense of blockages in another road; under these conditions, cars may seek alternative routes, overloading minor pathways that are not intended to carry heavy traffic. This kind of analogy may carry some meaning when it is considered that the meridian system is somewhat like a road network. Chakras may be considered analogous to large roundabout systems, where a number of roads intersect. When traffic travels freely around the circle, in the correct direction, there is optimum flow—but mis-timed traffic signals (like a state of neurological and energetic disorganisation), or reversals of flow will cause traffic build-up. The state of mind of the car drivers will alter according to the road conditions. When traffic is blocked or very slow, drivers experience irritation, rage, and depression—but when traffic moves optimally, drivers experience a sense of well-being.

In using energy psychological methods, we activate the information in the energy field relating to the target problem, and then we clear the information that constitutes the perturbation in the field—analogous to smoothing the ripples on a water surface after a stone (a trauma) has been dropped in. The ripples express the transmission of energy through the water, but also contain information regarding the original impact of the stone. Some methods incorporate a direct thought signal. For example, in TAT the client touches two meridian points, a chakra, and the occipital area of the skull whilst holding in mind a series of thoughts relating to healing the problem. Similar use of a thought signal is found in BeSetFreeFast, Zensight, and related approaches.

Thus energy psychological methods seem to work with both energy and information. Informational or signal changes lead to changes in quantity or flow of energy, some of which are experiential—and which are also linked to shifts in emotional and physical states. On the other hand, a disorganised energy system makes informational change more difficult because the signals are mistimed or scrambled. Emotional wounds can leave *breaches* in the energy field, which can be experienced or observed in subtle form. They also generate informational *perturbations* in the energy field. Both perturbations and breaches can be healed through energetic signals, as employed in energy psychological methods. Energy toxins will disorganise the signals in the energy system. Thus we have to work with energy, signals, and disruptions of signals—and this juggling of tasks is the skill of the energy psychologist.

The scientific basis of energy psychology

Despite the converging evidence of the energy-informational regulation of life, it is still sometimes asserted that energy psychology lacks a scientific basis. Such reactions appear to stem from a difficulty in relating the phenomena and procedures of energy psychology to the more prominent models and theories that prevail in the realms of biology and psychology — assumptions and modes of thought that do not take account of the energy dimension. The prevailing paradigms may be compared to the home page areas offered by some internet service providers, containing a range of packaged options and information; venturing beyond this into the uncharted and unregulated oceans of the wider internet can reveal all manner of data that may be perplexing, ambiguous, and disturbing. Many within the scientific community seem to stay within the safe area, motivated by anxieties regarding peer group approval, status, employment, research funding, and other socio-professional concerns that, whilst completely understandable, function as interferences with true scientific enquiry. A number of the innovators whose work is described above have suffered rejection and hardship as a result of presenting data that is in conflict with the prevailing paradigms. However, the reality of the energy dimension must eventually be accommodated, no matter how challenging to our assumptions, and as Dr Callahan is fond of pointing out, Thought Field Therapy is 'on-line with reality'. Its clear and precise procedures, and their results, are highly replicable and predictable. The phenomena are not theoretical, nor inferred, but can readily be observed directly by anyone who has been trained in the method. A state of distress is encoded in the energy field; when the coding is accessed, through a precise muscle testing procedure, and then played back into the system by tapping a sequence of meridians, the state of distress collapses. Factors which interfere with this process, such as the presence of energy toxins, can be identified and eliminated or neutralised. In this way it has proved possible for us to have easy access, through non-invasive procedures, to the fundamental energy signalling system that regulates the body, brain, and mind. The many profound and exciting implications of this are only just beginning to be explored.

CHAPTER FOURTEEN

Freud, Reich, and bioelectrical energy—from libido to Qi

"In a meeting of the inner circle, Freud counselled foresight. We had to be prepared, he said, that one of these days the psychotherapy of the neuroses would meet a dangerous competitor, a future organotherapy. Nobody could as yet have an idea as to what it would be like, but one could already hear the footsteps of its exponents behind one, he said. Psychoanalysis would have to be placed upon an organic foundation." [Wilhelm Reich, 1960, p. 54]

Libido—the energetic interface of psyche and soma

A theme running throughout Freud's writings was the interface between the psychical and the somatic. One aspect of this interface is the unconscious mind. Thus, in a letter to Georg Groddeck, dated 1917, concerned with organic disease, Freud wrote:

"In my essay on the Ucs which you mention you will find an inconspicuous note: 'An additional important prerogative of the Ucs will be mentioned in another context.' I will divulge to you what this note refers to: The assertion that the Ucs exerts on somatic processes an influence of far greater plastic power than the conscious act ever can." [E. L. Freud, 1961, p. 323].

Freud himself did not explore in detail the implications of psychoanalysis for organic disease, but this hint indicates his intuition of the further possibilities of the psyche-soma interaction—a borderland now addressed by the field of energy psychology. Via the energy system, through kinesiology muscle testing, we have access to both the deep unconscious and the body.

The libido and its quasi-electrical character

A second aspect of this interface is Freud's libido theory—the body-energy dimension. It is a central feature of Freud's work that seems largely forgotten or ignored by many contemporary analysts, who appear to view psychoanalysis as essentially a theory of internalised personal relationships. Throughout his writings, Freud postulated the ego's essential function as one of dealing with, and discharging, the excitation of libido. For example, in a paper outlining the causes of the onset of neurosis [1912c], he wrote:

> "… the quantitative factor should not be left out of account in any consideration of the precipitating causes of illness. All the other factors—frustration, fixation, developmental inhibition—remain ineffective unless they affect a certain amount of libido and bring about a damming up of libido of a certain height." [p. 236]

Freud viewed libido as having quasi-electrical characteristics, as well as being quantitative and capable of flow This is clear in a quote from his early paper on The Neuro-psychoses of Defence.

> "I should like, finally, to dwell for a moment on the working hypothesis which I have made use of in this exposition of the neuroses of defence. I refer to the concept that in mental functions something is to be distinguished—a quota of affect or sum of excitation—which possesses all the characteristics of a quantity (though we have no means of measuring it), which is capable of increase, diminution, displacement and discharge, and which is spread over the memory-traces of ideas somewhat as an electric charge is spread over the surface of a body. This hypothesis … can be applied in the same sense as physicists apply the concept of a flow of electric fluid." [Freud, 1894a, pp. 60–61]

This was not a peripheral or fleeting feature of Freud's thinking. James Strachey, the editor of the Standard Edition of Freud's works, in referring to the above quote, describes it as the "most fundamental of all his hypotheses" [p. 63].

Idea, energy, and affect

In the same discussion, Strachey goes on to explain an apparent ambiguity in some of Freud's writings, showing that a distinction is made between instinctual *energies,* psychical *ideas,* and the experienced *affect.* Thus, in Freud's paper on Repression [1915d, p. 152], he states that the 'psychical representative' of an instinct consists of two elements, one of which is the idea that is 'cathected' (invested with instinctual energy) and the other is the energy that is cathecting it. Freud viewed *affects* as one possible transformation of the energies of instincts [1915d, p. 153]. In his paper on The Unconscious [1915e], Freud argues that affects "correspond to processes of discharge, the final manifestations of which are perceived as feelings" [178]. Thus, clearly implicit in Freud's formulations, that informed his entire writings, are attempts to distinguish thought, energy, and affect, and the interrelationships between them. Freud considered that an idea is problematic *because of its connection with instinctual energy*—a formulation that, despite many differences of overall perspective, has clear points of contact with the TFT concept of the *thought field,* which consists of the idea combined with the energy field of the body.

The sexual origins of neurosis

Part of Freud's reason for his emphasis upon the sexual energy of libido as the key to psychoneuroses was because sexuality so clearly involves both the mind and the body. Thus he wrote in his Introductory Lectures [1916–17]:

> "Let me remind you of one of the very first objections that were brought up against psycho-analysis. It was said then that it was occupied in finding a purely psychological theory of neurotic phenomena and this was quite hopeless, since psychological theories could never explain an illness. People had chosen to forget that the sexual function is not a purely psychical thing any more than it is a purely somatic one. It influences bodily and mental life alike." [pp. 387–388]

Freud arrived at the view, based on his clinical observations, that disturbances in the development and flow of libido always lay at the heart of neuroses. He distinguished those due to current disturbances of sexual life (the 'actual neuroses' — the term 'actual' meaning current) from those that were due to traumas and psychological conflicts that were interfering with libidinal life. Thus, in one of his encyclopaedia articles, he wrote:

> "It [the sexual origins of neurosis] was discovered in the course of the prolonged search for the traumatic experiences from which hysterical symptoms appeared to be derived. The more carefully the search was pursued the more extensive seemed to be the network of aetiologically significant impressions, but the further back, too, did they reach into the patient's puberty or childhood. At the same time they assumed a uniform character and eventually it became inevitable to bow before the evidence and recognise that at the root of the formation of every symptom there were to be found traumatic experiences from early sexual life. Thus a sexual trauma stepped into the place of an ordinary trauma and the latter was seen to owe its aetiological significance to an associative or symbolic connection with the former, which had preceded it. An investigation of cases of common nervousness (falling into the two classes of *neurasthenia* and *anxiety neurosis*) which was simultaneously undertaken led to the conclusion that these disorders could be traced to *contemporary* abuses in the patient's sexual life and could be removed if these were brought to an end. It was thus easy to infer that neuroses in general are an expression of disturbances in sexual life, the so-called actual-neuroses being the consequences (by chemical agency) of contemporary injuries and psychoneuroses the consequences (by psychical modification) of bygone injuries to a psychological function which had hitherto been gravely neglected by science". [1923a, p. 243].

Toxic libido

Freud considered that disturbances of libido can be toxic. For example, in his discussion of the General Theory of the Emotions (Introductory Lectures 1916–17) he states this very clearly:

> "The 'actual' neuroses, in the details of their symptoms and also in their characteristic of influencing every organic system and every function, exhibit an unmistakable resemblance to the pathological states which arise from the chronic influence of external toxic substances and from a sudden withdrawal from them — to intoxi-

cations and conditions of abstinence. The two groups of disorders are brought together still more closely by intermediate conditions such as Grave's disease which we have learnt to recognise as equally due to the operation of toxic substances, but toxins which are not introduced into the body from outside but originate in the subject's own metabolism. In view of these analogies, we cannot, I think, avoid regarding the neuroses as results of disturbances in the sexual metabolism, whether because more of these sexual toxins is produced than the subject can deal with, or whether because internal and even psychical conditions restrict the proper employment of these substances." [p. 388]

Narcissism and hypochondria as 'actual neuroses'

In his paper On Narcissism [1914c], Freud posits hypochondria as a third actual neurosis, alongside neurasthenia and simple anxiety neurosis:

"Hypochondria, like organic disease, manifests itself in distressing and painful bodily sensations, and it has the same effect as organic disease on the distribution of libido. The hypochondriac withdraws both interest and libido—the latter especially markedly—from the objects of the external world and concentrates both of them upon the organ that is engaging his attention. A difference between hypochondria and organic disease now becomes evident: in the latter, the distressing sensations are based upon demonstrable [organic] changes; in the former, this is not so. But it would be entirely in keeping with our general conception of the processes of neurosis if we decided to say that hypochondria must be right: organic changes must be supposed to be present in it too. But what could these changes be? We will let ourselves be guided at this point by our experience, which shows that bodily sensations of an unpleasant nature, comparable to those of hypochondria, occur in the other neuroses as well. I have said before that I am inclined to class hypochondria with neurasthenia and anxiety-neurosis as a third 'actual' neurosis ... Now the familiar prototype of an organ that is painfully tender, that is in some way changed and that is not diseased in the ordinary sense, is the genital organ in its states of excitation. In that condition it becomes congested with blood, swollen and humected, and is the seat of a multiplicity of sensations. Let us now, taking any part of the body, describe its activity of sending sexually exciting stimuli to the mind as its 'erotogenicity', and let us further reflect that the considerations on which the theory of sexuality was based have long accustomed us to the notion that certain other parts of the body—the erotogenic zones—may act as substitutes for the genitals and behave analogously to them. We have only one more step to take. We can decide to regard erotogenicity as a general characteristic of all organs and may then speak of an increase or decrease of it in a particular part of the body." [pp. 8384]

Freud goes on to posit that the damming up of libido in the body and mind is experienced as unpleasurable. He hypothesises that this is why it is necessary for mental life to pass beyond narcissism and attach libido to others whom we love: "A strong egoism is a protection against falling ill, but in the last resort we must begin to love in order not to fall ill, and we are bound to fall ill if, in consequence of frustration, we are unable to love." [p. 85] In narcissistic megalomania, it is the ego itself that is invested with libido, whereas in the case of psychoneurotic people there is an excessive directing of libido towards unreal or phantasised figures.

The actual neurotic core of the psychoneuroses

A further aspect of the relationship between the two forms of neurosis (the actual and the psychoneurotic) is stated in Freud's Introductory Lectures [1916–17], where he explains that an actual neurosis may form the kernel of a psychoneurosis:

"A noteworthy relation between the symptoms of the 'actual' neuroses and of the psychoneuroses makes a further important contribution to our knowledge of the formation of symptoms in the latter. For a symptom of an 'actual' neurosis is often the nucleus and first stage of a psychoneurotic symptom. ... In such cases they play the part of the grain of sand which a mollusc coats with layers of mother-of-pearl." [pp. 390–391].

In 1925, in his Autobiographical Study, Freud states his position clearly:

"I was thus led into regarding the neuroses as being without exception disturbances of the sexual function, the so-called 'actual neuroses' being the direct toxic expression of such disturbances and the psychoneuroses their mental expression." [1925d, p. 25]

And he adds a few lines later:

Since that time I have had no opportunity of returning to the investigation of the 'actual neuroses'; nor has this part of my work been
carried on by anyone else. If I look back today at my early findings,
they strike me as being the first rough outlines of what is probably a
far more complicated subject. But on the whole they seem to me to
still hold good." [p. 26]

Freud concluded there was little more that psychoanalysis could
offer in relation to the actual neuroses:

"What characterises psycho-analysis as a science is not the material
which it handles but the technique with which it works. It can be
applied to the history of civilisation, to the science of religion and
to mythology, no less than to the theory of the neuroses, without
doing violence to its essential nature. What it aims at and achieves is
nothing other than the uncovering of what is unconscious in mental
life. The problems of the 'actual' neuroses, whose symptoms are
probably generated by direct toxic damage, offer psycho-analysis
no points of attack. It can do little towards throwing light on them
and must leave the task to biologico-medical research." [1916–17,
p. 389]

Traumatic over-stimulation as an actual neurosis

In Freud's final reformulations of his theories of anxiety [*Inhibitions,
Symptoms and Anxiety*, 1926d], he still wrote in passing of the actual
neuroses, but now incorporating the idea that the excessive excitation of trauma could form the basis of an actual neurosis—again
assuming a model of the mind in which the ego has formed to
manage excitation:

"… it must be remembered that in the experiences which lead to a
traumatic neurosis the protective shield against external stimuli is
broken through and excessive amounts of excitation impinge upon
the mental apparatus …" [p. 130]

and he adds a few pages later

"Analysis of the traumatic war neuroses … would probably have
shown that a number of them possess some characteristics of the
'actual' neuroses." [p. 141]

Thus it is possible to discern in Freud's thinking the idea of two sources of actual neurosis—two ways in which a person's ego may experience difficulties in managing the energy in the psycho-somatic system. One way is when the flow of internal libido is blocked, either due to behavioural limits to its expression or as a result of psychodynamic conflict. The other way is through traumatic impingement that violently infuses unmanageable levels of excitation from outside. It is worth noting within this model that sexual abuse of children will combine these aspects—generating libidinal energetic overload as a result of infusion by the adult's libido which also over-stimulates that of the child.

Since Freud's original work on the actual neuroses, which he never repudiated, most psychoanalysts have ignored this aspect of psycho-somatic life. There have been some exceptions, such as Blau [1952] and Zucker [1979]—and Fink [1970] draws attention to the way in which some of Freud's observations on the actual neuroses were supported by the later work of Masters and Johnson in their research on human sexual response.

Wilhelm Reich pursues Freud's concept of the actual neuroses

It was left to Wilhelm Reich to explore the phenomena and implications of the actual neuroses further. Reich describes two cases he worked with in 1920 that helped give rise to his impressions of the need for deeper consideration of these aspects. The first was a young student, referred to him by Freud, suffering from compulsive ruminations, compulsive anal phantasies, excessive masturbation and severe neurasthenic symptoms including pains, headaches, lack of concentration and nausea. Initially the treatment seemed stalled, as compulsive rumination was transformed into compulsive associating. Reich describes what transpired as follows:

"After some time, an incest phantasy broke through, and for the first time the patient masturbated with satisfaction. With that, all the symptoms disappeared suddenly. In the course of a week they gradually returned. When he masturbated a second time, the symptoms disappeared again, only to return again after a short time. This was repeated for several weeks. Finally it was possible to analyse his guilt feelings about masturbation and to correct some practices and attitudes which interfered with complete gratification. After that his condition improved visibly. After nine months of treatment, he was discharged, considerably improved, and able to work. He kept in touch with me for over six years; he married and remained well." [1960 (1948), p. 27]

The second case was a waiter who suffered from a complete inability to have an erection. In the third year of treatment a reconstruction of a 'primal scene' was possible. When he was two years old, his mother had another child and the patient had observed from another room. His impression was of a big bloody hole between his mother's legs. This corresponded to a feeling of emptiness in his own genitals. In a manner consistent with psychoanalytic knowledge at the time, Reich had connected the feeling of emptiness with phantasies of the castrated female genital and so forth. However, he later recognised that this feeling of emptiness, in this patient and others, reflected a "withdrawal of biological energy from the genital". Reich's analysis of the patient was considered correct by his senior colleagues at the time—but the impotence was unchanged. Subsequently, Reich considered the patient's difficulties as being to do with his pervasively rigid character structure.

Reich built his theorising explicitly on the basis of Freud's original concept of the actual neuroses—and the notion that there is an 'actual neurotic core' to the psychoneuroses:

> "In the actual neuroses in Freud's sense, biological energy is misdirected; it is blocked from access to consciousness and motility. The anxiety and the immediate vegetative symptoms are, as it were, malignant growths which are now nourished by the undischarged sexual energy. But on the other hand, the peculiar psychic manifestations of hysterias and compulsion neuroses also looked like biologically meaningless malignant growths. Where did *they* derive their energy from? Undoubtedly from the 'actual neurotic core' of the dammed-up sexual energy. This, and nothing else, could be the source of energy in the psychoneurosis. No other interpretation would fit Freud's suggestion … There could be no doubt: *The psychoneuroses had an actual neurotic core and the actual neuroses had a psychoneurotic superstructure.*" [ibid. pp. 32–33]

The idea and the excitation

Pursuing the relationship between the psychic *idea* and the somatic *excitation*, Reich noted that the idea of sexual intercourse is vivid and forceful if one is in a state of sexual excitement, but becomes "dim, colourless and vague" after sexual gratification. It is the endowment of an idea with excitation that makes it vivid and forceful. Reich explains the implications of this as follows:

"If, as in the case of the stasis neurosis [Reich's term for the actual neuroses], the idea of sexual intercourse does not arise in conscious-ness, due to moral inhibition, the excitation attaches itself to other ideas that are less subject to censorship. From this, I concluded: the stasis neurosis is a somatic disturbance caused by sexual excitation which is misdirected because it is frustrated. However, without a psychic inhibition, sexual energy can never become misdirected. I was surprised that Freud had overlooked this fact. Once an inhibi-tion has created the sexual stasis, this in turn may easily increase the inhibition and reactivate infantile ideas which then take the place of normal ones. That is, infantile experiences which in themselves are in no way pathological, may, due to a present-day inhibition, become endowed with an excess of sexual energy. Once this has happened, they become urgent; being in conflict with adult psychic organisa-tion, they have to be kept down by repression. Thus, the chronic psychoneurosis with its infantile sexual content, develops on the basis of a sexual inhibition which is conditioned by present-day cir-cumstances and apparently 'harmless' at the outset. This is the nature of Freud's 'regression to infantile mechanisms'. All cases that I have treated showed this mechanism. If the neurosis had developed not in childhood but at a later age, it was shown regularly that some 'normal' inhibition or difficulty of the sexual life had created a stasis, and this in turn had reactivated infantile incestuous desires and sexual anxieties." [ibid. p. 36]

Orgastic impotence

Reich found that all his patients displayed a severe disturbance of genital sexuality. They might be capable of sexual activity, and in the case of men, might be very erectively potent, but their orgasm was accompanied by little pleasure or surrender.

"Orgastic potency is the capacity for surrender to the flow of biologi-cal energy without any inhibition, the capacity for complete discharge of all dammed-up sexual excitation through involuntary pleasurable contractions of the body. Not a single neurotic individual possesses orgastic potency." [ibid. p. 43]

Sexual energy drives the neurosis

Reich concluded that psychic conflict and somatic stasis reinforce each other. The psychic conflict blocks the flow of sexual energy, forcing it back into earlier paths, thereby energising infantile sexual desires and intensifying the conflict and inhibition. Reich states:

> "The central psychic conflict is the sexual child-parent relationship. It is present in every neurosis. It is the *historical* experiential *material* that furnishes the *content* of the *neurosis*. All neurotic phantasies stem from the infantile sexual attachment to the parents. But the child-parent conflict could not produce an enduring disturbance of the psychic equilibrium if it were not continually nourished by the actual stasis which this conflict itself originally produced. Sexual stasis is, there- fore, the etiological factor which—constantly present in the immediate situation—affords to the neurosis, not its content, but its *energy* ... *The pathogenicity of the Oedipus complex*, therefore, depends on *whether or not there is a physiologically adequate discharge of sexual energy*. Thus, actual neurosis (stasis neurosis) and psychoneurosis are interwoven, and cannot be thought of as independent of each other." [ibid pp. 52–53]

What is the sexual energy? Reich's studies of bio-electricity

Reich puzzled about the nature of the sexual energy, and its observable and experienced manifestations when it broke through a patient's muscular character armour as a result of therapy. He found that when he was able to bring about a dissolution of charac- terological inhibitions and attitudes, and more especially a chronic muscular tension, "one of three basic biological excitations made its appearance: anxiety, anger or sexual excitation". [1960 (1949), p. 120]. Pondering whether these resulting 'vegetative currents', characterised by a sense of flowing movement, might reflect move- ments of body fluids, he concluded that purely mechanical move- ments could not account for all the sensations experienced, such as the melting quality of preorgastic sensations of pleasure. Moreover he noted that in cases of orgastic impotence, the genital may be engorged with blood and yet be without pleasurable excitation. He concluded that "The unknown 'something' I was looking for could be nothing but bio-electricity." [1960 (1949), p. 123].

Reich's explorations of this bio-electricity are described in a col- lection of his articles republished in 1982, under the title The Bioelec- tical Investigation of Sexuality and Anxiety.

"In the sexual act, two bioelectrically highly charged organisms come into contact with one another. The higher psychic functions cease temporarily. Everything is concentrated on the discharge of vegetative high tension. Two bodies experiencing orgastic ecstasy are nothing more than a quivering mass of plasm. ... The surface of the penis must be seen as one electrode and the vaginal mucosa as the other. The contact between the two is made by the acidic female secretion acting as an electrolyte." [1982, p. 13]

He reports a variety of electrical measures of shifting voltages on the body surface in response to pleasurable and unpleasurable stimulation, showing the electrical manifestations of sexual excitation.

Reich arrived at the view that anxiety and sexuality represent opposite flows of bio-electrical energy. In sexual arousal, the flow is outwards towards the world, the genitals expand, and the parasympathetic reaction predominates, whereas in a state of anxiety the flow is away from the world, the genitals shrink, and the sympathetic reaction predominates. Moreover, he postulated an antithesis between the body centre and the periphery:

"When the body's periphery is excited, sexual sensation is generated; when the centre, the area around the heart and diaphragm, is excited, anxiety is experienced. ... the idea of a functional antithesis between body centre and body periphery ..." [1982, p. 32].

Whilst many psychoanalysts have viewed aggression and destructiveness as primary drives, Reich did not. He states:

"Destructiveness is a biological reaction to the denial of sexual gratification ... a destructive act is the substitute for unattainable gratification in love." [1982, p. 37]

However, he saw both sexuality and destructiveness as directed 'towards the world'—and considered that the true antithesis of both these is anxiety, which is a flight 'away from the world'.

Harold Saxton Burr's studies of L-fields

Around the same time that Reich was exploring the bio-electric aspects of the human psychosomatic system, another researcher, Dr Harold Saxton Burr was also using a voltmeter to map the electrical charges on the surface of the body and to correlate these with states of health and sickness. Burr called these electrodynamic fields of life, L-fields. In a manner startlingly similar to Rupert Sheldrake's formulation of morphogenic fields that organise life forms, Burr wrote:

"Most people who have taken high-school science will remember that if iron-filings are scattered on a card held over a magnet they will arrange themselves in the pattern of the 'lines of force' of the magnet's field. And if the filings are thrown away and fresh ones scattered on the card, the new filings will assume the same pattern as the old.

Something like this, although infinitely more complicated — happens in the human body. Its molecules and cells are constantly being torn apart and rebuilt with fresh material from the food we eat. But, thanks to the controlling L-field, the new molecules and cells are rebuilt as before and arrange themselves in the same patterns as the old ones." [Burr, 1972, p. 12]

Burr found that measuring L-fields, by finding the difference in voltage between two points on the body, can give early warnings of illness. Diseased parts of the body show alterations in patterns of polarity, as is also found during a woman's menstrual cycle. In a psychiatric study, his research team also found abnormal voltage patterns on the bodies of those with serious mental illness:

"Results of the study showed clearly enough that the group consisting of those markedly deviated from normal behaviour by psychiatric examination also showed a similar deviation in electro-metric examination." [1972, p. 86]

He proposes:

"… the fascinating possibility that psychiatrists of the future will be able to measure the intensity of grief, anger, or love electrically — and as easily as we measure temperature or noise levels today. 'Heartbreak', hate, or love, in other words, may one day be measurable in millivolts." [1972, p. 17].

With such a remark, we are reminded of Freud's comment quoted earlier, that "in mental functions something is to be distinguished — a quota of affect or sum of excitation … which is spread over the memory-traces of ideas somewhat as an electric charge is spread over the surface of a body. This hypothesis ... can be applied in the same sense as physicists apply the concept of a flow of electric fluid." [Freud, 1894a, pp. 60–61] What Reich and Burr demonstrated was that this excitation is not only spread over the 'ideas' of the psyche, but is indeed also spread over the surface of the body, having electrical qualities that can be measured.

TFT explorations of the body's electricity

Much more recently, Dr Callahan and others within the TFT community, have been exploring the possibilities of measuring psychological reversal as shifts in electrical potentials on the body, using simple modern voltmeters. Although the readings have an inherent instability, a striking trend is often observed. Disturbing thoughts bring about a shift in mini-voltage measurements, as is also found when an electrode is placed on an area of disease in the body. There have been reports of practitioners detecting physical illness before it had otherwise become apparent, through these shifts in voltage patterns.

The meridians and the energy circuits

At this point we can begin to relate these observations and theories to the meridian energy fields of traditional Chinese medicine, one of the frameworks that inform contemporary energy psychology. Within this perspective, meridians are channels that carry the flow of subtle energy, known as Qi (pronounced 'Chee'; it has various other names in different traditions—for example, prana in the Hindu system). These form a closely-knit network that connect the internal organs with the body extremities, and are thought to play an important part in regulating the functions of the body. There are twelve main bilateral channels running up and down either side of the body and two central vessels running up and down the midline.

One kind of analogy is to think of the meridians as like electrical circuits, in which the current of Qi flows against various resistances and capacitances. In a state of dis-ease, a short circuit occurs, causing too much Qi to flow across some points and diminished supply to other areas. The acupressure points, where the meridians are thought to flow near the surface of the body, are known to be points of diminished electrical resistance.

Another kind of analogy is to envisage Qi as flowing along meridians, in a similar way to the flow of water along a riverbed. Smaller branches and streams irrigate the surrounding areas—and thus the whole of the body is supplied with Qi. When there is physical or mental dis-ease, the channels of Qi become blocked. This can result in diminished flow of Qi along one meridian, with flooding above the blockage, or perhaps excessive flow along other meridians, just as would be the case with any flowing liquid.

These analogies are helpful, but probably should not be taken too literally. The meridians may not be entirely equivalent to physical channels, but may have a more dynamic, fluctuating, and indeed elusive, quality. Nevertheless they give some hints of the kinds of problems or disturbances that can occur within the energy circuits.

The energy circuits are also considered to be transmitters of information. Cell biologist, James Oschman [2000] proposes that meridians are like the main transmission lines in the biochemical fabric of the body:

"Every part of the body, including all of the molecules so thoroughly studied by modern science, as well as the acupuncture meridians of traditional East Asian or Oriental medicine, forms a continuously interconnected semiconductor electronic network. Each component of the organism, even the smallest part, is immersed in, and generates, a constant stream of vibratory information. This is information about all of the activities taking place everywhere in the body." [p. 71]

Energy, flow, blockage, and symptoms

In common with the observations and insights of Freud and Reich, we find as we consider meridians, the following notions: an *energy* which has bioelectrical qualities; a natural *flow* of this energy; *information* in the flow of energy; *blockages* in the flow; and the physical and mental disturbances that may *give rise to* these blockages, or may *result from* them. The concepts of libido, orgone energy, and Qi seem in many ways interchangeable. When these are blocked, physical and mental symptoms arise. Taking these overlapping frameworks together, it would appear that blockages may occur as a result of various factors: physical or emotional trauma; energy toxins; infectious agents; psychodynamic conflict. Once a blockage has occurred, it may give rise to further symptoms—just as Freud indicated in his

outline of the interplay between the actual neuroses and the psychoneuroses, and as elaborated by Reich.

The association between the meridians and mental and physical
dis-ease is now well established by the remarkable effectiveness of
Thought Field Therapy. In this procedure, a person holds a troubling thought or idea in consciousness and then taps on a particular
sequence of meridian points; usually this results in a rapid drop in
distress (providing other factors are not impeding this shift). The idea,
in a state of excitation, is invested with both emotion and meridian
energy. As the person taps on the meridian points, the excitation falls
away, along with the emotion. When the person then thinks of the
same idea, it no longer evokes excitation or emotion.

Energy and information—controversy

Here we enter an area of seeming controversy and conceptual difficulty. Dr Callahan emphasises the importance of the correct
sequence of meridian points to be tapped for the particular problem
and for the particular individual—although 'off the shelf' algorithms
often work quite well. He considers the sequence as analogous to the
code that releases a combination lock; tapping the wrong sequence is
useless, according to this principle. Practitioners of TFT can readily
verify from their own experience that sequence is important—that
tapping one sequence may have no effect whatsoever but tapping
another sequence brings a rapid drop in subjective distress. On the
other hand, Gary Craig, developer of the TFT derivative, Emotional
Freedom Techniques (EFT), argues that sequence is not important
and that tapping on the points in any order will bring results. The
thousands of EFT practitioners around the world know, also from
their own experience, that EFT works well—and certainly is an
improvement on therapeutic endeavours that do not include energy
tapping. Craig postulates that "the cause of all negative emotions
is a disruption in the body's energy system" [stated on his website
and training materials www.emofree.com]. However, this is not a
view shared by Dr Callahan. He argues that the energy field is not
in a state of disruption, but contains highly organised information—
'perturbations'—which generate emotional and physiological states.
The meridian sequence coding of the perturbation can be found
rather precisely through muscle testing. Moreover, he points out that

the physiology of anxiety, for example, is not a disorganised or disrupted state, but is highly organised. Thus, he argues that the energy field is carrying encoded information, which is cleared as the precise meridian code is tapped. For Callahan, it is not a matter of blocked meridians, or of disruptions in the energy flow.

The coding in the flow

How can we reconcile these seemingly divergent and incompatible perspectives? Acupuncture and traditional Chinese medicine do consider that physical and mental problems are associated with disruptions in the flow of Qi. This is also similar to the insights of Freud and Reich. On the other hand, Dr Callahan discovered how the energy field does indeed appear to contain precisely coded information—a meridian sequence that can be derived through a standard procedure of muscle testing. So is the issue essentially one to do with *flow*, or with *information*? Once the question is posed this way, it is easy to see a possible answer. The information is encoded in the sequence of on-off flows of Qi in the meridians. We might suppose that a meridian is digital in its informational encoding: thus it can be open or closed. We may further suppose that when we experience an emotion that does not become fixed but is processed normally, there is a natural flow of energy through the meridian circuits—perhaps particularly through those meridians that are linked with that specific emotion, as indicated in the work of John Diamond. It may be that particular emotional experiences are associated with a particular patterning of meridian flow. When the flow is blocked for some reason, then the patterning in the energy system remains stuck—and the stuck pattern is reactivated whenever the person thinks of the troubling idea or memory. If the person taps on their meridian system in the appropriate sequence, then the blockage is cleared, the energy can flow in its specific pattern until it is dispersed; this dispersal coincides with the collapse of subjective feelings of distress.

To take a simple example, Dr Callahan's patient, Mary, who was completely relieved of her severe phobia of water by tapping only on the stomach meridian under the eye, presumably experienced a build up of energy in her stomach when she thought of water and this was associated with the state of intense anxiety. When the meridian was cleared, the accumulated Qi presumably flowed away rapidly so that the tension in her stomach dissipated and her anxiety collapsed. She stated that she had previously experienced the anxiety as located in her stomach. In most cases, the emotional states and accompanying meridian patternings are more complex. Muscle testing indicates that one meridian must be addressed before another, perhaps corresponding to layerings of emotions in the particular constellation of distress the person is experiencing.

Blockage in the informational-energy flow

The blockage in the patterned flow of Qi may occur for various reasons—and some may as yet be unknown to us. One reason, familiar within the classic Freudian paradigm, is that the conscious mind cannot tolerate processing the associated emotional experience, or perceives unconsciously that there is danger in becoming conscious of a potential emotion or impulse, and so the process is shut down; this would be a blocking of the informational-energy flow as a result of psychodynamic conflict. A second reason is the presence of psychological (or psychoenergetic) reversal; a literal reversal of the normal voltage polarity and direction of energetic flow. Such a reversal would obviously block the normal discharge of the patterned energy flow. A reversal may be the result of psychodynamic conflict, or blocking beliefs (i.e. factors within the psychological realm), but it can also result from the influence of individual energy toxins (factors within the biochemical or electromagnetic realms). If an energy toxin is causing reversals or other disruptions in the system, then attempts to clear a patterned blockage in the meridians will tend to be continually thwarted unless the toxin is removed or neutralised. This tends to be what we find when toxins are present—that in trying to work through the perturbations in the meridians, muscle testing reveals a long, seemingly endless, patterning of meridians to tap and a clear resolution is not achieved. When the toxin is identified and then removed or neutralised, it is often quite a simple tapping sequence that clears the perturbations.

One rather fundamental problem in our understanding must be acknowledged here. When we use TFT muscle testing diagnosis to ascertain a sequence of meridian points to be tapped, we do not know exactly what the muscle test means, other than that we should tap on a particular meridian. The client 'therapy localises' to various meridian 'alarm points' until one is found that makes the muscle strong. We do not know what this means at the energetic level— whether the meridian is blocked, or has too much energy flowing, or something quite different that we have not thought of. All we know is that tapping on the treatment point will help towards clearing the perturbation. The procedure is clear and fairly reliable. Following it leads to good clinical outcome in terms of relief of distress. But exactly why and how remains, in part, a mystery.

How does this model of meridian flow sequence as patterned information sit with Gary Craig's approach to EFT, where any or all of the meridians are tapped in any sequence? There are some differences in the technique of TFT and EFT. In the latter, there is great emphasis upon focusing on aspects—the sensory, cognitive, or emotional components of the target memory or feared situation. EFT is recognised not to work well if it is applied too broadly. The specific aspect is identified and continually emphasised by the procedure of the client speaking a phrase relating to this at each tapping point. In EFT there is quite an emphasis upon using the right language, whilst there is less emphasis upon finding the right sequence of tapping points. By contrast, with TFT it seems more possible to target an experience relatively globally. The specific aspects are picked up through muscle testing for the specificity of the sequence. This still does not quite explain how it is that EFT works as well as it does—since, according to Dr Callahan's theory and the daily observations of TFT practitioners, it should not do. Perhaps there is an additional element that plays a part. It is often noticed, particularly in EFT where the universal sequence becomes familiar and routine, that the tapping procedure is quite comforting. A hypothesis that is often proposed, and supported by substantial research evidence in relation to acupuncture [Stux et al. 2003], is that tapping on the extra-sensitive acupressure points brings about a relaxation response and the release of endorphins, just as is sometimes suggested in relation to acupuncture with needles. Tapping on the meridian points seems to make the whole psycho-somatic-energy system somehow more plastic and fluid, able to release stress and relinquish rigid attitudes and thought patterns. Although not an entirely satisfactory position in terms of theoretical clarity, it would appear that whilst the specific sequential tapping of TFT is the most efficient way of freeing the trapped patterns of energy in the meridian system, the more general tapping and talking of EFT is also able to bring about rapid change—and in the latter case, the psychotherapeutic skills of finding the optimum therapeutic focus and choice of words are crucial.

Perhaps the concept of the 'radiant circuits' provides a clue as to what might be happening in the non-specific methods such as EFT. These, less commonly cited patterns of energy, have also been termed the 'strange circuits' because of their odd behaviour, shifting around rather than remaining in relatively fixed channels. David Feinstein (2004) in his 'energy interactive CD' suggests they behave sometimes like hyperlinks on a webpage, jumping instantly to areas of need. Donna Eden, his clairvoyant partner in their work, cannot see meridians in primitive organisms, but can see the radiant circuits in them. They hypothesise, therefore that meridians are the energy paths left by the long term flow of radiant circuits. The radiant circuits appear to be particularly involved in positive emotional and energetic states, such as joy, and in healing and psychic phenomena. It seems possible, then, that in methods such as EFT, the radiant circuits play a role, bringing about energetic flow and healing wherever directed by the thought field and the client-therapist's intention.

One of the important contributions that Thought Field Therapy can add to the perspectives of Freud, Reich, and traditional Chinese medicine is that energy within the human system not only flows and can be blocked, but also carries information encoded in its pattern of flow or impedance of flow. This was not recognised before. In general acupuncturists do not appear to know about the significance of sequence of meridians.

Another illuminating discovery through TFT and other forms of energy psychology is that of psycho-energetic reversal. Although there had been earlier observations of 'reversal of the body's morality', reported by John Diamond, it was Dr Callahan who identified most clearly the phenomenon of psychological reversal and explored its implications. Again, it is not generally known by acupuncturists, or by many kinesiologists. In a state of general, or massive, reversal, a person's mood is negative, he or she is self-sabotaging, and experiences attractions and desires towards that which is destructive or even perverse. It is a condition comparable to Freud's [1920] description of the death instinct. Profoundly destructive states of mind and their associated ideologies of hatred and perverse life-denying religions may be viewed as dense concentrations of reversed energy.

What is the energy of energy psychology?

But what exactly is this energy of Qi, libido, or orgone? Certainly it has electrical qualities, measurable by conventional voltmeters, as shown in the work of Reich, Burr, and Callahan. Moreover, the acupoints and energy meridians of the body have different electrical resistance compared to other parts of the skin. Becker and Seldon (1985) also reported research suggesting a bodily energy system responsible for the organisation and healing of the body. On the other hand, this bio-energy and its energy fields appear to have other qualities that go beyond those of electricity.

Stanford physicist, William Tiller (1997) reported at length on the detection and measurement of subtle energy fields. Whilst these energies seem to have something in common with conventional electromagnetic fields, they also appear somewhat different. For example, one study showed that both conventional high intensity magnetic fields and the subtle energy fields of healers consistently accelerated the activity of enzymes, but no significant magnetic activity could be detected around the healers' hands.

Oschman [2000] reports on studies by Dr John Zimmerman of the biomagnetic field produced by the hands of practitioners of therapeutic touch. A SQUID magnetometer was used, designed to study weak human biomagnetic fields. As the therapeutic touch practitioner went into a meditative state, a huge biomagnetic field emanated from his hands: "The field was so strong that the amplifiers and recorders had to be readjusted so that a recording could be made." [p. 78]

Some studies point to qualities akin to light. It seems that the body's internal system operates by means of tiny amounts of biologically generated light. This is the case at the microlevel of cell structure and function. Marco Bischof has written a book called *Biophotons—The Light in Our Cells* (not yet available in English). In his summary, he writes:

> "According to biophoton theory ... the biphoton light is stored in the cells of the organism—more precisely in the DNA molecules of their nuclei—and a dynamic web of light constantly released and stored by the DNA may connect cell organelles, cells, tissues, and organs within the body and serve as the organism's main communication network and as the principle regulating instance for all life processes ..."
> [www.transpersonal-de/mbischof/englisch/webbookend.htm]

Is the sexual energy of libido the same as the energy emanating from healers? One male client reported that as energetic clearing of perturbations took place, during Thought Field Therapy and related methods, he often experienced a slight sensation in his genitals. Another client reported a strong sensation of energy emanating from his hands following a tapping exercise that had relieved deep perturbations and left him feeling more positive and free than he had for years. Observations such as these lead me to hypothesise that essentially the same energy is involved at all levels, but is refracted through the lenses of each particular chakra or other energy transformer or way-station. There is a need for energetic flow throughout the meridian, chakra, and other circuits; blockage at any level or area can lead to malfunction or limitation of optimum personal development.

Pearsall's summary of L energy

In his book *The Heart's Code*, Paul Pearsall (1998) summarises various characteristics of what he calls 'L energy', drawing on diverse sources of information. His studies are inspired by work with heart transplant patients, who have been found often to develop memories and attitudes characteristic of the heart donor. There is evidence that the heart itself can feel and think, and is the locus of a subtle and powerful form of energy.

Pearsall [p. 43] reports an experiment carried out in 1993 under the auspices of the U.S. army intelligence command. White blood cells taken from the mouth of a volunteer were centrifuged and then placed in a test tube. A probe was placed in the test tube, connected to a polygraph. Then the person who had donated the cells sat in another room and was shown a film with many violent scenes. As the volunteer watched the scenes, the cells in the test tube showed signs of extreme excitation. When the experiment was repeated several times, with the cells up to 50 miles away from the donor and up to two days after the donation, the same effect was shown. The cells were energetically and informationally connected to the donor despite the gap in space and time. This is another instance of the non-local, action at a distance, recognised in quantum physics—notably through Bell's Theorem, a quantum physics law that states that once connected, objects continue to affect one another forever regardless of distance and time.

Pearsall notes that L energy appears to travel faster than the speed of light, radiating out everywhere simultaneously, accounting for the 'nonlocal' effects of occurrences such as telepathy, remote healing and the the power of intercessionary prayer. It is not only nonlocal (everywhere) but also negentropic, formative, and organising in its effects—the exact opposite of the effects from Newton's second law of thermodynamics and its prediction of entropy. L energy is often accompanied by an electromagnetic field and others of the four known forms of energy (gravity, and weak and strong nuclear energy) but is different from all these forms of energy in its power, measurability, conduction, speed and reception.

Although it is not usually detectable through the senses, L energy occasionally reveals itself in various observable ways, such as spirals, a cloud surrounding the body, glowing etheric webs etc. and sometimes there seems to be tracings of its presence as if it is flowing back and forth from one person to another. Some sensitive people are able to perceive this more clearly.

Tachyon energy, sex and the sacred

L energy, or subtle energy, may also be related to the idea of tachyon energy (Jell, 2000; Wagner & Cousins, 1999)—regarded as the first formed, faster than light, energy that emerges at the interface of the zero point field and the quantum level of the physical universe. Tachyon energy can be viewed as the messenger between the formless zero point source and the quantum realm of the physical. It is omnipresent and travels faster than the speed of light. According to the principles outlined by Einstein, *the speed of light forms a kind of barrier*— nothing that is travelling below the speed of light can be accelerated beyond the speed of light, and nothing travelling faster than light can be reduced to the speed of light. However, physicist David Wagner, inventor of a process of creating tachyon antennae cells, claims that tachyon interacts with the quantum field, in a complex way, to manifest our physical world. Tachyon energy contains the potential for all frequencies. It interacts with what Gabriel Cousens [1987] has called the Subtle Organising Energy Fields (SOEFs) that determine the form of all physical and living entities, giving these increased energy.

Wagner postulates an 'energetic continuum', whereby the source energy of the zero point field condenses down into decreasingly slow frequencies, culminating in what we experience as the dense physical world. As the tachyon energy emerges from the zero point source, it interacts with the Subtle Organising Energy Fields (SOEFs), which then organise it into the various bodies, from the most subtle to the most dense. The SOEFs channel tachyon into the quantum energy field, forming the basis of the atomic and molecular structure of our three-dimensional physical world. Wagner describes how the tachyons interact with the SOEFs for each subatomic particle, transforming them progressively into more dense particles—thus, for example, transforming a pion into a muon (having an orbit 10 times higher than a pion), which is then transformed into an electron (having an orbit 207 times that of a muon)—and so on, all the way down the energetic continuum.

It becomes possible to see that this energy, in its various forms, whether it is called libido, orgone, or Qi, or tachyon, is the very essence of life. Sex and the sacred appear as different forms of the same energy that courses through the chakras, meridians, and subtle organising fields of mind and body, infusing the spectrum of human motives and potentials, from the highest strivings for spiritual awareness to the most basic instincts of survival. Moreover, this energy is benign, and life-seeking—negentropic, as Pearsall notes. Intense and perverse destructiveness, so readily a feature of human society, appears not to be a feature of this energy in its healthy form, but an expression of its literal reversal. Reversed energy, with its links to destructiveness, chaos, and entropy, is parasitic on healthy Qi. Unlike the benign tachyon energy flowing from the source in the zero point field, reversed energy has no source of its own.

Qi and sexual abuse—devastation of the energy circuits

Freud's intimations of the role of libido in psychosomatic life began with his explorations of the effects of sexual abuse on a child's development. Whilst many of the psychological, and even neurobiolgical, effects of childhood sexual abuse are now well-known (Mollon, 2002), the damage to the child's energy system is less appreciated. This damage occurs even when there are no other traumatic elements associated with violence, intimidation, and pain. When a child is exposed to premature sexual stimulation by an older person, his or her libidinal circuits are overloaded. The combining of the libidinal excitation arising within the child's own system with that irradiated from the other person's body, creates an intensity of energy that is both confusing and potentially terrifying. Its quantitative aspect cannot be managed by the child's ego, nor can its meaning be processed. The child's energy circuits can be literally blown apart, but this devastating yet subtle damage is relatively hidden. Emergency shutting down of the energy system may occur, giving rise to deep and pervasive inhibitions in subtle energetic flow, alternating with experiential states of feeling wide open and energetically leaking. Dissociative vacating of the body may occur, creating a sort of energetic firewall between the body and the experiencing self, that can block healing methods until this is addressed. In addition, the hypersexualised circuits of the abused child mean that he or she then becomes an energetic beacon attracting further abuse, as so often seems to happen. The energetic dimensions of trauma effects are worth further consideration.

CHAPTER FIFTEEN

Is the 'energy' concept necessary? A cognitive model of Emotional Freedom Technique

T he following article was written as a basis for discussion within NHS settings, where the concept of 'energy' has appeared troubling and problematic for some people. It seems that a minority of individuals react with alarm and anxiety to the idea of subtle energy and other phenomena that are not easy to measure. The quality of argument driven by these emotional reactions is usually poor, often consisting of little more than the assertion that the method "sounds wacky".[1] Nevertheless, it seemed a valuable exercise to explore to what extent it is possible to frame an energy psychology method entirely within concepts that are familiar in other forms of psychological therapy. This outline of a cognitive model manages to avoid any reference to purported energy systems. As a model, it works reasonable well as a plausible account of EFT. It cannot, however, take account of the energy phenomena (nor the derived theory) on which Thought Field Therapy is based—the clear encoding of a thought-emotion structure in the energy field of the body.

A Cognitive Model of Emotional Freedom Technique [EFT]

Abstract

The components of EFT are readily conceptualised as sharing constructs and strategies with cognitive-behaviour therapy –such as exposure, desensitisation, and cognitive reframing. Procedurally it is very similar to EMDR, a therapy also developed within a cognitive-behavioural framework. Desensitisation through tapping on the body appears to involve a disruption in the previous patterning of cognitive-emotional response when the distressing stimulus (image or thought) is activated. This increases entropy in the sequence of mental states (the 'state vector') and lowers the strength of the previous attractor fields. The points on the body used in EFT are characterised by sensitivity, higher electrical conductivity and density of mechanoreptors—and are found to bring about changes in the areas of the brain controlling emotional responses. The therapeutic process of EFT can be understood not only in terms of the simple cognitive model of theorists such as Foa and Kozak (1986) and Rachman (1980), but also the metacognitive theorising of Wells (2000). The meta-beliefs, postulated by Wells to prevent lower level cognitive process of information incongruent with the fear response, are recognised in EFT in terms of the various 'psychological reversals' that must be addressed before emotional desensitisation can take place. Finally, the observational stance inherent in the EFT procedure can be seen to have some points of contact with the mindfulness activity employed in some recent versions of cognitive therapy. It is concluded that EFT may be regarded essentially as a particularly synergistic and efficient combination of elements that bring about emotional desensitisation and cognitive restructuring, all of which are found in other therapeutic approaches.

Emotional Freedom Technique [EFT] is a popular method for relief of emotional distress (particularly anxiety) that involves tapping on the body whilst focussing on a target problem (such as a phobia/anxiety or other troubling emotion).[2] This brings about desensitisation. Affirmations of self-acceptance in relation to the target problem are also a feature of the approach. It is now widely used, both professionally within the context of psychological therapy, and by clients and laypersons generally as a self-help tool for stress relief. Whilst presented by its founder within an 'energy psychology'[3] paradigm, its components can readily be conceptualised within some of the same constructs and strategies as cognitive (or cognitive-behavioural) therapy.

The following components make up the EFT procedure:

- A target 'problem' or symptom is identified—along with its history and form.
- This target is broken into its various cognitive, sensory, imaginal, affective, and temporal aspects.
- Each aspect is then targeted for desensitisation.
- The client is asked to rate the degree of distress of each aspect, using the Subjective Units of Disturbance scale (SUDS), as developed by Josef Wolpe.
- The desensitisation is brought about by having the client tap on their body at points found to have a calming effect. This is done *whilst thinking of the distressing event*. The tapping appears to disrupt the usual patterning of cognitive-emotional response. At certain moments the tapping is accompanied by eye movements, humming and counting—a constellation of multisensory activities that appears to increase the disruption of the cognitive-emotional response.
- The tapping is initially accompanied by the client's making a statement of self-acceptance in relation to the target problem—along the lines of "Even though I feel/have (the problem/symptom/emotion) I completely accept myself". This functions to undermine a common obstacle to resolution: the presence of negative meta-belief/self-condemnation that otherwise continually generates more anxiety and distress because of having the problem.
- After a round of tapping, the client is asked again to rate the level of disturbance on the SUD scale. Tapping is continued until the SUD is at zero for each aspect.
- Maladaptive belief systems, including affectively negative self-related cognitions may also be targeted (as in EMDR). These are rated using the Validity of Cognition Scale (VOC). Cognitive change appears to take place quite readily—perhaps again because tapping interrupts the usual cognitve-affective sequence. The aim (as in EMDR) is to work until a positive cognition has a high VOC rating and the negative cognition has low rating.
- Testing the results is a key feature of the method. The client's subjective experience is continually and immediately monitored, using the SUD scale. When the work seems complete, the client is asked to think as fully as possible about the target problem to

check that all the SUDS are at zero. The client is asked to report back on his or her experience in vivo when the target situations are faced in reality. If further SUDs are reported subsequently, then the work is continued—often addressing new aspects that were not apparent initially.

- In checking the SUDs the client is asked to scan for body sensations.
- Sometimes the desensitisation has to be done in vivo (in the actual situation that evokes distress).
- As one target issue is successfully resolved, another may then present in the client's consciousness—for example, a thematically related traumatic memory from an earlier time. This in turn can be targeted for desensitisation. In practice the movement through issues and aspects may be quite rapid (but nevertheless thorough).
- Sometimes the desensitisation may be blocked by a meta-belief—for example, that it is not safe to overcome the problem—or by some other emotional investment in the problem. Usually these are unconscious or only partially conscious for the client. The solution is to have the client tap (disrupt the pattern) and say "Even though I want to keep (the problem) I completely accept myself". Following this, the desensitisation may often proceed easily.

Those familiar with Eye Movement Desensitisation and Reprocessing [EMDR] will recognise the procedure as very similar to that used in EMDR (and there has been much implicit cross-fertilisation between these two approaches [Hartung & Galvin, 2003]). Indeed it may conceivably be argued that EFT is a variant of EMDR, especially since tapping on the body is sometimes a feature of EMDR (rather than eye movements). In both EMDR and EFT, a process of 'dual attentional stimuli' is involved—which may function to disrupt the usual maladaptive patterns of cognitive-affective response, allowing the shift to a more affectively positive state. As with EMDR, other psychotherapeutic approaches can be used integratively. Many of the same principles of the clinical use of EMDR are applicable to EFT (Shapiro, 2001; Mollon, 2005)—but a key difference is that, with EFT, abreactions and client distress are very rare. Thus EFT appears to be an exceptionally safe means for clients to desensitise to memories of trauma without becoming retraumatised in the process.

The danger of retraumatisation in the process of talking about traumatic experience is one of the core clinical dilemmas in efforts to help patients with PTSD or extensive childhood abuse-trauma. Often talking of trauma will lead not to desensitisation but to sensitisation—a phenomenon van der Kolk (2002) has likened to neurobiological 'kindling'. EFT provides a solution to this dilemma.

How does tapping on the body bring about desensitisation/pattern disruption?

Tapping on points on the body appears to induce a relaxation response. In addition, it may function as a disruption or distraction— rather like the idea of 'dual attention stimuli' in EMDR—thereby interrupting the normal neurobiological patterning of cognition and emotional state.

The tapping points used in EFT are known to be locations of lowered electrical resistance to conductivity and have a high proportion of mechanoreceptors—specialised receptors that respond to mechanical forces such as tapping, massaging or holding. Stimulation of some of these is found to send electrochemical impulses to areas of the brain that govern fear and the stress response, demonstrated in fMRI studies (Hui et al. 2000). Numerous investigators have used neuroimaging methods to identify acupuncture-associated brain responses (Napadow et al. 2006). Thus it seems likely that tapping on the body, particularly at these sensitive points, sends a signal to the limbic and cortical regions that introduces 'noise' or disruption into the previously coherent organisation of the emotional response. Ruden (2005) hypothesises that the multisensory stimulation of tapping with eye movements, humming and counting (the so-called 9-gamut sequence used in EFT) provokes release of serotonin in the prefrontal cortex and the amygdala, which then interacts crucially at the moment of imaginal activation of the fear response. The phenomenon of neural plasticity is also relevant. When an image capable of evoking an emotional response is brought to mind, neurobiological changes occur, such that the memory becomes active and labile, susceptible to taking in new information (Nader et al. 2000; Debiec, 2006)—of course the common response of avoidance is what prevents new information being taken in. Tapping the body during these moments of neural plasticity appears to disrupt the previous response and allow an easier updating of information into the patterning of emotional response to the memory or image. Changes in brain frequency ratios have been reported following successful treatment with EFT and related methods (Andrade and Feinstein, 2003; Diepold & Goldstein, 2000; Lambrou et al. 2003; Swingle & Pulos, 2000; Swingle et al. 2004); digitised EEG scans showing 'before and after' changes following energy psychology treatments are posted on the www.innersource.net website. Mechanoreceptors are distributed all over the skin surface, so that some will be stimulated wherever the tapping takes place, but the points used in EFT are known to have a greater density of these.

If EFT can be viewed as a particularly effective method of pattern disruption, somewhat related to EMDR, it becomes possible to see more clearly how it fits into an overall cognitive-behavioural paradigm.

A succinct description of cognitive-behavioural therapy and the place of EFT within it

The following seems a reasonable broad-based description of cognitive-behavioural therapy.

'CBT' examines the interaction between thoughts/beliefs and emotion, how this give rise to mood disorders and anxiety, and how the person has evolved malfunctional strategies for avoiding anxiety. The content and the childhood origins of cognitive-emotional structures (such as automatic thoughts, core beliefs/schemas/fantasies/ working models of relationships, and so forth) are explored as part of the process of intrapsychic review and with the aim of the person becoming free of unhelpful beliefs. Disturbances of realistic thought are identified—including splitting, or 'black and white' thinking. Acceptance of the contents of the mind is encouraged, facilitating the development of an 'observing ego' and the practice of 'mindfulness' (adapted from Zen Buddhist practice)—thereby lessening the tendency for internal condemnation and repudiation of disturbing thoughts and feelings. The client is encouraged to speak freely of the contents of mind, including those that are felt to be shameful or abhorrent. Reframing of the problem in a variety of ways helps to modify the persisting unexamined loops of thought and emotion—e.g. the person with OCD may be helped to construe the self as excessively responsible rather than as excessively evil. The client is encouraged to face internal stimuli (thoughts, images, feelings etc.) and external situations that evoke anxiety, without resort to his or her usual strategies of avoidance—thus facilitating habituation, desensitisation, and extinction of the anxiety response. Behavioural experiments may be carried out to test beliefs and facilitate exposure to feared situations so that desensitisation can take place. Desensitisation and extinction of anxiety may be enhanced through EFT. Attention is also paid to manifestations of dysfunctional beliefs and behaviours in relation to the therapist and the therapy—these are used as further examples and sources of data. Methods of stress relief and affect regulation may be taught to the client; these may include EFT. In processing trauma, a procedural principle is as follows: the emotional information-processing system is activated, with accompanying affect and anxiety, then new realistic information is incorporated; a method such as EMDR or EFT may also be included at this point in order to disrupt the usual looping patterns within neuro networks. Installation of positive psychological resources (such as feelings of safety and confidence) may be brought about by means of guided imagery or pattern disruption methods such as EMDR or EFT.

Viewed within this framework, it can be seen that EFT is not an *alternative* to a cognitive-behavioural approach but a crucial additional component that greatly enhances its efficacy when used skilfully. Three major functions of EFT, within this perspective, are those of affect regulation, desensitisation, and pattern disruption.

Desensitisation through disrupting attractor fields

In a book called *The Neurophysics of Human Behavior*, Furman and Gallo (2000) model the action of a variety of psychological therapies, including EFT, in relation to a framework of the movement through states of mind that are captured by 'state attractors', mediated and triggered by automatic thoughts or 'memes'.[4] The term 'state vector' is used to refer to the trajectory of movement through the different states of mind. The various states of mind act as 'attractors', which 'capture' the state vector.

For example, one subject in their research would experience a state of uncertainty whenever he became excited about doing something new; the state of excitement would trigger the automatic thought/meme 'Look before you leap'—which would then cause the state vector to be captured by the state of uncertainty, resulting in a state-bound behaviour of hesitation—which then triggered another conflicting meme 'He who hesitates is lost'; the conflicting memes perturb both state attractors, so that the state vector is soon captured by the state of confusion; this triggers another meme, 'Successful people make quick decisions'; the subject then resolves the confusion by making a quick decision, which activates the excited attractor, which is soon perturbed, transitioning to the guilt attractor and then confusion.

Such patterns, and those commonly encountered amongst patients presenting for psychological help, may acquire a high degree of organisation and order, becoming very resilient and automatic. One component of what is needed for therapeutic change is an intervention which increases entropy and disrupts the pattern. The stability of the attractors needs to be perturbed so that they have less power to capture the state vector. Thus, Furman and Gallo describe the effect of the tapping used in EFT as one of "perturbing the stability of the attractors, thereby shallowing them and freeing the state vector to form new 'healthier' trajectories".

Another component sometimes included in the EFT sequence is known as the 'nine gamut'—nine different activities of eye movements, counting, and briefly humming a few notes, whilst simultaneously tapping—often assumed to have a 'brain balancing' effect. Furman and Gallo describe this as follows:

"The technique simultaneously destabilises trajectories and attractors in visual, auditory, and somatosensory modes. The eye movements destabilise visual mode representations via ocular-motor perturbation, humming destabilises auditory dialog, and tapping provides both tactile and motor perturbations to the associated attractors."

Other therapeutic methods may include actions that *increase* pattern and order. This may be the case, for example, when EMDR or EFT are used to enhance performance by coupling thoughts of the target situation with thoughts and emotions associated with confidence and success. In such ways, the old state vector pathways are disrupted/broken (increased entropy), whilst new and more positive vector paths are installed (increased order).

The opening phase of the tapping sequence of EFT may be used to reframe the client's presenting negative thoughts, in such a way as to offer a more positive view of self and the world: e.g. a victim of assault might be invited to say "Even though I was assaulted, and felt so helpless, and so ashamed, I managed to survive, I did the best I could, and I completely accept myself". This is actually similar to the process within EMDR of the installation of the positive cognition. Tapping seems to 'loosen' the patterns so that new and more positive states become attractors. To some extent this will occur naturally as positive states are sought since they are pleasurable and rewarding—but this cleavage of the old pathway (to the affectively negative state) and recombining in a new pathway (to an affectively positive state) can be helped with appropriate cognitive offerings from the therapist.

It is interesting to compare other psychiatric interventions in terms of this framework. For example, Electroconvulsive Therapy is clearly a broad-focus intervention bringing about temporary or even permanent increase in neurocognitive entropy. Similarly, pharmacotherapy is extremely broad in its neurocognitive pattern-altering effects. Psychological therapies can be more focused. Furman and Gallo (2000) comment:

> "Over the last three decades, numerous schools of brief therapy have arisen which make use of a much more tightly focused arsenal of entropy-increasing tools. Some of the more successful of these are NLP, EMDR, and various energy psychology approaches." [p. 187]

EFT in relation to overall models of cognitive therapy

Clearly a key component of EFT is the reduction in fear/anxiety as a result of exposure (combined with relaxation/distraction) to the target stimulus (such as a traumatic memory, or an anticipated phobic activity). This has been described as 'emotional processing', defined by Rachman (1980, p. 5) as "a process whereby emotional disturbances are absorbed and decline to the extent that other experiences and behaviour can proceed without disruption". Wells (2000), following an earlier suggestion by Foa and Kozak (1986) argues that effective treatment requires that [1] fear structures be accessed and then [2] incongruent information (such as evidence of present safety) to be incorporated into them. Factors that may interfere with emotional processing include high arousal and cognitive avoidance. EFT accesses and activates the fear structures by asking the client to think of phobic situations or to narrate experiences of trauma. As soon as fear arises, the client engages in tapping until the fear dissipates—thus the fear structures are activated but now encounter the incongruent perception of a lack of physiological arousal in the body. The tapping itself also provides stimuli incongruent with a 'reliving' of the trauma as it is recalled. Whilst reaching into the traumatic past, the client retains a foothold in the present through the current sensory stimulation of tapping.

Foa and Kozak point out that many patients fear that once an anxiety response has been initiated it will persist indefinitely—a fear of perpetual anxiety, which tends to become a self-fulfilling expectation. The rapid disruption or cessation of anxiety as a result of tapping provides the client with information that anxiety is time-limited and relatively easily dissipated.

Wells (2000) presents a Self-Regulatory Executive Function (S-REF) model of cognitive-emotional regulation. This comprises three interacting levels of cognition: [1] a stimulus-response lower level (perhaps derived from classical conditioning of fear responses); [2] an 'on-line' conscious appraisal of events, with control of action and thought; [3] a store of beliefs, including metacognitions, that comprise plans or instructions for processing. In this model, the metacognitive beliefs—such as "I need to worry in order to be safe"—may crucially impact on any attempts to modify emotional processing at a lower level.

Certain metacognitive beliefs may be encountered in EFT when it is found that a client is not experiencing rapid relief of distress/ anxiety in the way that is normally expected. It may often be ascertained that a metabelief is blocking the processing—for example, a belief that it is not safe to be free of the problem, or that the person does not deserve to be free of it, or that his or her identity will be threatened if the problem is resolved. Sometimes there may be a meta-motivation holding the symptom in place—such as a wish to punish others through having the symptom. These meta-beliefs and motivations (called, within EFT, 'psychological reversals') are addressed through having the client tap and say, for example, "Even though I feel it is not safe to let go of this anxiety, I completely accept myself".

In one example, a client in a workshop was being guided through a tapping treatment for her anxiety about driving on a motorway, a problem she had had for twelve years since experiencing a panic attack whilst driving. Initially, as the original panic attack was targeted, the SUDs dropped only minimally, which led the therapist to enquire why this might be. A meta-belief was found, to the effect that she felt it would be dangerous to overcome the anxiety because she might drive on the motorway and kill someone—a belief deriving from the thought when she had the panic attack that she "might have killed the children". This was rapidly reframed in terms of a desire to be able to drive safely on the motorway. The SUDs then dropped easily and the whole successful treatment took no more than ten minutes (with subsequent reports of success in driving on the motorway without undue anxiety).

Common meta-beliefs are along the lines of self-condemnation for having the problem: e.g. "I am a pathetic person for being depressed/not being able to cope/being damaged goods" etc. These would effectively block the EFT treatment unless addressed in the opening affirmation according to the formula "Even though I have this problem, I completely accept myself". This can be adapted and focused in various ways—e.g. "Even though I feel I am a pathetic person for having this problem, I completely accept myself" (using the client's own form of words). Thus, a correction for meta-belief blocks is inherent in the EFT procedure.

The lower level of Wells' S-REF model, that of stimulus-response classical conditioning, responds well to the EFT desensitisation/ pattern disruption method of tapping. This is advantageous, since one of the weaknesses of cognitive therapy is that it often lacks an effective means of desensitisation or facilitation of emotional processing. EMDR processes emotion very well, but runs the risk sometimes of evoking unmanageable levels of affect, resulting in traumatisation and sensitisation rather than desensitisation. EFT not only processes emotion but also runs very little risk of retraumatisation—and also contains procedures for minimising this risk further, such as Gary Craig's 'tearless trauma technique'. In that procedure the client is asked to think of the trauma only in a partial way and to keep looking at the therapist during the tapping, so that he or she does not defocus the eyes and become fully immersed in internal information relating to the trauma. From a cognitive therapy perspective this can be viewed as an effective way of accessing the fear structure (partially) whilst simultaneously accessing incongruent information (of safety) by staying focused externally in the present. The familiar and soothing nature of the tapping seems also likely to be a factor in establishing a sense of safety, incongruent with the sense of danger inherent in recall of a trauma. Tapping and touching the body is something that human beings do naturally as a means of self-soothing—and mothers will often sooth a baby by gently tapping on his or her body.

Mindfulness

Recently, some cognitive therapists have introduced mindfulness training, based on a Buddhist meditative practice (Teasdale, 1999; Segal et al., 2002). Part of the purpose of this is to de-centre the person's relationship to negative thoughts. By adopting an observing stance towards thoughts and emotions, the person can appreciate that thoughts are not facts. Both EFT and EMDR implicitly contain elements of mindfulness in the form of continually asking the client to observe their thoughts, feelings and bodily sensations through the therapeutic process. At the end of a round of tapping, or a set of eye movements, the client may be asked to assess their SUD and to report on feelings, thoughts and bodily sensations. The opening sequence of the round of EFT tapping—"Even though I feel ... etc."—also helps to evoke an observing stance, creating some distance from the emotion.

A stance of mindfulness may help the client to achieve a more meta-perspective on his or her own self. In some of the author's work, combining psychoanalytic and energy perspectives, a patient had been exploring over several sessions his profound cleavage within his personality, into a performing compliant 'false self' and a hidden and depleted 'true self'. Various 'energy' methods had been used, including Mindful Energy Scan—where the client observes the inner experiences of energetic tension whilst at the same time observing his breathing (somewhat similar to the Mindful meditation prescribed by Segal et al.). He began to report a new sense of peace with himself. As this was explored, what emerged was that he had achieved more of a meta-perspective such that he could accept that he was this person with a 'false' performing self *and* a much more hidden and depleted 'true' self and that he could accept how this had come about (this having been clarified further during the therapy). From this meta-perspective he was in neither the 'false' *nor* the hidden 'true' self, but in a position with an overview of both—a place from which he could experience some peace and acceptance.

Conclusion

Although the procedure of EFT, involving having the client tap on the body whilst thinking of the emotionally disturbing image or memory, can appear to some to be a little strange, a examination of the components of the method reveal these to be familiar elements of other therapies. Whilst the configuration of components may be innovative, the components themselves are not (and the therapy is not actually 'new', being presented first in 1995, and derived from the earlier work of Callahan, developed from 1980 onwards). EFT may be best viewed as a particularly efficient synergistic combination of strategies of emotional desensitisation and cognitive restructuring.

Notes

1. I have noticed certain qualities amongst those, often vociferous, commentators who style themselves 'sceptics'. They usually appear to be 'firm believers' in their particular model of reality, actively 'disbelieving' accounts that violate these models. Their discourse is frequently characterised by hostility, sarcasm and ridicule, and a sort of competitive-triumphant mode of argument. Personally, I do not *believe* in anything, preferring instead to operate with working hypotheses, ever-ready to be discarded in the light of experience and evidence. The belligerent 'sceptics' remind me of the devotees of the 'Helmholtz school' which influenced Freud in the 19th Century. In their opposition to vitalistic biology, they "pledged a solemn oath to put into power this truth: no other forces than the common physical-chemical ones are active within the organism ... reducible to the force of attraction and repulsion." [quoted in Sulloway, 1979, p. 14]. Rupert Sheldrake has established a website to provide critical information about well-known professional sceptics: www.skepticalinvestigations.org.

2. EFT is one of a family of related methods, which have evolved from an approach called Thought Field Therapy [TFT], developed by clinical psychologist and cognitive therapist, Roger Callahan in the 1980s.

TFTgrew out of the field of Applied Kinesiology, developed by chiropracter, George Goodheart, in the 1960s and 70s.

3.   see www.energypsych.org

4.   Memes might be regarded as 'thoughts' that do not involve true thinking – ready packaged or clichéd ideas that inhabit the individual mind and the wider human culture. These become self-replicating information patterns, or plans: "ideas, beliefs, religions, and scientific practices compete with each other for the limited space and copying resources of the human brain." [Furman & Gallo, 2000, p. 46]

CHAPTER SIXTEEN

Energy psychology perspectives and therapies for borderline and other personality disorders

L ike many diagnostic concepts in psychiatry, that of 'personality disorder' is often used rather loosely. Usually the term refers to psychopathology that pervades the personality, and which renders psychological therapy, of whatever kind, difficult or prolonged. Whilst many presenting problems will respond rapidly and satisfactorily to treatment with Thought Field Therapy or related methods, in some cases this does not occur and we find that the work is complex and difficult.

Sometimes, as Dr Callahan emphasises, the complex and stubborn nature of a problem may be due to individual energy toxins, which have to be identified and neutralised before progress is made. The role of energy toxins in generating anxiety, depression, anger, negative and self-destructive attitudes, should not be underestimated. Moreover, sensitivities or addictions to *internally* generated hormones (and perhaps other naturally occurring biochemical products), such as adrenaline, may play a part in many entrenched psychological problems and it can be crucial to address these.

Inherent contradictions

However, in other cases, the difficulty appears to lie in the very fabric of the personality—fundamental dysfunctions and contradictions in the basic beliefs and 'software' of the biocomputer. One clue to this, I find, is when the client announces, more or less at the first encounter, the view that their problems are unlikely to resolve easily—a statement that perhaps expresses a vague awareness of presenting some kind of impossible dilemma, or an intuition that their true agenda is not actually resolution of the presenting problem.

When this is the case, the client often appears reluctant to engage with energy psychology methods precisely because they work effectively. This effectiveness conflicts with the client's agenda of seeking idealised illusory gratifications—their illusory nature meaning that resolution has to be indefinitely postponed and psychotherapy has to be interminable. Salman Akhtar describes this as follows:

> "Fantasies whose core is constituted by the notions of 'someday' and 'if only' are ubiquitous in the human psyche. In severe character pathology, however, these fantasies have a particularly tenacious, defensive, and ego-depleting quality. The 'someday' fantasy idealises the future and fosters optimism, and the 'if only' fantasy idealises the past and lays the groundwork for nostalgia." [Akhtar, 1999, p. 226]

These fantasies can be hidden in long term conventional psychotherapy, but come more rapidly to the fore when energy methods are offered.

Another indicator is the sense of mild (occasionally strong) irritation that the therapist may feel during the work with the client—a therapist countertransference affect that is independent of the form of therapy. This irritation appears to be a response to inherent contradictions or incompatibilities in the client's presentation—these being either *within* the client's internal agenda or *between* the client's agenda and reality.

Sometimes the contradiction may lie in the fact of apparently seeking help whilst holding a fundamental attitude or belief that is at odds with this. One example is the person with an avoidant personality disorder who ostensibly wishes for help with overcoming his or her anxieties whilst maintaining a core belief that it is better to avoid thoughts, emotions, or situations that evoke anxiety. Such a client may become annoyed or reproachful towards the therapist for endeavouring to draw their attention to the avoided areas. A person with a dependent personality disorder may try to create an unhealthy state of dependence on the therapist that is at odds with the ostensive intention of overcoming his or her psychological difficulties. In the case of a person with narcissistic personality disorder, he or she may become depressed when confronted with their own imperfections and unrealistic expectations of self and others—the contradiction here being between expectation and reality. Although generalised anxiety disorder is not normally classed as a personality disorder, I would suggest in some cases the condition could quite reasonably be termed 'anxious personality disorder', since it appears to rest on a fundamental belief that in order to be safe it is necessary to be anxious all the time. Such a person ostensibly seeks help with their anxiety, whilst actually holding a belief that it would be inappropriate to feel calm. Clients with obsessive-compulsive personality disorder display a preoccupation with perfectionism, precision, and certainty, in ways that are incompatible with the vagaries of reality, and will often endeavour to distort the therapist's work into another obsessive-compulsive system. The client with a borderline personality disorder may hold contradictory and incompatible desires and internal models of relationships, these being maintained in separate states and structures of mind. The therapist may be confronted at different times by mutually contradictory relational stances whilst the client appears unaware or unconcerned about the iconoclastic nature of these.

Whilst psychodynamic conflicts between opposing wishes and fears are ubiquitous, and psychological reversals are found more often than not in relation to a client's presenting problems, there is an additional quality observable in those who may be described as suffering with personality disorders. It is the impression that the client, or some part of the client, is fundamentally opposed to the therapeutic work. The difference between them and other clients may be that the psychological reversals in their system do not clear easily, despite attention to individual energy toxins.

It can be noted that, by this kind of criteria, not all forms of psychopathology that pervade the personality need be described as 'personality disorders'. There are many clients whose difficulties are complex and multilayered, yet they do not present the inherent contradictions that tend to block the work and evoke feelings of irritation in the therapist. Such people will attend sessions reliably and engage in constructive work of examining and resolving their difficulties, even though this may take place over a relatively long period.

Personality disorders cause disruption of the work

By contrast, clients with personality disorders will present diffi-culties that interfere with the work, even though the energy psy-chology interventions are, on a session-by-session basis, effective. These difficulties might include: missing sessions (particularly in the case of avoidant personality disorder), profound suspicion of any approach to areas of emotional vulnerability (paranoid per-sonality disorder), fears of any therapeutic method that might result in genuine improvement (dependent and histrionic person-ality disorders), profound unease in relation to methods where the conscious mind is not fully in control and fully understanding the situation (narcissistic and obsessive compulsive personality dis-orders), fears of approaching areas of profound traumatic experi-ence (borderline personality disorder), chaotic presentation and challenges to the normal boundaries of therapy (borderline per-sonality disorder). All these forms of disruption can be explored and addressed.

Many clients whose early experiences have included significant deprivation in relation to needs for care, attention, protection, and general nurturance, may become preoccupied with the therapist in ways that interfere with the therapeutic task. Similarly, if there have been high levels of trauma in the childhood background, a client may be unconsciously motivated to avoid accessing his or her past experiences directly, and instead, therefore, will focus on desires and fears in relation to the therapist in the here-and-now. Whilst areas of transference, and other forms of personalised preoccupation with the therapist, need to be addressed at times in the course of the work, it can be detrimental to emphasise these as having privileged impor-tance. The implicit (and sometimes explicit) message to the client should be that the crucial work is that of identifying areas of distress, past traumas, dysfunctional beliefs, programmes, and behaviours—and of clearing the associated information encoded in the energy field. This work takes place *within* the client's psycho-somatic-energy system, rather than in the relationship *between* client and therapist. The aim is to empower the client and to facilitate autonomy by clearing the energetic obstacles to these, and, with this intention, to discourage dependence or other forms of personalised preoccupation with the therapist that are known to be at times potentially very damaging (Bates, 2006).

Clients with avoidant personality disorder will also often show a characteristic reaction to TFT in relation to phobic anxiety. Complete diminution of anxiety may be achieved in the consulting room, but the client may then suggest that this is because he or she is not in the situation that evokes anxiety (despite having experienced anxiety just a few minutes previously when merely thinking of the phobic situation). On the other hand, if efforts are made to suggest that the person seek out the phobic situation in order to carry out in vivo desensitisation with TFT, he or she may strongly resist this. This may at times come across as a kind of stubbornness, as if expressing a fundamental determination not to relinquish the anxiety.

Those who have experienced significant early trauma or deprivation may have established a protective layer of internal guards around the vulnerable core of the personality (Mollon, 2002b) . These function to keep others, including the therapist, away from this core—and may become quite aggressive when change in the fundamental emotional equilibrium is threatened. Often this may be viewed as the hidden paranoid core of the personality. It may not easily be revealed in conventional verbal psychotherapy, other than in the slow progress of the work—but comes much more quickly into view when energy psychology methods are used.

Although problems that are embedded within personality disorders can be more difficult to treat and may require longer work than those which are not rooted in such complexities, good results can still be obtained with energy psychology methods, much more rapidly than with other approaches. In order to resolve personality disorder, it is necessary to address various components, including core beliefs and fears, programmes, traumas and deep wounds to the self, inherited traumas, parts of the self, and warded off painful affects such as shame—as well as the non-psychological elements such as individual energy toxins, chronic hyperventilation and neurological disorganisation.

Core beliefs and schemas

An important component of the work with people with personality disorders is to resolve the core anxieties and the beliefs that generate the anxieties. These core beliefs, or schemas (Young, 1999; Clinton, 2005), are not necessarily in consciousness, nor do they usually form part of the client's presenting problem. However, they can usually be discerned by the skilled therapist and brought into the client's conscious awareness without too much difficulty. Examples of such core beliefs and schemas are:

> **Obsessive-compulsive personality**: "I must be perfectly in control of myself and my world and I must never make a mistake, or something terrible might happen."

> **Passive-aggressive personality**: "People will always try to dominate and exploit me, but asserting myself or being in conflict with others is dangerous."

> **Dependent personality**: "I am inadequate and lack the resources to cope on my own; it is not safe to attempt any independent initiative."

> **Avoidant personality**: "I cannot cope with painful emotions or anxiety and must avoid them—and I must avoid engaging with others because they might reject me and I would not be able to cope with that."

> **Narcissistic personality**: "I must maintain an image, for myself and others, of being unique, important, and special—to lose this image would be a catastrophic humiliation".

> **Histrionic personality**: "Since I am inadequate and unable to cope on my own, I must continually seek attention from others by performing and entertaining."

> **Paranoid personality**: "People are malevolent and deceptive and I must be continually vigilant for indications of this."

> **Schizoid personality**: "It is not safe to experience emotion or to allow other people to matter to me."

> **Borderline personality disorder**: "I cannot cope on my own and cannot manage my emotions on my own—but involvement with others is dangerous since they will always abandon me."

Sometimes the nature of an underlying dysfunctional belief, and its source, will become apparent during the process of TFT tapping for the symptoms and problems arising from the belief. For example, a man reported a sense of a black area at the back of his head, which he felt represented a constellation of anxieties and feelings of stress. As we began to work through a diagnosed sequence of tapping, he suddenly remarked that it had just occurred to him that his anxieties were based on an underlying belief that he cannot cope and will always be overwhelmed by the tasks of life. Then, as he continued tapping, he said he had suddenly realised where this belief had come from—it was that when he was young his father would regularly announce to all and sundry that his son was useless and could not do anything. As Lipton (2005) has pointed out, the young child's brain state is such that he or she is, in effect, hypnotically receptive to the repeated messages, about self and the world, provided in the early environment.

Some core beliefs can be particularly hidden. This is often the case with the paranoid belief that it is not safe to trust anyone. One man who had undergone many years of conventional psychoanalytic therapy, suddenly realised, during an energy session, that his fundamental assumption was that no-one could be trusted. This had been so pervasive and basic to his stance in the world that he had never thought to question it. For him it had appeared simply a feature of reality, yet it had powerfully influenced his relationships with others, including that with his psychotherapist, and had prevented him from forming an intimate attachment.

All these dysfunctional beliefs and associated anxieties can function as the basis of psychological reversals that block progress in various areas—i.e. they are the source of feeling that it is not safe to overcome a presenting problem. They can be cleared using energy methods. However, there will often be further reversals linked to these beliefs and anxieties, based on a fear that it is not *safe* to be free of the dysfunctional belief (which is, of course, perceived by parts of the client's system as profoundly functional), or that the person's *identity* is threatened by a change in core belief. These reversals have to be cleared in the normal way, by voicing them and tapping the side of the hand. The aim is to work to a point where the client's system provides a positive muscle response to the statement "all parts of me are willing/I have 100% inner willingness to modify or delete this belief that ...". Once the internal objections are thus removed, it is then relatively easy to clear the core belief. A diagnosed sequence of tapping is preferable, combined with brief phrases such as "clearing this belief that ...". However, simple EFT tapping on all the points will also often work perfectly well.

Some or all of the chakras can be addressed as the belief is cleared, using a circular tapping, *counter-clockwise* as the front of the body is pictured as a clock facing outwards; this direction of chakra movement helps to eliminate selected beliefs and attitudes. For issues of basic security, the root chakra may be most relevant—and here, because of the physical and social awkwardness inherent in its position on the perineum, the client can be asked simply to imagine the tapping movement. Beliefs relating to sexuality, generativity and creativity may be best addressed through the sacral chakra. Those relating to personal power may be cleared through the solar plexus. Fears relating to the giving and receiving of love are best addressed through the heart chakra. Problems in expressing oneself can be cleared through the throat chakra. Fears of seeing people and issues clearly may be best located through the third eye chakra. Combinations of these may often be relevant—and nothing is lost, other than a small amount of time, by tapping all of them in a counter-clockwise movement. Sequences of chakras may also be diagnosed through muscle testing, as with meridian points. Training in Seemorg Matrix provides a detailed and thorough method of working with traumas and beliefs encoded in the chakras.

After this work of tapping on meridians and/or chakras, muscle testing can be used again to check whether the belief has been cleared: "There is a belief in my system that ...". If the response is now in the negative, it should be followed up with "It has been cleared from all parts of me ..." and "... from all layers of me". A further check is to the statement "I want the belief back" and "some part of me wants the belief back". If any of these tests indicate that the belief is still in the system in some area or in some form, or that some part of the person wants the belief back, then this is treated as a further reversal (essentially like a 'mini-reversal') and can be cleared by voicing it and tapping the side of the hand.

Sometimes anxiety following the clearing of a dysfunctional belief may be quite conscious. For example, a woman presented with generalised anxiety and a tendency to feel stressed all the time, despite her relatively comfortable lifestyle. It became apparent that behind this state of chronic stress lay a belief that she was responsible for everyone's else's well-being and happiness: "if it rains I feel it is my fault!". As we continued tapping and exploring, she very insightfully suggested that this might have stemmed from having felt that she had been born into a role of making her mother feel better; this idea was based on having been told that she had been conceived on the doctor's advice to her mother to become pregnant as soon as possible following an earlier birth of a still-born sibling. We used tapping methods to clear the belief and associated role of always being responsible for other people's happiness and well-being. Muscle testing indicated that it was indeed cleared—but also indicated a desire to have it back. She exclaimed "What will I do without it? Life will be so boring!". We then used EFT Choices tapping: "Even though I feel lost without this role of being responsible for others' well-being, I choose to find something better to do with my life"—which enabled her to feel more positive about this change.

Traumas behind the core beliefs

It will also be necessary to clear the perturbations and energetic residues associated with the traumas and adverse experiences that have given rise to the dysfunctional core beliefs. Often large areas of these can be cleared rapidly, simply by asking the client's system to target these, using a phrase such as "the traumas behind this belief that …", and then diagnosing a tapping sequence. Before doing so, it will be necessary to check for, and clear, any internal objections or reversals against clearing these traumas. Muscle testing will indicate whether they have been cleared.

Areas of severe early trauma may be protected by internal 'guards'. It may be necessary to seek their permission in relation to healing the areas of trauma and also to healing the guards themselves. Muscle testing may indicate an initial denial of permission, but this can be treated as a reversal, which will normally clear in the usual way by tapping the side of the hand and voicing the objection; muscle testing will then indicate whether the objection has been rescinded. Subsequent tapping, whether by universal algorithm or by diagnosed sequence, will then remove the perturbations linked to the traumas, allowing the healing of both the traumas and the guards.

Resistance to changing core beliefs: the totalitarian ego

Often people can be quite resistant to modifying core beliefs or schemas. There is a general human tendency to try to maintain cognitive structures, the core constructs and assumptions about the self and the world (Mollon, 1993). Greenwald (1980) introduced the concept of the 'totalitarian ego', presenting a variety of experimental evidence for the way in which people consistently distort information to make it congruent with their illusions, beliefs and expectations. Epstein (1987) argued that the motive to maintain a particular view of self and the world can be considered on a par with the pleasure-pain principle. It may be a feature of personality disorders in general that cognitive structures are maintained with particular rigidity, preventing the person optimally learning from experience and modifying their constructs and beliefs in the light of changing situations. Once identified, this rigidity may itself be targeted for energy interventions—treating it as a reversal and tapping the side of the hand whilst saying "Even though I want to keep my basic beliefs and assumptions ... even though I want to be always right in my predictions ... even though I do not want to consider alternative ways of thinking ... I completely accept myself".

Other forms of psychological reversals

As in all forms of psychopathology, psychological reversals can be very important blocks to progress unless identified and resolved. In addition to those based on the core beliefs described above, personality disorders may contain reversals based on conflicts between improvement and basic beliefs about one's position or role—or against the struggle to escape from a particular role. Sometimes the underlying conflict may arise only after some progress has been made, taking the form of a mini-reversal. For example, a woman who had received Thought Field Therapy for various phobic anxieties relating to driving reported that she was "85%" better. Muscle testing revealed a reversal for being over the remaining 15% [i.e. her muscle went weak to "I want to be completely over this" and strong to "I want to keep the remaining 15% of the problem". When she thought about why, it occurred to her that if she did not have these anxieties her extended family might be even more inclined to lean on her and regard her as the strong one who has no problems. Thus her symptoms of phobic anxiety had been protecting her against this assigned role within her family. After this mini reversal was corrected, she responded well to further TFT and was quite unable to locate any anxiety when she thought of the driving possibilities that a few minutes previously had caused her significant alarm. This is an example of how a seemingly isolated problem (driving anxieties) is rooted in the overall personality and role in a family system.

Deep reversals are usually involved where there are complex dysfunctional patterns in a person's life. Without resolution of these, the pattern will inevitably recur despite temporary apparent improvements. Crucially these may relate to anxieties that resolution of the pattern will result in loss of connection to mother/father/family/ancestors/tribe, or to the 'home' culture. Such anxieties may be essentially unconscious, and may be present even when the conscious attitude is a wish to be free of such ties to family and ancestors. The attachment tendency is primordial and powerful, probably serving fundamental survival agendas in earlier evolutionary times—and may overrule conscious wishes to be free of a particular problem. The core belief may be "We are the kind of people who … (have this problem)." It may be revealed by muscle testing as the client says something like "Mother—I will remain lovingly connected to you and my ancestors if I resolve this problem"; if the muscle goes weak, then this indicates a deep reversal of this kind [Schusterman, 2005]. These intergenerational reversals can be corrected in the usual way, often quite easily. The approach of Seemorg Matrix also addresses deep level reversals through systematic testing of many different core beliefs and anxieties.

Deep level reversals can be very pervasively and powerfully sabotaging. A man was chronically frustrated by his inability to overcome blocks to progress in his life. He tended to procrastinate, frittered away his time and his career opportunities, and experienced himself as chronically inauthentic. In his relationship with his long-term girlfriend he vacillated between feelings of love and withdrawal. Eventually he realised that he had established a deep psychological contract with his mother, such that he would never put anyone or anything in a higher place of importance. This meant that he felt guilty if he thought he might love his girlfriend more than he loved his mother. Similarly he felt he could not believe in God, even though he attended a church, because that would be placing a

Being in a higher place than his mother. Most pervasively of all, he felt guilty if he were to become his more authentic self because he believed that what had been important to his mother had been his outward behaviour as opposed to his inherent feelings and desires (see my discussion of 'psychic muder syndrome'; Mollon, 2002b).

Addictions to pain and anxiety

Often, people who have suffered interpersonal trauma in childhood may have parts of their system that have developed an addictive relationship with pain. This can be apparent in those common situations of repeated patterns of abusive and hurtful relationships. It can usually also be identified as a reversal in relation to being free of patterns of painful relationships. One woman showed a parts reversal to being completely over a rape that had taken place in her early teens. This reversal did not clear with the usual tapping the side of the hand. I asked her if she had any idea why there might be this internal objection to being completely over the rape trauma. She replied that her sexual fantasies sometimes involved rape. After tapping the side of the hand, with the statement "Even though my sexuality was hijacked by this rape trauma, I completely accept myself", the subsequent muscle test to the statement "All parts of me are willing to be completely over the rape trauma providing I can still have my rape fantasies" registered as positive and we were then able to clear the perturbations fully. Addictions to anxiety and adrenaline are also frequent sequelae of childhood abuse trauma.

Programmes

Because personality disorders operate with broad patterns and themes of emotional and behavioural response, it can be important to address the underlying programmes that have derived from adverse childhood experiences. These are different from the core beliefs or schemas, since they are the generators of behaviours based on the beliefs. Muscle testing to the statement "there is a programme in my system that generates ... [the anxiety and associated behaviour]" will identify whether or not there is such a programme. The system's willingness to delete or modify this can then be checked. Once the internal agreement/lack of reversals has been obtained, then a simple tapping sequence, accompanied by a phrase such as 'clearing the programme for …' will usually clear the programme. Checks can then be made as to whether it remains in the system in deleted form, whether it can be reinstalled, and whether the system wants it back. If any of these elicit a positive muscle response, then tapping the side of the hand whilst voicing the issue will normally clear this.

The role of insight

It is often assumed that energy methods do not relate to the role of insight as emphasised in traditional psychoanalytic therapy. This is not actually correct. Profound insights do occur in the process of energy work—but these tend to accompany or follow the energetic shifts rather than being a *cause* of the shift.

Some of the energy methods are more inclined to give rise to insight than others. TAT and Seemorg Matrix are both somewhat meditative in their process, allowing a mental space within which new perspectives can emerge—sometimes startlingly so. For example, a woman was undertaking TAT in relation to persisting feelings of depression and lack of confidence after a period off work from stress in her job as a teacher. Following the TAT she reported an entirely new train of thought relating to the function of her depression; it occurred to her that she had never wanted to be a teacher, this had been her mother's choice of career for her, and she feared that if she recovered from her depression she would be expected to return to teaching. She found this spontaneous insight astonishing and illuminating. Previously we had undertaken energy work focused on her experience of feeling dominated and controlled by her mother.

Another client was undertaking Seemorg Matrix, focused on clearing the energetic imprints of her mother's hostility and envy towards her. Further nuances of the childhood situation were emerging in her awareness as she proceeded, and she began to see more clearly how she had felt that she must not surpass her mother in any field of achievement. Then, as we addressed some residual anxiety using TFT, she suddenly and with astonishment 'realised' how her mother had colluded with her father's sexual abuse of her because it had diverted his sexual attention.

Clearing the repeating energetic patterns of trauma

A common phenomenon, somewhat mysterious without an energy perspective, is the way in which patterns of trauma in a person's life seem to be repeated—including family and ancestral patterns (Ponomarava, 2003). It is as if other people, and life circumstances, are somehow mysteriously recruited as players in a repeating drama that is the unfortunate individual's life. From an energy perspective, this is not mysterious, but exactly what is to be expected. The patterns encoded in a person's energy system do tend to reproduce thematically similar events, drawing others, through energetic resonance, into enacting parts in the energetically encoded drama. Once it is accepted that human beings are not isolated entities encased within flesh and bone, but are interconnecting, information-rich, fields of energy, then it becomes easier to appreciate, at least in general terms, how these energetic transactions take place. A common example of this is the way in which psychotherapists will often find that they inadvertently (initially unconsciously) re-enact, in some thematically similar way, damaging experiences from their client's childhood.

Some of the dysfunctional information is derived not from the individual's own history of trauma but is 'inherited' from the parents—imbibed with the mother's milk, so to speak. For example, Roger Callahan, drawing on biologist Rupert Sheldrake's ideas of morphogenic fields, has emphasised that phobias are often inherited—not genetically but through the energy field. If the mother or father is very anxious, or has suffered much trauma, then this information may be transmitted into the child's energy system.

For the pattern of a person's life to change, it is important to clear the energy sequences that maintain or reproduce these. Seemorg Matrix and Tapas Acupressure Technique (and probably many other methods) appear able to address broad energetic patterns encoded at this deep level.

Dysfunctional energy sequences

These are internal patterns of fear, encoded energetically, that are evoked if basic developmental strivings are activated. For example, there may be a terror of abandonment or annihilation in response to strivings for independence or autonomy—or in response to expressions of emotional need. Another common pattern is that of terror evoked by failing to comply with the mother's image of herself and her child. Whilst these were once *interpersonal* patterns, between child and mother, they are now *endopsychic* structures of internal reaction, encoded energetically. The basic pattern is that the person makes the beginnings of some positive change, developmental step, or personal initiative—and then sabotages it, perhaps by engaging in discouraging internal talk, in a way that mirrors how the mother or other significant caregiver originally responded.

Transference-countertransference in the consulting room

From an energy perspective, transference phenomena not only involve the client's assimilation of aspects of his or her perception of the therapist to patterns rooted in childhood experience, but also include actual transactions between the energy systems of client and therapist. The therapist, especially when attuned to the client, will be energetically cued into feeling and behaving like a figure from the client's past. It is important for the therapist to be monitoring these energetic vectors, and their associated emotions, impulses and fantasies. For example, a therapist may suddenly be aware of experiencing a sadistic, or lustful, or exploitative impulse towards the client; this may not necessarily reflect the therapist's own psychological agenda but may indicate how a particular 'energy gestalt' (perhaps another term for what used to be called an 'internal object') within the client's energy field, and derived from childhood traumatic experience, is resonating within the therapist's energy field. These energy patterns and gestalts, associated with the phenomena of transference and countertransference, need to be cleared—using a method such as Seemorg Matrix.

Complexities of Borderline Personality Disorder and its Treatment

Whilst many or all of the above features may apply in the case of borderline personality disorder, there are some additional factors that often complicate the clinical picture with BPD. These include the following realms: the structure and experience of self; split images of the self and other; false self and related syndromes; disorders of information processing; dysfunctional interpersonal interactions; the use of the other for affect regulation; the use of addictive substances or addictive activities for affect regulation; the mechanisms/ strategies of defence, including defensive inhibitions of mentalization; dysfunctional energy sequences; complex developmental post traumatic stress disorder.

All of these disturbances arise in the context of interpersonal trauma and/or dysfunctional early attachment relationships. Innate psychobiological abnormalities may also play a part. Energy Psychology methods can help with all these.

Structure and experience of self

Whilst there are a number of components of the sense of self (Mollon, 1993), a core feature is the identification with words, images, and roles available or given within the family and culture that the person happens to be born into (Mollon, 2001). For example, a baby is born and is assigned a sound, a word, and the developing child learns that he or she *is* this word. Gradually the child, adolescent, and adult, identifies with further images, roles and words available in the wider cultural and economic world—a point inherent in much of the Lacanian writings (e.g. Gurewich & Tort, 1999). The establishment of a viable and somewhat stable sense of self, derived from these words, images and roles, is crucial for adequate functioning in the social world. A 'person' needs to know who and what he or she is in terms of parentage, family lineage, role and place in the world, and so on.

When a person grows up in a very disturbed and disordered family the sense of self may be incoherent. Split images of self (as 'good' and 'bad') may alternate, linking also to split images of the other (the phenomena of the Kleinian paranoid-schizoid position). The splitting, or dissociation, of images of self (and other) may be particularly pronounced when the child has experienced repeated and severe trauma from caregivers. Another source of negative self-images is the way in which dysfunctional families may *impose* an identity on the child (Mollon, 2001), such as the bad 'black sheep', or the crazy one. Commonly, images of self as *excrement* arise from severe abuse—"I am a bag of shit". These negative self-images are intolerable to conscious awareness and give rise to vigorous efforts at defence. Extensive matrices of negative cognitions and self-images may arise from experiences of abuse, trauma, or neglect.

Split images of the other

One of the core dilemmas for the child who grows up to have a borderline personality disorder may be that the mother who was experienced as a source of love and gratification was also experienced as abandoning and rejecting when strivings for independence and autonomy (or other natural developmental initiatives) were activated [Masterson & Rinsley, 1975]. The loving and abandoning aspects of the mother were experienced as mutually incompatible—and therefore remain dis-integrated or split.

The person with BPD believes that he or she can only be loved in a manner that is highly conditional—this is the fundamental core dysfunctional cognition. Thus love, which is felt to be vital to life, is perceived also as deadly—indeed, paradoxically, as hatred. This profound confusion is not tolerable and results in entrenched splitting of the images of the other (and also of the self)—maintaining the person in the Kleinian paranoid-schizoid position. There may then be marked oscillations between positive and negative images of self and other.

Failures of mentalization

Mentalization is the capacity to interpret one's own and other's behaviour in terms of underlying mental states—to have a 'theory of mind'. Fonagy and colleagues (Fonagy et al. 2002; Bateman & Fonagy, 2004) have elaborated on the idea that the child who develops a borderline personality disorder may find the awareness of a caregiver's malevolent intention to be essentially intolerable—with the result that the child defensively shuts down his or her capacity to mentalize. This defensive strategy is undertaken in the service of maintaining the attachment to the caregiver—a goal which may take precedence over all others. This may have a bearing on the juxtaposition (or alternation) of intense neediness and intense fear of emotional involvement shown by many people with BPD.

False self and psychic murder syndrome

The belief in highly conditional love can be associated with false self developments—compulsive chameleon-like adaptations to what is perceived as the desires and expectations of the other. In extreme cases this can amount to what I have termed 'psychic murder syndrome' (Mollon, 2002b). This arises when the child believes that the mother wishes to 'murder' the true self and substitute a version that fits her image of her ideal child—this psychic murder then, through processes of identification, being continued internally. The result is that any potential expression of authentic mental life (such as desire, emotion, or expression of true experience) is 'killed off'—a kind of serial murder of the self.

There may be other complex forms of destructive internal organisation. Hallucinatory internal voices, often of a controlling and destructive nature may be experienced. These may reflect trauma-based dissociative organisations and may also be linked to psychotic areas within the mind. Sometimes organisations of inner 'guards' may have a positive protective function in relation to a vulnerable core of the self, whilst in other cases they appear to be essentially destructive and anti-life and anti-sanity.

Disorders of information processing

People with BPD often show disturbances of emotional perception and information processing—sometimes grossly so and sometimes subtly. Partly this seems to reflect the assimilation of experience to internal schemas and models of interpersonal trauma and abuse. Thus the person may perceive others, including the therapist, in a 'paranoid' way, determined by earlier experiences of trauma and betrayal. In addition, an important factor may be the energy phenomena of 'neurological disorganisation' and polarity reversal. A disorganised or reversed energy system may cause the person to be emotionally 'dyslexic', perceiving a negative message when this is not intended by the other person.

Neurological disorganisation and psychological reversal will also lead to incoherence of internal communication, and an inability to pursue goals coherently. Because human beings are, in addition to physical bodies and brains, interconnecting energy fields, an energy disorganised person may have a disorganising effect on the energy field of another person. This may be experienced as aversive by the other person, evoking hostility.

The use of the other for affect regulation

Because of the proneness to overwhelming states of affect, the person with BPD will tend to turn to others for soothing, with a marked intensity of need. This need for 'selfobject' functions (Kohut, 1971; Mollon, 2001) is driven by the presence of trauma within the person's psycho-somatic-energy system. The problem is that in childhood the caregiver who is sought intensely as a source of soothing may also be the source of interpersonal trauma and overwhelming negative affect. Intense need of the other may coexist with intense fear. Terrors of engulfment may alternate with those of abandonment.

The addictive use of others for soothing and affect regulation will always lead to crises, because human partners are always imperfect and will fail.

Complex developmental post traumatic stress

People with BPD usually suffer from long term developmental post traumatic stress, arising from interpersonal trauma (often including sexual abuse). As a result, they are often preoccupied (consciously or unconsciously) with avoiding traumatic memories. When such memories are triggered by associative cues (e.g. media references that remind him or her of the trauma), the person can be overwhelmed with negative affect. For similar reasons, such a person can be over-whelmed and destabilised by a psychotherapeutic consultation; the attentiveness of an empathic listener may lead the person to speak of and remember traumatic events that are otherwise avoided.

Trauma, and its associated mood disturbance and anxiety, is at the very heart of the problems of borderline personality disorder.

Treating elements of BPD with energy methods

A psychoanalytic perspective is valuable in relation to work with borderline personality disorder, with its complex origins in trauma and disruptions of normal development. However, conventional psychoanalytic therapy, even though rooted in sound psychodynamic principles, may in some cases continue for a considerable time without crucial early trauma being revealed and addressed (as is also the case with other purely verbally based methods). This is because a traumatised person's psyche is often organised around avoiding thoughts that may lead to memories of trauma and may therefore remain in this avoidant stance indefinitely. On the other hand, if childhood trauma is focused upon, the client may become re-traumatised. Energy methods help counter this in two ways: first, by collapsing surface layers of disturbance as the more superficial trauma are addressed, the deeper layers move closer to the 'surface' (in a manner analogous to the movement of items in a spring-loaded dispenser, so that as the uppermost one is removed the next shifts into its place); secondly, the gentle and relatively non-distressing nature of the methods mean that the client begins to feel safer (consciously and unconsciously) about allowing access to the deeper trauma.

Neurological disorganisation

Many patients with BPD will be found to be neurologically disorganised (which can be revealed with muscle testing). The correction methods from applied kinesiology (the precursor of energy psychology) may be useful for the patient on a regular basis. These include Cooks Hookups, the Wayne Cook posture, collar-bone breathing, the navel-K27 massage—and a number of variations on these. Patients who are prone to ND often find that Cooks Hookups is a particularly calming and coherence-inducing exercise.

Treatment of trauma and anxiety

The patient with BPD will have many areas of trauma and anxiety, usually including childhood trauma. All these can be targeted with energy methods. As the therapeutic work continues, the patient will gradually become relatively free from the traumas of the past.

Thought Field Therapy is an excellent means of clearing the perturbations arising from trauma. In addition, for treating deep patterns of trauma and dysfunctional cognition, including ancestral patterns, Seemorg Matrix may be appropriate. This works with the chakras rather than the meridian system—and may therefore be addressing more core forms of encoding of trauma and belief. Part of the Seemorg approach is to link adult traumas with thematically related 'originating' traumas of childhood, and to target the relationship between these and also the matrixes of dysfunctional cognitions arising from the traumas.

The 'linking beliefs' between childhood trauma and later patterns may also be targeted with Seemorg. An example of these might be: "Because my mother rejected the real me, I have rejected the real me" (for a patient who experienced chronic disconnection from his true desires and feelings). Another example might be "Because I was neglected and abused as a child, I neglect and abuse myself now and expect to be treated this way by others".

Constellations of trauma may be addressed. An example might be: "All the times I experienced my mother as abandoning me". Another might be: "All the times my father hit me". Muscle testing can be used to guide whether these constellations can be addressed as a whole, or whether the individual experiences must be targeted.

Tapas Acupressure Technique is also able to address deep patterns and constellations of trauma, but is simpler in method than Seemorg.

Changes in the trauma-related cognitions

As with all personality disorders, the trauma-related cognitions are important to address in borderline personality disorder. These are likely to be generating profound feelings of distrust in relationships, intensely negative self-images, and pervasive discouragement and hopelessness. Of all the energy approaches, Seemorg Matrix most explicitly addresses the deeply rooted core cognitions and belief systems—providing 105 matrices of core beliefs (with potentially unlimited further matrices). This combined approach of clearing the energetic residues of trauma, and concurrently the associated core beliefs is powerfully effective—and may be particularly important in the case of borderline personality disorder, where underlying beliefs about abandonment, abuse, exploitation, helplessness, and being unlovable, may be exerting a profound effect.

Tapas Acupressure Technique also works with cognitive components stemming from trauma—for example, using simple ideas such as "it was a long time ago" and "its not happening now" to bring about shifts in the internal perspective on a past trauma.

Whilst Roger Callahan does not believe that Thought Field Therapy works directly to change cognitions, it is apparent that cognitive change usually follows the collapsing of the perturbations in the thought field that have given rise to the disturbance in the body.

Emotional Freedom Techniques do work with cognitive components, sometimes introducing affirmations, using tapping to eliminate the 'tail enders' that would typically undermine the affirmation, and also incorporating the 'Choices' method as developed by Patricia Carrington.

Energy methods for self-help

A common feature of BPD is a deficiency in the capacity for affect regulation—such that anxiety, anger, and other negative affects may easily spiral out of control. This tendency may be rooted in innate factors and/or childhood experiences with caregivers who not only failed to provide consistent soothing, but also may have fuelled the state of agitation and have further overwhelmed the child with negative affect. One result may be that the adult with BPD is ambivalently dependent on others for soothing, often experiencing frustration and rage when this is not forthcoming.

Some of the easier forms of energy therapy, such as EFT or simple TFT algorithms (without the full TFT diagnostic approach guided by muscle testing), are readily learned and used by clients. These can then form an effective and instant means of affect regulation that is under the client's own control.

Clients can also learn the process of EmoTrance (as developed by Silvia Hartmann), becoming able to focus on the experience of energetic tension in the body, allowing this to 'soften and flow' so that it is released—a skill with many applications once learned.

It is also possible for some clients to learn simple forms of self muscle testing—for example, forefinger raising, forefinger pressing on middle finger, the 'O' ring test, or the 'sticky-smooth' finger-thumb test. These can then provide a readily available means for the client to seek information and guidance from his or her own energy system.

The use of Be Set Free Fast (BSFF)

Although derived from energy psychology methods, by a clinical psychologist, Larry Nims, who had originally trained with Roger Callahan in Thought Field Therapy, the BSFF method now dispenses with tapping or in any other way physically stimulating the energy system. Instead, the method involves the 'installation' of a rather comprehensive instruction to the subconscious mind, stating that on thinking of an agreed code word, or trigger word, the identified emotional problem will be resolved. The same formula and trigger word is used whatever the emotional problem. Once the programme has been installed, the client simply has to identify a problem and say or think the trigger word—the unconscious mind then gets to work resolving it. Thus the method is simple in the extreme, albeit somewhat subtle. Many clients do find it to be very helpful. As with other methods, the process can be guided by muscle testing—but this is not essential.

Because of its simplicity and effectiveness, it seems sensible to use this routinely with clients with BPD, in addition to other approaches. The availability of the trigger word means that the client always has, instantly, a means of accessing internal resources and creativity to bring to bear on any problem that he or she becomes aware of.

Energy toxins and toxic relationships

Energy toxins are often a factor in complex forms of disturbance such as BPD. Roger Callahan's Thought Field Therapy draws attention to the way in which common foods and substances may affect the individual's energy system, causing reversals and neurological disorganisation, preventing therapeutic progress, or causing a relapse after seemingly successful treatment. TFT contains well established methods for detecting and (temporarily) neutralising these. Other methods, such as Radomski's 'allergy antidotes' [www.allergyanti-dotes.com] and Tapas Acupressure Technique [www.tatlife.com], are also used to address energy toxins.

An impressionistic observation is that patients who have experienced a great deal of trauma in childhood, such as some of those with borderline personality disorder, often seem to suffer with many food intolerances and substance sensitivities. It is as if the person has come, as a result of extensive trauma, to register the world in general as 'toxic'—a kind of generalised phobic response of the body to the world and its chemical contents. Another possibility is that people who have experienced overwhelming amounts of stress and trauma have fewer resources available within their system for dealing with energy toxins.

I have found that muscle testing will sometimes reveal that certain persons or relationships are also experienced as energy toxins, having effects (such as neurological disorganisation and recurrent psychological reversal) that are strongly analogous to the effects of toxins. For example, a person may muscle test strong to "I want to be well" but weak to "Jim—I want to be well", thereby indicating that 'Jim' is causing a reversal. For many clients, the phrase 'my mother' will cause a reversal. These energy toxic relationships may need to be dealt with in ways similar to those used for energy toxic substances.

Energy toxins are often at the root of addictions to substances. The addictive substance is an energy toxin, causing reversal, and thus 'tricking' the system into responding as if it were desirable and good. For example, a smoker may muscle test strong to 'tobacco', but weak to "tobacco—I want to be well"—indicating a reversal revealed only through the second level of testing. People with BPD often suffer from addictions to harmful substances and harmful relationships.

Integrating energy methods with psychotherapy

Particularly in relation to work with people with borderline personality disorder, energy methods are not to be considered 'stand alone' therapies. They must be integrated with an overall approach, based on broad psychobiological, psychodynamic, developmental and systemic perspectives. The ongoing interaction between client and therapist must be continually monitored, since the client's internal disturbance is frequently likely to be expressed and played out in relation to the therapist. If there is a prominent unresolved issue in the therapeutic relationship, this is not an appropriate time to undertake an energy treatment. On the other hand, the most efficient way of responding to transference may be to endeavour to understand it and shift its content out of the transference and into recollections of childhood (where it truly belongs). In this respect, the approach is closer to the original one of Freud than to that of many contemporary psychoanalytic fashions (Mollon, 2005).

Clinical Example [a composite case]

Gail was a twenty five year old woman, who presented with a history of traumatic and unstable relationships, periods of depression and self-harm (superficial cutting and a couple of overdoses). She would form intense but volatile relationships with men, expressing strong fears of abandonment and deep insecurity, often triggered by subtle vacillations in the man's availability. Gail's childhood was characterised by an emotionally intense but chaotic relationship with her mother, her father being a more distant figure. The mother would at times be loving and attentive, whilst at other times would be critical, rejecting, and remote. On occasion her mother would leave the household following rows with the father. Gail recalled feeling terrified that her mother would never return. In her early adolescence, the parents separated and Gail continued to live with her mother. Gail disclosed some degree of sexual abuse by a neighbour when she was aged between seven and nine; this appeared to have taken place during babysitting, and involved sexual touch but not penetration. In adolescence, Gail had started drinking alcohol, which would lead her to angry and violent outbursts, with damage to objects and sometimes to herself; this was when her pattern of cutting began. She was still prone to bingeing on alcohol occasionally, but did not routinely drink heavily. Currently Gail had a boyfriend and, despite its rather stormy course, she tended to feel positive about the relationship; however, she often dissociated during sexual activity. Gail also at times experienced periods of anxiety and panic, including claustrophobic anxieties.

Gail had initially expected to be offered some kind of 'counselling' or psychotherapy. It was explained to her that although verbal psychotherapy can be helpful in facilitating understanding and insight, it is not always able to bring about fundamental shifts in the emotional patterning in the mind and body, whereas the adjunctive methods of energy psychology can often do precisely this. Gail expressed relief and enthusiasm on hearing this. She had experienced 'counselling' before and had not found this helpful. Although she thought the actual procedures of the energy methods seemed somewhat strange, she was very happy to give them a try.

Installing preliminary resources

As a first step, the Bc Set Free Fast programme was 'installed', by simply asking Gail to read the 'instructions to the unconscious mind', as developed by Larry Nims. This incorporates a 'trigger word', chosen by the client, which can activate the healing programme whenever a problem is noticed and the trigger word used. Gail's chosen trigger word was 'angel'. To her surprise, Gail began to notice that when she used this method the problems she was experiencing did somehow lessen; she would find herself behaving somewhat differently or would arrive at a subtly different perspective on the situation. The effect would not always be obvious immediately—but in retrospect Gail began to appreciate a pattern of change that she could discern.

Another initial step was to teach Gail to use EmoTrance (Hartmann, 2003). This method, which is focused on the 'existing energetic realities' rather than meridians or chakras, involves the client in becoming more aware of where and how an emotion is experienced in the body. For example, she reported that her experience of agitation that would sometimes lead to cutting was often located as a feeling of ballooning energy in her chest. She was invited to consider this as a form of 'trapped energy'—and then to use intention to allow this energy to 'soften and flow', so that it could become a 'liquid' finding its way out of the body wherever it might, much as a river finds it way to the sea. As Gail became proficient in the use of this method she found it very helpful as a new means of releasing tension from her body, which she could employ in place of the old method of cutting. She was surprised at how easy it could be to transform her bodily experience in this way, and how unpredictably the energy would flow—for example, sometimes pouring out down the arms and hands, sometimes out of the throat and mouth, sometimes out through the soles of the feet, and sometimes just dissipating from the surface of the skin.

Gail was also taught the basics of EFT. This is easy to learn, highly adaptable, and an enormously valuable tool for affect regulation. Gail was amazed and very relieved to discover that she could use this simple method at any time for any kind of distress that she was experiencing.

Neurological disorganisation

Muscle testing revealed that Gail's energy system tended to be both disorganised (neurological disorganisation) and in a general (or massive) state of reversal. She was taught corrections for neurological disorganisation, particularly the exercise known as Cook's Hookups, which she found very calming; this involves sitting with left foot over right, and right hand over left, hands entwined and drawn down and under and up to rest on the chest, tongue on the roof of the mouth. 'Collar bone breathing', as developed by Dr Callahan, was also found helpful. Such exercises facilitate the cross flow of energy. Standard treatments for psychological/energetic reversal were used; tapping side of hand, and/or rubbing the neurolymphatic reflex points on the chest. When these corrections for disorganisation and reversal were employed, Gail's mood became more positive. However, without the corrections, Gail tended to become easily argumentative, hostile, self-sabotaging, perseverative in her speech, and often misperceiving the emotional signals of other people, registering negative affect when none was intended (a kind of emotional dyslexia).

Routine use of TFT and EFT

As the work proceeded, Gail would speak of various stressful or troubling events and issues in her current life—such as turbulence in her relationship with her boyfriend, arguments with her mother, and disputes with a neighbour. In addition to the two methods described above, these problems were addressed with Thought Field Therapy. Precise tapping sequences were derived, which usually led to a rapid collapse of her anxiety or anger. Psychological reversals were frequently found, and these had to be addressed through the usual means of tapping the side of the hand (small intestine) or the neurolymphatic reflex point on the left side of the chest.

Often, Gail would begin to speak of troubling circumstances and experiences during her childhood and adolescence. When she became upset, the therapist would invite her to tap on various points derived from Thought Field Therapy—usually the basic anxiety algorithm of under eye, under arm, collar bone, but sometimes with the addition of the eyebrow point, because of its role in trauma, and sometimes with the addition of the chin for shame, and the little finger for anger, or the outside of the eye for rage. Other points would sometimes be relevant and the therapist worked somewhat intuitively in finding these. Gail was surprised to find that she could "talk about all of that without feeling worse"; previously she had felt like cutting herself after talking of childhood traumas.

The Thought Field Therapy was embedded in the ongoing therapeutic discourse. Often this meant that rather than focussing just on one specific and isolated memory or troubling issue, the process was one of exploring a network of related ideas and experiences. After a sequence of tapping, the therapist might ask "What comes to mind now?". In this way, the TFT functioned to facilitate the free-associative flow of psychodynamic material.

Treating the sexual abuse trauma

It was apparent that the childhood sexual abuse by a neighbour was still exerting an effect, not only on her sexual relationship with her boyfriend, but also in terms of subtle residual symptoms of PTSD. The latter included anxiety and dissociative reactions to mentions of sex, panic when she began to think of certain periods of her childhood, as well as pervasive feelings of shame. Gail agreed, with some trepidation, to use Thought Field Therapy to eliminate the distress associated with the memories of abuse. Muscle testing revealed a reversal to the prospect of overcoming this problem—specifically to do with safety. Therefore she was asked to tap the side of her hand, whilst stating "Even though I feel it is not safe to overcome this problem because I need to be on my guard at all times, I completely accept myself". The following tapping sequence was derived: eye brow; collar bone; under eye; under arm; collar bone; chin; little finger; outside of eye; collar bone; index finger; collar bone. Her subjective units of distress [SUDs] dropped from 9 to 5. Following the '9 gamut' sequence of eye movements, counting and humming, the SUDs dropped further to 2. Muscle testing revealed a mini-reversal at this point, as is commonly the case—the client is happy to release most of the distress, but responds as if wanting to hold on to some of it. She was asked to tap the side of her hand whilst thinking of the 'remainder' of her distress. A further round of tapping then reduced the SUDs to zero—expressed in her comment that she could no longer think about the experiences of abuse. She acknowledged that she could still remember the events, but they seemed more distant and no longer held any emotional charge for her. This was tested by asking her to recount the events of being sexually molested— which she could then do without any emotional distress. It was also apparent that Gail's self-related cognitions had changed in relation to the experience of molestation. Previously she had tended to believe that in some way she had been responsible, through not saying no, and this had been associated with both shame and guilt. Following the TFT, Gail could now clearly and congruently see that the responsibility for the abuse was that of the perpetrator. The TFT was consolidated with the Seemorg Matrix method, clearing the traumatic energy imprints from the chakras, and then targeting cognitions from the Seemorg 'sexual abuse matrix'. Following this work, Gail found that her sexual relationship with her boyfriend improved and she no longer dissociated during love-making.

Treatment of claustrophobic anxieties

Gail had often experienced some degree of claustrophobic anxiety in certain situations—but mostly managed to avoid circumstances that would trigger this. One day she mentioned that when staying in a hotel room recently she had felt a sudden panic at the thought of the door being locked and a fantasy of being trapped in the room. TFT was applied to this experience. Gail then shifted to thoughts of medical procedures in the past, fears of being restrained, memories of being given gas at the dentist as a child. Further TFT led her to think of vague childhood memories of panic, and fears of intruders in her bedroom. She thought of recurrent childhood dreams of seeing a figure in her bedroom doorway and experiencing overwhelming panic. It was apparent that what was being accessed here was a layering of related experiences and anxieties; as the emotional intensity of one layer was removed with TFT, the next layer emerged to be addressed. The impression of childhood anxieties about intruders in her bedroom remained obscure. It was never possible to know with any certainty what exactly these feelings and images were based

378 PSYCHOANALYTIC ENERGY PSYCHOTHERAPY

on—and the relative balance between real experience and fantasy. Gail became somewhat tormented with this uncertainty, wondering who, if anyone, might have been the culprit in generating her childhood panic. TAT was used at this point. The first step, whilst in the TAT pose, was for Gail to acknowledge that she had these various related fears of being trapped and fearing an intruder of some kind; the next step was to entertain the thought that whatever these fears were derived from, it was a long time ago and was not happening now; then a third step was to allow the thought that "all the roots and origins of these fears are healing now". Gail reported a great sense of peace following this—and cautiously expressed a new feeling that it did not seem to matter too much if she never knew what had given rise to her fears of being trapped.

Identifying and treating energy toxins

Gail reported that at times she would drink alcohol to excess—and indeed that even small amounts of alcohol would have a bad effect on her. She would become argumentative and oppositional, perseverative in her speech, and would tend to perceive her boyfriend's remarks and behaviour in the most negative light. Muscle testing confirmed that alcohol not only weakened her energy system but also caused a general/massive reversal. Gail was taught the '7 second' toxin neutralisation technique as used in TFT, which she could use before or after she drank alcohol. As a result she became able to drink moderate amounts of alcohol without becoming disturbed and without experiencing a compulsion to continue drinking.

Sometimes Gail would complain of panic attacks or states of generalised anxiety. Usually these did not appear to be derived from any obvious psychological content. Therefore the hypothesis that they were triggered by 'energy toxins' was explored, since the findings of TFT are that these often play a part in panic attacks. Muscle testing (following the TFT protocol) revealed sensitivities to various common foods, including wheat and chocolate—and these were treated with the TFT toxin procedure and Gail was advised to avoid them for a few weeks. However, the crucial culprit turned out to be some of Gail's toiletry products. Certain perfumed products caused her energy system to become reversed and disorganised and to cause a general weakness. This effect was apparent only with some

of her perfumes; others caused no problem. The TFT toxin procedure was used for the problematic products and Gail was advised
to avoid these particular ones. As these various energy sensitivities
were addressed, Gail experienced a marked lessening in her anxiety
and panic.

Traumas and reversals in relation to mother

In addition to the traumas of sexual molestation, another crucial
area to apply energy desensitisation was Gail's experiences of her
mother's threatened abandonment. There were many such experiences throughout Gail's childhood. She had continually feared that if
she displeased her mother she would be abandoned. Gail was asked
to think of a series of representative instances of this, which were
then targeted with Thought Field Therapy. Seemorg Matrix, which
works with the chakras, was then used to address "all the times I
feared my mother would abandon me". The Seemorg 'traumatic
connections' protocol was used to address the connection between
the childhood traumas and Gail's adult behaviour: i.e. "Because I
was afraid my mother would abandon me, I am insecure in my adult
relationships and fearful of asserting my needs". Following this, the
Seemorg core beliefs protocol was used, drawing upon cognitions
from the 'abandonment matrix'.

It was apparent that Gail had fearfully perceived her mother at
times as neglectful and abandoning. These perceptions had been
intolerable. She had preferred to see herself as bad and undeserv-
ing. EFT was applied to this anxiety-laden perception of her mother,
beginning with the setup phrase: "Even though I saw my mother as
neglectful and abandoning, I completely accept myself". This helped
to relieve Gail's difficulties with 'mentalization' (Fonagy et al., 2002),
whereby she displayed at times selective difficulties in grasping her
own and other's states of mind.

A further aspect of reversals derived from her early experiences
with her mother related to 'psychic murder syndrome' (Mollon,
2002b). A pattern became apparent whereby Gail would abruptly cut
off from emotional connection—with her boyfriend, with the therapist, and with her own vulnerability and need. A move towards
authentic communication of vulnerable emotional need would be
followed by a sudden cutting off, in ways that were sometimes rather

bewildering. It was as if she could not bear to be authentic in her emotional expression. We clarified that this expressed her identification with her experience of her mother's desire to replace her real self with a compliant but false 'Stepford child'. Thus Gail had become a 'serial killer' of her own authentic self. Once clarified, it was possible to address this using Seemorg Matrix, using the traumatic connections protocol: "Because I felt my mother wanted to kill off my real self, I have kept killing off my real self". TAT was also used similarly; step 1 being to hold in mind the problem, that she had felt her mother to be hostile to her authentic self; then step 2 being that she need no longer apply this pattern to her own self; step 3 being that the roots and origins of this problem are healing now; step 4 being that all the places in her mind, body, and life where this pattern has been stored are healing now; step 5 being forgiveness of self and other in relation to this problem.

Although Gail made much progress, there was often an impression of some kind of unconscious sabotage still taking place as she endeavoured to move forward in her life. Indeed it seemed at times that progress in the work would be followed by a 'negative therapeutic reaction'. Muscle testing was used in an effort to throw light on this. Gail tested weak to 'my mother', indicating that the thought of her mother weakened her energy system. Moreover, her arm went weak also to "my mother—I want to be well", indicating that the thought of her mother threw her into deep 'intergenerational reversals' involving fears of losing the core attachment to the family line. Gail was tested when she stated "mother—if I move on in my life and become happier I will remain connected to you and my ancestors". Her muscle showed weak to this (and strong to the converse). These very fundamental intergenerational reversals had to be corrected before Gail could consolidate and maintain the positive changes in her life. Following these reversal corrections, Gail was more easily able to envisage becoming happier and more successful in her life than her mother had been able to be.

The work described here took place with Gail over a period of several months, seeing her once per week. Slowly but steadily over this time, her life became more settled, enjoyable, and productive. Her relationship with her boyfriend deepened and flourished.

CHAPTER SEVENTEEN

A systematic review[1] of the evidence base for energy psychology methods

I n this review, studies of all varieties of meridian-tapping and somato-sensory stimulation that are used to disrupt dysfunctional cognitive-emotional patterns are outlined. However, there are a number of differing theories and hypotheses about the mechanisms underlying the observed therapeutic effects—and, indeed, different methods may operate through slightly different, albeit related, processes. These competing hypotheses are a matter of ongoing debate and research.

Summary

- Thought Field Therapy (TFT) is based on Dr Roger Callahan's observation that when particular sequences of acupressure points are tapped an associated anxiety or other psychological distress is eliminated; the roots of this discovery lay within the field of Applied Kinesiology. Emotional Freedom Techniques (EFT), a derivative of TFT, is a widely used method of rapid emotional desensitisation, with similarities to EMDR, which also contains a tapping procedure. Many EMDR practitioners incorporate EFT and related methods into their work. All the components of EFT are found in other widely used psychological methods. The modes of action of EFT and TFT, although related, may be somewhat different. In addition to TFT and EFT, there are many other approaches within the broad field of energy psychology.

- Like other cognitive, behavioural, and psychodynamic methods, EFT involves close and detailed attention to the thoughts which give rise to dysfunctional emotions and behaviour. By contrast, TFT seeks more precisely the encoding of the psychological problem in the energy field of the body. These may be considered complementary emphases.

- TFT, EFT, and related methods, are easily learned by clients as simple self-help tools of affect regulation.

- For best results with complex mental health problems, TFT and EFT should be incorporated within a wider therapeutic framework using cognitive, behavioural and psychodynamic principles.

- TFT and its derivatives have been used for 25 years—with much clinical knowledge accumulated during this time.

- Evidence for the efficacy and clinical effectiveness of TFT, EFT, and related methods includes the following:

  o Thousands of brief case studies

  o Systematic clinical observation studies

  o Randomised controlled studies

  o Brain scan data

  o Studies of effects on Heart Rate Variability

  o Field studies of treatment of PTSD in disaster areas

○ Audio-visual recordings showing behavioural change.

○ A large 14 year audit in South America, incorporating numerous randomised, controlled, double blind trials.

○ Uncontrolled pilot studies

• Randomised controlled trials have demonstrated the efficacy of TFT and EFT, maintained at follow-up months later.

• Various uncontrolled clinical studies report good results for TFT, EFT, and related methods with a variety of clinical problems.

• A large scale 14 year audit, incorporating double blind trials, in South America, provides strong support for the effectiveness of TFT/EFT type of methods, suggesting their superiority over other cognitive behavioural and medication treatments.

• It is concluded that there is a much greater research evidence-base for energy psychology methods than for most other interventions within mental health services.

What are TFT and EFT?

Thought Field Therapy is derived from Applied Kinesiology, and is based on observations of the encoding of emotional distress in the energy fields of the body. Emotional Freedom Techniques, a derivative of TFT, is a constellation of procedures for rapid desensitisation/relief of emotional distress. These include exposure, desensitisation through tapping on the body, and cognitive restructuring/reframing. There are clear similarities with the procedures of Eye Movement Desensitisation and Reprocessing [EMDR],[2] but without the hazards of the latter; tapping (which is also used at times in EMDR) is less eliciting of emotional material than eye movements (Omaha, 2004). Both EMDR and EFT appear to disrupt the repetitive 'looping' of cognition, image, and emotion that are present in psychopathological states—thereby allowing a rapid shift towards more positive states and new perspectives on life situations. Many EMDR therapists incorporate EFT into their practice since they combine very well (Hartung & Galvin, 2003; Mollon, 2005).

EFT is the most widely used of a family of therapeutic approaches sometimes called 'energy psychology'—but theoretical positions that do not rely on assumptions about an energy system have also been proposed to account for the observed effects of somato-sensory stimulation. In clinical practice, EFT and related methods are combined with, or embedded within, other psychological therapies. Like EMDR, *it is not a 'standalone' therapy*, but is to be used by psychological clinicians within their overall field of competence. EFT is a simplification of more complex procedures from which it is derived. This simplification makes it easily learned by clients.

The TFT procedure

1. The client is asked to think about the problem, whilst he or she taps a sequence of meridian points. These sequences may be either the regularly occurring 'algorithms', or more individual meridian codings found through muscle testing.
2. Checks may be carried out, using muscle testing, to ascertain resistances within the energy system to releasing the perturbations generating the distress. If found these are corrected, using an energy tapping procedure.
3. The procedure is followed until the subjective distress drops to zero. This may also be confirmed by muscle testing.
4. If the distress does not rapidly drop, muscle testing may be used to identify energetic factors that may be interfering; these factors may include substances and foods that may function as 'individual energy toxins'.

The EFT procedure

1. a target image or memory is identified, which evokes anxiety or other distressing emotion;
2. this is dissected into its various components or aspects—which might be cognitive, affective, sensory, imaginal, or temporal;
3. the client is asked to think of these whilst a desensitisation procedure is followed, involving tapping on the body (the client tapping on his or her own body);

4. the tapping appears to disrupt the previous patterning of cognitive-emotional response, inducing a dissipation of distress;
5. the tapping is accompanied by a statement of self-acceptance in relation to the target problem (which reduces a common tendency to resist the desensitisation);
6. sometimes additional levels of resistance to desensitisation are identified; these take the form of meta-beliefs (Wells, 2000) or meta-motives that lead the person to believe that recovery from the emotional problem is dangerous in some way.
7. tapping may, at certain points in the process, be accompanied by eye movements, humming and counting (a constellation of multisensory activities which further disrupts the previous cognitive-emotional patterning) a procedure known as the '9 gamut'.
8. the tapping is continued until subjective distress is eliminated;
9. another aspect of the target problem may then be addressed.
10. the work is continued until all cognitive and emotional aspects of the target problem have been resolved.
11. Single traumas and anxieties may be targeted. In addition, by working systematically through a range of key instances of a network of thematically related memories, the emotional charge can be taken out of a significant areas of personality impairment (for example, a range of experiences underpinning low self-esteem).

The practitioner closely monitors the client's progress from moment to moment, by careful observation and by asking the client to provide ratings of the Subjective Units of Disturbance [SUDs]. This feedback is used to guide the process.

TFT and EFT do not retraumatise

These methods may be used by skilled psychological therapists who are able to track the client's progress through the layers of anxieties, dysfunctional cognitions, and traumatic memories. They may also be readily employed by the client as a simple stress-relief and affect-regulation tool. The methods do not require the client to relive emotional trauma—nor require him or her to talk in detail about the experience. This is a considerable advantage in working with traumatised patients who may become overwhelmed by simply talking of the traumatic experience. Adverse reactions appear extremely rare.

TFT and EFT may be combined with other methods

TFT and EFT may readily be combined with other psychological methods, including other cognitive-behavioural strategies. In clinical practice the actual tapping procedure is likely to be embedded within much more activity of a conventional verbal cognitive or psycho-analytic (or other) nature. Through the ordinary discourse of psychotherapy, the practitioner will identify the affective, cognitive, and psychodynamic areas to target with TFT or EFT. For example, most of a psychotherapy session may consist of verbal enquiry and exploration, with TFT/EFT taking up the last few minutes after the crucial issues have been clarified and understood. On the other hand, it is possible to work more free-associatively with 'tapping and talking' since the process appears to allow a more free emergence of psychological material.

TFT and EFT help to reduce states of being emotionally overwhelmed

Those clinicians who combine TFT/EFT with EMDR tend to use eye movements if there is a need to elicit cognitive-emotional material — and to use tapping methods if the client is likely to become emotionally overwhelmed (Hartung & Galvin, 2003; Mollon, 2005; Omaha, 2004). The qualities of being soothing and non-eliciting of emotional intensity make TFT/EFT ideal as a self-help tool for affect regulation, as outlined in popular books such as Lynch and Lynch (2001).

Benefits of TFT and EFT

The benefits of TFT and EFT, as commonly reported by its practitioners, are that:

1. It is often highly effective.
2. It is often extremely rapid in its effects.
3. Patients report immediate benefit in terms of relief from emotional distress

4. It does not require the patient to relive trauma with depth and intensity.
5. In general, it does not cause distress to the client.
6. Clients often like to use the method on their own and report benefit in doing so.
7. It can be used both as a simple stress relief method and as part of complex psychological therapy.
8. It can be combined with other psychological therapies.

The different levels of evidence

A range of different kinds of evidence may be relevant in evaluating a therapeutic approach. At the most basic level, case studies and anecdotal reports are crucial. Systematic observation, involving gathering data from routine clinical practice is another form of evidence. This may sometimes be thought of as 'practice-based evidence' — often an important balance to the evidence provided by trials in more refined and restrictive research settings (Barkham & Mellor-Clark, 2000). Tests of efficacy, involving good research design, help to demonstrate that the therapy actually does something beyond a placebo effect. Large scale randomised controlled trials may compare the effectiveness of different therapeutic modalities on clinical problems. Most treatments within mental health services are not based on the latter form of evidence.

Case studies and anecdotal reports

There is a great deal of evidence of this nature. Workshops, special interest groups, and conferences, within the UK and the USA, are one source of clinical reports and discussion of cases. The hundreds of brief case examples, with discussion, on the www.emofree.com website have already been mentioned. Writing within the auspices of the Association for Comprehensive Energy Psychology (ACEP), Dr David Feinstein comments:

> "Estimates based on informal interviews by the author with a sampling of the ... [association's] ... members are that more than 5000 'strikingly effective' cases (more rapid and more favourable outcomes than the therapist would have predicted had standard treatments for the conditions been employed) are documented in the membership's clinical records". [Feinstein, 2005]

In a later paper, he adds that in general energy psychology methods are "backed by more than thirty thousand documented cases" [Feinstein, 2007]. As well as the clinical accounts in the present book, there are also a number of other texts with case examples and discussion (e.g. Connolly, 2004; Diepold, Britt & Bender, 2004; Gallo, 1999; 2002; Hartung & Galvin, 2003; Mollon, 2005; Quinn, 2004). A detailed personal account is provided by Schaefer (2002).

Examples of cases from the www.emofree.com website

Many of the cases reported on Gary Craig's www.emofree.com website are interesting and persuasive. For example, Mair Llewellyn gives an account of a single session treatment of depression in a young man in his early twenties. Initially his voice was flat and his face expressionless. He was very unhappy because he had split up from his girlfriend and was also worried about his job. When asked about his family and childhood, his emotions began to emerge—and he agreed to tap whilst they continued talking. He talked of his feeling of powerlessness as a child and about his parents continually arguing. He mentioned a time when his mother had left and how frightened he felt. It seemed he had felt he was to blame, that he was unlovable. As he continued tapping, the sadness cleared and he began talking with new insight and clarity. She quotes him as follows:

> "It wasn't my fault about Dad and Mum arguing, as I was only a little kid, too young to be responsible. No wonder I felt insecure throughout my relationships, and devastated when they failed. All my life I have been frightened and sad about life. Now for the very first time I feel as if the clouds have lifted and the sun is shining ... That's a strange feeling given that the girl I love has left me and my job is coming to an end, but that is actually how I feel ... I won't need to feel those sad feelings ever again"

This remarkable shift in mood and cognition, with real mutative insight, came about simply through talking and tapping in a single session. Gary Craig comments: "This cognitive shift is one of the most fascinating features of the tapping procedures. Literal belief changes happen behind the scenes and clients see the whole scenario through a different set of glasses (beliefs). It often takes years (sometimes decades) of talk therapy or other conventional procedures to arrive at this enviable healing place. With EFT it is often simultaneous. This feature is so important that I often use it as evidence that EFT has been successful. In a way it is the ultimate evidence." http://www.emofree.com/Depression/textbook.htm

Carol Solomon presents a case of a corporate executive who became afraid to fly in the months following 9/11, saying that he had watched too much news coverage. He had a history of panic attacks prior to this. His worst fear was of experiencing another panic attack. Dr Solomon identified a large number of aspects of her client's anxiety, each of which was addressed using a specific tapping statement. She incorporated 'choices' phrasing into some of these. Thus, for the general anticipatory anxiety, she invited him to tap using a number of statements such as: "Even though I get anxious just thinking about the plane flight … Even though I am afraid of having another panic attack …"; then interweaving these also with positive choices statements such as: "Even though I am worried about the flight, I choose to know I can calm myself" and "Even though I am not certain how things will go, I choose to let it be fun and easy." For specific fears, she suggested phrasing such as: "Even though I am afraid I won't be able to breathe …" and "Even though I am terrified to get on the plane …", then with choices statements such as: "Even though I am afraid of suffocating, I choose to know there is plenty of air and I can breathe freely" and "Even though unexpected things can happen, I choose to stay relaxed and confident". For physical symptoms, the phrases included: "Even though my chest and gut feel tight/my palms are sweaty/I feel like I can't breathe". There was considerable general improvement through working on these aspects, but some element of the problem remained. Therefore Dr Solomon asked if there might have been events in childhood during which he might have had similar feelings. He spoke of times when his older brother would pin him down under the bed covers, and he would be in a state of complete panic, feeling that he could not breathe or move—and that he was what he called 'enveloped'. EFT then continued with phrases including: "Even though I felt panicked and had to get out … Even though I felt enveloped … Even though I couldn't breathe" etc. but then shifting to the possibility of letting go of the anger at his brother: "Even though I was terrified and afraid

I would never get out, I am open to the possibility of forgiving my brother." Work on these issues covered several months, reducing his anxiety to zero. Four and a half years later, the client reported that he regularly flies, with no anxiety at all. http://www.emofree.com/Panic-anxiety/911-anxiety.htm

These two cases were selected at random, with little searching, from the archives on the www.emofree.com website. There is an inherent plausibility to the accounts because the underlying structure of the problem is unravelled in the course of the treatment. There are thousands of such examples, succinctly described. The sheer weight of numbers of clinical anecdotes is a powerful indication of the efficacy and value of the method.

Systematic clinical demonstration methodology

The 1994 'Active Ingredient Project'—Florida State University. [reported in Carbonell and Figley, 1999].

This study demonstrated the efficacy of Thought Field Therapy, from which EFT was derived

Trauma researcher Dr Charles Figley and colleagues were concerned in the early 1990s at the apparent absence of effective and efficient psychological therapies for treating trauma—treatments that were much in need for the many veterans of the Vietnam war. For example, a 1992 meta-analysis of all published studies (Solomon et al.) found that no treatment approach reported even a partial success rate greater than 20% after 30 hours of treatment—and Seligman (1994) noted that only 'marginal' relief is possible for those diagnosed with PTSD:

> "[there are] ... almost no cures. Of all the disorders we have reviewed, PTSD is the least alleviated by therapy of any sort. I believe that the development of new treatments to relieve PTSD is of the highest priority." (Seligman, 1994, p. 144)

Moreover, patients would find that speaking of their trauma was difficult and would cause as much suffering as the original trauma, often without any relief from doing so. Against this bleak background, Figley and colleagues established a programme to examine and evaluate innovative methods of treating traumatic stress. They chose to use a 'systematic clinical demonstration methodology' (Carbonell & Figley, 1996; Liberman & Phipps, 1987)—essentially small scale measures of efficacy.

In order to select 'innovative and promising methods of treating symptoms of post-traumatic stress', a survey was sent to 10.000 members of an Internet consortium of therapists, asking them to nominate treatments that were extremely efficient and could be observed under laboratory conditions. In addition, the authors contacted hundreds of clinicians to solicit treatment nominations. An advisory board of traumatologists then examined nominated treatments to select some for further investigation. Four promising approaches were identified, each of which were in clinical use but at the time had a paucity of research examining their effectiveness. These were: Traumatic Incident Reduction (a kind of focused Rogerian counselling); Visual Kinesthetic Dissociation (an NLP strategy); EMDR; and Thought Field Therapy (the precursor of EFT). Carbonell and Figley (1999) add "Other approaches were noted, such as various exposure-based, behavioural and cognitive treatments." The innovators of each of these four approaches were invited to send a treatment team to the research laboratory for 7-8 days and to treat clients under conditions of the research design. Two symposia were held for each of the treatment approaches, with discussion by clinicians and researchers, both of the method (its history, theory, procedure, indicators of success, requirements for training etc.) and the outcomes of the therapy.

Each patient was identified as having a trauma history and symptoms of traumatic stress. They were all given the Brief Symptom Inventory, before and 6 months after treatment—a 53 item self-report inventory with ratings of distress on a 5 point scale, which is known to be sensitive to change. The Impact of Events Scale and the Subjective Units of Disturbance ratings were also used. Participants were also asked to keep a diary of ratings on a daily basis for the next 6 months.

The length of each session was determined by the therapist, but the research design limited the therapy to one week. The length of each session varied from 4 hours for the Traumatic Incident Recall, to 20 minutes for Thought Field Therapy. The average duration of treatment per client, in minutes was 254 for TIR, 113 for VK/D, 172 for EMDR, and 63 for TFT.

Results

All four treatments produced a drop in scores. For reasons of varia-tion amongst the levels of severity of symptoms of the patients in the four groups, as well as the relatively small numbers of subjects, the study could not be taken as a comparative measure of effectiveness. However, the authors note in relation to the SUD scores: "Nonethe-less, it appears that EMDR and TFT produced the largest drop in scores."

There are two further points suggestive of the value of TFT. First, the treatment time was shortest for TFT (average 63 minutes, compared to 172 minutes for EMDR) — although further randomised controlled studies are needed before this can be taken as reliable comparison. Second, the TFT team treated all 12 patient assigned to them. By contrast, the EMDR team agreed to treat only 6 of the 15 subjects assigned to them on the grounds that most were consid-ered inappropriate for the treatment or would need more therapy before commencing EMDR.

Carbonell and Figley (1999) speculate about the common factors in all four of these successful therapies — and focus on the simultaneous exposure to the traumatic memory and the reduction in distress.

> "Essentially, in all of the approaches, the trauma is recalled in the presence of relaxation (or if not relaxation, the absence of stress) and thus is not 're-lived' as it is remembered because the negative affect associated with the trauma is not re-experienced with the memory of the event".

Commenting further on this project, in a foreword to Gallo (1999), Charles Figley writes:

> For the last four years we have investigated a large number of treat-ment approaches that purport to cure these trauma-based problems. Among the most exciting and different treatment approaches we studied was Thought Field Therapy. Exciting because the treatment was simple, fast, harmless, and easy to teach both clients and clini-cians. It was different because little talking was involved. ... The directions involved tapping ... while performing other activities such as certain eye movements, humming and counting. I must say we found the procedure very peculiar.

Our investigations showed that this method worked dramatically and permanently to eliminate psychologically based distress in a substantial number of people. We have shared our findings with colleagues ... and continue to be confident that such therapy does succeed in counterconditioning, similar to cognitive-behavioural methods". [p. viii]

Two randomised controlled demonstrations of efficacy

The study of EFT by Wells and colleagues (2003)

The first randomised and controlled study of EFT, is that by Wells et al. (2003). Participants with phobias of small animals—such as spiders, rodents, or cockroaches—were randomly assigned to two groups. One group received a 30 minute treatment with EFT [n. 18]. The other received training in a procedure called diaphragmatic breathing [n. 17], which has been shown to produce physiological changes consistent with deep-relaxation (Lehrer et al. 1999). Thus, the control group treatment did contain active ingredients likely to induce relaxation and therefore likely to facilitate desensitisation. Moreover, the deep-breathing condition was designed to parallel as closely as possible the EFT condition. Whilst the EFT group tapped on the meridian points, repeating the reminder phrase (e.g. "this fear of spiders") at each point, the deep-breathing group was asked to repeat this phrase between each breath. Each emotional aspect of the problem was addressed with 'rounds' of deep-breathing, paralleling the rounds of meridian tapping with EFT. Levels of fear were assessed by taking SUDs at different stages of a Behavioural Approach Task (BAT). The BAT involved 8 points at progressively distances nearer to the feared animal. A further measure was how far the participant could tolerate approaching the animal on the BAT. Follow-up measures were taken 6 months or more later. The results were that the EFT treatment produced significantly greater improvement than did the deep-breathing condition, as measured behaviourally and on self-report measures. The improvement was found to be largely sustained at follow-up.

The significance of this study is that it contained a control condition for comparison, and it was randomised—thus meeting the highest research standards. The choice of a control condition that mimicked the procedure of EFT in all details except for [a] the use of a self-acceptance statement, and [b] tapping on the meridian points, suggests that the effective factors did have something to do with the ingredients specific to EFT. Since deep-breathing does induce relaxation, the superiority of the EFT condition must be due to more than induction of an ordinary relaxation response.

11 additional participants were also assigned to an EFT group treatment. Similar improvements to the individual treatment condition were found.

Baker & Siegel 2005. A partial replication and extension of the Wells et al. study. 'Can a 45 minute session of EFT lead to a reduction of intense fear of rats, spiders and water bugs?'

This study is contrasted with that of Wells et al. 2003. In addition to the EFT condition, Baker and Siegel inserted a no-treatment control condition. For the other comparison condition they used a supportive interview similar to Rogerian nondirective counselling. Thus there were three groups.

The results supported the Wells study. Participants improved significantly in their pre-post test ability to walk closer to a feared animal after EFT, whilst the other two conditions showed no improvement. The EFT group showed significant decreases on the SUDs measure of fear, and on the Fear Questionnaire, as well as on a new questionnaire designed for the study. Participants in the other two conditions [no treatment, and the supportive interview] showed no decrease in fear on these subjective measures.

Measures of heart rate showed a large but equal change for each condition—thus indicating that relaxation alone is not the active ingredient.

A check for the influence of suggestion was included. The participants were told which of the three conditions they would be assigned to and were asked to rate the degree to which they expected this described condition to help reduce their fear. The EFT and Supportive Interview participants did not differ significantly in their mean expectation scores—but despite these equal expectations, they did differ markedly in outcome, with EFT showing superior results. Participants in the no treatment group (sitting and reading for 45 minutes) did not think this condition would reduce their anxiety.

Despite the expectation of improvement in the Supportive Interview condition, these participants did no better than the no treatment group.[3]

A follow-up was conducted of participants 1.4 months after the original testing. On most measures the significant effects of one sessions of EFT held up and remained superior to that of the two comparison conditions.

Dr Patricia Carrington reports on a series of studies planned or in progress, building upon these studies, by one of the co-authors, Dr Harvey Baker, and colleagues (www.eftupdate.com/ResearchonEFT.html): [1] a controlled study in a clinical setting, comparing EFT with two control groups; this will involve three groups, an EFT treatment group, a psychoeducational intervention group, and a no treatment group receiving only medication; [2] a comparison of EFT and a sham variant (no true acupoints being tapped) examining the effect on maths anxiety; [3] a study of the effect of EFT versus two control conditions on basket ball skill; [4] a study of the effect of EFT on alcohol addiction in a small village in India; [5] a comparison of EFT using the standard tapping points with a version using tapping on other body locations; a study of the effect of EFT on fears of public speaking, using a virtual reality programme to test this.

Other controlled studies

EFT compared with Progressive Muscle Relaxation [Sezgin & Ozcan, 2004]

32 students in Turkey were treated for test anxiety in relation to the university entrance exam. Each half of the group was given a lecture on the modality to be used, either EFT or muscle relaxation, and were given instructions on how to apply these. The groups were asked to carry out the modalities three times a week for two months, particularly when feeling anxious about the exam. Whilst both groups showed a decrease in anxiety, measured on the Test Anxiety Inventory, the decrease with EFT was significantly greater than that in the progressive muscle relaxation group (p < .05).

Group treatment with EFT. [Rowe, 2005]

102 individuals were treated with EFT, modified for a group, and showed highly significant improvement (p .0005) on a test of psychological stress. These improvements held up at 6 month follow-up. A within-subjects design used the subjects as their own controls. The Derogatis Symptom Checklist-90 (SCL-90-R SA 45 short form) was given one month prior to the workshop, immediately prior, immediately after, one month after, and six months after. Scores showed a decrease in the checklist's global measure of distress, as well as on all nine subscales and held up at six month follow-up (p < .0005).

Various forms of tapping [Waite & Holder, 2003]

This randomised controlled study used 119 university students to investigate the impact of brief EFT tapping for fears. Three treatment conditions were used: [1] tapping on the twelve standard EFT points, accompanied by the usual EFT statements and the 9 gamut sequence of eye movements, humming, and counting; [2] tapping on twelve points not used in standard EFT; [3] tapping with the fingers on twelve points on a doll rather than on the subject's own body. A no-treatment control group were given the task of making a toy out of paper. The tapping treatments were very short, involving just two rounds of the procedure. Each tapping condition produced statistically highly significant drops in SUD ratings of fear of 18%, but there was no drop in SUDs for the control group. This substantial drop in fear after just a couple of minutes of a tapping procedure is striking—and supports those who argue that it is the sensory stimulation of tapping rather than any connection with purported acupressure points that disrupts the fear response.

TAT for weight loss [Elder et al., 2007]

A randomised and controlled study, at the Center for Health Research, Kaiser Permanente in Portland, provided support for the use of Tapas Acupressure Technique as a helpful approach for maintaining weight loss.

The aim of the study was to compare TAT with two other interventions for helping people maintain weight loss after they had successfully lost excess weight (at least 3.5 kg) on a behavioral program.

TAT was compared with Qigong and Self-directed support (a simple cognitive-behavioral approach with advice and encouragement). All three approaches involved 10 hours of instruction over a 12 week period. The outcome measure was weight gain. 92 adults were involved in the study.

After three months, the group using TAT had not gained any weight, but the Self-Directed Support group gained an average of 0.35 kg. At 6 months the Self-Directed Support group had gained 1.5 kg., but the TAT group had gained only 0.25 kg. Qigong was found too difficult for the participants to practice, and this group gained the most weight of all. There were no adverse effects of TAT.

The authors conclude:

> "TAT was a feasible intervention, warranting further study as a potential weight maintenance intervention."

A summary of the research is published as Mist et al. 2005—and also available at: http://journals.medicinescomplete.com/journals/fact/current/fact1005a13a60.htm

Doctoral dissertations demonstrating efficacy

[NB. Doctoral dissertations, by their nature, are expected to be of a high academic standard and to be suitable for publication as peer reviewed literature].

Schoninger 2004

48 individuals with public speaking anxiety were randomly assigned to a treatment group or a waiting list control group. They were then required to give a speech in front of a small audience, followed by the administration of measures of anxiety [the Clevenger and Halvorson Speaker Anxiety Scale, and the Speilberger Trait and State Anxiety Scale] as well as self-report [SUD ratings]. No significant differences between the groups were found prior to the treatment. The treatment group was given a single TFT session focussed on public speaking. Following this, they gave another speech in front of an audience. Scores on the three measures were significantly lower compared to pre-treatment scores (at the .001

level). By contrast, the anxiety scores for the control group after giving a second speech (following a two week delay) increased slightly. This waiting list group was then given a TFT session, producing improved scores similar to those of the original treatment group. Participants in the study showed decreased shyness, confusion, physiological activity, and post-speech anxiety, as well as increased poise and interest in giving a future speech. These gains were retained at 4 month follow-up.

Darby 2001—needle phobias

20 patients who had been unable to receive necessary medical treatment because of intense needle phobia showed significant immediate improvement after one hour of TFT and at one month follow-up. Measures used were the Wolpe and Lang Fear Survey Schedule and SUD ratings. Significance was at the .001 level

Wade 1990—phobias and self-concept

This study investigated the effects of TFT on anxiety and self-concept with 28 subjects with a phobia. The TFT reduced the phobias substantially, as indicated by SUD ratings, and significant improvement was found on standardised measures of self-acceptance, self-esteem, and self-congruency (the Tennessee Self Concept Scale and the Self Concept Evaluation of Location Form). A waiting list control group of 25 patients did not show any improvement.

Salas 2001—specific phobias

22 subjects were used as their own controls for a study of treatment of specific phobias, half receiving EFT first, followed by Diaphragmatic Breathing, the other half receiving Diaphragmatic Breathing followed by EFT. The Beck Anxiety Inventory, a modified Behavioural Avoidance Test, and SUD ratings were administered prior to treatment and after each treatment. EFT produced a significant decrease of anxiety on all three measures regardless of whether it was the first or second treatment. By contrast, the Diaphragmatic Breathing produced a significant drop in the SUD ratings but not the other two measures, and only when it was the first treatment.

Schulz 2007. Therapists' views on integrating energy psychology in work with survivors of childhood sexual abuse

12 psychologists in private practice were surveyed regarding their use of energy psychology with adult survivors of childhood sexual abuse. 5 of these used energy psychology as their primary modality, whilst the other 7 combined it with talk therapy, CBT, and/or EMDR. All 12 therapists considered energy psychology methods to be the most effective treatment for the anxiety, panic, and phobias suffered by survivors of abuse, and also reported improved relationships, mood and self-esteem in these patients as a result of using energy psychology methods. 10 of the interviewees attributed decreases in the dissociative symptoms of their clients to energy psychology, with better self-care and less self-harming behaviours also being reported. One therapist summarised the common experience as follows: "My life and work have been enriched beyond measure … I have been able to help people in ways I never imagined possible. The speed and depth of change can be astonishing." [Schulz, 2007b].

Studies including brain scan data

Swingle, Pulos & Swingle 2004 Road Traffic Accidents Trauma

This studied the effect of EFT on 9 road traffic accident victims suffering from PTSD. EFT was taught to the subjects in two sessions and they were given tapping home-work. Three months after this intervention the accident victims showed significant positive changes, both in brain scan measures and in self-reported symptoms of stress. Measures used were the Beck Depression Inventory, the Beck Anxiety Inventory, ten anger items from the Spielberger State-Trait Anxiety Inventory, and a questionnaire to assess avoidance of driving or riding in vehicles. These were administered 10-24 days before treatment and again within 70 to 160 days following EFT treatment. In addition an eyes-closed qEEG assessment of 19 brain locations was carried out. The SUD ratings dropped significantly for all nine subjects (initial SUD averaged 8.3; following treatment they averaged 2.5 (p < .001) and a global reduction of symptoms was found at follow-ups, not all the gains held for 4 of the 9 subjects at follow-up. Brain wave data showed differences between the five whose improvement held and the four whose did not. The latter showed increased arousal of the right frontal lobe, considered to be an indicator of depressed mood ($p < .02$). On the other hand, the five who sustained improvements showed increased theta/beta ratio changes, following treatment, in the occipital region (an indicator of central nervous system quiescence) and increased theta/sensory motor rhythm amplitude over the sensory motor cortex (a measure of somatic quiescence). A further interesting factor was that the four whose improvements were not sustained did not comply with the tapping home-work.

Swingle 2000 [conference presentation] Reductions in the frequency of seizures

EFT was used as a treatment for children with epilepsy. They were given EFT by their parents whenever they thought a seizure might occur. Swingle found significant reductions in frequency of seizures among these young children, as well as extensive improvement in their EEG readings after two weeks of daily in-home EFT.

Lambrau, Pratt, & Chevalier 2003. Treatment of claustrophobia—with brain scan data

Four subjects suffering with claustrophobia were treated with TFT in a thirty minute session and pre- and post-treatment EEG readings were taken, along with physiological measures and SUD ratings. These were compared with those of four non-phobic control subjects who were given a thirty minute relaxation treatment. All subjects were asked to enter and remain in a small metal lined enclosure for as long as they could tolerate, up to 5 minutes. This was repeated after the TFT or relaxation treatment. The results were that although the claustrophobic subjects' theta activity EEG scores were higher than those of the control subjects ($p < .001$), along with physiological and subjective measures, after the TFT treatment these decreased to the same level as the non-phobic subjects. Reduced anxiety remained at 2 week follow-up.

Diepold & Goldstein 2000. TFT effect on qEEG measures maintained at 18 months

An individual's qEEG measures were taken before and after a TFT session, and again at 18 month follow-up. When the subject thought of the targeted personal trauma prior to the TFT statistically abnormal brain-wave patterns were observed, but not when thinking of a neutral event. Following the TFT, the brain waves were normal when thinking of the same trauma. This improvement held at 18 month follow-up.

Andrade and Feinstein—digitised EEG scans in Generalised Anxiety Disorder [www.innersource.net]

An individual with Generalised Anxiety Disorder (GAD) was studied with EEG scans prior to TFT treatment and again after 4, 8, and 12 sessions. Patients with GAD are known to have distinctive brain wave ratio signatures (Lubar, 2004). With the TFT treatment the symptoms of GAD subsided and the EEG patterns normalised. These images are posted on the www.innersource.net website. When a group of scans of patients with GAD who received TFT were compared with a group who were treated only with medication, the TFT group showed a normalisation whilst the medication group did not, even though both groups experienced a lessening of anxiety. These studies formed part of the large South American audit.

Systematic clinical observations with outcome data

Sakai et al. 2001 Tapping methods in medical and psychiatric services

Seven TFT trained therapists applied TFT to 714 patients at the Kaiser Behavioral Medicine Services (with referrals from primary care) and Behavioral Health Services (a specialist psychiatry/mental health service). The purpose was to establish, for this health maintenance organisation, the potential of TFT in relation to a variety of clinical conditions. A wide range of symptoms and disorders were treated — including, for example, acute stress, anxiety, OCD, phobia, depression, anger, food cravings, chronic pain, panic disorder, and PTSD. Statistically significant within-session reductions in self-reported stress were obtained with 31 problems/symptoms in 1594 applications with 714 patients. Pre and post-test SUD ratings were significant at .001 level of probability for these, except for alcohol cravings, major depressive disorder, and tremors, which were at the .01 level of probability. Six case studies were included in the report. Three of these case descriptions included data on changes in heart rate variability, often used as an objective measure of physiological change with TFT.

The methodology of this study is criticised by Lohr (2001), but some of his arguments seem a little odd, based apparently on his perception of TFT and its rationale as implausible. Lohr's complete dismissal of the study seems a little harsh, especially in view of the authors' own comment in the abstract: "These ... are preliminary data that call for controlled studies to examine validity, reliability, and maintenance of effects over time." [p. 1215]

Comparison of TFT data with a study of CBT–effects on heart rate variability in severely depressed patients

Dr Callahan is enthusiastic about the use of Heart Rate Variability (HRV) as an objective, reliable, and placebo-free measure of the effectiveness of TFT. He became interested in this after being contacted by a cardiac specialist, who had been using TFT for stress relief amongst his patients, noticed a remarkable improvement in HRT, which is usually rather difficult to influence. Abnormally low HRV is a strong predictor of mortality (Nolan et al. 1998). The most stable measure of the variability is the SDNN (standard deviation of normal to normal intervals). Improvements in SDNN of about 20% can be brought about by interventions such as stopping smoking for a period of time, or exercising for six months or more. Most drugs have a negative effect on SDNN. However, Dr Callahan has repeatedly found that often TFT can produce improvements in SDNN of much greater than 20% in a matter of a few minutes. For example, he describes the case of a physician who had suffered with depression for 20 years, not helped by any medications or previous psychotherapies: prior to TFT he rated his depression at a SUD of 10 and his HRV SDNN score was a very low 32.3 ms.; immediately following a few minutes treatment with TFT his depression completely disappeared and his HRV increased to 144.4 ms. (Callahan & Callahan, 2003, p. 28).

Carney et al. (2000) studied the effects on HRV of cognitive behaviour therapy carried out with severely depressed patients who also had cardiac problems. After up to 16 CBT sessions, the patients reported some improvement in depression symptoms, but the SDNN score did not improve, but in fact declined somewhat. The mean scores were:

Pre-therapy SDNN: 103.4

Post-therapy SDNN: 98.9. (a decrease/worsening of 4.5%)

Carney and colleagues concluded: "It is possible that heart rate and HRV never return to normal once there has been an episode of major depression" (pp. 645–646).

Dr Callahan (Callahan, 2001c) selected 8 cases from the TFT organisation's files, of people who had suffered severe depression and for whom they had pre- and post-therapy SDNN scores. The pre-therapy average SDNN was much lower/worse than those in the Carney study. After just one treatment with TFT the SDNN scores rose markedly and the depression was also eliminated. The scores were:

Pre-therapy SDNN: 57.5

Post-therapy SDNN: 105.7 (an improvement of 84%).

Field Studies with PTSD in war and disaster areas

Johnson et al. 2001 [reported also in Feinstein 2006] Tapping methods helped with war trauma

In the year 2000, five separate trips to Kosovo were made by clinicians from the Global Institute of Thought Field Therapy to treat those traumatised by war. 105 trauma patients were treated, with ages from 4-78—almost all referred by their physicians. 249 separate traumas were treated, including gang rape, witnessing massacres, sadistic torture, and being involved as perpetrators of military misconduct. Due to Albanian taboos on displays of emotional suffering, the SUDs scale could not be used, nor the word 'trauma'. The translation of the phrase 'bad moments' was used—and the complete absence of distressing emotion and somatic disturbance was taken as the measure; thus the patient might say, thorough translation: "Yes, at this moment it is completely gone ... if the way I feel at this moment becomes all moments I will be completely satisfied". For 103 of the 105 patients, and for 247 of 249 traumatic memories, the treatment was successful. The authors comment:

"In addition to the self-report of complete relief, their spontaneous expressions provided confirming clues. People gave that look of astonishment, hugged, put their hands to their temples, and looked up to the heavens in gratitude... Also it was typical for them to feel great energy, then disappear long enough to return with a bag full of peaches or nuts."

Follow-up data ranged from 1 month to 9 months. All treatment successes endured without relapse.

This report was criticised by Rosner (2001), on the grounds that [a] only superficial information about the sample was provided, [b] diagnostic information was absent, [c] the self-report measure of distress was rather crude, [d] the description of TFT was rather short. However, the reviewer does note that "doing research in a postwar society is more than difficult" and that "it is only to be expected that methodological standards should be of lesser importance than in a review of laboratory research performed in safety in a rich country." [pp. 1241–1242]. By contrast, Hartung and Galvin (2003) comment: "Scientists can criticise this study's lack of randomisation of subjects, use of nonstandardised measures, failure to account for competing hypotheses, and the like. Practicing psychotherapists, on the other hand, ... will more likely feel exhilarated when reading about this work. A report of 98% recovery from trauma, even if informal, is likely to encourage a clinician who is dedicated to alleviating the suffering of trauma victims." [p. 60]

One of the main therapists in the Kosovo work was Carl Johnson, a clinical psychologist with a background as a PTSD specialist with the Veteran's Administration. He made four further visits to Kosovo following the publication of the original account, mainly in order to train local health care practitioners in Thought Field Therapy. He was able to obtain follow-up information, from two physicians, on 75% of the people he had treated during his first five visits. In almost every case, the improvements following the initial TFT treatments had been maintained; for each treated traumatic memory, the subjective distress had been eliminated. The physicians did ask Johnson to see two patients for further treatment of some additional memories that had not initially been addressed. In a letter of appreciation, the chief medical officer of Kosovo, Dr Skkelzen Syla (a psychiatrist), wrote about these results:

> "Many well-funded relief organisations have treated the post traumatic stress here in Kosovo. Some of our people had limited improvement but Kosovo had no major change or real hope until … we referred our most difficult trauma patients to [Dr Johnson and his team]. The success of TFT was 100% for every patient, and they are still smiling until this day."

Johnson's records of his work in Kosovo show that a total of 189 patients were treated for a total 547 traumatic memories. Of these, 187 people and 545 traumatic memories were treated successfully with complete cessation of distress in relation to those particular memories. His reports of his use of TFT in other disaster areas are as follows: South Africa: 97 clients were all treated successfully for a total of 315 traumatic memories; Rwanda: 22 clients were all treated successfully for a total of 73 traumatic memories; Congo: of 29 clients, 28 were treated successfully for a total of 77 out of 78 traumatic memories. Johnson himself acknowledges that treating traumatic memories is only one aspect of healing PTSD (Feinstein, 2006).

In an article in The Thought Field (Callahan, 2001), Dr Callahan responds to a common reaction of disbelief experienced by those unfamiliar with TFT on hearing of the impressive results reported by Johnson. One commentator had questioned whether the traumatised people could truly be smiling, as stated in the letter from Dr Syla. Dr Callahan had asked Dr Johnson to explain more and to clarify the reported findings.

Dr Johnson explained that Dr Syla's letter had been to do with an additional group of patients, following those referred to in the journal article. He had been asked back to Kosovo following the earlier work, partly in order to train local doctors in the method. During two trips in 2001, he treated a total of 50 patients, with a total of 150 traumas. The results were recorded by Dr Syla, and the success rate was 100%. Dr Johnson further explained his approach as follows:

"Many of these traumas involved the death of loved ones. I learned early, back in the Kosovar refugee camp in Oslo, that it is not possible to treat such a trauma in the same way as others. If you set a goal of reducing the suffering or the problem, etc. the person resists—because they fear losing the last aspect of their relationship, even though that is suffering. So now I present it in a different way. When the person tries to recall the good times with the lost one, it hurts too much ... so they must push all of the memory away. This is a block which prevents the presence of the lost loved one—the sweet memories, the wisdom, the closeness in the heart that would be possible even now. I ask if the patient would want me to remove this block so that they might have the loved one back, to this extent. Always the answer is yes.

When all perturbations have been removed and the problem is soothed, I check for the various reversals ... and then, prior to the final testing, I have the patient say something like "Finally I have my father with me again." After treating other types of war trauma I finish by treating the war as a whole, and at the end the patient says 'Finally I have freedom from that war!!' Invariably, after making these statements (the trauma has been soothed) the patient shows a wonderful smile and usually hugs me. They are smiling about the lost one without pushing the memory away. They are not respond-ing to the trauma memory with a smile. But if I see a patient on the street and ask if the treatments are still holding strong, they will say 'po [yes] ... meir [it is good] ... faleminderit [thank you]' and give me a very nice smile." [Callahan, 2001—quotation from online journal].

Radio phone-in programmes—treatment of the general public

Two studies (Callahan, 1987; 2001; Leonoff, 1996) have reported the results of radio phone-in programmes, where callers were treated over the phone for various problems, such as phobias, anxieties, addictions, guilt and marital problems. Callahan treated 68 callers over the phone, reporting a success rate of 97%, with an average improvement of 75.9% (indicated by immediate SUD ratings), and an average treatment time of 4.34 minutes; Leonoff also treated 68 people, reporting 100% success rate, with an average improvement of 75.2%, and an average treatment time of 6.04 minutes. Whilst many questions can be raised regarding the reliability and accuracy of the data, these studies may still have some merit. As Hartung and

Galvin (2003) comment, the clinicians deserve some credit for having the courage to expose their method so publicly: "After all, it might have turned out the other way: ninety per cent of the callers could have announced to thousands of listeners that they did not feel any better and that TFT is a hoax." [p. 61].

Callahan himself notes:

"Why radio shows? In treating sceptical strangers one may minimise positive expectations associated with one coming for help and paying for it. Also it avoids the secrecy element associated with psychotherapy claims in the past. Fraud has been known to occur in science and a public demonstration helps avoid some of these problems ... Audio tapes of all treatments were made and are available for review." [1995 paper, revised 1998]

Audio and video recordings of energy psychology treatments

As Dr Callahan notes in his discussion of radio show data, the recording and making public of treatments using TFT and other methods is, in many respects, ultimately a more persuasive demonstration of effectiveness that the presentation of dry reports or abstract numbers. There are now many such recordings available.

For example, the EFT website (www.emofree.com) offers over 200 EFT sessions on various DVDs produced as educational materials. These include work with 6 inpatients at the Veteran's Administration Hospital in Los Angeles, suffering from severe PTSD. One exert shows a patient with a severe height phobia, linked to memories of 50 parachute jumps in a war zone. In addition he suffers with flashbacks of traumatic memories and insomnia, despite psychotherapy over a period of 17 years. After five minutes of tapping, he reports a complete absence of fear when thinking of heights, even though initially he experienced extreme discomfort. The therapist invites him to walk out onto the fire escape on the third floor; he experiences no anxiety (but much astonishment). Three of his most intense traumatic memories of the war are then addressed. He is taught how to tap on his own to deal with further memories. Two days later he is interviewed again and he reports having slept through the night for the first time for many years. He is able to recall without anxiety the traumatic memories that had been treated.

David Feinstein has posted a video on the internet showing rapid treatment of a severe height phobia. Prior to treatment a woman is seen shaking with fear when on a 4th floor balcony, but following half an hour of energy psychology work she is able to lean over the railing without discomfort. A two and a half year follow-up, also videoed, indicates that her fear has not returned. This can be found at   http://video.google.com/videoplay?docid=5507061960927141022 &q=height+phobia+video&hl=en [or go to www.video.google.com, then type 'height phobia' into the search field.]

Studies exploring whether it matters where the client taps

An area of continuing debate and study

Carbonell 1997
Treatment of acrophobia.
One study by Carbonell and colleagues conducted a randomised double-blind study, comparing TFT with a placebo treatment in which the subjects who suffered from fear of heights tapped points not used in true TFT, although including some components of TFT such as the '9 gamut' tapping sequence with eye movements etc. The subjects in the true TFT condition showed significantly greater improvement than the placebo group (using both SUD ratings and scores on the Cohen Acrophobia Questionnaire).

Waite & Holder 2003
[also discussed above, as a randomised controlled study]
These researchers assigned participants to one of 4 treatment conditions: 1. normal EFT; 2. tapping on the arm, using the normal EFT verbalisations; 3. tapping on a doll, using the usual EFT verbalisations; 4. making a toy out of paper. Two minutes of each treatment were conducted. Pre and post-test SUDs were taken. The first three conditions showed a drop in fear of 18%. The 4th, control, condition showed no drop in fear. Waite and Holder concluded that the benefits of EFT do not depend on tapping the specific points used in EFT.

Baker and Carrington [2005] have discussed this paper. They point out that in all three tapping conditions the decrease in fear occurred very quickly: "We know of no scientific studies of procedures characteristic of more traditional therapies which show an 18% decrease in fear in so short a time". This finding by Waite and Holder is also consistent with the hypothesis that it is the tapping on mechanoreceptors, which are present all over the body, that is important rather than the stimulation of energy meridians [e.g. Ruden, 2005].

Large scale outcome study with randomised controls

The South American Studies: A large scale audit and preliminary trial of EFT methods over 14 years—The study by Joaquin Andrade MD and colleagues from Uraguay

"No reasonable clinician, regardless of school of practice, can disregard the clinical responses that tapping elicits in anxiety disorders (over 70% improvement in a large sample in 11 centers involving 36 therapists over 14 years." [Maarten Aalberse & Christine Sutherland. *The South American Studies. Summary and Discussion of the Clinical Data.* www.bmsa-int.com]

[The data from this study are discussed in Andrade & Feinstein, 2004, Feinstein 2007, and in a website article by Aarlberse & Sutherland www.bmsa-int.com]

Dr Joaquin Andrade introduced TFT-related methods to 11 allied clinics in Argentina and Uruguay after being trained in this approach in the U.S.A. Previously he had studied traditional acupuncture in China, which he had used in medical practice for 30 years. Interestingly, Andrade no longer accepts the 'energy' theory, but instead hypothesises the effects of tapping in terms of neuro-biological effects of sensory-kinaesthetic stimulation, acupressure points being dense concentrations of mechanoreceptors—describing the approach as Brief Multi-Sensory Activation Therapy (www.bmsa-int.com).

The staff had no funding for research but decided to track the outcomes of the new treatments and compare them with the cognitive-behavioural and medication methods they were already using. Over a 14 year period, 36 therapists were involved in treating 29,000 patients. The patients were assessed by 'blind' interviewers, mainly by telephone, at close of treatment, and follow-ups at one month, three months, six months, and twelve months. The most prominent diagnosis was 'anxiety disorders'—which included panic disorder, post-traumatic stress disorder, specific phobias, social phobias, obsessive-compulsive disorders, and generalised anxiety disorder. Pre and post treatment scores on standardised measures such as the Beck Anxiety Scale, The Spielberger State-Trait Anxiety Index, and the Yale-Brown Obsessive Compulsive Scale, were also used to supplement the assessors' ratings. In many cases pre and post-treatment functional brain scan images were also used as an objective measure of change.

The interviewers had a record of the diagnosis and intake evaluation, but not of the treatment method. Both patients and raters were instructed not to discuss the therapy procedures that had been used. The raters were asked to assess whether the patient was now asymptomatic, showed partial remission, or had no clinical response to treatment. Psychological testing and brain mapping were carried out by other staff who were neither the patient's therapist nor rater.

Of the 36 clinicians, 23 were physicians (5 of whom were psychiatrists), 8 were clinical psychologists, 3 were mental health counsellors, and 2 were nurses. All had extensive experience in treating anxiety disorders, with varying levels of training and experience in Thought Field Therapy and derivative methods.

The ratings of the interviewers, supported by the psychometric data, indicated that the TFT/EFT type of methods were more effective than the existing treatments for a range of conditions. However, a number of more detailed sub studies were conducted employing a randomised design with the existing treatments, of 'CBT with medication' as a control, and using double blind assessment.

5000 patients with anxiety disorders

The largest of the sub studies followed 5000 patients with anxiety disorders over a five and a half year period. Half of these received TFT/EFT type of treatment without medication, whilst the other half received CBT with medication. Diagnoses included panic disorder, social phobias, specific phobias, OCD, generalised anxiety disorder, PTSD, acute stress disorder, somatoform disorders, eating disorders, ADHD, and addictive disorders.

Results of the sub-study of 5000 patients:

- Positive clinical responses (ranging from complete relief to partial relief to short relief with relapses) were found in 63% of those treated with CBT and medication and in 90% of those treated with TFT/EFT (p < .0002).
- Complete relief from symptoms was found in 51% of those treated with CBT and medication, and 76% of those treated with TFT/EFT (p < .0002).
- At one year follow-up, the patients in the tapping group were less prone to relapse than those in the CBT and medication group.

Comparison of numbers of sessions required

There was a difference in the number of sessions required to achieve positive outcomes. 96 patients with specific phobias were treated with CBT and medication, whilst 94 with the same diagnosis were treated using TFT/EFT combined with the NLP method of visual-kinaesthetic dissociation (watching an internal movie of the phobic situation). With approximately 95% of the patients, functional brain imaging was used in addition to the clinical ratings and pre and post-treatment test scores. The results were:

- Positive results were obtained with 69% of patients treated with CBT and medication within 9-20 sessions, with a mean of 15 sessions.
- Positive results were obtained with 78% of the patients treated with TFT/EFT and visual-kinaesthetic dissociation within 1-7 sessions, with a mean of 3 sessions.
- The brain mapping correlated with the raters' conclusions and with the psychological test data. Those patients showing the greatest improvement showed the largest reduction in beta frequencies. These beta frequency reductions not only persisted at 12 month follow-up, but in fact became more pronounced.

Comparison between medication alone and TFT/EFT

30 patients with generalised anxiety disorder were prescribed diazepam, whilst 34 patients with the same diagnosis were given TFT/EFT.

- 70% of the medication group experienced positive results.
- 78.5% of the TFT/EFT group experienced positive results.
- About half the medication patients experienced side effects or a recurrence of anxiety on stopping the medication. This did not happen with the tapping group.

Comparison of strict versus varied sequence of tapping

The importance of sequence in tapping was investigated. 60 phobic patients were treated with a standard 5-point algorithm; another group of 60 patients were treated with the order of tapping varied.

- Positive responses were experienced by 76.6% of the standard algorithm group and by 71.6% of the varied order tapping group. This was not statistically significant.
- The treatment team formed the impression that for many disorders a wide variation in the tapping protocol can be employed, whilst for certain conditions more precise protocols are required for optimum clinical response.

Tapping compared with acupuncture needles

40 patients with panic disorder were given tapping treatments focused on pre-selected acupuncture points. 38 patients with the same diagnosis received acupuncture stimulation using needles on the same points.

- Positive responses were experienced by 78.5% of the tapping group but only 50% of the needle group.

Effectiveness for different clinical groups

Ratings of effectiveness for different clinical groups were given in four categories: 1. Much better results than with other methods; 2. Better results than with other methods; 3. Similar to the results with other methods; 4. Lesser results than expected with other methods; 5. No clinical improvement or contraindicated. The findings were as follows.

Much better results than other with methods

Panic disorder, with and without agoraphobia.
Agoraphobia without panic disorder.
Specific phobias.
Separation anxiety disorders.
PTSD and Acute Stress Disorders.
Mixed anxiety-depressive disorders.
Adjustment disorders.
ADHD.
Elimination disorders.
Impulse control disorders.
Problems relating to childhood abuse and neglect.
Other emotional problems: fear; grief; guilt; anger; shame; jealousy; rejection; painful memories; loneliness; frustration; love pain; procrastination.

Better results than with other methods

Obsessive compulsive disorders.
Generalised anxiety disorders.
Anxiety disorders due to general medical conditions.
Social phobias.
Learning disorders; communication disorders; feeding and eating disorders of childhood.
Somatoform disorders.
Factitious disorders.
Sexual dysfunction.
Sleep disorders.
Relational problems.

Similar to the results expected with other methods

Mild to moderate reactive depression.
Learning skills disorders.
Motor skills disorders.
Tourette's syndrome.
Substance abuse-related problems, including anxiety.
Eating disorders.
[It was found that for these conditions, it is best to combine a number of approaches.]

Lesser results than expected with other methods

Major endogenous depression.
Personality disorders and dissociative disorders.
[tapping methods are considered a useful adjunct to other methods].

No improvement or contraindicated

Psychotic disorders.
Bipolar disorders.
Delirium.
Dementia.
Chronic fatigue.
[although it is recognised that there are many anecdotal reports of people with these diagnoses being helped by tapping methods with a number of life problems.]

[NB. Although these categorisations are interesting, clinical expertise has moved on since this work was undertaken. Skilled clinicians have found ways of helpfully incorporating Thought Field Therapy, or other tapping methods, into work with a very wide range of clients.]

Brain scan images

Brain scan images from this study, showing results before and after energy tapping, can be found at www.innersource.net/energy_psych/epi_neuro_foundations.htm

Status of the South American studies

This examination of data from the 11 clinics was essentially an audit for the purpose of internal validation of procedures and protocols rather than a formal research study. Nevertheless, the large number of patients involved, the long period of time covered, the range of data obtained, the variety of clinical conditions treated, and the double blind, randomised, and controlled nature of the investigations, combined with the startling results, all combine to make a powerful case for the role of 'energy psychology' or somato-sensory tapping methods in routine mental health care.

Andrade and Feinstein comment:

"These were pilot studies, viewed as possible precursors for future research, but were not themselves designed with publication in mind. Specifically, not all the variables that need to be controlled in robust research were tracked, not all criteria were defined with rigorous precision, the record-keeping was relatively informal, and source data were not always maintained. Nevertheless, the studies all used randomised samples, control groups, and double blind assessment. The finding were so striking that the research team decided to make them more widely available." [Andrade & Feinstein, 2004, p. 4]

Pilot studies, without control groups

Reduction of dental anxiety with EFT

Graham Temple conducted a study of EFT with 30 patients suffering with high levels of dental anxiety, and who required invasive dental procedures. The EFT took place in the dental surgery and lasted no more than 6 minutes. SUD ratings were taken before and after EFT, which was immediately followed by the dental treatment. The mean SUD rating prior to EFT was 8 and after EFT was 3. All patients experienced reduction in anxiety. The reduction in anxiety is impressive since the second SUD rating was taken just before the dental treatment. http://www.emofree.com/Research/graham-temple-dental-study.htm

Sports performance improvement with EFT

Sam Smith conducted a simple study of skills in kicking a ball, before and after EFT, at a fundraising event on a sports field. 37 volunteers showed an overall improvement of 80.7% in rugby penalty kicks following EFT. After the first kick, the volunteers were asked to state two factors that they believed may have impeded their success. These comments, which were then used as EFT statements, included such ideas as: "I'm not strong enough"; "too many people were watching"; "I'm no good at this kind of thing". Whilst some of the improvement could be due to a simple practice effect, it seems unlikely that the magnitude of the pre and post-EFT difference could be due entirely to this. http://www.emofree.com/Research/rugby-kicking-contest.htm

Eyesight improvement with EFT

Carol Look conducted an 8 week pilot study of improvement in various eyesight problems, using EFT instructions given by post. 400 participants initially signed up for the study, having been recruited through newsletters and conferences. Only 120 of these completed the full 8 week course. Each week, the participants were sent instructions for EFT tapping in relation to various emotional issues that could have a bearing on visual problems. 75% of participants reported improvement in various eyesight problems. SPSS statistical software, with t tests and ANOVA was used. http://www.emofree.com/pdf-files/eyesight-experiment.pdf

Before and after photographs of blood Rouleaux—illustrating the psychosomatic effect of EFT

Rebecca Marina reports on studies of her own blood cells, using a darkfield microscope, before and after using EFT—illustrating not only the effect of EFT but also the relationship between emotions and physiology. The work was carried out in collaboration with her physician. http://www.emofree.com/Research/rouleaux.htm

Research in relation to the meridian system

Although there is debate in relation to the questions of the importance of tapping on traditionally recognised acupressure points (as opposed to random tapping on the body), and whether a theory of energy is required to account for the therapeutic effects of tapping, the evidence for the existence of meridians, and for the potency of acupuncture, is worth noting. Even if theories of energy are put aside, acupoints are noted to be close to nerve bundles or nerve endings, and thus appear to be regions of increased sensitivity (Stux, Berman, & Pomeranz, 2003) that deliver enhanced signals to the brain when stimulated.

Evidence for the existence of the meridian system

French researcher, Pierre de Vernejoul, injected radioactive isotopes into the acupuncture points and tracked their movement using a gamma ray camera. The injected isotopes followed exactly the same pathway as the meridians as traditionally conceived. As a control, injections were also made into nearby non-meridian locations, and also into blood and lymphatic vessels; these did not diffuse in the same manner as the injections at meridian sites. These studies were carried out on 250 healthy subjects and 80 patients with renal pathology. Another interesting finding was that injections into the bilateral kidney meridian diffused faster on the health side and slower on the diseased side. [Darras, J-C., de Vernejoul, P., & Albarhde, 1992].

Acupressure points show lowered electrical resistance than other areas (Becker, 1991; Bergsmann & Woolley-Hart, 1973; Cho, 1998; Cho & Chung, 1994; Liboff, 1997; Syldona & Rein, 1999). Changes in brain function are associated with stimulation of specific acupressure points (Cho, 1998; Darras, 1993; Hui, 2000; Omura, 1989, 1990).

Evidence for the effect of acupuncture/acupressure[4]

The World Health Organisation lists over 50 conditions that may be helped by acupuncture. Many of these are mental health problems, including anxiety, depression, addictions, insomnia, and hypertension. The British Acupuncture Council reviewed seven controlled clinical trials of acupuncture for anxiety or depression, as well as four studies that did not include control groups—and concluded: "The findings from these studies suggest that acupuncture could play a significant role in the treatment of depression and anxiety" [British Acupuncture Council, 2002, p. 11).

Most studies of the effects of acupuncture have addressed its analgesic properties. This effect is marked—and is also found in relation to animals, thus casting doubt on explanations in terms of placebo effects. Stimulation of sham acupoints does not produce the same analgesic effect. There is evidence that acupuncture analgesia is related to endorphin release (Stux, Berman, & Pomeranz, 2003).

Evidence for the effectiveness of Therapeutic Touch

Therapeutic Touch is a simple form of energy-based physical touch, derived from Applied Kinesiology, that has been used extensively in nursing contexts, including psychiatric nursing. It has been found effective in reducing physical pain and anxiety (Gagne, 1994; Heidt, 1981; Hughes, 1997; Peck, 1997).

Evaluation of the research basis for energy psychology methods

There has been a significant amount of research into both the efficacy (achieving an effect in a laboratory context) and the clinical effectiveness (being helpful with clinical populations) of TFT, EFT, and related methods. Considerable clinical knowledge has been accumulated since the first exploration of TFT in 1979 (Callahan, 1981). This clinical knowledge is shared amongst colleagues internationally in books, conferences, and websites. The effectiveness with a wide variety of clinical problems has been reported in a huge number of case studies and systematic clinical observations, as well as field studies in disaster areas. Heart Rate Variability is a most interesting new outcome measure that has been explored with TFT; preliminary results suggesting that whilst other psychological therapies, such as conventional CBT, do not improve HRV, TFT produces a marked improvement. Although the very large and long term South American study lacks some of the rigour of formal research (being designed for internal audit rather than publication), its findings from double blind studies are very strongly suggestive, not only of the value of TFT type of methods, but their superiority to cognitive and behavioural methods that lack some of the components of TFT or EFT.

This research evidence-base is considerably more than is the case for most interventions in psychiatry and psychotherapy. Although drugs are obviously subject to careful trials of efficacy and safety, many other activities within a mental health service, such as most group activities, art therapies, occupational therapies, supportive activities etc., have little or no research evidence-base. As Roth, Fonagy and Parry (1996) comment, "… there are over 400 different named therapies, which can be seen as variations on the basic themes within a smaller number of families of theories and techniques. The vast majority of these 'brand name' therapies are totally unevaluated" [p. 40].

The efficacy of EFT has not only been demonstrated to exist, but to be considerable. A marked reduction in anxiety, under laboratory conditions, was found to result from a short session of EFT—*and to be sustained at 14 month follow-up*. This effect did not occur in the two control conditions and was not due to suggestion. Most psychological therapies have not had such efficacy demonstrated. For example, there are no studies demonstrating the efficacy of a psychoanalytic interpretation, or a cognitive therapy 'Socratic question', in terms of its immediate effect on the client's level of anxiety. By contrast, the use of the SUD scale enables the EFT/TFT clinician to monitor the client's level of distress from moment to moment, and to know more or less immediately whether the tapping intervention is working or not.

Some directions that would be valuable for future research in relation to energy psychology therapies would be: further exploration of HRV as an outcome measure, with comparisons between different therapies; further dismantling studies to determine which components of the TFT & EFT procedure are crucial to efficacy (e.g. whether particular tapping points are important, whether the verbal statements of self-acceptance are important, whether the presence of the therapist makes a difference compared to the condition of the client performing TFT/EFT alone, etc.); second, randomised controlled studies comparing TFT and EFT with other therapies for clinical populations.

Notes

1. A systematic review aims to "find all relevant studies, published and unpublished, assess each study, synthesise the findings from individual studies in an unbiased way, and present a balanced and impartial summary of the evidence." [Davies, H.T. O. & Crombie, I.K. 2005]
2. EMDR, once considered a strange procedure, is now the most highly researched treatment for trauma, is well established as an immensely useful method, and features in the NICE guidelines for treatment of PTSD.
3. It is often proposed that the effect of seemingly unusual methods might be due to suggestion or a placebo effect. In addition to the control for this included in the Baker and Siegel study, Callahan makes the following apt point:

    "It is generally believed that treatments require confidence or optimism in order to work (Seligman, 1994, p. 253). However, no belief or confidence is needed in the TFT treatment; in fact, it typically works in the face of extreme militant scepticism. The procedure itself does not inspire confidence. Even when it works some people don't believe it! (see Apex problem)." [1995]

4. Many scientific studies can be found at www.accupunctureinmedicine.org.uk

CHAPTER EIGHTEEN

Case studies

The following case studies have been selected for their illustration of a variety of clinical presentations and how these might be addressed using energy psychology methods. Some are lengthy and detailed accounts, whilst others are brief vignettes. The first three are contributed by other practitioners and clients.

Facilitation of work with complex problems and fragmented or dissociated self-states

In work with some of the most profoundly compromised states of self, involving fragmentation or dissociation, the judicious use of energy psychology interventions at certain points can facilitate and ease the process to a remarkable degree.

Humpty Dumpty Tells A Story [Contributed by Edina Dzeko]

Some time ago I was in my office reading the referral letter regarding this patient whom I will call B. I was about to meet her for the first time and could not help but wonder who she really was. Her personal history questionnaire gave the impression of her being a very young child. There were various diagnoses stated in the reports—psychotic depression, severe anxiety, self harm, social phobia and ME. There was very little information about her family background and upbringing; mainly just details regarding her recent engagement with the mental health services. What I could gather was that B was a 20-year-old white European and the eldest of three children. Her parents came to live in England, when B was 7 because of her father's job. B could not remember much of her childhood, but stated that it must have been a happy one. Although the family planned to go back to their country of origin at some point, this did not happen as they all settled in and voted in favour of staying in England permanently. After passing her A level exams, B took a gap year which she spent with her grandparents and got to know her extended family. Her parents stated that B enjoyed the gap year, she returned home feeling excited and full of good memories. The onset of her depressive symptoms started whilst at University and she was admitted to a psychiatric hospital. Nobody noticed what was going on for her at the time and B could not recall any significant event that may have triggered the onset. She in fact could not remember much, her parents gave most of the information and also brought her to the appointment.

I walked to the reception area and called her name. B followed me to my office and sat down playing with beads in her hands. She looked scared, tense and anxious. She had a frozen look on her face, her eyes fixated and on each question I asked she kept saying 'I don't know' in a childlike voice. She had no language to describe anything nor could she stay in the room for more than twenty minutes. She looked like a frightened little girl who had got lost and could not find her way back home. I spoke to her the way I would speak to a very young child and asked her whether she would like to come again. She nodded.

In the beginning B spoke very little and needed a lot of prompting. She said she had no energy to do daily activities and spent most of her time sleeping. She had just returned from University following the onset of her symptoms. She was unable to talk about the precipitating events, she appeared to have lost the ability to speak, and thus I decided to allow her to use the therapeutic space in whatever way she was able to do so. She brought pen and paper to the sessions and started drawing. This was the only way she could communicate how disturbed she was at the time. Her drawings were chaotic and fragmented, thus describing her state of mind. B used a black pen only and the images she drew looked as if from horror movies, some were scary and showed sharp objects. They all looked disorganised, persecutory and confusing. At times she would take the pen and scribble on the paper as if she was a one year old child who could only draw lines the way her hand moved. Other times she would draw as if it represented a substitute for self-harm, as if she were attacking the paper.

During this time we would analyse her drawings and their relation to the way she may have felt, even though she always stated that she felt nothing, that she was unreal and everything and everybody were distant to her. Slowly, I was beginning to understand her world, which she described as if living in a bubble where she felt safe and away from people. Nobody could hurt her as long as she lived in the bubble. Months later into therapy, she drew two little circles away from each other but joined with a line in between. She circled the one circle and wrote: this is one me — it is hurting, it cries, it feels stuck and people do not get to this one. It is far, far away from everyone. She then wrote her nickname in the other circle and said this is other me — it is scared of people and does not know what to say and do, does not feel, cannot keep going but keeps going anyway like an auto pilot. For the moment she seemed to be examining what she wrote on the paper, she looked at me and then wrote again: Who am I? Who is B? Where do I belong? Where is home?

Gradually B started to talk more in the sessions, although still very little. Her English was basic. There was a sense of chaos in her stories and it was difficult to make any sense of what was going on for her. She still presented in a child-like manner, scared and feeling confused. On a number of occasions we tried exploring how 'one me' got hurt, but she always stated that she did not know. She would shrug her shoulders and would dismiss any of my attempts to engage her in such exploration. It seemed obvious that she was struggling to talk about herself. It seemed that B was only content when engaged in her world of drawings, so I encouraged her to do more at home. A few sessions later, B brought a Humpty Dumpy which she made of clay. It was wrapped carefully in her favourite t-shirt. I was struck by the beautiful image she presented to me, the image that described her internal world, which was fragmented and broken. We had no idea as to how it got broken, what the trauma was and why her world felt distant and unreal. I tried talking to her about the story of Humpty Dumpty and what it meant to her. It meant nothing to her. However, she told me that she heard children making new rhymes in which Humpty Dumpty was put back together. On hearing this B got very angry that they could think of something like this. For her Humpty Dumpty was meant to stay broken and nothing and nobody could put him back together. This was the first time that B showed some feelings and I commented on this and that I thought the image she made represented her inner world. She did not say anything but went on to draw more and wrote: "Nothing is indestructible. You can take anything apart but sometimes you can't fix it back together". B was describing her broken world and how she did not believe that she could be helped. Maybe part of her wished to remain broken. She got up from her chair and took a few pens which were on my desk and started breaking them. She was struggling but managed to do so. She then looked at me; she had a winning smile on her face. The broken pieces were left on the table. I waited a moment and said that perhaps she thought that only if I was also broken, as she was, only then I would be able understand her.

From her experience nobody understood her, at least this is how it seemed to her living in her little bubble. Her parents did not seem to pay much attention to her problems; nothing was ever spoken about in the house and doctors struggled with making a diagnosis. Each time she saw a new doctor it appeared that she presented in a different manner and therefore was given a different diagnosis. Drawing from the image of Humpty Dumpty and the way she related to me in the sessions, I got the impression that she may have presented each fragment of her self to each clinician she saw at the time. This may have created confusion in understanding who she was and what she presented with. I found myself reading once again the reports written on her, trying to find clues as to what had happened that caused her to become fragmented and broken as Humpty Dumpty is. I was searching but without much success. Time passed and we made very little progress in therapy. B still spoke little, presenting like a scared little girl lost in her world. I was beginning to feel confused, there was so much of the unknown. In desperation to find a way of helping her, my thoughts turned to energy methods.

When the appropriate moment arrived in the session I introduced energy methods to her. I explained the technique, the significance of being specific and described tapping on the body energy system. She was a bit reluctant. However, B and I had a good therapeutic relationship, she trusted me and therefore she was in agreement to give it a try.

As already mentioned, B was very anxious and scared of people, she had no friends and the aim was to help her engage with the outside world. She wanted to work on this. On a scale 0-10, she rated the anxiety of meeting people at 10. She could not identify any specific memory with regard to her anxiety, so we started tapping on "Even though I feel anxious about meeting new people, I am ok". I noticed that B was rather slow in following the tapping sequence; it felt as if there was no energy in her body whatsoever. There was no rhythm in the way she was tapping. On a few occasions she paused as if needing to take a rest. When it came to do the 9 Gamut point as part of the tapping sequence, B suddenly stopped as she found this part difficult to do. After a few attempts she managed to complete the sequence. Also, whilst tapping on her body B spoke in a child-like voice, often hardly audible. There was a sense of energy flow being heavy. She looked shy. After the first round B rated her anxiety at 8, so we continued tapping until her anxiety level dropped down to 2. When we reached this point B stated that her anxiety level was ok at this level, she felt safe and in control. She did not want to go any further in dealing with her anxiety, but stated that she felt extremely lonely living in her bubble. So we started tapping on 'feeling lonely'. I noticed that she was now tapping with more energy, and after completing the sequence she paused, looking very sad and said that she wished she had friends. She stated that she could only make friends with 'little people' and not grown ups, as she was scared of them. I used a metaphor of her being a little girl living in grown-up's body, she smiled and we continued tapping. In spite of her initial difficulty in engaging with EFT, B found tapping very exciting and she reported feeling more energised for the first time in ages. She agreed to tapping at home for a few minutes each day.

Although I had hoped that using EFT would make a shift in the therapeutic process, I did not envisage that this session would make such a dramatic change in her. The following session, B brought colour pens and started drawing. Unaware of the image she was producing I was aware of the calmness she presented with. For the first time B sat quietly and appeared to be in deep thought. To my amazement the image she drew was an image of a rather big baby opening her arms as if waiting to be picked up and given a hug. Away from the baby was the image of a mother, her arms being stuck to her body. I was still speechless by the shift in her drawings, when she looked at me saying "lets make some words, make some language". I was surprised by the sudden flow of words. The story of her life started to unfold.

On asking her to tell me about the drawing, B told me that that she does not remember being hugged by her mother. If she did get a hug now it would feel strange. On one level she wanted a hug from her mother more than anything else, on another she was scared of being hugged. She also recalled a childhood memory of playing in the garden whilst her mother was watching TV in the living room. There was a glass door separating them. She remembers looking through the glass door hoping to get her mother's attention. On remembering this significant memory, B looked sad, there were tears in her eyes. I invited her to do tapping on 'feeling sad'. We did only one round this time, following which B looked at the drawing again. After a few minutes of silence, she talked about her relationship with her mother, who was described as cold and critical of her. She recalled that once when she was very young despite her being so ill she was sent to school. The teachers contacted her mother and sent her back home. Even when ill her mother did not take care of her.

B and I carried on using EFT in the following sessions. Sometimes we were tapping on very specific issues, and sometimes on more general issues. We tapped on whatever came to her mind. We followed the flow of energy in the room. She became more talkative and also continued drawing. Her drawings were colourful, coherent and beautiful images. She also started doing breathing exercises (alternate nostril breathing) every morning for a few minutes. This she found extremely helpful in feeling calm, relaxed and reported it stimulated her thinking. She opened up, in that she started expressing herself more and more; she had started attending groups run by Day Services and made friends. It felt things were changing rapidly. B had more energy to do things, started swimming, riding her bike, something she had not done in years.

The world was beginning to feel more real, at least sometimes. We continued tapping on 'even though the world still does not feel real, even though there are parts of me that still feel distant, even though I don't know who I am'. Then in one of the sessions, whilst telling me about what she had done that week, she drew something. Although I could not see what she was drawing, I could see that she was using lots of colours, and that her facial expression was different, she was looking like a curious child who had just made a discovery. Then she lifted the paper and said: this is me! And it was a mirror image of her on that day. But the body was divided in two parts. I noticed that she drew some tears on one side of her face and I commented on it. She looked at the picture saying that she cannot cry, but if she did everything would be calmer. So we tapped on 'even though I cannot cry now, I am ok'. After a few rounds of tapping, what emerged was that she was scared of crying as this triggered memories of having been admitted to a psychiatric hospital.

B went on to tell me about this experience and each time she felt disturbed by a specific aspect of her memory we tapped on it. What I learnt was that she started having some difficulties whilst in the first year at the University. She was living in the student accommodation and did not get on with the people she was sharing with. She was missing home and felt unable to cope with the course work. Consequently she started withdrawing from friends and became depressed. She spent most of the evenings in her room crying. She wanted to go back home, but felt scared to tell her parents, especially her mother, as their expectation was that she needed to study for a degree, even though she may not have been ready for that challenge. Being unwilling to turn to her parents and having no close friends to turn to she went to see her GP. After seeing her cry uncontrollably and expressing some fleeting suicidal idea, the doctor contacted local psychiatric services. During this appointment B admitted to self harming behaviour, her left arm covered in scars. Understandably, the GP was concerned about her.

The following is her account of events. She attended a local psychiatric unit for an assessment. It was a Friday afternoon and the assessing doctor felt she should be admitted for the weekend. He said that he would see her on the following Monday and discharge her, so she agreed to an informal admission. However, on Monday this doctor was not to be seen and the weekend turned into a three week long admission. On the psychiatric ward, she kept saying that she was scared of staff as they were strangers to her. She said that she was being watched 24 hours a day. On one occasion she tried to take keys from the staff in a bid to escape. To make matters even worse, the staff wanted to do a blood test without knowing that she had a phobia of needles. B felt overpowered. She felt shattered, she could not recognise where she was and who she was. Her arm stopped being her arm, and she was self harming as if this were the only way she could prove to herself that she still existed. After a few days of being on the ward and with no possibility of escape, she dissociated. She stopped talking and everything became unreal.

In talking about this in the following sessions, B almost cried. She spoke about how petrified and misunderstood she felt at the time. It felt like being in a strange place, where she did not feel she belonged. We carried on using EFT on 'feeling petrified'. What emerged from this was that it reminded her of the time she moved to England, when she felt lonely and due to the language barrier people could not understand her and she could not understand them. B also described some disturbing memories about having to change school and learn a new language following the move. She hated the change, felt different to others and had no friends. She felt isolated and lost. Eventually she settled in and adjusted to the new life style.

Whilst tapping on her body B became very playful and words started pouring out of her—"Even though I don't do feelings, even though I still feel broken, even though the world is a scary place, even though I don't do angry"—to hear herself say this word 'angry' was surprising to her. She paused and repeated—"I don't do angry, never have done". She then went on to tell me that ever since she was young she had to be a good girl, she would do everything to avoid getting in trouble, she always had best grades in school so as not to be criticised. She constantly felt criticised by her mother. Whatever she did was never good enough. When she tried rebelling she was told off. Her father was always busy working and spent very little time at home.

This was rather difficult for B as she felt that expressing any feelings towards her mother would be betraying her. She said it was difficult for her to put her feelings in words but continued tapping without using words. Each time an image came to her mind or she had some disturbing feelings, B would tap on her body. During this period in therapy, she would still at times present in a child-like manner, at times saying that the tension in her body was too overwhelming and that she had an urge to self-harm. I introduced the Cooks Hookups position to her. Each time she felt the tension she would sit quietly for a few minutes. The first time she sat in this position she kept moving her fingers and kept rolling her eyes. She kept saying "they cannot keep still, they have to move". We tapped on "even though some parts of my body have to move, even though some parts of my body do not want to listen". Eventually, B reached the state of calmness, commenting that once she almost fell asleep whilst sitting in CH position. Her anxiety level was initially at 10, then 2 went to 0. She had tears in her eyes. The world was becoming more real to her.

From this moment, B become more proactive in the sessions; she was asking for structure and homework. She was not presenting as a child any more, but a young woman who was trying to make sense of her world and what had happened to her. The therapy holiday breaks were described as either ok or too long, giving a sense of her being aware of the time. The drawings she had done were examined almost during every session but she had no need to draw as she now had a language to express herself. Nevertheless, the pen and paper were still in the room.

Having found words to describe her life, B pointed out that "we now have one big picture". On asking her to explore who 'we' are, she took two pieces of paper, glued them together and drew two circles, one in the other, describing the whole picture as her bubble. What in the beginning of therapy were two separate circles away from each other, were now together and B had words to describe them. She positioned people in her life, near or away from the bubble, depending on who they were. She wrote down some words as well. The two parts were almost together. We decided to tap on "narrowing the gap between the two". After a few rounds of tapping, B stated that on the day there is no gap, she will feel real. She also took the broken pens, looked at them and said they should not be broken into pieces, and left them on the table. There was also a wish to be hugged. B hugged herself, sitting in the chair, feeling calm and relaxed.

Not only did she draw a big picture describing her bubble, but she also had a mental picture in her mind. As we continued tapping and talking about narrowing the gap, B initiated having more structure in her daily life. From being someone who always needed others to tell her what and when to do, she started taking responsibility for organising her daily activities. It seemed that having internal structure in place, she was able to think of external structure. There were still times when she reported feeling lost and not knowing what to do. At those times she would sit quietly and do the breathing exercise, as we agreed, and would let her mind wonder. Whilst in this almost meditative position, she was able to achieve a state of peacefulness and calmness.

One day whilst doing the tapping sequence at home, she got the idea of building Lego. So she went shopping and bought herself some. On hearing this in the session the first thought that came to my mind was that she was still a child wishing to play. I wondered whether she was telling me she was not ready to make a change. However, as she was so excited in talking about the way she built Lego, it occurred to me that this was her way of putting fragmented pieces together the way she felt they were meant to be. She was ready to put things into perspective, broken pieces were put back together, Humpty Dumpty was put back together. It seemed as if she found her true self by doing this. She no longer talked about "one me or the other me", but everything became 'Me'. She found the answer to her question 'Who am I?'. In exploring the Lego image with her, it was also obvious that the image she built did not necessarily need to stay intact—the Lego blocks could be arranged and rearranged if necessary. Her persona in the session changed as well. She would often take her shoes off and sit comfortably in the chair, as if almost lying. Her tone of voice changed and she became playful, talkative and more confident. What fascinated me was her sudden spontaneity in the way she spoke about herself. She no longer had a need to look in her diary to remind herself of the activities she had done during the week, she had a sense of time. She would attend sessions saying things like "I have been thinking". She also started asking her parents questions about her upbringing, which not only provided her with the details of what she was like as a child, but made the whole family examine the way they related to each other. They became closer as a family. She has now begun to tell me about her relationship with her siblings.

B recently visited a local library and started reading books on Mind, Body and Spirit. She also became interested in knowing about dissociation. One day she found a few books on dissociation, but they made no sense to her as they were textbooks and thus written in a rather academic language for her to understand. She asked if I could explain it to her. Whilst I was contemplating what to say, B looked at me asking why do not I write something that would be helpful in understanding what it feels like when the world one lives in is not real, but a dream and when one is broken into pieces. This is how the idea of writing this chapter was conceived and I am grateful to her for being brave enough to share her story.

At the time of writing, therapy continues. We still use EFT on issues that unfold in the sessions and we talk about them. There is very little need to draw. Sometimes B likes to go through her drawings, as if reminding herself of where she was and where she is at now. In this regard she recently made a life chart, describing major events in her life. From looking at the chart, she said that soon she would be ready to return to University. I know she will tell me when therapy is to end.

Reflections

I am aware that there are still many pieces in her story missing. The picture is not complete and there is no magical happy ending. We are continuing to work together. Even on the day that therapy comes to an end, there will be no ending. She may need and wish to seek further help at some point in the future. At the present moment, B is making another Humpty Dumpty, which she said would like to leave in my office to sit on the window sill for ever. I wonder whether it means that she is now ready to tell me about her early years, up to the age of 7. I also wonder whether it means that she is now ready to tell me about what may have happened at University to trigger her breakdown. I wonder why B has never had an intimate relationship. During our last session she said: "my thoughts are coming by themselves".

The story continues.

[Edina Dzeko is a chartered counselling psychologist, with a particular interest in trauma and the psychological problems of refugees. She works within the Hertfordshire Partnership NHS Trust.]

Multiple Modalities for Multiplicities
[Contributed by Dr Shoshana Garfield PhD]

This self-written case history details some of the excellent benefits of energy psychology. I came to Dr Mollon as a doctoral student aged 38, referred from another therapist with whom I had ended treatment a few years before and with whom at time of writing I still meet in session once or twice a year. The background of trauma included sexual abuse as an infant, sexual abuse at age 3, ritual abuse (RA) for, possibly, just under a year (aged 5), and a general environment of neglect, maternal competition, paternal violence, instability, unpredictability, highly inappropriate boundaries and drugs, including drug dealing. Extreme dissociation was my main strategy, and I had a multiple personality with only one alter. Nevertheless, I consistently did well at school and despite a great lack of social skills was passably functional.

It was my deliberately inadequate second suicide attempt at age 11 at summer camp that procured me therapeutic services for the first time (the first one, at age 6, was quite intended to kill). After that, I received 20 years of therapy from 5 different therapists, all trained differently. It was with the last therapist that I made the most progress, and it was in my 17th year of treatment that I integrated my multiple personality. When this last treatment ended, I had already begun to explore energy work with Reiki and spirit healing. I was also aware that despite the end of the funding for therapy, I could have benefited from further treatment.

In one of my infrequent follow-up sessions with this last and superb therapist, I was referred to Dr Mollon. What had inspired this was that I had just endured an experience with a child care provider ('Mary') I had hired; Mary was emotionally unstable and I had held back from firing her to appease those around me, most notably including Mary and my husband. Indeed, I had allowed my doubts about hiring her in the first place to be overridden by others. It turned out that Mary quit with a week's notice, moved in with one friend of mine, and told her and another friend half-truths and lies that cost me both relationships. I had been devastated that neither friend had been particularly interested in my account, that I had let the boundaries of my relationships with Mary be so sloppy, and above all, that I had tried so hard for so long to try to please others instead of going with my own instinct on the matter.

In my first appointment with Dr Mollon, I described these events in great detail, with additional detail of my background. It was clear to both of us that early events (not just the RA) had led me to develop a strategy of appeasement, as doing otherwise risked not only tortuous punishment, but to my unconscious, a genuine threat of physical and/or psychical death. Although I was strongly dubious that a single appointment could genuinely address such a deeply held pattern, my comfort level with working with energy was high through my practitioner experience with Reiki, spirit healing and reflexology, and through my client experience in numerous energetically-based modalities (e.g. shamanism). In short, if it might help, whether or not it would meet all its claims and even if it were fringe and not evidence-based, I was willing to give it honest engagement.

The in-person appointment with Dr Mollon was approximately 2 hours, of which the first hour was spent talking. In the beginning of the second hour, I was taught muscle testing to which I took quickly; it was necessary to learn because I did not want to be touched in session (it had taken me 17 years of therapy just to be able to lie down on the couch and I was not about to consent to touch with a therapist at a first session), and the ability to self-test was later to prove invaluable in my own independent work. I had already downloaded an EFT manual (www.emofree.com) to familiarise myself with the points and general process. Another issue of great relevance to the success of the treatment was that Dr Mollon used his energy modalities as well as his psychotherapeutic skills to create safety; one of the first things we tapped on was that I would pace myself and release safely without distress, and reassured my—I cannot say it any other way—being that wholly unconscious releases were entirely acceptable. This was a truly new concept to me as even with my own energy work as either practitioner or client I most often sought to translate into words what was going on energetically. With Dr Mollon, my entire system experienced permission to release because of this initial work on safety, pacing and beliefs. The rest of the session, which was mainly with a TFT-based modality, was to resolve the appeasement pattern within the context of keeping the opening promise to release safely without distress.

It was the night of that first appointment that I realised something profound and vastly important had occurred. I was visiting late with a neighbour, and she offered me chocolate. I do not have a weight or food problem, and I was able to easily realize I simply did not want it although it looked delicious; the hour was just too late. I was also instantly aware that my hostess was invested in my eating the chocolate: she wanted to eat it and wanted to justify her own desire by having me eat it too; she was slightly overweight and wanted me to eat it for sabotaging reasons, and, as she was also simply being a generous hostess by offering refreshment, a rejection might somehow offend. I declined the chocolate, and did so without even the smallest flicker of doubt or worry that I would suffer negative consequences for satisfying my own true choices. It partly was a sobering event for showing me the depth and expansiveness of my former appeasement pattern (it was just chocolate after all), and, demonstrated how effective the treatment with Dr Mollon had been (I would have previously experienced agonising self-doubt in the condensed moments before verbalising my decision, and would have most likely have dutifully eaten a large portion of something in which I had no interest).

The success of that appointment deeply inspired me to continue. I wanted more success in releasing the remains of my trauma; I did not know at the time how much may be left, yet I so very much wanted to be truly and completely free. After that first, in-person appointment with Dr Mollon, I worked with EFT on my own, intensively and daily—7 days a week, sometimes 2 hours a day of tapping—for about 6 months. During that time, I would have ad hoc telephone appointments with Dr Mollon to work on issues on which I was stuck or just knew I could not handle alone. I felt incredibly empowered by the ease with which I could engage EFT independently, and felt profoundly supported by the additional sessions, however loosely structured, with Dr Mollon. I was delighted that I could release so much without bringing material to consciousness; it was such an especial contradiction to my 20 years of psychotherapy experience.

It was the ad hoc nature of the appointments that underscored an important difference between my previous therapy experiences and my energy psychology experience. Partly because there was so much time spent actually tapping rather than talking, partly because the appointments were 'as needed', like aspirin, and partly because of Dr Mollon's working stance on transference, the transference relationship was minimal and transference work was simply non-existent.

I also had two episodes of extreme overwhelm during those 6 months that highlighted the difference between EFT and TFT. In the first, I had arrived at my office on a weekend to continue my work on my doctorate. As had become my habit, before I started work I tapped on the intention to be highly productive, but on this day, fear started coming up. I tried tapping on the fear, but it kept mounting until I was in a full-fledged body memory of terror and panic. EFT often requires specific language regarding events, and my tapping was only 'tapping into it' like a vein of ore in a mine and made it worse despite language of asking for unconscious release. Something from my unconscious mind was demanding healing, but I was clearly unable to handle it. It took immense effort and force of will to even call up the verbal functionality to telephone Dr Mollon to let him know of my state, and after the call, I crawled under my desk and curled up there for whatever safety I could conjure and just gave in to the experience until Dr Mollon could call me back. I was fortunate that he was able to call me on a Saturday within an hour or so, and he used TFT to bundle together whatever was going on. The phone call was short—less than 20 minutes. It is almost a year later and I have not had another such experience since.

The second episode was during a phone session with Dr Mollon. I could feel something rising energetically in me, which I shared, and Dr Mollon identified it as terror. I then recognised it, and it accelerated and started to threateningly rise. Dr Mollon was able to keep me tapping throughout and with TFT derail the terror and heal it completely. I have not had a rise of terror since (again, almost a year later at time of writing), not even in my dreams/nightmares, which is even more significant than the previous example as the nighttime terrors were highly frequent and regular before this healing. In short, an entire structure had collapsed with this treatment.

Another critical moment of my treatment with Dr Mollon came up when we tripped over RA programming.[1] This was our longest phone session; it was 45 minutes. During this time, I released the initial issue as well as the programming. I did not require the details of the programming to release it with Dr Mollon, and I was exuberantly pleased with how effective his treatment was, although I also had to tap on feeling guilty (my issue; Dr Mollon was fine with it) on taking so much time when we were both expecting a shorter session based on previous experience. I felt truly lucky to be able to happen upon the RA programming in session, as it is generally deeply buried and stubbornly persistent. It was clear that the modalities of EFT and TFT were allowing me to access, and heal, a variety of traumatised and damaged areas that had been hitherto inaccessible.

A last point in discussing my experience of the actual treatment, both on my own and with Dr Mollon, is that healing often continued after a session. It was often sufficient to set an unconscious process in motion which would then have enough momentum to carry itself through to unconscious completion. This is entirely congruent with that crucial opening promise to my being to release safely and without distress at my own pace.

I could have been so satisfied with the success of the first appeasement session that I did not pursue further treatment. It was my ongoing commitment to truly heal, feel whole (which I did not quite experience despite integration), and love myself freely that inspired me to the profound commitment to continue the work. It has been the EFT and TFT which has finally enabled me to achieve these long-standing goals and to be able to transition from healing work to peak performance work. I can look myself in the mirror now, and tell myself I love me without any squirming resistance, demurral or refusal. I feel whole. I feel joy daily. Much of this achievement was based on the foundation of the incredibly hard work in psychotherapy I, and my therapists, have done in two arduous decades; it is the psychotherapeutic energy modalities which have ultimately made this achievement possible.

What I had received with psychotherapy had not been enough. It was not the practitioners; my therapists, despite the differences in their training, all made a significant and positive impact on me, most notably the last. I would also not have done better with a therapist from another strand of analysis. Psychotherapy was certainly not deficient as an experience because I was a deficient client. In my opinion, having experienced excellence in both traditional, talking-only psychotherapy and in energy psychology, the modality that attends only to the mind and not concomitantly to the energy system, psychotherapy, runs the danger of not only inadvertently limiting but actually preventing the true healing that I know most analysts genuinely wish for their patients. In writing this, I feel compelled to state that the fact of my speaking of these energy modalities in such superlative terms is a statement of their superlative efficacy in the right hands. The beauty and power of releasing unconsciously and the empowerment of doing so much work of my own cannot be overstated. Trauma and pain are often indescribable (Herman, 1992; Scarry, 1985); I find the experience of healing to the level achieved with energy psychology equally ineffable and beautifully so.

Herman J (1992) Trauma and recovery: The aftermath of violence from trauma to recovery. New York: Basic Books.

Scarry E (1985) The body in pain: The making and unmaking of the world. New York: Oxford University Press.

[Dr Shoshana Garfield, PhD in Psychology, is an energy psychology practitioner, mainly in the fields of EFT and Theta DNA healing. For more information, see www.shoshanagarfield.com.]

Energy Therapy: A Personal Perspective [anonymous contribution]

I am a former lecturer in a scientific field related to psychology and have suffered a number of depressive and manic episodes during the past 4 years. I attempted suicide three times and spent over 4 months on a psychiatric ward of a general hospital. I have been on various types of medication, including Venlafaxine, Fluoxetine and Lithium. I now remain on Lithium alone. And I tap ...

When I was admitted into hospital I was unable to talk about my problems. Indeed, I did not even know what they really were. I did not feel ill; I had simply had enough and wanted to die. I even argued with the doctors about whether I was ill at all. My consultant psychiatrist felt that medication alone was not working sufficiently well and that I would benefit from psychological intervention. I agreed simply because I wanted to get out. I did not think I needed a psychologist and I knew I would be unable to talk to one. I was in for quite a surprise.

I cannot remember what we discussed in the first session but I do remember expecting something along the lines of cognitive-behavioural therapy; and certainly some form of talking therapy. But this was not to be the case. I was hugely relieved at this as the stress I had felt at the prospect of having to talk was almost as great as the stress of the problems themselves. I was also aware that, despite the fact I had problems, I did not think them sufficient to cause such depression. Basically, I did not really know why I was depressed. I can see now that recognising I was depressed whilst denying I was actually ill reflects somewhat dissonant thinking; but it did not seem at all inconsistent to me at the time.

When the psychologist, PM, explained to me the form the sessions would take, I was amazed, particularly when he showed me the tapping technique. Frankly, I thought he was mad. I could not for the life of me see how tapping away at parts of my anatomy, irrespective of whether they corresponded to meridian points, could possible help me deal with my problems. Furthermore, I felt vaguely ridiculous tapping and I certainly could not see any therapeutic value in the repetition of phrases such as "Despite X (the problem), I deeply and completely accept myself". It was clear to me that I did not accept myself and I felt this was all utterly pointless. I told PM this, who informed me that I did not have to believe in these phrases, I just had to repeat them.

Occasionally, while tapping about an area, I became highly anxious and/or distressed about things I didn't even know were disturbing me. PM would pick up on whatever it was, ask me what I was thinking and then we would tap through that. I can remember being surprised, on several occasions, about becoming upset about a particular area, and even more so when there seemed to be a number of different layers for one basic issue. At times I felt like a Russian doll.

One of the methods that struck me with incredulity was muscle testing. PM would request that I hold my arm outstretched before me and ask if I minded whether he touched my wrist. He told me to resist his attempt to push my arm down. He informed me that this was to test the degree to which I believed something to be true. I still do not really understand how this works, but remember that on one occasion he instructed me to say "All parts of me want to be well" as he pushed on my wrist. My arm plummeted so quickly that we both laughed. I could not believe it. After a while it became clear that part of me did, indeed, wish to remain ill: it was safe being ill, not having to return to the real world. My illness became like a protective cover—I could hide behind and not have to deal with reality.

It became standard for me to leave the Energy Psychology sessions feeling 'zonked'—rather as though I had smoked cannabis—and to lie on the floor of the quiet room and sleep. The sessions made me feel immensely calm for a time afterwards. Unfortunately, this feeling did not seem to last for more than a few hours at a time and I could not see how it was going to help me in the long term. I still wanted to get out of hospital to kill myself. However, a couple of sessions had quite a striking effect on me. After a particularly distressing session, I wrote the following in my diary:

I think I feel more pain after PM touched on something that really hurts. That seems obvious, except that we don't *deal* with issues, as such, we just tap. And reiterate phrases, tailor-made phrases. And yet something happens. Something very definitely happens.

One further session had such an intensely calming impact that I shall never forget it. PM had told me to imagine stagnant energy draining through my body, out through my arms and legs. As usual, I felt zonked but calm afterwards. What was different about this was that the effect lasted for a long time. I can remember lying on my back in bed that night, with my legs outstretched and my arms lying straight by the side of my body. I swear I could feel energy, bad energy, foul, putrefying energy, flowing down my arms and legs, and out through my fingertips and toes. It was an incredibly intense experience. I wanted to know more about Energy Psychology.

PM gave me a couple of papers to read. It was unlike any form of psychotherapy I had ever read. As a former hard-nosed scientist I could not believe the effect the therapy had on me. I became less sceptical about the therapy although remained determined to kill myself once I got out. I realise now (but didn't at the time) that by asking for information about Energy Psychology, I was, at some level, accepting two things. First, that this therapy was having an impact on me and, second, that I needed it. I was indeed ill. After my initial reluctance to talk, I ended up laying myself bare to PM. I told him things that I had never previously told anyone. He never pushed me to disclose more than I could cope with which actually led me to disclose more each time. It was a safe environment in which to examine my life.

I often wonder why I was able to talk when I had never previously been able. I rather suspect that the therapy, because it induced a state of calm, relaxed me to a degree that enabled me to release those issues which had remained trapped for so long. Furthermore, I think the calm feeling enabled me to have the courage to face those issues; to allow them to come to the surface. At times, we spoke about them; at others I was unable and we simply tapped. It took a long time for me to come to terms with some of the issues, which leads me on to the subject of just what hard work Energy Psychology is for the patient.

After some sessions, I would feel exhausted. When I mentioned this to PM he said it was because I was working hard during the sessions. The following diary entry exemplifies this:

PM then came to collect me. A really hard session—he trying to get me to express, release the anger, and me trying hard not to. He got me standing whilst tapping and it carried on and on and seemed to get faster and faster until I almost shouted at him to stop. I did beg him to stop and sat down and wept and tried to scream and tried not to scream—I don't know. I'm not sure now whether I screamed or not.

And the next morning I wrote:

Slept better last night. Don't feel quite so desperate this morning, but can still feel all this emotion in my stomach. I'm having difficulty identifying the emotion. In particular, I'm not sure where the low mood stops and the anger starts. Or perhaps the feeling is just a mixture of the two.

On reading this entry, I realise now that I was actively working on issues outside the sessions. But there were one or two issues that I was frightened to face alone. I needed PM in order to progress. When he went on holiday I wrote, "Miss PM as I find I don't really want to confide in anyone else now". I couldn't. His office was a safe haven in which I could examine my demons. I trusted him. And this was during a time when I had no trust in anyone else.

PM showed me how to use the technique on my own. I used it often, particularly when I was allowed leave to stay with my sister. In the mornings I would be anxious about having to live through another day and in the evenings I would be stressed about getting nightmares and images from my past. Tapping and repeating certain phrases helped a great deal. I have used Energy Therapy less and less as the weeks and months have passed. But I know it is there. I know I can utilise it if I need to.

All my senses seem sharper. I perceive colour with an intensity I have never before known. The sense of calm continues to this day. Of course, the lithium keeps my mood stable, but there is something more. I feel an inner peace that I have never before experienced. I actually feel comfortable in my own skin.

To a scientist of my background, anything which is not theory-driven is anathema. I was genuinely surprised after my sessions with PM that Energy Therapy is not based on any theory. However, and also to my surprise, I now consider this not to be a problem. I do not know why the therapy works: I only know that it worked for me. I intend now to carry out research into why Energy Therapy does apparently work. That it is not theory-driven should not mean that it should be ignored—or worse, ridiculed. I am gradually returning to academia and I am viewing psychological therapies with a fresh and, most importantly, open mind.

Sexual addictions and obsessions

Sexual addictions and obsessions are both common and distressing, although not always easily acknowledged by clients. These may have complex roots—in sexualised representations of repeated childhood traumas, in the use of sexual stimulation to relieve anxiety and depression, and in the use of sexuality to express a variety of essentially non-sexual needs and desires.

John—treatment of a sex addiction

This case in interesting, in that it illustrates the targeting of various traumatic experiences that lay behind the problem, but also describes the layers of issues that begin to unfold as the areas of distress are cleared. Some temporary negative reactions to improvement are shown (the 'negative therapeutic reaction'), as deeper patterns and attachments are inevitably challenged by the forward movement. The sessions were about a month apart. Earlier sessions were approximately an hour in length, but the later ones were shorter as there was less to do.

John was a successful car salesman in his early 40s. He presented with a longstanding problem of sex addiction—"my whole life is consumed by sex". Over a period of about 10 years he had received various forms of therapy, including individual and group, prior to embarking on Thought Field Therapy. Some of the roots of his excessive preoccupation with sex were clear enough: sexual abuse by a teenage female babysitter when he was age 7, and various other experiences of sexual over-stimulation in the rather dysfunctional childhood family. He said he could not get close to anyone emotionally, and would always have several women 'on the go' at any one time, having sex with them, without love, whilst they always wanted a relationship. He described his mother as having been abusive and hurtful in various ways—and his ex-wife as similar.

Initial muscle testing indicated a reversal against giving up the sex addiction—and a part of him believing that it was not safe to be close to a woman. Muscle testing also indicated that this fear of women was rooted most strongly in his relationship with his ex-wife—rather than in his relationship with his mother, as we had initially assumed. He recalled that when he first met his wife he had been capable of being close to her, but had become withdrawn in response to her violence and criticism.

We used a TFT diagnostic sequence to heal the part of him that felt it was not safe to be close to a woman.

Session 2

John reported that he had felt low since the first session, and that he was not having sex in the way that he used to. He said he was seeing one lady that he had known for some time and had given up all the others. I commented that he appeared to have given up his sex addiction. He looked surprised, but then agreed that this was the case—and that his underlying depression was now in view.

John went on to talk of his wish to be free of his ex-wife—and he referred to ways in which she had been abusive and traumatising, mirroring some of his earlier experiences with his mother.

We agreed to target some of the traumas with his ex-wife with TFT. He was dissociated from affect about these—but muscle testing suggested a SUD of 8 (out of a maximum of 10). His first target was an experience of begging his wife to stop her relentless abusive tirade. This rapidly collapsed to a SUD of 0 with the following sequence: eb c ue a c un a ch if c lf oe g50. Then he thought of other instances of "what came out of her mouth—like the bottom of a barrel—evil stuff"—and muscle testing indicated a SUD of 9. With a further tapping sequence, he was smiling and laughing with a SUD of 0 (eb oe c ue a c if ch oe if lf c).

We then proceeded to addressing traumas with his mother. He recalled how she would beat him, and if he put his arms up or cried she would beat him more. We targeted a specific incident of this, diagnosing the following sequence: ue a c eb oe c lf a eb if lf g50 c a ue c. He was again smiling at the end of this.

He was impressed with the results of the TFT and asked in amazement "how did someone learn to do this?", adding "I've been in therapy for years—it helps—but it doesn't get rid of the feelings".

Session 3

John reported that he no longer felt bothered about his ex-wife, his mother, or sex. These three areas had been satisfactorily addressed.

However, he said he still felt unhappy with himself and his self-esteem—"I'm so used to feeling shit about myself". He went on to speak of his negative views of himself, despite the fact that people seem to like him. He felt that he had always been depressed—adding "sex was an escape—now I don't escape".

The following long tapping sequence was used in relation to this depression and low self-esteem: sh c eb un a ue c g50 oe ue a c if mf if oe eb ue a c 9g if a ue c. He was then asked how he felt at that moment and he replied: "I don't feel like I did! No—I feel relaxed—I can't explain how I feel". The following sequence was then used: un c un if c ue a c eb oe a ue un lf mf ch if lf 9g. He then reported feeling definitely better and was smiling broadly.

Next John spoke of his low self-esteem to do with his difficulties in reading and writing and how his mother used to tell him he was stupid. We used the following sequence whilst he thought of this: eb oe ue un ch a c liv th if mf g50 lf sh. He then reported "I feel OK". I asked him to recall his mother telling him he was stupid and asked how he felt—he said he felt nothing now.

I asked if there was anything more he wished to address at this point (since the work so far had only taken half an hour). He said the only thing left bothering him was his teenage daughter, who is in some ways like his mother (John's ex-wife). Whilst he thought of this we used the following sequence: eb if oe ue a c un eb ue g50 9g. He smiled and said he was feeling a lot better than when he came in. I asked what he now felt when he thought of his daughter. He replied: "I love her dearly—she's a great kid—I feel quite emotional—it brings a tear to my eye—I seem to be getting quite emotional these days—watching films and so on—it's difficult to hold it in". I commented that perhaps he was feeling much more and he said this was definitely the case. He spoke of how he was getting on with his girl-friend better than at any point during the previous 4 years, seeing more of her and being open with her.

I said there had been a lot of change rather quickly. He replied "Yes, its been amazing".

Session 4

John reported that he had just had a very good weekend—his mind was not racing in the way it used to—but he then talked of the many problems in his life. He said he was feeling very angry because his ex-wife was trying to "worm her way back in", partly through contact with their daughter. He conveyed some continuing ambivalence towards her—wanting to be free of her, yet still feeling some kind of connection and pull back to her. We used the following sequence whilst he thought about his ex-wife: sh eb a ue c eb oe mf if un ch c. He said he now felt 'nothing' when he thought of his ex-wife—and went on to speak of his relationship with his girlfriend, which he said was the best it had ever been. However, he showed a mini-reversal, muscle testing weak to "I want to be completely free of my ex-wife". After correction for this, we tapped the following sequence: sh eb oe ue a c un ch eb a ue c if mf c. Then he showed level 2 reversal regarding the future, testing weak to "I will be free of my ex-wife". Following level 2 correction, we tapped the following sequence: eb c oe ue a c un ch c oe sh if c 9g c. He remarked: "I feel rather good—its amazing—unbelievable" and went on to speak of his astonishment, and that of his family, at how much change there had been for so little time and work. He said his brother was still a sex addict and had had years of therapy in France.

Session 5

John reported that he had been feeling very much better. However, he was aware of stress and physical tension. Exploration of this revealed his tendency to be perfectionist, which created inner pressure and a sense of never being good enough. I asked where he thought this originated. He replied that it was from his mother—"whatever I did was never good enough".

We used EFT in relation to his perfectionism. He reported feeling calm, with his shoulders relaxing. We then used a specific sequence to clear the remnants of the roots of his perfectionism in his mother's words to him: sh eb c ue a c un ch chakras if eb c. Following this, he reported "a weight off my shoulders" and said he could no longer detect any distressing feelings about his mother.

However, he then spoke of his awareness that he cannot easily relax and be happy. As we start to tap whilst he focused on this problem he thought of his difficulties in relaxing with his mother, having to be on his guard the whole time. Following this he was smiling and said he felt OK.

Session 6

John reported feeling depressed. His ex-wife had been in touch with him, harassing him, and he had been obliged to change his mobile phone number.

Muscle testing indicated that he felt it was not safe to be happy — and a specific intergenerational reversal, that if he were happy he would lose the connection to his depressed mother. We then tapped the following sequence: eb a ue a c oe if c. He responded by saying: "I feel different already—I don't feel like I did when I walked in". Then he remarked that he thought he took after his mother. Muscle testing revealed a reversal against being different from his mother. This was corrected, resulting in "that brings a smile to my face".

Further muscle testing indicated a reversal on the basis of not feeling *allowed* to be happy—and not feeling allowed to have his own life and to take his own initiative. These were corrected.

John then went on to talk of his anger and feelings of depression about his wasted years.

It was then possible to understand more about the internal sequence of events that had led to his more depressed state. Feeling better had involved a break with his previous self in relation to his mother—an internal move that in itself provoked a reversal concerning losing this connection to his mother and to his previous self. Then, in addition, he had felt rage about his wasted years. The outcome had been a state of depression following feeling better.

Session 7

John reported that he felt irritable today—things had been going wrong. However, he emphasised that he did not feel troubled by thoughts of the past anymore. Yesterday had been a good day—and he had woken up today feeling OK but then things had gone wrong at work, there had been various frustrations and he had felt irritable. He had used some EFT himself and had felt better.

It seemed that in this session John was confirming the overall good progress, but we were left with problems inherent in his basic temperament, such as his irritability and low frustration tolerance. His need seemed to be to develop more self-acceptance in relation to this basic temperament. We used the following TFT sequence for this: oe ue a c lf c. Following this he was smiling again.

Session 8

John reported feeling low. He said he had been having a very difficult time with his daughter and also problems with his ex-wife. His daughter had been expelled from school, was stealing and lying, and generally appearing immune to benign influence. She was "just like her mother" and the situation was "a nightmare". John spoke of feeling deeply disappointed in his daughter's behaviour—and remarked: "the three people who have meant something to me have been a disaster: my mother, my wife, and my daughter".

We applied TFT to these feelings. He reported feeling more relaxed—"still low, but better than when I came in".

Session 9

John reported that he had been through a period of feeling depressed and had taken a week off work. There had been continuing problems with his daughter—it had been "one thing after another". However, he had experienced a spontaneous recovery from his depression a few days previously. He was now experiencing no troubling thoughts and "nothing is bothering me today". He explained that he had been applying stricter boundaries to his daughter, and that these had seemed to be bearing fruit in better behaviour.

What struck me in John's account of his reactions here was that he had experienced depression in response to very difficult circumstances, and he had taken some time off work to recover—and he had then recovered. It is not depression in itself that is pathological, since it is a normal emotional response to certain kinds of events. Depression can only be legitimately regarded as pathological if it is persistent, not appropriate to the circumstances, and the person does not show a normal capacity to recover.

Session 10

John said he was not feeling on top of the world, but not as bad as he had previously felt. The situation was somewhat better with his daughter. He felt his normal state was to be somewhat miserable. We talked about his current relationships with women. He felt he did not want a regular partner at the moment and was trying to reduce the amount he saw his woman friend. Significantly, he mentioned that he had remained free of his original sex addiction; thoughts of sex no longer dominated his life. We used TFT to address his current mood and self-esteem and he reported then feeling much better.

John felt able to continue without further therapy at this point.

Jeremy—erotic obsessions

Jeremy was a 50 year old man who presented in a state of depression and desperation associated with distress regarding his sexual obsessions. His preoccupations were of a general anal nature, but particularly focused on watching and hearing a woman defecate. He recalled having such an interest all his life, with memories from age 3 or 4 of liking to watch little girls defecate and of listening at toilet doors, particularly to his mother. This obsession was all-consuming and a source of enormous shame, guilt, and anxiety—which he had tried to alleviate with a pattern of heavy drinking. His wife had tolerated this to an extent over the years, but he feared his marriage was nearing its end as a result of his compulsive interest in anal matters. When able to work, Jeremy held a good job as a software engineer.

Jeremy described having felt lonely and neglected as a child. He said his mother had been busy looking after his handicapped younger sister and his father had been emotionally absent. During our first meeting, Jeremy mentioned images of his uncle "doing things to me on the toilet, with his trousers down" when he was aged three. He thought he had stayed with this uncle when his mother had been pregnant. Interestingly he described fluctuating recollections of this: "I remembered—then I forgot—then I remembered again".

Following the initial assessment, Jeremy reported a sense of horror at how much his life has revolved around his sexual preoccupations. However, he described how this had given way to a feeling of peace as he had accepted this is how it had been. We targeted what appeared to have been the sexual abuse trauma by his uncle, using TFT focused with the simple phrase "sexual trauma with my uncle". The aim of this was not to elicit further details of this possible memory, but to clear the perturbations or energetic residues that may have been left by such an experience. Using a diagnosed sequence of tapping, Jeremy expressed much emotional abreaction during this process which took just a few minutes. No clear content emerged, but the emotion was strong. He then reported feeling very calm.

At our third meeting he reported that the preoccupation with toilets had gone. He had also stopped drinking alcohol. His wife had commented that making love with him had felt completely different from previously. Guided by muscle testing, we identified his anger with women as the appropriate next target for TFT, which was carried out using a diagnosed sequence.

In the fourth session, more emerged regarding his childhood circumstances. He had a sister two years younger, his handicapped sister three years younger, and a brother five years younger. The births had taken place at home. It began to seem likely that Jeremy would have developed an infantile equation between birth and defecation—and that part of his motives for listening so intently when his mother visited the lavatory was to check whether she was producing another hated rival baby. His interest in anal matters seemed also to have been enhanced by his mother having to evacuate his handicapped sister's bowels manually. We used TFT to address these further aspects and roots of his anal preoccupations. Significantly, Jeremy reported that he was beginning to experience new (normal) feelings of revulsion regarding anal matters.

By the fifth session, Jeremy reported feeling "very well" and said he was "astonished" at how much better he was feeling. He was no longer preoccupied with toilets. Interestingly, he described this loss of addictive compulsion as follows: "I feel I could be interested if I chose to be—but I feel like I am making a choice not to be. I still register the opportunity to listen at lavatories, but I choose not to". He was getting on much better with his wife and reported that they made love most days. His initial high CORE score of 85 had dropped to a low score of 22.

Over the next few months, Jeremy chose to attend several more sessions addressing other aspects of his life, career, pattern of drinking etc—but the anal preoccupation did not return.

Apparently severe personality difficulties cleared easily

Although severe and pervasive 'personality disorders' may involve complex and relatively prolonged therapeutic work, sometimes a person who presents with what appear to be very entrenched problems can be helped rather easily. A pervasively disturbed state of mind may sometimes be related to a specific trauma—and, once this is effectively addressed, the disturbance goes.

Josephine—trauma of father's suicide

Josephine was a 22 year old woman who presented with a recent history of overdoses, anxiety, nightmares and difficulties in concentrating. These problems had been present since the death of her father by suicide on her 20th birthday. Her childhood had been troubled, with an early parental separation and subsequent sexual abuse by her father. During her early childhood she had been 'Daddy's little girl', but after the parental separation, from the age of 13, he would come into her bedroom and molest her. She described him as disturbed—"he wasn't right in the head"—and gave accounts of how he was paranoid and controlling, and on some occasions violent, threatening to kill her and himself with a knife. Despite these experiences, it seemed that Josephine had managed to maintain feelings of love for her father. She explained that she had managed to put these traumatic events behind her, but the horror had all come back to her on her 20th birthday when he committed suicide. He had asked her to visit him, and when she went, accompanied by his sister, she found him hanging from the banister.

Josephine was keen to try TFT, which she had heard about. We tried an initial sequence of tapping, focussed on her current level of anxiety. She responded well to this, remarking: "It feels really weird—I feel so calm—it's so strange—I feel really relaxed".

We moved straight on to using TFT for the target experience of encountering her father's dead body hanging. Her initial SUD was 9. After a diagnosed sequence of tapping, the SUD dropped to 6—but then stuck around 5. I asked her what aspect she was thinking of. She said he was the first dead person she had seen—his eyes had been open—and he had looked blue. A further round of tapping, using a sequence for trauma and anxiety led to a SUD of 3—and then a subsequent round dropped the SUD to 0. She was asked to think further about what she saw and experienced in relation to her father's body—her SUD remained at 0. She remarked: "I don't feel anything—it's really weird—it's really strange—I can't explain it." At a follow-up session a couple of weeks later, Josephine reported feeling completely fine. Some of her remarks were as follows:

> "I feel OK—its weird—just doing that thing and I feel OK—the main problem was with my Dad and now its OK—I haven't really thought about my father since—I still have the memory but not the exhausting intensity—its strange—I feel happy with myself—really I'm quite happy. It's an unusual method but very effective. When I left last time I felt relaxed but completely drained—I went home and slept for four hours—then I felt brilliant—so calm and relaxed. I felt a slight embarrassment—it was such a big thing, but I just haven't felt the emotions that were attached to it. I'll be able to go to my father's grave now and put flowers and at last feel at peace with my Dad rather than being a screaming wreck. My friends think I look different—more at peace. It is so strange—I have the memory but the feeling is not there—I just feel calm. Its hard to explain—when I bring up the memory it is just calm."

Josephine's original CORE score was high (83). After the TFT, as measured at the second meeting, it had dropped to a very low score of 12. At a further follow-up 7 months later, Josephine reported feeling very happy and her CORE score was a mere 4—very low indeed.

Sexual difficulties following trauma

Sometimes sexual difficulties have deep and complex roots, requiring extensive work to unravel and treat. On the other hand, it is common for sexual problems to arise from relatively simple traumas that can be cleared rather easily. Traumatic perinatal experiences form one such category.

Mrs. Jones—sex aversion following traumatic birth

Mrs. Jones was referred by her GP because of a strong aversion to sex with her husband following a traumatic birth of her son a couple of years previously. She had become depressed post-natally, had recovered from this, but still felt unable to have sex—an indeed described the idea as 'unbearable'. Moreover she did not want another baby. Despite this, she reported a good relationship with her husband and said their sexual activity used to be enjoyable.

We used TFT, targeting first the trauma of the birth, and then the thought of sex with her husband. Diagnostic muscle testing was used to discern the sequences. After a few minutes work she experienced no anxiety when thinking of the birth, nor on imagining having sex with her husband. The prospect of intercourse now appeared desirable to her.

This single session was all that was required. In a subsequent letter, she wrote: "Dear Dr Mollon, I just wanted to say how interesting I found the whole experience—the best thing being that it seems to have worked!".

Physiological and psychological trauma

Sometimes a person may suffer severe physiological reactions to toxic substances (including individual energy toxins)—which, in turn, functions as a psychological shock trauma. The experience of disorientation and panic, produced by the toxin, generates further anxiety around the fear of re-experiencing this. Both levels of the trauma and anxiety need to be cleared.

Panic following drug misuse

A young man presented with a history of panic attacks that had become very disabling over the past couple of years. He had become increasingly restricted, fearful to go out in case he was overwhelmed with anxiety. Associated with the panics were anxieties about his heart—palpitations triggering fears of a heart attack. In addition he had become sensitive to many foods and substances; caffeine or sugar would be likely to provoke anxiety or panic, with racing heart. All of this dated from a time when he had overdosed on cocaine and had collapsed. Prior to this he had taken cocaine, Ecstasy, LSD, and 'magic mushrooms' on a regular basis, especially Ecstasy.

Muscle testing indicated that his energy system was disorganised and tending towards massive reversal. He was strong to wanting to be sick, and weak to wanting to be well; he was weak to palm down on the head and strong to palm up (a reversal of the normal pattern). This was corrected with tapping the side of the hand, along with hand on navel and taps on thymus, collar bone, chin, under nose and forehead. A reversal regarding safety was apparent—again easily corrected.

Muscle testing then showed a strong response to the idea that the cocaine overdose had constituted a trauma to his system (a physical and psychological trauma). Diagnostic TFT was then used to clear this. We also cleared 'all the residues of cocaine, Ecstasy, LSD and magic mushrooms', again using diagnostic TFT. Muscle testing then indicated that these were cleared and that he was free of the panics. Moreover, the substance sensitivities had also cleared, without needing to be specifically addressed.

He was asked to try to locate any remaining traces of anxiety. This led him to voice the fear that he might become ill and collapse and doctors would not know what was wrong and might give him the wrong treatment that would worsen his heart problems. He explained that this thought stemmed from the fact that doctors had not been able to cure his heart palpitations and panic. With further TFT, he then reported the thought that doctors are highly paid because they are trained to know what they are doing and to be able to make good judgements. Thus his fearful thought was replaced with a realistically positive one. A similar process happened when he spoke of claustrophobic anxieties that he might be trapped on a tube train in London. After tapping he said he was now thinking that it was unlikely to happen because he was rarely in London anyway!

He could locate no further sources or aspects of anxiety—and said he felt calm but tired.

The clear impression is that the cocaine overdose had been a traumatic shock to his system, both physiologically and psychologically—resulting in his defensive programmes shifting into high alert.

Treatment of chronic and complex difficulties in a small number of sessions spread over a few months

Often there is not a specific single trauma, or even a specific series of traumas, that underlie the presenting state of mind. Rather complex

and pervasive problems may need to be addressed. These may sometimes be effectively dealt with in just a few sessions spaced perhaps
at monthly intervals.

Mary—chronic depression

Mary was a depressed Irish lady in her early 40s. She said she had
felt depressed for as long as she could remember, and certainly since
early childhood. As a teenager she had made a suicide attempt.
She was intelligent and, despite her difficulties, she had performed
reasonably well academically and had a good job in a commercial
company. She lived with a man. Her initial CORE score was 96,
which is high and indicates pervasive psychological distress. Previously she had undergone counselling, which she had found to be of
no help: "I just talked of how bad my childhood was".

In her initial consultation she talked of how she frequently entered
a dark place in her mind, and there she would be filled with fear, desperation, and insecurity. She feared she would lose her job and her
house. She talked of wanting people to like her, but would ruminate
every day about what she might have done wrong.

Following her agreement to engage in TFT we found general
reversals to do with safety and guilt in relation to feeling better. This
led her to speak of how she felt she had a hurt child inside her and
she had never cried when she was young. She talked of missing her
father. We addressed these using diagnosed TFT. Further sessions
were roughly a month apart.

In the second session, she spoke of a change following our first
meeting: "Strangely enough, I have felt better about myself—I
remembered when I was little and I was called 'plumpy' and everything was OK then—I had forgotten about that before." She also
explained that although she still felt worried, her anxieties were more
focused on particular issues, such as finance and her relationship
with her partner David. We applied further TFT to these worries,
which left her with what she described as "a nice warm feeling". Her
CORE score had dropped to 51.

In the third session she reported that the previous day had been
the first time for years that she had woken up not feeling panic—and
this had felt strange because it was unfamiliar. She talked of her finan-
cial worries as being at the heart of her anxieties; she had been made

redundant twice and her partner had business difficulties. They did not earn enough between them. As we explored these thoughts and feelings, she began to speak of how her mother would tend to be very negative and critical and used to tell her that she would never be good enough to have a job. We applied a long diagnosed TFT sequence to this constellation, after which she felt better. She then talked of her anger with her partner—how he doesn't seem to worry and this worries *her*. She felt she was wasting her life on him and had given up hope of having a child. Whilst she thought he was a very kind person, she felt she had made the wrong decision in staying with him so long. We applied further TFT to this. She then commented that she had been thinking for three years that she would like to leave David but she had not done so because she felt she needed his help in her flat; she now thought this was a crazy reason for staying with him. At this point her CORE score had risen again to 70.

By the fourth session she reported that her panic had gone and she no longer felt terrified like she used to. However, she noticed that she would wake up feeling worried (rather than terrified) and *angry*. She spoke of a fear of losing her job. Her CORE score was up to 87. I asked why she thought this might be when she was reporting improvements in her mental state. She replied:

> "I can see what is happening—I feel more responsible for it. Before, I used to think I was just ill and a pill would sort me out—now I see more what the situation is—I am fighting more—previously I gave up—now I try to pull myself out, but it is painful. Maybe it was better when I had no hope—people think I seem better, but it is painful to have hope."

I asked what the hope was, and she said it was hope of being like a normal person, of having children, of planning holidays. "At the moment I don't know how to answer people when they ask what I did at the weekend—I just stayed in bed. Compared with others I feel more angry with myself. I feel more pain without the medication." We applied more TFT. There were reversals to do with parts, deservedness, and shame. We also addressed 'programmes' to do with being anxious and hopeless. Following this she reported feeling more positive.

In the fifth session she said she was definitely feeling better, with no panics. She said she was aware of experiencing worries that related to insecurities from her childhood. We used TFT to clear inherited trauma and pain from the maternal line. She spoke of hating her mother, and of feeling hated by her—this giving way to a sense of forgiving her mother. We also addressed and cleared pervasive feelings of shame and guilt about being born. She recognised that her father had loved her. She then began to talk of a sense of wanting to push at boundaries and limits—and of wanting to catch up with lost time—a state that we likened to that of someone who had just woken up after being in a coma for years. Her CORE score was 47.

The positive trend continued in the sixth session. She again reported that she felt she was getting better, feeling less anxious, and more alive. Moreover she felt her partner was happier—but she still felt she would like to leave him eventually. She wanted babies and was aware of time passing. She concluded "I can feel myself healing".

At the seventh session we agreed to stop. She said she was feeling a lot better. Her CORE score was 21—i.e. showing no clinical level of psychological distress. The treatment process had covered about 6 months.

Emotions in the body

It is a commonplace of energy psychology work to address emotions expressed in the body—in bodily sensations, symptoms, and physical illness. This has been a line of exploration particularly within EFT— see, for example, Gary Craig's two DVD series on working with serious physical illness.

Suzanne—anger in the gut

Suzanne, a woman in her late thirties presented with a history of depression and excessive use of alcohol—in the context of an unhappy marriage. She had separated from her husband but felt constrained by his reluctance to set her free and agree to a divorce. He had an illness that led her to feel guilty at the thought of 'abandoning' him. Her adolescent daughter lived with her and she experienced the usual tensions and irritations common to such relationships. In addition to stress and depression, Suzanne complained of various somatic problems.

As we began to work through a tapping sequence for 'the way I feel at the moment', guided by my proxy muscle self-testing, I sensed that her system seemed to be sticking on the large intestine index finger point—it did not seem to be clearing. I asked if she had any problems with her gut. She told me that she did—sometimes irritable bowel and other similar problems (she had not referred to this before). Therefore I muscle tested her directly, first in the clear (strong) and then having her touch the 'alarm' test point for the large intestine, followed by the small intestine alarm point. Both tested very weak. The stomach meridian alarm point tested moderately weak. This indicated a disturbance in these specific meridians, and possibly in their associated organs (consistent with her report of problems in her gut). We then applied the basic TFT muscle testing procedure, but taking these disturbed meridians (each in turn) as the target. Thus we muscle tested for the sequence to tap to correct the problem in the large intestine, looking for meridian points that would make the arm strong when she thought of the large intestine. This sequence began with the treatment point for the governing meridian, under the nose—as did the sequence for the small intestine meridian. The target meridians themselves did not come up as needing to be tapped until quite late in the sequence. We worked through these sequences until the two intestinal meridians and the stomach meridian all tested strong when therapy localised to their alarm test points.

Since the governing meridian had come up as the first point in the sequence for the two dysfunctional intestinal meridians, I put to Suzanne the hypothesis that frustrations to do with not feeling she was the governor of her own life were being expressed through disturbances in her gut. She found this extremely plausible and talked of her feeling that she was not in control of any aspect of her life. We were then able to clear various areas of tension in her body by identifying the anger and frustration trapped there: e.g. "Even though there is anger in my shoulders I completely accept myself", followed by a sequence of tapping. More generally we then tapped on the opening words "Even though I feel I have no control in any area of my life I completely accept myself". At the end of this session Suzanne felt calm and intrigued by the information revealed through energy checking. She reported that her body felt free of tension.

This session illustrates the way in which information regarding a problem is communicated from the body through energy checking (muscle testing) and then healing information is put back into the body through tapping the meridian points revealed through the body's energy code.

Physiological remembering

The following case illustrates how memories of events may at times be experienced physiologically—sensations and body reactions at the time of the original event may be re-experienced without a clear awareness of the originating context (Mollon, 2002a). It can be important to be alert to these processes that may emerge during tapping (as well as at other times).

Jennifer—abortion trauma

I had been working with Jennifer, a 40 year old woman who presented with anxieties and panic, for some months when the following session took place over the phone. She told me of recent dreams of abortions, miscarriages, and blood. These seemed to have been triggered partly by having been reading about post traumatic stress disorder. Her association to the dream was to an abortion 25 years previously. There had been bleeding, with blood all over the bed. She recalled changing her mind about the abortion, just as the anaesthetic was starting to take effect, and trying to speak of this but her words being lost in her throat as she sank into unconsciousness. She mentioned that it had been following this that her anxieties and panic started. In particular she had become afraid of the dark and could not sleep. She recalled a moment when she looked out of the window of her apartment and feared there was somebody there in the darkness—and had feared she was going mad.

Initially she showed a psychological reversal to being over this trauma, based on guilt. This was corrected and a long tapping sequence was applied—covering traumatic shock, anxiety, guilt, anger, and shame [eb c ue a c ch if eb oe un lf ue a c]. Her initial response to this was an expression of disgust and guilt, and to wonder why she had allowed herself to become pregnant. The further short sequence for guilt was applied [if c]. She then recalled that her boyfriend had not wanted the child and had indeed wanted her to have an abortion.

With further tapping, Jennifer then began to complain of a sensation in her throat—"like a lump". I suggested that this sensation represented the words and emotions stuck in her throat that she had not been able to utter because of the anaesthetic. She agreed but then reported feelings of panic as she focussed on the idea of words stuck in her throat. As we continued tapping, I put to her that perhaps this was a recollection of the panic she had felt at it being too late to stop the abortion—a panic that had been subdued by the anaesthetic, like a ghost stuck in her throat—and, furthermore, that this may have given rise to her fear of the ghost 'out there' (outside the window), of the aborted fetus and her own scream coming back to haunt her. She replied that this made much sense and that she felt some relief.

Then Jennifer said she recalled another reason why she had not been able to express her feelings fully about the abortion. When she had come round from the anaesthetic, her boyfriend was sitting in the room crying—so that she felt she was not allowed to be upset as well.

As the tapping continued, Jennifer suddenly reported feeling woozy—"like I've been drinking". I put to her that perhaps this was a recollection of the anaesthetic—of her feeling on coming round, along with the panic at realising the abortion had taken place. This made sense to her. With further tapping she felt very calm.

Relating to childhood parts

The following two cases are, each in their own way, fairly typical instances of how the client may come to access a dissociated child self (or part) in the course of energy psychology work. By going with the emerging images and emotions, still tapping, and perhaps engaging in internal dialogue with, or expressions of love for, the child, it is often easy for the client to resolve deep divisions in the psyche and experience new feelings of peace.

Joining up with the childhood self

A woman sought help with trauma-based reactions that had been stirred up during her training in psychotherapy. She was aware of a childhood involving witnessing violence between her parents and some degree of sexual abuse from her father. This picture was based partly on direct memories and partly on reports from her mother. However, her explicit conscious memory of her childhood was very patchy. During the first session, various childhood traumas were addressed and muscle testing indicated that these successfully cleared, even though the traumas were not fully accessed consciously.

At a follow-up session several weeks later, she reported feeling much better, lighter, and more peaceful. Whilst very pleased with this change, she said she would like to be able to remember more of her childhood. Muscle testing indicated psychological reversal to remembering more, based on fears regarding safety. As she thought about this it occurred to her that probably neither her father nor her mother would be able to cope with her discussing her childhood with them—so she reasoned that if she did remember more, she would have to keep it to herself and not share it with them. Further tapping around these issues then led her suddenly to remark that she was aware of an image of her child self. I asked what the child was doing. She said the little girl was standing with her arms outstretched. With further tapping she saw herself bending down and embracing the child and picking her up. As she continued tapping she became very emotional at this joyful healing moment.

As we reflected on what had happened, it became clear that her agenda had subtly changed. From an initial idea that she wanted to remember more of her childhood—with an expectation that this would involve recollecting much that was painful—her spontaneous process had shifted to one of reconnecting with and healing her lost childhood self. This joyful reunion with herself had been quite unexpected—but extremely welcome. Remembering actual events now seemed much less important.

Lucy—deep roots of panic

Lucy, a young woman in her early twenties, presented with strong reactions of anxiety, panic, and dissociation in response to sexual situations with her husband. These appeared to contain components of traumatic stress, but she was unsure what events these might relate to. After resolving certain reversals to do with safety and parts, we proceeded to tap simply to the thought of "the roots and origins of this anxiety". During the tapping she reported seeing an internal image of her child self—a terrified little girl. Whilst continuing the tapping, I encouraged her to comfort her little girl self, which she did. She described picking the child up and holding her until she was calm—all the time continuing the tapping sequence.

When Lucy came for a follow-up session several weeks later, she reported a sense that the terrified little girl had indeed been healed (confirmed through muscle testing) but described further anxiety to do with an image of a "girl in a black room" who had been protected by the terrified girl. She said the girl in the black room was very much more damaged, having two components—a mutilated body and a completely detached spirit floating in a disembodied state. After muscle testing for safety, deservedness, and willingness of this 'girl in the black room' to be healed, we proceeded to tapping to "the girl in the black room and all that has been done to her". Following this, Lucy reported that when she pictured the girl in the black room she no longer felt any distress, as if this was now just an image with no emotional charge. Muscle testing confirmed that this girl part was now healed.

Working through the invasion of projective identification

Being the recipient of projective identification—the process whereby one person projectively and manipulatively (but unconsciously) evokes an unwanted feeling in the other, with which the recipient identifies—is a common feature of human interaction. If the projectively evoked feeling and negative self-image meets with a receptive and congruent substrate in the recipient, it may be quite difficult to dislodge, even with interpretation and understanding. TFT or EFT can often greatly help with the 'detoxifying' of such invasions.

For example, a professional trainee talked of her self-doubts regarding her capacity to continue competently with her training. She felt that perhaps she was not suited to this particular profession. After she had spoken at length of various events and circumstances in her training schedule during the previous week, describing certain distressing interactions with a supervisor, it became apparent that the supervisor was a troubled man who probably felt inadequate himself in his role. He appeared to have made various remarks unconsciously designed to evoke such feelings and self-image in his trainee. As these experiences were explored and discussed during the session, the trainee was able to appreciate the understanding and perception of the process of projective identification—but this did not alter how she felt. It was only with meridian tapping that her mood and her identification with the projection began to shift. There were layers to this. After a first sequence of tapping she expressed anger with herself for having succumbed to the supervisor's criticisms. Then she expressed anger with him. Finally she expressed anger that she had spent so much time and energy on this man. I then took her through a tapping sequence beginning with the statement "I wasted so much time and energy on this idiot"—following which she reported that she just wanted to laugh, which was a very marked contrast with her mood just a few minutes previously.

Basically the same principle and process can be applied to the more repeated and chronic projective identifications of childhood. A child may be born into a particular phantasy in the mother's or father's mind, and then identifies with this assigned role. Many variants and theories regarding this kind of process have been described over the years in the psychoanalytic and family therapy literature (Grotstein, 1981). To some extent this process is normal and unavoidable, as Lacan's work describes: each child is assigned a name, a sound with multiple complex meanings and associations, and is obliged to identify with this sound and its connotations (Mollon, 2001). No human being can exist entirely outside the realm of culture, with its shared language and meanings. Human identities are always socially and culturally constructed identities—always, in a sense, 'false' selves. It is a matter of degree. We can aim for a state of relative freedom from the potentially imprisoning effect of persistent projective identifications in childhood—these are the ones which define us negatively and restrictively, which say "you are this bad kind of person and you cannot be anything other than that". Tapping on the meridian system (or holding the chakras) whilst these projective identifications are held in mind is enormously effective in clearing the negative programming imbued in childhood.

*Physical issues—recovery from toxic medication
evidenced through heart rate variability.*

TFT is as applicable to physical as it is to psychological issues. I am grateful to Robin and Mary Ellis, both TFT practitioners, for providing the following material. The measure used was Heart Rate Variability (HRV), which, in his review of the relevant research, Dr Callahan has found to be not only a sensitive and important measure of physical and psychological health, but also the best predictor of death (Callahan, 2001e, 2001f, Callahan & Callahan, 2003). It can reveal the effects of toxins even before these are apparent through other symptoms.

Mary developed a Deep Vein Thrombosis, leading to a medical crisis and admission to hospital. She was given three drugs: a diuretic, an anti-arhythmic, and an anti-coagulant. In the short term, these worked well, allowing Mary to return home. This happened to coincide with Dr Callahan's asking, on the TFT web serve, whether anyone had information on Heart Rate Variability in relation to drug toxicity. Being familiar with this measure, Robin and Mary decided to take HRV readings every day, using the software and heart beat finger sensor linked to an ordinary computer. In order to ensure a clear reading reflecting the effects of the medication, they checked (in the normal TFT way, using muscle testing) for every conceivable toxin in foods or products that Mary was using—either eliminating these or neutralising them with the TFT '7 second' toxin treatment. Then, with these other toxins out of the picture, HRV readings were taken which were more likely to reflect just the effects of the prescribed medication. Two days after being home, the SDNN reading was 82 (too low); after '7 second' toxin treatment for the medication, the reading rose to 102 (somewhat better). Three days after being home, the SDNN had dropped to a worrying 23—rising to 174 after '7 second' treatment. Five days after being home, the SDNN was 31—and the '7 second' treatment could raise this only to 35. The situation was looking ominous. Over the next week, Mary continued to become more and more ill. A fortnight after being home on the medication, Mary's SDNN reading was a seriously low 12, rising to 51 after '7 second' treatment. Her heart rate was becoming very irregular and she was showing signs of jaundice. At this point, Robin and Mary decided to stop all prescribed medication and changed to a herbal treatment, using well-researched products designed to clear and prevent embolisms (containing an enzyme called Protease). Within a week she felt normal. The SDNN stabilised around 180—now slightly on the high side, but then normalising further as they continued TFT treatment of toxins. Five weeks later, Mary saw the cardiologist, who greeted her with the words "You do look very well!". Mary told him she had stopped taking his drugs four weeks previously. After some simple routine tests of blood pressure and heart rate, the cardiologist stated that Mary had made the right decision in coming off the drugs, adding "it looks as if we overdid it a bit". Robin's view was that the HRV readings were clearly indicating that if Mary had continued with the prescribed drugs she would have been heading for cardiac arrest.[2]

Whilst no practitioner of TFT or energy psychology methods would recommend a client to withdraw from medication except under medical supervision, this case is an illustration of the significance and value of measures of Heart Rate Variability, as explored by Dr Callahan, as well as a sobering indicator of the potentially toxic nature of some prescribed drugs (even though these might be life saving and essential at certain points).

Notes

1. **Note on programming, provided by Dr Shoshana Garfield.** The following information is based on a discussion with master trainer in neuro-linguistic programming (NLP), Jamie Smart (www. saladltd. co. uk). Hypnosis in general is subject to many misunderstandings. It is not like the popular comedy show sketch of *Little Britain* where a hypnotising magician waves his fingers around and around while saying, "Look into my eyes, look into my eyes, you are going into a trance ..." People constantly use hypnotic language and hypnotic tones of voice, especially for induction of light trances (deeper trances are more rare). Inducing a hypnotic trance, whereby the person in trance is suggestible and the person who induced the trance, deliberately or not, has the power to provide a programme, is actually very common. It is, in fact, ubiquitous. Since we are born without the genetic patterns of behaviour that most animals are born with, and since our cultures are so varied, we humans have evolved to have mechanisms of receptivity that allow

us to be socialised into the normative expectations of our individual and cultural environments. The social rules and abilities that we absorb and often subsequently pattern are originally stored unconsciously and hence parallel the internal working models of attachment theory (Cortina & Marrone, 2003). Hypnotic receptivity is fundamental to this process of socialisation simply because of time pressures; we are young for a relatively short period of time yet need as humans to learn such vast quantities just to be able to comprehend, however unconsciously, the highly complex expectations of behaviour to which we are subject and which shape our ability to be in the world. An example of non-judgmental, socialising, parental hypnotic language to a small child would be 'I see you are drawing on the floor with a blue crayon. What you want to do is draw on the paper. We draw on paper. [Gets paper] Here's paper. [Provides paper] Draw on this. We like drawing on drawing paper.' An example of implanting a suggestion hypnotically in an adult is when a medical doctor says to a cancer patient, 'You only have about 3 months to live' and then the patient receives it unconsciously as a directive to only live 3 months. Therefore, parents as well as other people in authority have extra permission to implant and suggest. Parents are hypnotically and regularly programming their children, and most are most often well-meaning and well-intentioned, even when doing such programming unconsciously. Nevertheless, given human imperfection, even well-meaning and loving parents will unintentionally implant and programme negatively. A common example is how parents often convey conditionality of their love and acceptance when socialising children to behave in expected ways, such as the use of the terms 'good boy/girl' and 'bad/naughty boy/girl', which implies globalising judgment of self-worth based on current behaviour (I do this behaviour now = I am a bad/naughty/good child; Mummy and Daddy don't like/love naughty/bad children…). For a fuller discussion of this, see Rosenberg (2003). Moreover, that there are some who deliberately use NLP/hypnosis techniques seems not only plausible, but inevitable. Of course, all programming is subject to reprogramming. The character of the Little Britain hypnotist works because we are familiar with people who use whatever skills or tools are at their disposal to fashion their own lives as they choose without engaging with the needs of others, and in fact do so at the expense of others. In this context of this brief discussion, implantation of self-destructive or other-harming programming found in ritual abuse is simply another use, albeit a morally reprehensible one, of pervasive human practice.

Cortina M, Marrone M. (eds) (2003) *Attachment theory and the psychoanalytic process*. London: Whurr Publishers. Rosenberg M (2003); *Nonviolent communication: A language of life*. USA: PuddleDancer Press.

2. Mary told me of a sequel to this experience. Following an injection of adrenaline (necessary for an acute condition) she had developed heart fibrillation. Her heart rate was 171 — but after treatment of the adrenaline reaction with the '7 second' Callahan Techniques method, this dropped immediately to 100. With further TFT her heart rate was normal the next morning. She had declined medication. The cardiologist was astonished at this rapid improvement.

Ethical aspects of energy psychological work–dangers of idealisation and illusions of knowing

"In developing right affiliations, we are speaking about establishing appropriate, healthy, outreaching, caring, and mindful relationships. These relationships differ markedly from inappropriate ones that are ruled by arbitrariness, self-righteousness, perfectionism, or self-centeredness." [Hover-Kramer, 2006, p. 10]

Practitioners of energy psychology methods know, from their experience that they usually work well, rapidly, gently, with minimum distress, are non-invasive, and mostly have no adverse side-effects. Clearly they are the treatment of choice in many cases. However, their effectiveness and (for most people) their seemingly innovative nature, present new ethical and professional practice considerations (discussed extensively by Dorothea Hover-Kramer, 2006). These can include the following:

- Informed consent, particularly insofar as the methods may not correspond to the client's prior expectations. This also concerns the nature of the explanations given to the client.

- Scope of practice issues—the extent to which use of energy methods legitimately falls within a practitioner's scope of practice within their designated profession.
- Management of the slightly altered, and sometimes disoriented, states of mind entered by clients (and sometimes practitioners) during energy-based work.
- Maintenance of an appropriate therapeutic relationship that minimises excessive dependency, transference, idealisation, and other distortions in the client's view of the therapist. These concerns can be somewhat at odds with some principles and assumptions found in traditional, psychoanalytically-oriented psychotherapy.
- Caution regarding the use of intuition, muscle testing, and other forms of non-verbal sources of data.

Of course, all the normal ethical, professional and legal considerations that are relevant in traditional forms of psychotherapy also apply in relation to energy modalities. The stunning effectiveness of energy methods makes the necessity for the highest standards of ethics even more central to our work. Professor Michael Cohen, expert in ethics, law, and medicine, puts this as follows:

"On one level, energy therapies share the same ground as other health and mental health professions in terms of the propensity for boundary violations. Caregiver and client meet in a unique space: one in which the client offers vulnerability and receives wisdom, knowledge, and nurturing. The therapeutic relationship is deep and exhilarating; prior limits, it feels, can be transcended in the healing space of understanding and empathy between therapist and client. This very freedom allows space for abuse for those who are unwary. Humans who have not fully done their own psychological and spiritual work, it seems, can be tempted to turn the grace of a sacred encounter into an unwelcome and profane violation; the safety of therapeutic intimacy into terrifying violation. Whilst energy therapies share this potential danger zone, boundaries are perhaps even more easily penetrated in energy therapies than in psychotherapy, because the work can move quickly through deep emotional layers and, in the experience of many healers and clients, even further, to spiritual layers that may have been previously hidden." [2006, pp. xv–xvi]

Much of this revolves around the need for the therapist to be cautious, honest, self-aware, observant, continually monitoring results of the work, generating and revising hypotheses in the light of emerging evidence. Whilst it should obviously go without saying that a practitioner should not make misleading claims about his or her work and its effects, the excitement of discovering the potency and astonishing range of application of energy psychology methods can lead some, particularly those new to the field, to make claims that are both simplistic and misleading. Energy psychology methods do not operate by 'magic', they do not produce 'miracles', in the sense of bypassing work that needs to be done. Instead, they seem to enable the necessary work to be targeted and carried out much more efficiently than purely talk-based methods. Nevertheless, complex problems remain complex, and many layers, strands, and networks of cognitive, emotional, and energetic issues may need to be addressed. The speed of change may be alarming and disorienting to some clients. Such aspects require astute and sensitive, empathic and energetic, observation of the client's shifting states of mind and body. Appropriate explanation needs to be given, and this will vary from client to client. Some may like extensive and detailed discussion of the nature of the work, the principles and history behind it, and so forth. Others may be happy with a very brief and general explanation, their essential concern being with finding relief from the presenting problem. It can be important to avoid a misleading impression of certainty regarding the mode of action of energy psychology methods. Thus, it may not be appropriate for a practitioner simply to repeat a dogmatic explanation provided by the founder of one of the methods. Instead, it may be best to acknowledge that we are far from fully understanding the mode of action of energy psychology methods, that they are based on observation rather than theory, and that a range of hypotheses have been proposed. Indeed, I would go further, and suggest that the practitioner should aim to avoid dogmatism even in his or her private beliefs. Our most favoured assumptions and beliefs can often turn out to be flawed and in need of revision. So whatever perspective or theory appears most apt and relevant at one point is best viewed as merely a provisional working framework and series of hypotheses. This allows us to retain an essentially scientific stance of enquiry. If we can manage to hold on to this position, of tolerating not knowing (all such 'knowing' being illusory), we are less likely to utter misleading claims to clients, colleagues, or the general public. We are also less likely to idealise our own 'knowing' and inadvertently foster the client's idealisation.

Illusions of knowing do indeed cause all manner of problems. They can lead us to overlook evidence that is incongruent with our assumptions, or ignore client's expressions of doubt or concern, or fail to modify and develop our understanding in the light of evidence; they can also lead to a grandiose identification with the power of energy methods. In the case of the 'cynics' who are certain of their own beliefs, that exclude the possibility that energy psychology methods can work, the illusion of knowing prevents them being open to new and valuable information that is potentially of benefit to their clients.

Transference, idealisation, denigration and disillusion

The realm of transference, and its associated distortions in the perception of the therapeutic relationship, deserves particular consideration. Here I will state some observations and conclusions that seem to me obvious but are at odds with pervasive assumptions within the psychoanalytically derived forms of psychotherapy. In that field, it has somehow come about that 'transference' is viewed as the most crucial focus of psychotherapy—but transference seems to be a source of some of the most terrible twistings and malign transformations of the relationship between client and therapist.

The practice of conventional psychotherapy is difficult. It requires a discipline of relationship with the client, such that professional boundaries are maintained whilst being maximally open emotionally to his or her communications of need, desire, hope and fear. Into this receptive vessel of the therapeutic frame comes the potentially explosive force of the transference—containing the thwarted desires and needs of childhood, combined at times with trauma and potential despair. In the case of clients who have experienced extensive and severe childhood trauma or neglect, this transference can be profoundly difficult to manage. The 'logic' of the transference is that the therapist will at some point potentially be perceived as being as bad as the original abuser, this alternating or coexisting with an image of the self as overwhelmingly bad. Such perceptions will create enormous anxiety in both client and therapist—and both may be motivated to ward these off. A common reaction is for the client to try ever harder to show that he or she is not bad, abusive, exploitative, uncaring etc., and also to demonstrate that the client is not utterly bad, by endeavouring to express love by accommodating the client's expressed 'needs' for special gratifications or reassurances that extend the normal boundaries of the frame. With such situations the two possible outcomes of these pressures tend to be either that the client breaks off the therapy, or some kind of serious violation of the usual boundaries takes place. Although these are the more difficult instances of the impact of transference, they are essentially just stronger expressions of the normal features of work that is focussed in the relationship between therapist and client.

Boundary violations in psychotherapy tend to be regarded as expressions of inadequate discipline, awareness, training, or ethical standards in the therapist. Of course such factors may be components of the situation, but I think the problem that is revealed in these more extreme circumstances of boundary derailment is one inherent in psychotherapy generally, whenever there is an implicit assumption, on the part of either therapist or client, that the relationship itself is to be healing or reparative. Freud did not view the therapeutic relationship in this way. His method was that of free-association as a means of revealing repressed childhood memories, desires, phantasies, and fears, which he aimed to bring into the light of consciousness in order that the ego might deal with these in a more reality-based way. He found that often the patient would repeat, rather than remember, childhood constellations in relation to the analyst—and that this was the patient's way of remembering. This transference relationship was to be viewed not as real but 'as if', a form of memory that contained information about the patient's childhood developmental past. Although this strategy of making use of the transference as memory can work reasonably well in relation to a small spectrum of relatively well-functioning patients, for many people it is unfeasible. In such cases there is simply too much childhood trauma and unmet needs that become downloaded into the relationship with the therapist—and these cannot easily be contained within the boundaries of the therapy. Too much is expected of the therapeutic relationship, leading to rage and disillusionment in the patient and, at times, burn-out in the therapist. Excessive focus on the here-and-now and interaction between client and therapist is often seen as necessary in response to this onslaught of childhood trauma and need, and yet this attention to the relationship may only serve to stimulate the client's endeavours to seek gratification and nurturance from the therapist.

One of the many advantages of the energy psychology methods is that they redirect the therapeutic focus back to the internal dysfunctional information within the client's own mind-body-energy system. It is this dysfunctional information, encoded in the client's energy field, that has brought him or her to seek help—rather than because the client has a problem in relation to the therapist. The therapist becomes a facilitator of change in the informational energy field of the client, rather than a receptacle of transferred desires, needs, and images from infancy. As a result, there is less strain on the therapeutic relationship. The energy psychology perspective on transference is succinctly stated by Dorothea Hover-Kramer (2006): "Transference happens when the client personalises the professional relationship with the therapist which diminishes the effectiveness of the therapeutic relationship." [p. 43] She adds that "The more disorganised, disempowered, and lacking in internal resources clients are, the more susceptible they will be to transferences." [p. 43]. I believe this is actually startlingly close to Freud's original view of transference as 'resistance', a truthful perspective that has become lost in some contemporary approaches. Minimising the intrusion of preoccupations with the therapist enhances the speed and effectiveness of the therapy, in my experience.

Whilst helping to counter some of the excesses and imbalances in contemporary psychoanalytic approaches, there are, on the other hand, other dangers for the therapist's attitude and state of mind inherent in energy psychology. The most obvious of these is that of mania and illusions of omnipotence. Most people who encounter the rapid and profound shifts brought about by energy psychology methods, unless striving to ward off a full awareness of the implications, are likely to become filled with enthusiasm, eager to tell and demonstrate the phenomena to all who will listen (and many who will not). Along with this enthusiasm there can be impatience with those who refuse to believe the paradigms-challenging accounts. It can be easy to slip into thinking that one can heal anything using these methods—and indeed it is true that most physical and psychological problems can be helped to some degree using TFT, for example, since there appears always to be a corresponding encoding in the energy system which, when tapped, makes some contribution to the alleviation of illness or distress. Idealisation of self, the method, and the originator are common results of identification with these powers of healing. As a counter to these, it is good to remind oneself that we are mere technicians of the energy system. We know what to do to bring about a certain result in some, but not all, cases. This does not mean we are anywhere near a real understanding of the phenomena—nor that we can help everyone with these methods.

Idealisation of the originator of a method can stifle innovation since any deviation from the founder's own style or protocol may be viewed as heresy or betrayal, provoking denouncement or even 'ex-communication'. The condemnation of deviance is not necessarily carried out by the founder, but may be the function of those who strive to receive the founder's blessing. In place of genuine scientific and rational assessments of the value of innovative ideas, there is a judgement based on 'herd' thinking and concern for status within the group. Such dynamics are found within psychoanalytic, clinical psychological, and other professional and scientific groups, as well as within the energy psychology fields.

The flip side of idealisation is disillusionment and denigration. Sometimes those who have been the most enthusiastic proponents of energy psychological methods become ardent opponents— denouncing a once idealised founder and the methods themselves as fraudulent. The rigid idealisation is replaced by an equally rigid and restricted denigration. Neither position allows for the truth of the *imperfection* of the methods, our understanding of their nature, and the personal qualities of the founders. It is sobering and helpful to remind ourselves that whatever methods and understanding we have evolved at any one point will inevitably be viewed as primitive by future generations. All we can do is our imperfect human best.

Communicating with colleagues—the use of bridging concepts

Obviously it is necessary, for both scientific and professional reasons, to integrate the findings of energy psychology into the rest of our knowledge and theories of how the material and human world is. On the one hand, it is important not to minimise what is new and surprising in energy psychology, when compared to traditional approaches—but, on the other hand, we need to make use of bridging concepts that help us and our colleagues in other fields make links to more familiar domains. Moreover, we need to do so in such a way as to facilitate our own critical examination of energy psychology methods and theoretical frameworks. EFT is an interesting example here. If we look at any of its individual components—such as taking a history, identifying crucial formative experiences, linking adult and childhood traumas, finding recurrent core conflictual themes, identifying automatic negative thoughts and limiting beliefs, reframing and cognitively restructuring the client's relationship with the problem, using body-based forms of desensitisation, use of in vivo desensitisation, testing the results, and so forth—these can all be found in other well-established therapeutic methods, including those found in the UK guidelines from the National Institute for Clinical Excellence (NICE). Nevertheless, there seems to be something in the overall gestalt of EFT that goes well beyond the sum of its constituent parts. TFT, by contrast, in its attention to details of the energy system as originally revealed in Applied Kinesiology, seems to present phenomena that are less easily conceptualised within other frameworks. I feel it is important to allow these epistemological and conceptual tensions to remain open, not rushing to premature conclusions or pseudo understandings. At one pole is the danger of simplistic formulations of energy psychology methods that have a superficial and seductive appeal—whilst at the other pole is the dismissal of reports of energy psychology effects because they do not fit conventional paradigms. Neither position facilitates true enquiry and the furtherance of knowledge.

Perhaps the best we can say to our colleagues in neighbouring fields is that many of us, having worked for years with other, psychoanalytic or cognitive, methods, find that energy psychology appears to offer results that are more rapid, deep, and gentle than we or our clients have hitherto experienced. We have struggled with our own perplexity and scepticism, including the natural and almost ubiquitous tendency to reject whatever violates our fundamental assumptions, and we find ourselves embracing this developing field of therapeutic enquiry with persisting enthusiasm and astonishment.

REFERENCES

Andrade, J., & Feinstein, D. (2003). Preliminary report of the first large scale study of energy psychology. www.emofree.com/research/ andradepaper.htm
Also published as 'Energy psychology: Theory, indications, evidence'. In: D. Feinstein (2004). *Energy Psychology Interactive. Rapid Interventions for Lasting Change*. Innersource. Ashland. OR: 199–214.

Akhtar, S. (1999). 'Some day' and 'if only' fantasies. In: J. F. Gurewich, & M. Tort. (Eds.), *Lacan and the New Wave in American Psychoanalysis. The Subject and the Self*. New York: Other Press: 203–233.

Baars, B. J. (1988). *A Cognitive Theory of Consciousness*. Cambridge: Cambridge University Press.

Bailey, A. (1993). *The Seven Rays of Life, from the writings of Alice Bailey*. London: Lucis Press.

Baker, A. H., & Carrington, P. (2005). A comment on Waite and Holder's research supposedly invalidating EFT. www.energypsycho.org/ research-critique-eft.php

Baker, A. H., & Siegel, L. S. (2005). Can a 45 minute session of EFT lead to a reduction of intense fear of rats, spiders and water bugs? A replication and extension of the Wells et al. (2003) laboratory study. Manuscript in preparation.

Barkham, M., & Mellor-Clark, J. (2000). Rigour and relevance: the role of practice-based evidence in the psychological therapies. In: N. Rowland

and S. Goss (Eds.), *Evidence-Based Counselling and Psychological Therapies. Research and Applications*. London: Routledge.

Bates, Y. (Ed.) (2006). *Shouldn't I be feeling better by now? Client views of therapy*. Basingstoke: Palgrave Macmillan.

Bateman, A., & Fonagy, P. (2004). *Psychotherapy for Borderline Personality Disorder. Mentalization-based Treatment*. Oxford. Oxford University Press.

Beck, A. T., & Emery, G. (2005). *Anxiety Disorders and Phobias. A Cognitive Perspective*. Cambridge, MA. Basic Books.

Becker, R. O. (1991). Evidence for a primitive DC electrical analog system controlling brainfunction. *Subtle Energies* 2(1): 77–78.

Becker, R. O., & Selden, G. (1985). *The Body Electric*. New York. Morrow.

Becker, R. O., Reichmanis, M., Marino, A. A., & Spadaro, J. A. (1976). Electrophysiological correlates of acupuncture points and meridians. *Psychoenergetic systems, 1*: 105–112.

Bergsmann, O., & Wooley-Hart, A. (1973). Differences in electrical skin conductivity between acupuncture points and adjacent areas. *American Journal of Acupuncture, 1*: 27–32.

Beutler, B. R., & Harwood, T. M. (2001). Antiscientific attitudes. What happens when scientists are unscientific? *Journal of Clinical Psychology, 57*: 43–51.

Bion, W. R. (1962). Learning from experience. In: W. R. Bion (1977) *Seven Servants*. New York: Jason Aronson.

Blau, A. (1952). In support of Freud's syndrome of 'actual' anxiety neurosis. *International Journal of Psycho-Analysis, 33*: 363–372.

Bloom, K. (2006). *The Embodied Self. Movement and Psychoanalysis*. London: Karnac.

Bollas, C. (2007). *The Freudian Moment*. London: Karnac.

Bowlby, J. (1980). *Attachment and Loss. Volume 3. Loss, Sadness, and Depression*. London: Hogarth.

Bradley, D. (1998). *Hyperventilation Syndrome*. London: Kyle Cathie.

Brand, N. (2007). *Fractured Families. The Untold Anguish of the Falsely Accused*. Bradford on Avon: BFMS.

Bray, R. (2006). Thought Field Therapy: Working through traumatic stress without the overwhelming response. *Journal of Aggression, Maltreatment & Trauma, 12*(No. 1/2): 103–123.

British Acupuncture Council. (2002). Depression, anxiety and acupuncture. The evidence for effectiveness. London: Author.

Burr, H. S. (1972). *Blueprint for Immortality The Electric Patterns of Life*. Saffron Walden. C. W. Daniel.

Callahan, R. (1981). A rapid treatment for phobias. Collected Papers of the Institute of Applied Kinesiology.

Callahan, R. (1985). *How Executives Overcome the Fear of Public Speaking and Other Phobias*. [previously titled *The Five Minute Phobia Cure*]. Wilmington, DE: Enterprise Publishing.

Callahan, R. (1995). A thought field therapy (TFT) algorithm for trauma: A reproducible experiment in psychotherapy. Paper presented at the annual meeting of the American Psychological Association, New York, August 1995.

Callahan, R. (2001). *Tapping the Healer Within. Using Thought Field Therapy to Instantly Conquer your Fears, Anxieties, and Emotional Distress*. New York: Contemporary Books.

Callahan, R. (2001b). Kosovo revisited. *The Thought Field, 7*(3). Dec. [www.tftrx.com]

Callahan, R. (2001c). Objective evidence of the superiority of TFT in eliminating depression. *The Thought Field, 6*(4). Jan. [www.tftrx.com]

Callahan, R. (2001d). Self-acceptance and Thought Field Therapy: A recommendation for complex cases. *The Thought Field, 7*(2). July. [www.tftrx.com]

Callahan, R. (2001e). The impact of Thought Field Therapy on heart rate variability (HRV). *Journal of Clinical Psychology, 57*(10): 1153–1170.

Callahan, R. (2001f). Raising and lowering heart rate variability: Some clinical findings of Thought Field Therapy. *Journal of Clinical Psychology, 57*(10): 1175–1186.

Callahan, R. (2006). Voltmeter and Psychological Reversal. www.tftrx.com

Callahan, R. J., & Callahan, J. (2000). *Stop the Nightmares of Trauma*. LaQuinta, CA: Callahan.

Callahan, R., & Callahan, J. M. (2003). *Sensitivities, Intolerances, and Individual Energy Toxins: How to Identify and Neutralise them with Thought Field Therapy*. LaQuinta, CA: Callahan Techniques Ltd.

Carbonell, J. (1997). An experimental study of TFT and acrophobia. *The Thought Field, 2*(3): 1–6.

Carbonell, J. L., & Figley, C. (1999). A systematic clinical demonstration of promising PTSD approaches. *Traumatology, 5*:1. Article 4. http://www.fsu.edu/~trauma/promising.html

Carney, R. M., Freedland, K. E., Stein, P. K., Skala, J. A., Hoffman, P., & Jaffe, A. S. (2000). Change in heartrate variability during treatment for depression in patients with coronary heart disease. *Psychomatic Medicine*. Sept. *62*(5): 639–647.

Caruso, W., & Leisman, G. (2000a). The clinical utility of force/displacement analysis of muscle testing in Applied Kinesiology. *International Journal of Neuroscience, 2001.* 1–12.

Caruso, W., & Leisman, G. (2000b). A force/displacement analysis of muscle testing. *Perceptual and Motor Skills, 91:* 683–692.

Charman, R. A. (2006). Foreword, in J. R. Cross. *Healing with the Chakra Energy System.* Berkeley, CA: North Atlantic Books.

Cho, S., & Chung, S. (1994). The basal electrical skin resistance of acupuncture points in normal subjects. *Yonsei Medical Journal, 35:* 464–474.

Cho, Z. H. (1998). New findings of the correlation between acupoints and corresponding brain cortices using functional MRI. *Proceedings of the National Academy of Science, 95:* 2670–2673.

Church, D. (2007). *The Genie in Your Genes.* Santa Rosa, CA: Elite.

Clinton, A. (2005). *Seemorg Matrix Work. The Basic Manual.* Canaan, NY: Seemorg LLC.

Cohen, M. H. (2006). Foreword to *Creating Right Relationships: A Practical Guide to Ethics in Energy Therapies,* by D. Hover-Kramer, Behavioral Health Consultants, Cave Junction OR.

Connolly, S. M. (2004). *Thought Field Therapy. Clinical Applications. Integrating TFT in Psychotherapy.* Sedona, AZ: George Tyrell Press.

Coulter, H. L. (1977). *Divided Legacy.* Volume 3. Washington, DC: Wehawken.

Cousens, G. (1987). *Spiritual Nutrition and The Rainbow Diet.* Berkeley, CA: North Atlantic Books (reprinted 2004).

Crawford, I. (1990). *A Guide to the Mysteries.* London: Lucis Press.

Cross, J. R. (2006). *Healing with the Chakra Energy System.* Berkeley, CA: North Atlantic Books.

Cuthbert, S. C., & Goodheart, G. J. (2007). On the reliability and validity of manual muscule testing: a literature review. *Chiropractic & Osteopathy, 15*(4) www.chiroandosteo.com/content/15/1/4

Cutler, E. (1998). *Winning the War against Asthma and Allergens.* New York: Delmar.

Darby, D. (2001). The efficacy of thought field therapy as a treatment modality for individuals diagnosed with blood-injection-injury phobia. Unpublished doctoral dissertation. Minneapolis, MN: Walden University.

Darras, J-C., de Vernejoul, P., & Albarhde, P. (1992). A study on the migration of radioactive tracers after injection at acupoints. *American Journal of Acupuncture, 20*(3).

Darras, J. C., Albarède, P., & deVeernejoul , P. (1993). Nuclear medicine investigation of transmission of acupuncture information. *Acupuncture in Medicine*, 11: 22-28 [www.acupunctureinmedicine.org.uk]

Devilly, G. J. (2005). Power therapies and possible threats to the science of psychology and psychiatry. *Australian and New Zealand Journal of Psychiatry*, 39(6): 437–455.

Davies, H. T. O., & Crombie, I. K. (2005). What is a systematic review. *What is…?* Vol. 1(5). www.evidence-based-medicine.co.uk.

Debiec, J., Doyere, V., Nader, K., & LeDoux, J. E. (2006). Directly reactivated, but not indirectly reactivated, memories undergo reconsolidation in the amygdala, Proceedings of the National Academy of Sciences, USA. 28.103(4): 3428–33.

Dennison, P. E., & Dennison, G. E. *Brain Gym. Teachers Edition.* Ventura, CA: Edukinesthetics Inc.

Diamond, J. (1978). *Behavioural Kinesiology and the Autonomic Nervous System.* Valley Cottage: Archaeus Press.

Diamond, J. (1979). *Your Body Doesn't Lie.* Enfield: Eden Grove (1997 edition).

Diamond, J. (1985). *Life Energy.* St. Paul, MN: Paragon House.

Diamond, J. (1986). *The Re-mothering experience. How to totally love.* Valley Cottage, NY: Aschaeus Press.

Diamond, J. (1988). *Life-Energy Analysis: A Way to Cantillation.* Valley Cottage, NY: Aschaeus Press.

Diamond, J. (2002). *Facets of a Diamond. Reflections of a Healer.* Berkeley, CA: North Atlantic Books.

Diepold, J. H., Britt, V., & Bender, S. S. (2004). *Evolving Thought Field Therapy. The Clinician's Handbook of Diagnosis, Treatment, and Theory.* New York: Norton.

Diepold, J. H., Jr., & Goldstein, D. (2000). Thought field therapy and QEEG changes in the treatment of trauma: a case study. Moorestown, NJ: Author.

Durlacher, J. V. (1994). *Freedom From Fear Forever. The Acu-Power way to overcoming your fears, phobias and inner problems.* Mesa, AZ: Van Ness Publishing Co.

Elder, C., Ritenbaugh, C., Mist, S., Aickin, M., Schneider, J., Zwickey, H., Elmer, P. (2007). Randomized Trial of Two Mind–Body Interventions for Weight-Loss Maintenance. *Journal of Alternative and Complementary Medicine*, 13(1): 67–78.

Epstein, S. (1986). A cognitive self theory. In: K. Yardley & T. Honess. (Eds.), *Self and Identity. Psychosocial Perspectives.* London: Wiley.

Fairbairn, W. R. D. (1952). *Psychoanalytic Studies of the Personality*. London: Routledge.

Feinstein, D. (2004). Energy Psychology Interactive CD. www.innersource.net with accompanying book: *Energy Psychology Interactive*. Ashland, OR: Innersource.

Feinstein, D. (2005). An overview of research in energy psychology. Association for Comprehensive Energy Psychology. http://www.energypsych.org/research-overview-ep.php

Feinstein, D. (2006). Energy Psychology in Disaster Relief. https://energypsych.org/article-feinstein4.php

Feinstein, D. (2007). Energy Psychology: Background, method, evidence. https://www.energypsychologyresearch.com

Figley, C. R. (1999). Editorial note to *Energy Psychology* by F. P. Gallo. Boca Raton, FL: CRC Press.

Figley, C. R., & Carbonell, J. L. (1995). Active ingredients project. The systematic clinical demonstration of the most efficient treatments of PTSD. Tallahassee, FL: Florida State University Psychosocial Research Program and Clinical Laboratory. Cited in F. P. Gallo (1999). *Energy Psychology*. Boca Raton, FL: CRC Press.

Fink, P. J. (1970). Correlations between 'actual' neurosis and the work of Masters and Johnson. *Psychoanalytic Quarterly, 39*: 38–51.

Foa, E. B., & Kozak, M. J. (1986). Emotional processing and fear: exposure to corrective information. *Psychological Bulletin, 99*: 20–35.

Fonagy, P., Gergely, G., Jurist, E., & Target, M. (2002). *Affect Regulation, Mentalization and the Development of the Self*. New York: Other Press.

Fried, R. (1999). *Breathe Well, Be Well*. Chichester: Wiley.

Freud, E. L. (Ed.) (1961). *Letters of Sigmund Freud 1873–1939*. London: Hogarth.

Freud, S. (1894a). The neuro-psychoses of defence. *S.E., 1*. London: Hogarth.

Freud, S. (1905d). Three essays on the theory of sexuality. *S.E., 7*. London: Hogarth.

Freud, S. (1912c). Types of onset of neurosis. *S.E., 12*. London: Hogarth.

Freud, S. (1914c). On narcissism: an introduction. *S.E., 14*. London: Hogarth.

Freud, S. (1915d). Repression. *S.E., 14*. London: Hogarth.

Freud, S. (1915e). The unconscious. *S.E., 14*. London: Hogarth.

Freud, S. (1916–17). Introductory lectures on psycho-analysis. *S.E., 15-16*. London: Hogarth.

Freud, S. (1920g). Beyond the pleasure principle. *S.E., 18*. London: Hogarth.

Freud, S. (1923a). Two encyclopaedia articles. *S.E., 18*. London: Hogarth Press.

Freud, S. (1923b). The ego and the id. *S.E., 19*. London: Hogarth.

Freud, S. (1925d). An autobiographical study. *S.E., 20*. London: Hogarth.

Frost, R. (2002). *Applied Kinesiology*. Berkeley, CA: North Atlantic Books.

Furman, M. E., & Gallo, F. P. (2000). *The Neurophysics of Human Behavior*. Boca Raton, Fl: CRC Press.

Gagne, D. (1994). The effects of Therapeutic Touch and relaxation techniques in reducing anxiety. *Archives of Psychiatric Nursing, 8*(3): 184–189.

Gallo, F. P. (1999). *Energy Psychology. Explorations at the interface of energy, cognition, behavior, and health*. Boca Raton, FL: CRC Press.

Goodheart, G. J. (1989). *You'll Be Better. The Story of Applied Kinesiology*. Geneva, OH: AK Publishing.

Green, A. (1995). Has sexuality anything to do with psychoanalysis? *International Journal of Psychoanalysis, 76*: 871–883.

Green, A. (2000). *The Chains of Eros. The Sexual in Psychoanalysis*. London: Karnac.

Greenwald, A. G. (1980). The totalitarian ego: Fabrication and revision of personal history. *American Psychology, 35*: 603–608.

Grotstein, J. (1981). *Splitting and Projective Identification*. New York: Aronson.

Gurewich, J. F., & Tort, M. (1999). *Lacan and the New Wave in American Psychoanalysis. The Subject and the Self*. New York: Other Press.

Hartmann, S. (2003). *Oceans of Energy. The Patterns and Techniques of EmoTrance. Volume 1*. Eastbourne: DragonRising.

Hartung, J. G., & Galvin, M. D. (2003). *Energy Psychology and EMDR. Combining Forces to Optimize Treatment*. New York: Norton.

Hawkins, D. (2002). *Applied Kinesiology*. Berkeley, CA: North Atlantic Books.

Hawkins, D. (1995). *Power vs. Force*. Sedona, AZ: Veritas.

Hawkins, D. (2001). *The Eye of the I*. Sedona, AZ: Veritas.

Hawkins, D. (2003). *I. Reality and Subjectivity*. Sedona, AZ: Veritas.

Hawkins, D. (2005). *Truth vs. Falsehood. How to tell the Difference*. Toronto: Axial.

Heidt, P. (1981). Effect of Therapeutic Touch on anxiety levels of hospitalised patients. *Nursing Research, 10*(1): 32–37.

Hodson, G. (1953). *The Seven Human Temperaments*. Adyar, Madras: Theosophical Publishing House.

Hover-Kramer, D. (2002). *Creative Energies. Integrative Energy Psychotherapy for Self-Expression and Healing*. New York: Norton.

Hover-Kramer, D. (2006). *Creating Right Relationships. A Practical Guide to Ethics in Energy Therapies.* Cave Junction, OR: Behavioral Health Consultants.

Hrobjartsson, A., & Gotzsch, P. C. (2005). Placebo interventions for all clinical conditions. *Cochrane Library.* Issue 2. http://www.cochrane.org/cochrane/revabstr/ab003974.htm.

Hughes, P. P. (1997). Therapeutic Touch with psychiatric adolescent patients. *Journal of Holistic Nursing,* 14(1): 6–23.

Hui, K. K. S., Liu, J., Makris, N., Gollub, R. W., Chen, A. J. W., Moore, C. I., Kennedy, D. N., Rosen, B. R., & Kwong, K. K. (2000). Acupuncture modulates the limbic system and subcortical gray structures of the human brain: Evidence from fMRI studies in normal subjects. *Human Brain Mapping,* 9(1): 13–25.

Hyman, R. (2003). How people are fooled by ideomotor action. http://www.quackwatch.org/01QuackeryRelatedTopics/ideomotor.html accessed 22.08.06.

Jacobs, G. E. (1981). Applied Kinesiology: An Experimental Evaluation by Double Blind Methodology. *Journal of Manipulative and Physiological Therapeutics,* 4(3): 141–145.

Jacobson, E. (1964). *The Self and the Object World.* New York: International Universities Press.

Jell, A. (2000). *Healthy with Tachyon.* Twin Lakes. WI: Lotus Press.

Johnson, C., Shala, M., Seddijaj, X., Odell, R., & Dabishevci, K. (2001). Thought field therapy — soothing the bad moments of Kosovo. *Journal of Clinical Psychology,* 57: 1237–1240.

Kaufman, M. (1971). *Homeopathy in America.* Baltimore: John Hopkins Press.

Kendall, H. O., Kendall, F.P., & McCreary, E. K. (1949). *Muscles — Testing and Function.* Baltimore: Williams & Wilkins.

Kennedy, R. (2001). *Ideas in Psychoanalysis: Libido.* Cambridge. Icon Books.

Kenny, J. J., Clemens, R., & Forsythe, K. D. (1988). Applied kinesiology unreliable for assessing nutrient status. *Journal of the American Dietary Association.* June. 88(6): 698–704.

Kirsch, L. T. J. (2002). The emperor's new drugs. An analysis of antidepressant medication data submitted to the U.S. Food and Drug Administration. *Prevention and Treatment.* (American Psychological Association) 5. Article 23.

Kleijnen, A. (1991). Clinical trials of homeopathy. *British Medical Journal,* 302: 316–323.

Klein, M. (1946). Notes on some schizoid mechanisms. In: M. Klein (1975) *Envy and Gratitude and other works (1946–1963).* London: Hogarth.

Kohut, H. (1971). *The Analysis of the Self*. New York: International Universities Press.

Krebs, C. (1998). *A Revolutionary Way of Thinking. From a Near-Fatal Accident to a New Science of Healing*. Melbourne. Hill of Content.

Lambrou, P. T., Pratt, G. J., & Chevalier, G. (2003). Physiological and psychological effects of a mind/body therapy on claustrophobia. *Subtle Energies and Energy Medicine, 14*(3): 239–251.

Langs, R. (1978). *The Listening Process*. New York. Aronson.

Lansdowne, Z. F. (1989). *The Rays and Esoteric Psychology*. York Beach, Maine: Samuel Weiser.

Lansdowne, Z. F. (1993). *Ray Methods of Healing*. York Beach, Maine: Samuel Weiser.

Lawson, A., & Calderon, L. (1997). Interexaminer agreement for Applied Kinesiology Manual Muscle Testing. *Percepual and Motor Skills, 84*: 539–546.

Lehrer, P. M., Sasaki, Y., & Saito, Y. (1999). Zazen and cardiac variability. *Psychosomatic Medicine, 61*: 812–821.

Leisman, G. (1995). Electromyographic effects of fatigue and task repetition on the validity of estimates of strong and weak muscles in Applied Kinesiology Testing procedures. *Perceptual and Motor Skills, 80*: 963–977.

Leisman, G., Shambaugh, P., & Ferentz, A. (1989). Somatosensory evoked potential changes during muscle testing. *International Journal of Neuroscience, 45*: 143–151.

Leonoff, G. (1996). Successful treatment of phobias and anxiety by telephone and radio: A preliminary report on a replication of Callahan's 1987 study. *The Thought Field, 2*(1): 3–4.

Leuchter, A. F., & Cook, I. A. (2002). Changes in brain function of depressed subjects during treatment with placebo. *American Journal of Psychiatry, 159*(1): 122–129.

Levy, S. L., & Lehr, C. (1996). *Your Body Can Talk. The Art and Application of Clinical Kinesiology*. Prescott, AZ: Hohm Press.

Liberman, R. P., & Phipps, C. C. (1987). Innovative treatment and rehabilitation techniques for the chronically mentally ill. In: W. Menninger & G. Hannah (Eds.), *The Chronic Mental Patient*. Washington, DC: American Psychiatric Press.

Liboff, A. R. (1997). Bioelectrical fields and acupuncture. *Journal of Alternative and Complementary Medicine, 3*. 577–587.

Lilienfeld, S. O., Lynn, S. J., & Lohr, J. M. (Eds.) (2003). *Science and Pseudoscience in Clinical Psychology*. New York: Guilford Press.

Lilly, J. C. (1974). *The Human Biocomputer*. London: Abacus.

Linde, K. (1997). Are the clinical effects of homeopathy placebo effects? A meta-analysis of placebo-controlled trials. *Lancet, 350*: 834–843.

Lipton, B. (2005). *The Biology of Belief*. Santa Rosa, CA: Mountain of Love.

Lohr, J. M. (2001). Sakai et al. is not an adequate demonstration of TFT effectiveness. *Journal of Clinical Psychology, 57*(10): 1229–1236.

Lubar, J. F. (2004). *Quantitative Electroencephalographic Analysis (QEEG) databases for neurotherapy*. New York: Haworth Medical Press.

Ludtke, R., Kunz, B., Seeber, N., & Ring, J. (2001). Test-retest reliability and validity of the Kinesiology muscle test. *Complementary Therapeutic Medicine*, September. 9(3): 141–145.

Lynch, V., & Lynch, P. (2001). *Emotional Healing in Minutes*. London: Thorsons.

Manaka, Y., Itaya, K., & Birch, S. (1995). *Chasing the Dragon's Tail: the Theory and Practice of Acupuncture in the Work of Yoshio Manaka*. Brookline, MA: Paradigm Publications.

Martin, A. (1997). *Your Body is Talking; Are You Listening?* Penryn, CA: Personal Transformation Press.

Martin, A., & Landrell, J. (2005). *Energy Psychology/Energy Medicine. The Practice of Neuro Kinesiology Psychoneuroimmunology in Exploring the Body/Mind Connection. 9th Edition*. Peryn, CA: Personal Transformation Press. www.transformyourmind.com.

Masterson, J. F., & Rinsley, D. (1975). The borderline syndrome: the role of the mother in the genesis and psychic structure of the borderline personality. *International Journal of Psychoanalysis, 56*: 163–177.

Meltzer, D. (1973). *Sexual States of Mind*. Perthshire: Clunie Press.

Mist, S., Elder, M., Aickin, M., & Ritenbaugh. (2005). A randomised trial of Tapas Acupressure for weight-loss maintenance. *Focus on Alternative and Complementary Therapies.10.38-39* [a quarterly review journal presenting evidence-based approaches to health care]. Abstracts of 12th Annual Symposium on Complementary Health Care. 19-21st September. 2005. Exeter, UK.

Modi, S. (1997). *Remarkable Healings. A Psychiatrist Discovers Unsuspected Roots of Mental and Physical Illness*. Charlottesville, CA: Hampton Roads.

Mollon, P. (1993). *The Fragile Self. The Structure of Narcissistic Disturbance*. London: Whurr.

Mollon, P. (2001). *Releasing the Self. The Healing Legacy of Heinz Kohut*. London: Whurr.

Mollon, P. (2002a). *Remembering Trauma. 2nd Edition*. London: Whurr.

Mollon, P. (2002b). *Shame and Jealousy. The Hidden Turmoils.* London: Karnac.

Mollon, P. (2005). *EMDR and the Energy Therapies. Psychoanalytic Perspectives.* London: Karnac.

Mollon, P. (2005b). The inherent shame of sexuality. *British Journal of Psychotherapy, 22*(2): 167–177.

Mollon, P. (2007). Debunking the 'pseudo-science debunkers'. *Clinical Psychology Forum, 174* June: 13–16.

Monti, D., Sinnot, J., Marchese, M., Kundel, E., & Greeson, J. (1999). Muscle test comparisons of congruent and incongruent self-referential statements. *Perceptual and Motor Skills, 88*: 1019–1028.

Moseley, J.B., & O'Malley, K. (2002). A controlled trial of arthroscopic surgery for osteoarthritis of the knee. *New England Journal of Medicine, 347*(2): 81–88.

Motyka, T., & Yanuck, S. (1999). Expanding the neurological examination using functional neurologic assessment Part 1. Methodological Considerations. *International Journal of Neuroscience, 97*: 61–76.

Nader, K., Schafe, G. E., & LeDoux, J. E. (2000). The labile nature of consolidation theory. *Nature Neuroscience Reviews, 1*(3): 216–219.

Nambudripad, D. S. (1993). *Say Goodbye to Illness.* Buena Park, CA: Delta Publishing Company.

Napadow, V., Webb, J. M., Pearson, N., & Hammerschlag, R. (2006). Neurobiological correlates of acupuncture. *Journal of Alternative and Complementary Medicine, 12*: 931–935.

Nelson, J. E. (1994). *Healing the Spirit. Integrating Spirit into our Understanding of the Mentally Ill.* Albany, NY: State University of New York Press.

Nolan, J., Batin, P., Andrews, R., Lindsey, S., Brooksby, P., Mullen, M., Baig, W., Flapan, A., Cowley, A., Prescott, R., Neilson, J., & Fox, K. (1998). Prospective study of heart rate variability and mortality. *Circulation, 48*: 1510–1516.

Null, G., & Dean, N. D. (2003). *Death by Medicine.* New York: Nutrition Institute of America.

Ogal, H. P. B., Stör, W. (2005). *The Pictorial Atlas of Acupuncture.* Marburg: Könemann.

Omaha, J. (2004). *Psychotherapeutic Interventions for Emotion Regulation. EMDR and Bilateral Stimulation for Affect Management.* New York: Norton.

Omura, Y. (1989). Connections found between each meridian and organ representation areas in the cerebral cortex. *Acupuncture and Electro-Therapeutics Research International Journal, 14*: 155–186.

Omura, Y. (1990). Meridian-like networks of internal organs. *Acupuncture and Electro-Therapeutics Research International Journal*, 15: 53–70.

Orloff, J. (2005). *Positive Energy*. New York: Three Rivers Press.

Oschman, J. L. (2000). *Energy Medicine. The Scientific Basis*. New York: Churchill Livingstone.

Owen, R. M. M., & Ives, G. (1982). The mustard gas experiments of the British Homeopathic Society: 1941–42. *Proceedings of the 35th International Homeopathic Congress*: 258–259.

Pearsall, P. (1998). *The Heart's Code. The True Stories of Organ Transplant Patients and What They Reveal About Where We Store Our Memories*. London: Thorsons.

Paterson, J. (1944). Report on Mustard Gas experiments. *Journal of the American Insitute of Homeopathy*, 37: 47–50, 88–92.

Peck, S. D. (1997). The effect of Therapeutic Touch for decreasing pain in elders with degenerative arthritis. *Journal of Holistic Nursing*, 15(2): 176–198.

Perkins, B. R., & Rouanzoin, C. C. (2002). A critical evaluation of current views regarding eye movement desensitisation and reprocessing (EMDR); clarifying points of confusion. *Journal of Clinical Psychology*, 58(1): 77–97.

Perot, C., Meldener, R., Goubel, F. (1991). Objective measurement of proprioceptive technique consequences on muscular maximal voluntary contraction. *Agressologie*, 32(10): 471–474.

Pert, C. (1999). *Molecules of Emotion. The Science behind Mind-Body Medicine*. New York. Simon & Schuster.

Peterson, H. M., Hoyer, D., & Ross, G. (1994). Muscle testing to provocative vertebral challenge and spinal manipulation: a randomised controlled trial of construct validity. *Journal of Manipulative Physiological Therapy*, Nov-Dec. 17(9): 620–621.

Pignotti, M., & Steinberg, M. (2001). Heart rate variability as an outcome measure for Thought Field Therapy in clinical practice. *Journal of Clinical Psychology*, 57(10): 1193–1206.

Ponomerava, N. (2003). Do we marry our parents? Unpublished MA dissertation. School of Psychotherapy & Counselling, Regents College. London.

Pothmann, R., von Frankenberg, S., Hoicke, C., Weingarten, H., & Ludtke, R. (2002). Evaluation of applied kinesiology in nutritional intolerance of childhood. *Forsch Komplementarmed Klass Naturheilkd*. December. 8(6): 336–344.

Profet, M. (1991). The function of allergy: Immunological defences against toxins. *Quarterly Review of Biology, 66*(1) March. 23–62.

Quinn, N. (2004). *Life Without Panic Attacks*. Eastbourne: DragonRising [e book: www.nicolaquinn.com].

Rachman, S. (1980). Emotional Processing. *Behaviour, Research and Therapy, 18*: 51–60.

Radomski, S. (2002). Allergy Antidotes Manual. www.allergyantidotes. com

Rapp, D. (1991). *Is this your child?* New York: William Morrow.

Redpath, W. M. (1995). *Trauma Energetics: A Study of Held-Energy Systems*. Lexington, MA: Barberry Press.

Reich, W. (1960). *The Writings of Wilhelm Reich*. New York: Farrar, Straus & Giroux.

Reich, W. (1982). *The Bioelectric Investigation of Sexuality and Anxiety*. New York: Farar, Straus & Giroux.

Reilly, D. T., Taylor, M. A., McSharry, C., & Aitchison, T. (1986). Is homeopathy a placebo response? Controlled trial of homeopathic potency, with pollen in hayfever as model. *Lancet*, October *18*: 881–886.

Rosner, R. (2001). Between search and research: how to find your way around? Review of the article 'Thought field therapy—soothing the bad moments of Kosovo'. *Journal of Clinical Psychology, 57*(10): 1241–1244.

Roth, A., Fonagy, P., & Parry, G. (1996). Psychotherapy research, funding, and evidence-based practice. In: A. Roth & P. Fonagy, *What Works for Whom? A Critical Review of Psychotherapy 'Research*. New York: Guilford Press.

Rowe, J. E. (2005). The effects of EFT on long-term psychological symptoms. *Counseling and Clinical Psychology, 2*(3): 104–111.

Ruden, R. A. (2005). Neurobiological basis for the observed peripheral sensory modulation of emotional responses. *Traumatology, 11*: 145–158.

Sakai, C., Paperny, D., Mathews, M., Tamida, G., Boyd, G., Simons, A., Yamamoto, C., Mau, C., & Nutter, L. (2001). Thought field therapy clinical application: Utilisation in an HMO in behavioural medicine and behavioural health services. *Journal of Clinical Psychology, 57*: 1215–1227.

Salas, M. M. (2001). The effect of an energy psychology intervention (EFT) versus diaphragmatic breathing on specific phobias. Unpublished thesis. Kingsville, Texas: Texas A & M University.

Schaefer, J. C. (2002). *The Pretzel Man. A True Story of Phobias and Back Problems*. Bloomington, IN: 1st Books.

Schmitt, W., & Leisman, G. (1998). Correlation of Applied Kinesiology muscle testing findings with serum immunoglobin levels for food allergies. *International Journal of Neuroscience, 96*: 237–244.

Schmitt, W., & Yanuck, S. (1999). Expanding the neurological examination using functional neurologic assessment. Part II: Neurologic basis of Applied Kinesiology. *International Journal of Neuroscience, 97*: 77–108.

Schoninger, B. (2004). Efficacy of thought field therapy (TFT) as a treatment modality for persons with public speaking anxiety. Unpublished doctoral dissertation. Cincinnati, OH: Union Institute.

Schulz, K. M. (2007). Integrating energy psychology into treatment for adult survivors of childhood sexual abuse: An exploratory clinical study from the therapist's perspective. Unpublished doctoral dissertation. California School of Professional Psychology, San Diego.

Schulz, K. M. (2007b). Integrating energy psych. into treatment for adult survivors of childhood sexual abuse. A summary of my dissertation findings. *The Energy Field. Newsletter of the Association for Comprehensive Energy Psychology,* Spring. Volume 8(1): 5.

Schusterman, D. (2005). Intergenerational and systemic psychological reversals. Presentation at the annual conference of the Association for Comprehensive Energy Psychology. Baltimore.

Segal, Z. V., Williams, J. M. G., & Teasdale, J. D. (2002). *Mindfulness-Based Cognitive Therapy for Depression.* New York: Guilford.

Seligman, M. E. P. (1995). *What you can change and what you can't.* New York: Knopf.

Sezgin, N., & Ozcan, B. (2004). A comparison of the effectiveness of two techniques on reducing test anxiety: EFT and Progressive Muscular Relaxation. Presented at the 6th Annual Energy Psychology Conference. Toronto.

Shapiro, F. (2001). *Eye Movement Desensitization and Reprocessing.* 2nd Edition. New York: Guilford.

Shapiro, F. (Ed.) (2002). *EMDR as Integrative Psychotherapy. Experts of Diverse Orientations Explore the Paradigm Prism.* Washington, DC: American Psychological Press.

Sheldrake, R. (1985). *A New Science of Life. The Hypothesis of Formative Causation.* London: Blond & Briggs.

Sheldrake, R. (1988). *The Presence of the Past. Morphic Resonance and the Habits of Nature.* London: Collins.

Sheldrake, R. (1999). *Dogs that know when their owners are coming home and other unexplained powers of animals.* London: Hutchinson.

Shmitt, W. H., & Leisman, G. (1998). Correlation of Applied Kinesiology muscle test findings with serum immunoglobulin levels for food allergies. *International Journal of Neuroscience, 96*: 237–244.

Smith, C. W. (1987). Electromagnetic effects in humans. In: H. Frolich (Ed.), *Biological Coherence and Response to External Stimuli.* Berlin: Springer-Verlag, pp. 205–232.

Solomon, S. D., Gerrity, E. T., & Muff, A. M. (1992). Efficacy of treatments for posttraumatic stress disorder. *Journal of the American Medical Association, 268*: 5. 633–638.

Spitz, H. (1997). *Nonconscious Movements: From Mystical Messages to Facilitated Communication.* Manwah, NJ: Lawrence Erlbaum.

Stevens, A., & Price, J. (2000). *Evolutionary Psychiatry.* London: Routledge.

Stibal, V. (2006). *ThetaHealing.* Idaho Falls: Rolling Thunder Publishing.

Stux, G. (2003). Additional methods of treatment. In: Stux, G., Berman, B., & Pomernanz, B. *Basics of Acupuncture. 5th Edition.* Heidelberg: Springer, pp. 326–334.

Stux, G., Berman, B., & Pomeranz, B. (2003). *Basics of Acupuncture. 5th Edition.* Heidelberg: Springer.

Sulloway, F. J. (1979). *Freud, Biologist of the Mind.* London: Burnett Books.

Swingle, P. (2000). Effects of the Emotional Freedom Techniques (EFT) method on seizure frequency in children diagnosed with epilepsy. Paper presented at the annual meeting of the Association for Comprehensive Energy Psychology. Las Vegas: NV.

Swingle, P. G., & Pulos, L. (2000). Neuropsychological correlates of successful EFT treatment of posttraumatic stress. Paper presented at the second international energy psychology conference, Las Vegas: NV.

Swingle, P., Pulos, L., & Swingle, M. (2000). Effects of a meridian-based therapy, EFT, on symptoms of PTSD in auto accident victims. Paper presented at the annual meeting of the Association for Comprehensive Energy Psychology, Las Vegas, NV. May 2000.

Swingle, P. G., Pulos, L., & Swingle, M. K. (2004). Neurophysiological indicators of EFT treatment of posttraumatic stress. *Subtle Energies and Energy Medicine, 15*(1): 75–86.

Syldona, M., & Rein, G. (1999). The use of DC electrodermal potential measurements and healer's felt sense to assess the energetic nature of Qi. *Journal of Alternative and Complementary Medicine, 5*: 329–347.

Tansley, D. (1972). *Radionics and the Subtle Anatomy of Man.* Rustington: Health Science Press.

Tansley, D. (1975). *Radionics Interface with the Energy Fields.* Saffron Walden: C. W. Daniel.

Tansley, D. (1984). *Chakras—Rays and Radionics*. Saffron Walden: C. W. Daniel.

Tansley, D. (1985). *The Raiment of Light. A Study of the Human Aura*. London: Routledge.

Teasdale, J. D. (1999). Metacognition, mindfulness and the modification of mood disorders. *Clinical Psychology and Psychotherapy, 6*: 146–156. *Special Issue. Metacognition and Cognitive Behaviour Therapy*.

Teuber, S. S., & Porch-Curren, C. (2003). Unproved diagnostic and therapeutic approaches to food allergy and intolerance. *Current Opinion in Allergy and Clinical Immunology*, June 3(3): 217–221.

Tiller, W. A. (1997). *Science and Human Transformation. Subtle Energies, Intentionality, and Consciousness*. Walnut Creek, CA: Pavior Publishing.

Tiller, W. A. (2003). Foreword. In: S. Yurkovsky. *Biological, Chemical and Nuclear Warfare*. Chappaqua: New York: Science of Medicine Publishing.

Travis, C., McLean, B., & Ribar, C. (1989). *Environmental Toxins: Psychological, Behavioral, and Sociocultural Aspects. 1973–1989*. Washington, DC: American Psychological Association.

Tschernitschek, H., & Fink, M. (2005). 'Applied Kinesiology' in medicine and dentistry—a critical review. *Wien Med Wochenschr*. February, *155*(3-4): 59–64.

Ullman, D. (1991). *Discovering Homeopathy. Medicine for the 21st Century*. Berkeley, CA: North Atlantic Books.

Van der Kolk, B. A. (2002). Beyond the talking cure. Somatic experience and subcortical imprints in the treatment of trauma. In: F. Shapiro (Ed.), *EMDR as an Integrative Psychotherapy Approach*, pp. 57–83. Washington: American Psychological Press.

Wade, J. F. (1990). The effects of the Callahan phobia treatment techniques on self concept. Unpublished doctoral dissertation. San Diego, CA. The Professional School of Psychological Studies.

Wagner, D., & Cousins, G. (1999). *Tachyon Energy. A New Paradigm in Holistic Healing*. Berkeley, CA: North Atlantic Books.

Waite, W. L., & Holder, M. D. (2003). Assessment of the emotional freedom technique: An alternative treatment for fear. *The Scientific Review of Mental Health Practice, 2*(1): 20–26.

Wade, J. F. (1990). The effects of the Callahan phobia treatment techniques on self concept. Unpublished doctoral dissertation. San Diego, CA: The Professional School of Psychological Studies.

Waite, W. L., & Holder, M. D. (2003). Assessment of the emotional freedom technique: An alternative treatment for fear. *The Scientific Review of Mental Health Practice, 2*(1): 20–26.

Walther, S. (1988). *Applied Kinesiology Synopsis*. Pueblo, Colorado: Systems DC.

Waska, R. *The Danger of Change. The Kleinian Approach with Patients Who Experience Progress as Trauma*. 2006. New York: Routledge.

Wells, A. (2000). *Emotional Disorders and Metacognition. Innovative Cognitive Therapy*. Chichester: Wiley.

Wells, S., Polglase, K., Andrews, H. B., Carrington, P., & Baker, A. H. (2003). Evaluation of a meridian based intervention, emotional freedom techniques (EFT), for reducing specific phobias of small animals. *Journal of Clinical Psychology, 59*: 943–966.

Whalen, E. (1995). Foreword, in D. R. Hawkins. *Power vs Force*. Carlsbad, CA: Hay House edition, 2002.

Winnicott, D. W. (1960). Ego distortion in terms of true and false self. In (1965) *The Maturational Processes and the Facilitating Environment*. London: Hogarth.

Young, J. E. (1999). *Cognitive Therapy for Personality Disorders: A Schema-Focused Approach 3rd Edition*. Sarasota, FL: Professional Resource Press.

Yurkovsky, S. (2003). *Biological, Chemical, and Nuclear Warfare. Protecting Yourself and Your Loved Ones. The Power of Digital Medicine*. Chappaqua, New York: Science of Medicine Publishing.

Zucker, K. (1979). Freud's early views on masturbation and the actual neuroses. *Journal of the American Academy of Psychoanalysis, 7*: 15–32.

INDEX

A
acupuncture
  conditions helped by, 417
  meridian points in, 62, 416
  tapping, 327, 412, 416
  website, 419
addiction, 111, 161, 229–30, 360,
  441–7
adrenaline, 238, 245
affect regulation, 367, 370
Akhtar, Salman, 350
alcohol, 224, 230, 378
algorithms, 49, 64, 101–2
allergies, 115–16, 240, 250
American Medical Association, 299
amygdalas, 234
anaphylactic shock, 244
Andrade, Dr Joaquin, 409, 415
anger, 102
anxiety
  addiction and, 111
  addiction to, 360
  arousal caused by, 124
  borderline personality disorder,
  368

Callahan, 111
case study, 425
chakras, 260–1
disorders, 410–11
Freud on, 315
Generalised Anxiety Disorder,
  401
hyperventilation, 126–7
reversal and, 143–6, 150–1
severe, 238
sexuality and, 320
subsuming of, 139
tapping and, 344
TFT and, 101–2, 368
apex effect, 54, 101, 157–9, 170, 202
Applied Kinesiology
  borderline personality disorder,
  368
  Callahan, 51–2
  development of, 32
  Diamond, 1, 11, 35
  Durlacher's contribution, 56
  energy psychology and, 11
  founded, 1
  Goodheart on, 1, 30, 348